Reaching Audiences

Reaching Audiences

A Guide to Media Writing

Third Edition

Jan Johnson Yopp
University of North Carolina at Chapel Hill

Katherine C. McAdams
University of Maryland at College Park

Boston   New York   San Francisco
Mexico City   Montreal   Toronto   London   Madrid   Munich   Paris
Hong Kong   Singapore   Tokyo   Cape Town   Sydney

Editor-in-Chief, Social Sciences: Karen Hanson
Senior Editor: Molly Taylor
Editorial Assistant: Michael Kish
Marketing Manager: Mandee Eckersley
Production Editor: Christine Tridente
Editorial-Production Service: TKM Productions
Composition and Prepress Buyer: Linda Cox
Manufacturing Buyer: Chris Marson
Cover Administrator: Kristina Mose-Libon
Electronic Composition: Omegatype Typography, Inc.

For related titles and support materials, visit our online catalog at www.ablongman.com

Between the time Website information is gathered and then published, it is not unusual for some sites to have closed. Also, the transcription of URLs can result in unintended typographical errors. The publisher would appreciate notification where these occur so that they may be corrected in subsequent editions.

Library of Congress Cataloging-in-Publication Data

Yopp, Jan Johnson.
    Reaching audiences : a guide to media writing / Jan Johnson Yopp, Katherine C. McAdams.—3rd ed.
      p.   cm.
    ISBN 0-205-35922-1
      1. Mass media—Authorship. 2. Mass media—Audiences. 3. Report writing. I. McAdams, Katherine C. II. Title.

P96.A86 M38 2002
808'.066302—dc21

                          2002024884

Printed in the United States of America

10 9 8 7 6 5 4 3 2 1   07 06 05 04 03 02

CONTENTS

PART TWO
Gathering Information

PART THREE
Other Media Writing Styles

PREFACE

Cable television. Video news releases. Databases. E-mail. Fax machin.
ellites. Web sites. Cell telephones. Networks. Internet. World Wide \

Technology continues to create a multitude of new ways to send ai
information. We are truly in an information age. Although many audienc
still rely on newspapers and television, they are drawn to a dazzling array of
faster, electronic sources of information and entertainment. Wave after wave
of invention invites attention, analysis, and adoption. Developments seem to
appear faster than they can be mastered.

Technology has enabled communicators to produce work more efficiently and quickly, just as it has allowed users to access information faster
and in greater quantities. Technology also has broadened the field for communicators. Writing markets have been created in publications and advertising for specialized audiences, online newspapers and services, specialty video
news releases, Web design, and literally hundreds of other jobs. Students in
journalism and mass communication programs have many career possibilities
beyond jobs on newspapers or magazines, in public relations or advertising,
and in radio or television.

Professors in journalism and mass communication teach specific styles of
writing. Students interested in print journalism first learn the inverted pyramid style of writing. Broadcast students follow a shorter and more casual
electronic communication format. Advertising students learn copywriting.
Public relations students practice writing news releases and brochures. Pho-
tojournalism students write cutlines. Graphic designers write legends. Each
format has its prescribed guidelines. And the fields are coming together.
Some print journalists write versions of their stories for the company's online newspaper. Electronic journalists also write for online sites. Advertising
and public relations personnel at times blend into integrated marketing.

Regardless of format or medium, today's students must learn to make
their writing clearer, more accurate, more relevant, and more appealing.
They must think constantly about their audiences. They must know their
audiences and their specific language uses and interests. Students need to understand the importance of good writing and be willing to take on the task.

must push students harder to pay attention to their writing and
skills. Today's students are the communicators of tomorrow—regard-
what technology has developed and what medium they ultimately use.
The key ingredient for success in any communications job is good writ-
g. In today's world, good writing often suffers. The proliferation of tech-
iology has diverted many communicators from their main task: good
writing. In the rush to produce and send information, people often overlook
the critical need for accuracy and proper spelling and grammar. Too many
communicators believe that the first draft is good enough and do not spend
time editing and rewriting. Such a philosophy can erode informative, entertaining, well-crafted writing. Technology has enabled anyone with information, no matter how the content is structured, to put it out for public view.
As a result, much information is poorly written and irrelevant to audiences.

Students need to learn the skills required to become good communicators, and they must be committed to the craft of writing. They cannot rely
more on spell-checkers and grammar-checkers housed in computers than on
their own knowledge. They must know the basics of proper sentence construction. They must know how to gather information, sort it, and put it in
a format that audiences will receive. Otherwise, communication does not
happen. Communication must get through to the audience to be complete.

The following chapters stress the basic writing skills essential to any student in any mass communications field: news-editorial, advertising, public
relations, broadcast and online communication, photography, graphic design, or multimedia presentation. The essentials of good writing apply, regardless of format.

Part One presents the basic components of the writing process and the
critical role of audiences. Students will learn the fundamentals of print journalism; how to write text for different formats, including the Web; and the
value of the inverted pyramid style of writing. Any informative writing must
be grounded in the tenets of basic newswriting, and it must be checked and
rechecked for precision and clarity. Specifically, Chapter 2 speaks to the need
for accuracy and provides diagnostic spelling, grammar, style, and math tests.
Specific tips are given to improve writing, from word selection to sentence
length to grammar and usage. Students also will learn the steps of editing, a
crucial part of the writing process, and how to avoid bias in writing.

Part Two reviews how to gather information through three principal
methods: research, observation, and interviewing. Students also are intro-

duced to online searches and resources as well as the dangers of libel and un-ethical conduct in newsgathering.

Part Three discusses other media writing: electronic communication, public relations, and advertising. Each has its particular formats and commu-nications tools for reaching audiences.

The appendices supplement the chapters with a list of abused words and the answer keys to the self-guided spelling, grammar, and math tests.

Mass communication at all levels demands writing that is accurate, com-plete, fair, and concise. Writers constantly must consider their audiences; they can no longer write solely for their own enjoyment. They must create messages that are well written and that will reach the intended audiences.

We clearly embrace technology. Without it, we would not have been able to produce our writing in this text efficiently and easily. Technology will not disappear, and no one would wish it away. But technology changes and fades. The importance of good writing does not.

Acknowledgments

Writing a book is never the work of just the individuals whose names are under the title, and so it is with this book and its third edition. A number of colleagues and friends have provided invaluable contributions.

The core of the book would not have been done without Kevin Davis of Macmillan, who saw the potential in our initial concept and encouraged us to write, and Karon Bowers, Molly Taylor, and Michael Kish at Allyn and Bacon, who guided and assisted on the third edition.

The third edition was written with the advice, counsel, and support of our colleagues at the School of Journalism and Mass Communication at the Uni-versity of North Carolina at Chapel Hill, especially Dean Richard Cole, Pro-fessor Harry Amana, Professor Phil Meyer, Associate Professor Bill Cloud, Associate Professor Cathy Packer, Associate Professor Carol Pardun, Associate Professor Charlie Tuggle, Librarian Barbara Semonche, Lecturer Val Lauder, and graduate students Victoria Ekstrand and Carol Wilcox Stiff; and at the College of Journalism at the University of Maryland, especially Professor Mau-reen Beasley, Professor Carl Sessions Stepp, Associate Dean Chris Callahan, As-sociate Dean Greig Stewart, and students Andrea Hoffman and Encarnita Pyle. We also thank Associate Professor Beth Haller, Professor Thom Lieb at Towson University, and Associate Professor Erik Bucy at Indiana University.

In addition, we gratefully acknowledge the following reviewers of this third edition: Renée Botta, Cleveland State University; Dennis R. Getto, University of Wisconsin–Milwaukee; Nancy Edmonds Hanson, Minnesota State University Moorhead; and Margaret Young, Bradley University.

Beyond our professional colleagues, we also acknowledge the contributions of our families for their moral support and ability to manage without moms for a while.

Reaching
Audiences

1

Writing for Today's Audiences

Each morning, Tom Adams rises at 6:00 A.M., showers, dresses, makes coffee, and walks down his driveway in suburban Maryland to retrieve the *Washington Post*. Today, the *Post* is 127 pages, with a 20-page health insert and three advertising circulars. He has cereal and toast while perusing the *Post*. CNN airs on television in an adjoining room.

At 7:00 A.M., Adams departs for work at an environmental consulting firm 19 miles from home. He tunes his car radio to the all-news AM station to catch a current traffic report. About 10 miles into his commute, his cellular telephone beeps; he recognizes a client's number from its screen and decides to answer as he carefully passes construction warnings posted on the roadside.

Once in the office and on the phone, Adams calls up the more than 30 e-mail messages on his computer, then starts to sort through the day's mail: two brochures on upcoming seminars, copies of the *Environmental Reporter*, the *Federal Register*, and the *Wall Street Journal*—42 pages today.

It is 8:30 A.M., and Adams already has processed hundreds of media messages—and ignored or missed thousands more. By the time he returns home at 6:30 P.M., he will have processed hundreds more messages—before he ever sits down to check the Weather Channel and watch his alma mater play on ESPN II.

Several hundred miles away, Lorayne Oglesbee begins her day scanning a copy of the *News & Observer*, a regional newspaper published in

Raleigh, North Carolina. In the background as she dresses is public radio's "Morning Edition." Oglesbee pauses from time to time when a sound byte catches her ear—or when one of her two school-aged daughters calls for help.

She says her goodbyes when the kids board their bus, then avoids news programs on the three-mile drive to work. She listens to classical music instead, relaxing before she begins what she knows will be a hectic day. She is an attorney for a local hospital.

Oglesbee spends most of her day reading and interacting with legal staff and other attorneys. She writes legal briefs, answers mail and phone calls, and prepares legal documents. At the end of a day filled with complex reading, she opts to spend leisure time watching television with her family or reading popular magazines. Some evenings, by necessity, are devoted to her laptop computer or to telephone business.

Like Adams and Oglesbee, people in the twenty-first century are bombarded by media messages. An overabundance of choices among and within media often confound people who already are pressured by needs for additional income and time.

Only a select few messages actually reach the average person, who is constantly tossing out messages judged irrelevant, unclear, or uninteresting. Messages must be carefully structured to reach an intended audience. Thus, the fate of any message lies in good writing that is streamlined to reach a busy and active target audience. This chapter discusses:

- How information overload challenges audiences,
- How audiences today evolve and change,
- How writers can understand and serve audiences,
- How to overcome roadblocks to reaching audiences, and
- Why the writing process is important for communicators.

Reaching Audiences

As we observed in the examples of Adams and Oglesbee, audiences are hard to reach because of heavy competition from various media and from busy lifestyles. Children and adults today—including you—have developed the skills to sort constantly what will and will not be read, watched, or heard in the limited time available.

Audiences have a nearly insatiable desire to be informed. How people seek out media was clearly evident in the terrorist attacks on the United States in September 2001. Television lost little time in getting live pictures on air. Americans and others watched as the second plane crashed into the second World Trade Tower and less than an hour later when the two towers collapsed.

People looking for additional information logged on to news Web sites but were shut out of some because of the volume of online traffic that day. For example, MSNBC.com had about 10 times its normal load capacity, and ABCNews.com had 7 times its normal daily users. People also used the Internet to connect with relatives.

Newspapers—even if they were morning newspapers—rushed to put out special editions by early afternoon. Word of mouth, the oldest medium of all, became another means of communication as students, friends, teachers, and relatives called one another with the news.

People in an uncertain and changing world are looking for information. They also are seeking leisure activities and looking to new media, such as Internet publications and electronic bulletin boards. They want and need information that will help them cope with or escape from everyday life.

How do writers get through the clutter of today's media and lifestyles to reach waiting audiences? They do it with good writing. They write messages that are simple, clear, and accurate. Audiences will not stick with messages that are confusing, incoherent, or unbelievable. Writers must craft, therefore, messages that attract and hold audiences with their content and structure and that are relevant and emotionally compelling.

Few communicators today write messages for pleasure or for the sake of the task. Rather, most writers today have a purpose in writing. They want to tell of a family's trauma during the attack on the World Trade Center. They want to inform voters about candidates. They want to entertain viewers of a late-night talk show. They want to highlight a product's usefulness. They want to sell a client's services. These writers want their messages to reach a destination, and they want audiences to pay attention.

Roadblocks to Reaching Audiences

A variety of obstacles exist between writers and their audiences:

- *Media and information glut.* More kinds of media become available almost daily. Each memo, letter, article, or news brief has infinitely more competition for an individual's attention than could have been imagined a decade ago. An overwhelming smorgasbord of media offers information. People use online services, direct mail, and an array of cable and satellite channels in addition to the traditional media. They are hungry for information, and they are able to choose media that are most relevant to their lifestyles.

• *Taxing lifestyles.* Audiences today, despite labor-saving devices, are busier than ever with multiple commitments to work and family. People are spending more of their leisure time on family activities and household chores and less on media consumption.

• *Diversity of audiences.* Audiences no longer resemble most writers. An increasingly diverse society has changed audience needs and interests from those of even ten years ago.

• *Unfriendly messages.* Poor writing interferes with messages getting through, just as do commuting, working, children, and too many media choices. A message that bores or taxes an audience or that takes too long to understand can be the greatest roadblock to complete communication.

Writing Is the Basic Task

Before they are printed, broadcast, aired, or distributed, messages are written. Communicators have to write first, regardless of what medium or technology they use. Consider these examples:

- A school principal writes the monthly calendar of activities before announcing it at a Parent-Teacher Association meeting or printing it in the school's monthly newsletter.
- A radio reporter types stories before she reads them on the 6:00 A.M. news show.
- A working mother who wants her teenage son to prepare dinner leaves instructions on the kitchen counter.
- An advertising copywriter creates a direct mail letter for customers of a sporting goods company.
- Three television journalists write their scripts before the weekly Sunday morning news program.
- The editor of the campus newspaper writes two editorials for each edition, then updates the paper's Web site.

All communicators—whether they are journalism or mass communication students, newspaper reporters, advertising copywriters, or school principals—must write a message before it is sent to its intended audience. Once writers let go of the message—that is, after the message is aired or distributed—they have little control over whether the audience absorbs the message. Although the message may have arrived, it might be crowded out, deleted, or ignored.

For audiences to pay attention, writers must create messages that are accurate, appealing, organized, readable, relevant, compelling, clear, complete, and simple. Audiences today require good writing. An audience will gain no new information or entertainment if the message fails to be read or heard because it was poorly written.

Media Glut

Writers must remember that today's world offers more to read, watch, and listen to than anyone could possibly consume. More than 30 years ago, Marshall McLuhan predicted today's trends, suggesting that new media would alter society in dramatic, unanticipated ways.

> *Electronic technology is reshaping and restructuring social patterns of interdependence and every aspect of our personal life. It is forcing us to reconsider and reevaluate practically every thought, every action and every institution formerly taken for granted. Everything is changing—you, your family, your neighborhood, your education, your government, your relation to "the others."*

He was right: Society has changed. McLuhan could hardly have envisioned the information explosion today.

No one person can possibly read or see the tiniest fraction of information that is available today. Media pervade daily life. Technology has overcome the barriers of geography and cost—almost anyone can buy the equipment to be in touch with anyone anywhere in the world. People in remote areas can tune in to events via satellite dishes; a sailboat captain in the Caribbean can receive a fax on board or view an online copy of the latest *Wall Street Journal;* viewers can watch real-time video on their laptop computers.

Changes in Media and Audiences

The need for information and entertainment is constant, and the preferred sources have changed—perhaps for the good. The change, however, has not been so good for traditional media, such as newspapers. Research has shown that fickle audiences may not return to a medium once they have abandoned it for another.

Newspapers have been hard hit by change as audiences have moved to other technology to get information and entertainment faster. In the last 25 years, the circulation of daily newspapers has dropped, and hundred of daily newspapers have closed. Critics of the newspaper industry have said that newspapers have not kept up with the technology and not changed enough to attract readers. Some newspapers have taken steps to reach out to readers, such as putting reporters' e-mail addresses at the end of stories and inviting readers to sit in on daily news meetings. Others have launched special reporting projects targeted to community interests. Newspapers such as the *Washington Post,* the *Wall Street Journal,* and the *New York Times* have established elaborate web sites that may be accessed easily at home or at work.

Watching television news is still a daily activity for most Americans. Although television appears to be the main source of news, it, too, has dealt with declining ratings and increased competition.

Media forms continue to evolve, taking audiences on a roller-coaster ride into an unimagined future of interactive and virtual reality. More specialized media, more ethnic media, more electronic media—in fact, more media of all kinds—are on the market. And all these media, old and new, compete fiercely for audience share and attention.

You saw in observing Adams and Oglesbee that audiences do not accept or assimilate every message that comes their way. They sift through messages and choose which ones they will hear and read. Successful communicators know that about their audiences. Writers must understand an audience's lifestyles, media preferences, interests, and language. That knowledge will aid them in selecting topics and polishing any message so that it fits an audience's needs and interests. Audiences change, just as society changes, and successful communicators take into account the impact of these forces on their audiences.

The 2000 census showed that most people in the United States lived in households but that less than half of those household groups were what was once considered a stereotypical family. Single-occupant, single-parent, and blended families were more common than the so-called typical family household. Neighborhoods and communities, increasingly diverse, were home to many racial and cultural groups.

The information revolution has directly affected audiences. New technology has given them greater access to information and entertainment.

Millions of people have quick access to multimedia Web sites that contain sound, film, and videotape, as well as text.

Today's media audiences are filled with people who have become accustomed to fast food, fast travel, and fast information. Today hundreds of millions of people worldwide have Internet access, and many of them regularly use Internet communication for daily tasks. Increasingly sophisticated audiences expect immediate, accurate, high-quality information.

Lifestyles and Diversity

Life today is complex with more sources of news that come from all directions. Media have proliferated, but no new hours have been added in the day to give audiences more time to use more media.

Even though some audience members search for information and use new media, others are more resistant. Caught in the demands of daily living, they still rely on the more traditional media for information. Perhaps they do not have the financial means to buy computers and software to go online. Writers must be aware, therefore, of how to communicate in both old and new media.

At the same time people's lifestyles are changing in the United States, the country is witnessing another trend that affects media use: cultural diversity. Demographic experts predict increasing shifts. The latest U.S. census data show that minorities make up a fast-growing one-third of the U.S. population. The traditional categories—African Americans, Asian Americans, Hispanic Americans, and Native Americans—lose meaning as new groups, such as Caribbean and Pacific Islanders, immigrate and as intercultural families become commonplace. Some young people of mixed heritage will no longer classify themselves in a single ethnic category.

Although ethnic- and gender-specific media have long had a role in this country, the changing complexion of the United States has meant an increase in media that address specific groups and individuals. The changes have meant new topics, new discussions, and new themes. Media, particularly general-interest newspapers, cover issues that for many years were carried only in specialized media, such as the black or Hispanic press.

Changing diversity has meant that media are also working to hire employees who represent differing groups so that newsrooms will more accurately reflect the makeup of the population in general. That has not been easy. African American, Asian American, and Hispanic American reporters, for example, are still few in number.

To attract and retain audiences, media executives have had to consider constraints such as money, lifestyles, increasing demands on time, and the lure of other media. Smart media managers have realized that they must adjust and be flexible to reach specific audiences. They have recognized that often they need to create a profile of their audience, by research and other means, to find out exactly who they are and what they need. Armed with knowledge about audiences, media leaders—and writers—can aim messages more specifically to their targeted destinations.

Knowing Audiences

People who write tend to read more than the average person does. They are likely to be more educated, have a larger vocabulary, and exhibit a greater interest in various topics. They may write to please themselves or to satisfy what they think audiences want to know. As lifestyles and diversity change, these writers might be out of touch with their audiences and not know truly who their audiences are.

Such ignorance is dangerous. Writers are at risk if they do not know who their audiences are or if they assume that they know who their audiences are. They also cannot assume that all audiences can grasp complicated, technical messages. Successful writers make an effort to know and to get in touch with their audiences.

Identifying Audiences

Few writers have a single audience, although many mistakenly write for what they call a mass audience. In today's world, *mass audience* is only a rough term used to describe a conglomeration of many smaller, specific audiences. Some may consider CNN, for example, to have a mass viewing audience. But even its audience can be broken into subgroups.

Members of small audiences have much in common. Some typical smaller audiences are veterans, working mothers, union members, and power company customers. An audience may be tiny (members of Temple Sinai) or it may be huge (Americans interested in better health care).

Regardless of size, every audience may be subdivided into smaller component audiences. For example, members of the congregation at Temple Sinai will include smaller audiences of children, teens, young adults, singles, marrieds, new parents, empty nesters, maintenance staff, grounds workers, and so on. Even a smaller audience in the congregation, such as immigrants from other countries, could be further divided into those from specific countries, such as Poland, Germany, or Israel.

Breaking an audience into its composite groups is an important activity for people who need to communicate essential messages. Each subgroup may have specific needs for information and a particular way of getting it. A university, for example, has many audiences, including students, faculty, staff, alumni, potential students, governing bodies, the press, and potential donors. No one message will effectively reach all of these audiences. Most universities spend a great deal of time and money developing specific messages that are targeted to their many audiences, such as the alumni newsletter for alumni, direct mail for potential donors, and news conferences for the media.

Writers must identify their audiences. A shortcut is to ask the question, "Who cares?" The answer will be a list of groups or audiences that are potential consumers of the message.

Let's try the "who cares?" method for listing audiences for a message. You are writing an article for your company newsletter on a new policy that provides preventive health care benefits to employees who have children. "Who cares?" yields this list:

- Married employees with children,
- Single employees with children,
- Employees thinking about having or adopting children, and
- Employees who have no children but who wish they had health care benefits.

Why is listing audiences important? Because even if writers go no further in getting to know their audiences, once they have at least listed them, they may change their writing approach. For the employee newsletter, your initial attempt at an introduction might have read:

```
A new company policy will provide health care benefits for
preventive medicine.
```

But after you list audiences, your introduction becomes more personal:

```
As a single parent, staff geologist John Payne has worried
about the extra expense of annual medical exams for his
```

three children and a doctor's visit if the children were only mildly ill.

But Mega Oil's new health benefits program will ease those worries. The plan will reimburse employees with children for preventive health expenses, such as well-child checkups.

As audiences are subdivided and defined, so are writing tasks. When writers take time to identify specific audiences, such as single parents, messages can be targeted for those audiences. The approach, structure, and language can be chosen to suit the audience, and communication becomes possible—and even likely.

The Writing Process Explained

Many people believe that good, skillful writing springs not from teaching and learning but from inborn talent that eludes most ordinary people.

Nonsense.

Writing a straightforward message requires no more inherent talent than following a road map. Author Joel Saltzman compares learning to write with learning to make salad dressing:

> *This is the only way I know to make a terrific salad dressing: Mix up a batch. Taste it. Mix again.*
>
> *The secret ingredient is the patience to keep trying—to keep working at it till you get it just right.*
>
> *Do most people have the talent to make a terrific salad dressing? Absolutely. Are they willing to make the effort to develop that skill? That's a different question.*

Good writing, like good salad dressing, can make even dry material palatable and can make good subject matter great. Like ingredients in a recipe, each word, sentence, and paragraph is selected carefully with one goal in mind: pleasing the consumer. The first bite will determine whether the diner eats more; good writing will sell a piece beyond the first paragraph. Like cooking, not every writing session will produce a masterpiece, but the end product must be palatable.

Writers today work in the same way as writers have worked throughout time—by following a regimen called *the writing process*. Once writers have identified their topics, they follow seven stages of the writing process presented here: information gathering, thinking and planning, listing, drafting, rewriting, sharing, and polishing.

Stages of the Writing Process

The same sequence of activities outlined here occurs in good writing of all kinds. All communicators must gather information, think about and plan the message, list key information, draft the message, rewrite the draft, share the message, and polish by checking and editing. Together, these separate stages of activity form the writing process: a set of behaviors common to all writers. The order of stages may vary, and some stages may be repeated, but each stage is essential to producing a good message.

Each stage in the writing process is briefly explained here; later chapters in this book will explain writing tasks in greater detail. You will be referred to relevant chapters as each stage is discussed.

Keep in mind that following these stages will produce successful writing in business, education, advertising, public relations, the new media and news media, and daily life. Throughout this text, you will learn what professional writers know: Writing is a skill that can be learned like other skills, one stage at a time. And the first stage is to go beyond yourself to gather information. Good writers are seekers.

Stage One: Information Gathering

Gathering information on your topic is the first stage of the writing process. To begin the search for information, you must answer questions that all people are prone to ask: Who? What? When? Where? Why? How? How much? Then what?

New technologies put many answers at our fingertips. Basic facts and figures are easy to obtain online, but every writer needs to go beyond superficial statistics. The Internet is just one tool.

Never begin to write without talking to other people or reading their work. Good writing requires basic external information. Once you know the questions, go outside yourself to find the answers. Even if you are an expert on your own topic, you must find other reliable authorities on it.

In writing an announcement of an art exhibit at a local art museum, for example, a writer might begin the questioning by talking with obvious experts—perhaps the curator and a local art teacher—who can provide answers and lead the writer to additional sources. For the exhibit announcement, aside from the basic *when* and *where* questions, the audience still needs to know the following: What types of artwork will be shown? Will prizes be awarded? Will any special guests appear at a reception?

The new questions will guide your next steps in your information search. Generally, steps in research lead to one of three sources:

1. *Interviews.* Talk, in person or by phone, to authorities or to people your initial sources suggest. Interviewing is discussed in Chapter 9.

2. *Library and online research.* Any kind of writing can require research in libraries, web sites, or databases. For example, if the art on display at the art museum celebrates Impressionism, the writer needs to find out about the Impressionists and their art. Basic research skills are included in Chapter 7.

3. *Other sources.* Brochures, publications, or archives can provide helpful information in old and new sources. For example, an article or brochure about last year's art exhibit could be located through a newspaper index or online archive. Chapter 7 explains how to use traditional and innovative reference sources.

It is important to gather information from a variety of sources. Ideally, a writer compiles more information than is actually needed so that he or she can be selective about which information to use.

Take notes on every source used in the information-gathering stage. A writer never knows when an important fact or statistic will emerge or when a quotable statement will be uttered. It is best to have a notepad always ready. In addition, careful notes enable writers to attribute interesting or unusual information to sources and to be accurate in what they have written.

Some writers refer to the information-gathering stage as "immersion" in the topic. Whatever it is called, this first stage of writing turns the writer into an informal expert on his or her subject matter.

Stage Two: Thinking and Planning

Once information is gathered, the writer studies the notes taken in Stage One and ponders them. He or she scans material to see what information seems most important and most interesting, then determines the angle and the focus.

A good writer always makes decisions about priorities, keeping in mind the audience that will receive the message. Successful writers actually picture the probable audience, hold that image in mind, and plan the message for that imaginary group. Some writers say they write for a specific person, such as a truck driver in Toledo or Aunt Mary in Hartford. Sometimes the thinking stage will allow the writer to see possibilities for creative approaches to writing.

In this stage of the writing process, the writer may realize that more information needs to be gathered before listing and writing can begin. Once the writer has gathered enough information, he or she will begin to evaluate and set priorities, asking, "What does my audience need to know first? What next?" and so on. If no further gaps in information become apparent at this stage, the writer takes pen and notepad in hand and moves on to Stage Three.

Stage Three: Listing

Listing requires writers to list the facts and ideas that must be included in the message. Some writers jot down key words; others write detailed outlines. Whatever form this activity takes, it yields one or more lists. Initial lists should be made by brainstorming, jotting down each important message element, and perhaps scratching out, adding, or combining items in the lists.

Once lists are committed to paper, the writer reviews them and attempts to rank the information. Imagine, for example, that the top priority item on the list is "student art shown." One of the top audiences listed is "parents," and one of the top audience goals is "nurturing our young people." Isolating these items guides the writer to structure a message that will feature student art, appeal to parents, and frame the event as a constructive, positive effort for young people.

In this stage, the writer imposes order and organization on the information. Chapters 4 and 5 deal with specific ways to organize messages.

Stage Four: Drafting the Message— As You Would Tell It

For most people, even experienced writers, writing seems somewhat unnatural. In contrast, conversational speech always seems to flow. So the efficient writer drafts a message by writing it as it might be told to a friend.

Checking the lists made in Stage Three, the writer would begin by "talking" about the first and most important element in the message—perhaps like this:

```
A student art show that displays the talents of 27 of the
city's young artists will open at 7 p.m. Wednesday at
Rockville Art Museum.
```

Once this telling process has begun, it continues easily. The writer will move smoothly through interesting aspects of the message to a stopping point after the listed priorities have been included.

By the end of this stage, the writer has created what is called a draft, rather than a message. The term *draft* distinguishes this version from a finished product. It is different from a polished message, and purposely so. Think of the draft as a raw lump of clay, in which substance is what counts. The stages that follow will shape the clay, giving form to the finished message. Drafting messages is discussed in Chapters 4 and 5.

Stage Five: Rewriting

In this stage, the conventions of the written language are imposed on the draft. Sentences are checked for completeness and coherence; paragraphs are formed and organized; and transitions and stylistic flourishes are added.

A good portion of this book is devoted to the skills involved in rewriting. Only through rewriting—sometimes repeated rewriting—can a message be streamlined to reach its intended audience. All good writers rewrite; great writers pride themselves on the painstaking reworking of their original phrases. Author E. B. White labored for three years over his slim classic *Charlotte's Web,* and he willingly revised much of his other work as many as 14 times.

Of course, writers on deadline cannot afford the luxury of spending years, or even hours, rewriting a draft. They develop shortcuts to rewriting as they become familiar with print formats, as described in Chapter 5. But no good writer ever skips the rewriting stage.

Rewriting is separate from polishing (Stage Seven), in which fine points of style, such as capitalization, are debated. If a writer stops in mid-draft to debate a style point, the train of thought is interrupted, and the writing process stops. Small decisions are left for the last stage—a stage that may be conducted by someone other than the writer.

Rewriting a draft is the bulk of the writing process. It is hard, time-consuming work; factors to consider in the process are discussed in Chapters 2 and 3. A rewritten draft is far from a finished work, however. Two stages remain in the writing process: sharing and polishing.

Stage Six: Sharing

The revised draft now must go to another reader—almost any other reader. By this stage, most writers have lost perspective on the message. They have become knowledgeable about the topic, and they may no longer be able to judge how the message would be received by an average member of the audience.

Sharing your work at this stage gives you a much better idea of how an audience member may react. Outside readers will quickly let you know whether the information is confusing or unclear, or whether any important details are missing.

It is a good idea to share your work with a naive reader—someone who knows far less about your topic than you do. Sometimes a colleague at work or a family member is an excellent choice for sharing because of that person's distance from your topic. In class, your instructor might allow peer editing of stories.

In large offices, outside review of your revised draft may be built in. For example, in big companies, drafts usually are reviewed by one or more editors and often by top management. Such an editing process is helpful in many ways, and certainly it saves the time and trouble of finding someone with whom to share your writing.

Regardless of who is sharing and commenting on your work, you as a writer must never forget that you did the initial research. You have expertise on your topic that your colleagues, family members, or even top managers may not have. Be sure to get feedback from your outside readers in a setting where you both can talk. You may need to explain why certain parts of your message are written as they are. Good editing is negotiation; no editor is an absolute dictator. You as a writer need to work with, not for, editors and outside reviewers. Together, you can produce clear, correct writing.

Stage Seven: Polishing

The final stage in the writing process is one that many people ignore or abhor. But editing or polishing is an essential and critical part of the writing process, and it is appropriately the last stage. Many young writers feel that all capitalization, punctuation, grammar, usage, and spelling must be perfect, even in an initial draft. Concentrating on perfection in all those areas is unimportant in the early stages of writing. You might spend 10 minutes looking in the dictionary for a word that you eventually decide not to use!

Working on word-by-word perfection at the early stages of writing is wasteful and even paralyzing. Writers who worry about every comma will find it difficult to get through the stages of drafting and revising. Writing becomes a much more comfortable and speedy task when polishing is put off until its proper place at the end of the process. After the important substance and form of the message have been established, then spend time with style books, dictionaries, and thesauruses.

All writers should polish their work. But in truth, this final stage of editing may well be performed by another person. An editor or editorial assistant may make the final checks for correctness and consistency and put a message in final form. The polishing process comes last also because it may come after the writer passes the message along. Confident writers welcome assistance with this final, cosmetic touch, knowing that letter-perfect writing will add to the credibility and clarity of their message.

Considering Audiences

E. B. White in the introduction to *The Elements of Style* explains that good writing is a writer's responsibility to the audience. He tells how his professor and coauthor, William "Will" Strunk, taught rules to writers out of sympathy for readers.

> *All through* The Elements of Style *one finds evidences of the author's deep sympathy for the reader. Will felt that the reader was in serious trouble most of the time, a man floundering in a swamp, and that it was the duty of anyone attempting to write English to drain this swamp quickly and get this man up on dry ground or at least throw him a rope. . . . I have tried to hold steadily in mind this belief of his, this concern for the bewildered reader.*

It is time to return to Strunk's wisdom. As a teacher in the early twentieth century, Strunk knew that audiences were hindered by poor type quality and low levels of literacy. Today, writers contend with new distractions Strunk could never have imagined. But the remedy in either era is the same: clear messages that show consideration for audiences.

The principles of effective communication are more important now than ever, regardless of the medium, as discussed in Chapters 10 through 12. Even essential messages are in danger of being crowded out in an increasingly competitive media marketplace and in an age of instant, constant communication. Challenges for writers have never been greater; at the same time, communication opportunities have never been so great. The potential power of media messages is unlimited in society, where people are confounded by change and unlikely to have traditional networks of family, church, and community.

Today's complex communication environment calls for simple, direct messages. The chapters that follow provide a guide to writing messages that audiences will search for and understand in the information age.

Wrap-Up

So where are we? In this chapter we have discussed the many changes in media and audiences, as well as how writing is critical to communication. Every day people are bombarded with dozens of messages from television, newspapers, mail, e-mail, faxes, flyers, magazines, Web sites, billboards, other people, and on and on and on. In today's information age, numerous messages cruise from writer to audiences. Many reach their destination—audiences—but are immediately discarded before they have a chance to be assimilated and acted on.

Writers and communicators must accept that getting messages to people in today's society is an unparalleled challenge. Writers have to accept that they cannot do much to change an individual consumer's lifestyle. They cannot reduce the number of media. They cannot modify society's diversity. They cannot alter the fact that only a few messages get through the daily clutter.

But they can control one aspect: the structure of the message. Trained writers know techniques for ensuring that messages reach their destination and are consumed. For some audiences, the succinct three-paragraph news brief will suffice. Others will seek the longer, more detailed, narrative account. Good writers know which techniques and which structures best fit their audiences.

In the next two chapters, you will look at standard equipment writers need to make messages, clear, complete, and accurate. They must know grammar, spelling, and style. In many cases, they need to calculate simple math problems. These specific skills are discussed in Chapter 2.

Chapter 3 expands on the stages of writing outlined in this chapter and gives some basic rules for clear writing. Knowing these rules will help when it's time to write—skills taught in Chapters 4 and 5.

EXERCISES

1. Keep a media log for a 24-hour period between today and the next class. Make a chart showing which media you used, how long you viewed or read, a summary of messages, and what else you were doing while using each medium. Indicate whether you had interference or distractions that prevented you from understanding the message. Be prepared to compare your media-use patterns with those of others in the class.

2. Interview a relative about his or her media use, formulating questions based on your log. Explore how his or her media use has changed during the last 5 years, 10 years. Where does the person get most news? Entertainment? Information that is dependable? In-depth information?

3. Write a few paragraphs describing the characteristics of the audience for your student newspaper. Then explain how you could follow Strunk and White's advice to help the audience use and understand the student paper better.

4. Choose a major national event that occurred within the past two weeks. Go to the library and select several sources that reported the event. Examples would be community newspaper, national newspaper, local daily newspaper, national news magazine, or online publication. Compare the way each introduced and developed the story. Look at writing style, language, length of story, anecdotes, and quotations. Does the format for presenting the news fit the medium's audiences? How?

5. Interview a classmate. Follow the stages of writing in producing a 30-line story about the person. Explain what you did in each stage. For example, in listing, you might list the person's accomplishments or extracurricular activities. In sharing, you might have another classmate read your draft.

REFERENCES

Ian E. Anderson, ed., *Editor and Publisher Yearbook*. New York: Editor & Publisher Co., 1997.

Associated Press Managing Editors Home Page. Available: http://www.apme.org.

"Internet Slowed but Unbowed," *Broadcasting & Cable,* September 17, 2001.

Irwin Kirsch, Ann Jungeblut, and Donald Rock, "Reading Newspapers: The Practices of America's Young Adults." Paper delivered to the Education Writers Association, April 1988.

Marshall McLuhan and Q. Fiore, *The Medium Is the Message: An Inventory of Effects.* New York: Bantam Books, 1967.

The Poynter Institute Media Diversity Beyond 2000 Home Page. Available: http://www.poynter.org/dsurvey.

Joel Saltzman, *If You Can Talk, You Can Write.* New York: Ballantine Books, 1993.

William Strunk, Jr., and E. B. White, *The Elements of Style.* New York: Macmillan, 1979.

U.S. Census Bureau Home Page. Available: http://www.census.gov/population.

2

Tools for Writers
Spelling, Grammar, Style, and Math

An advertisement tells readers that a local oratorio group is looking for sopranos, altos, and bases.

A news story reports that ultraviolate rays from the sun can cause skin damage and lead to skin cancer.

A company's annual report notes that revenues rose 10 percent in the last quarter.

A close check of all the above statements shows that the oratorio group isn't really looking for bases, like bases in baseball, but singers as in basses; the sun has ultraviolet rays that perhaps violate the skin; and because of a computation error, the revenues actually rose 19 percent.

Writers can gather information, write stories, and publish or air them. But if they aren't careful in checking their grammar, punctuation, spelling, numbers, or facts, they can damage their credibility with audiences—as well as their company's credibility.

For example, when President Ronald Reagan was shot in 1981, ABC newscaster Frank Reynolds announced that Reagan had died. Within seconds, he had to recant the story. Errors need not be that dramatic to cause audiences pause or dismay, however. In announcing the university's hiring of a prominent journalist, a campus newspaper headline billed him as a

"Pultizer Prize winner." Did you catch the typo? Another student newspaper in capturing the news after the terrorist attacks on September 11 noted retribution was "eminent." CBS reported on shark attacks along the North Carolina coast, and the map identified the location as Monteo, rather than Manteo. Often, such errors are caused by haste or carelessness.

Research has shown that when messages are perceived to be error free, they also are thought to be credible and well written. The perception of quality carries over to the writer and to the medium, be it newpaper, television, or online site. In other words, messages free of errors are thought to be of high quality and produced by professionals.

Students often argue that they don't need to know spelling, grammar, or punctuation skills. They believe that an editor—somewhere—will fix any errors, or that errors will be caught by spell-checkers or grammar-checkers. Wrong. As a communicator, you may be writer and editor. And as most of us know, spell-checkers don't catch the difference between *principal* and *principle* and any number of synonyms and homonyms.

Communicators who pay attention to their craft pay attention to detail. That means attending to spelling, grammar, punctuation, and style. Most media have style rules. They follow Associated Press style or they have developed style guidelines of their own. Adopting a specific style ensures consistency in all articles, regardless of who writes them or where they appear.

In addition to style, more and more writers today are expected to know basic math. For example, they need to know how to compute percentages, to figure out square footage, to determine whether poll data are representative, and so on.

In this chapter, you will learn

- What spelling pitfalls to watch for,
- Common adult grammar problems,
- Basic rules of Associated Press style,
- Copyediting symbols, and
- Bottom-line math skills.

Spelling in the Computer Age

Writers, BEWARE: Spelling skills are essential in the computer age. This warning might sound exaggerated because computers can check spellings of hundreds of words in minutes. But take heed. The following paragraph passed a spell-check program in less than one second without a hitch:

```
They're know miss steaks in this newsletter cause we used
special soft wear witch checks yore spelling. It is mower
or lass a weigh to verify. How ever it can knot correct
arrows in punctuation ore usage, an it will not fined words
witch are miss used butt spelled rite. Four example, a
paragraph could have mini flaws but wood bee past by the
spell checker. And it wont catch the sentence fragment
witch you. Their fore, the massage is that proofreading is
know eliminated but is berry much reek wired.
```

Although the example is exaggerated, it serves to remind that a spell-checker only "checks." It looks to see that all typed words correspond exactly to real words listed in the computer's dictionary. Here's how it works: Spell-checkers look at each word, then check for a match in the dictionaries stored in the computer memory. A spell-checker highlights only the words that have no match in the computer's dictionary, stopping the checking process at those words so that they may be manually checked by the writer or editor.

What Spell-Checkers Will (and Won't) Do

Memory-based checking systems are a great invention, virtually eliminating senseless typographical errors such as "scuh" and "typograpical," as well as common spelling problems such as "seperate" and "mispell." Unfortunately, however, it is not a perfect invention.

Here's the problem: If a computer merely finds a word in its dictionary, it "checks" that word, assuring the writer that the spelling is correct. Say, for example, the computer encounters this sentence: "Robin was going too the fare." The sentence checks. The words "too" and "fare" exist in the dictionary, so they pass muster. And if Robin happens to be spelled correctly "Robyn," that error will go unchecked because "robin" would be found in the computer's dictionary. Or perhaps the typo is an actual word, such as "count" instead of "court." The error would slip by as correct, and the writer would have created an immediate audience-stopper and confusion.

Remember that a spell–checker indicates only the words that have no match. So spell–checkers aid writers in only some spelling instances, not all of them. Some of the most challenging spelling tasks, which are listed in the next section, are still the writer's responsibility.

A Do-It-Yourself List

By now it should be clear that spell–checkers will not do everything. The writer has the hands-on, do-it-yourself responsibility of checking the following problems that spell–checkers do not correct.

HOMONYMS. Writers must distinguish among homonyms, or words that sound alike but have different meanings and are spelled differently. Any writer's credibility would drop if his or her readers saw these sentences:

```
Mrs. Margolis consulted two professional piers before
suspending the student.
```
Readers will see Mrs. Margolis conferring in a lakeside setting.

```
Barnes said he didn't want to altar his plans.
```
Will Barnes offer his plan during religious services?

```
All navel movements will be approved by the commanding
officer.
```
Whose belly buttons?

```
Investigators found millions of land mines sewn into the
earth.
```
Did someone use a needle and thread?

Such homonyms as "pier" and "peer," "alter" and "altar," and "sewn" and "sown" escape highlighting by the spell–checker, which recognizes each as a dictionary word. Writers who are overconfident in the ability of spell–checkers will undoubtedly leave simple errors in their writing. Some words writers should watch for include the following:

to, two, too	aid, aide
their, they're, there	it's, its
no, know	whose, who's

More subtle—but no less damaging—are the errors made when writers confuse other commonly occurring homonyms, such as those listed here. Good writers distinguish between or among homonyms.

affect (verb)

effect (noun, meaning result, verb meaning bring about)

a lot (colloquial expression substituted for "many" or "much")

allot (to distribute)

allude (refer to)

elude (escape)

altar (in a church)

alter (change)

altogether (adverb meaning entirely)

all together (adjective meaning in a group)

bare (naked, uncovered)

bear (animal, to support)

baring (showing)

bearing (supporting)

bore (to drill, to be dull)

boar (pig)

canvas (cloth)

canvass (poll)

capitol (building)

capital (city)

compliment (flattering statement)

complement (fills up or completes)

counsel (advise, legal adviser)

council (assembly)

consul (diplomatic officer)

dual (two)

duel (combat between two people)

flair (style; panache)

flare (torch)

guerrilla (person who engages in warfare)

gorilla (ape)

immigrate (come to a new country)

emigrate (leave one's country)

legislature (body)

legislator (individual official)

miner (in a mine)

minor (under age)

naval (of the navy)

navel (belly button)

pore (small opening; to examine closely)

pour (to cause to flow)

pier (water walkway)

peer (social equal)

principal (head, first)

principle (lesson, belief)

role (in a play)

roll (list)

stare (regard intensely)

stair (step in a staircase)

stationery (paper)

stationary (permanent)

vein (blood vessel)

vain (conceited)

vane (wind detector)

Note: There is no such word as "alot." "A lot" is two distinct words.

SIMILAR WORDS WITH DIFFERENT USES. No spell-checker knows the difference between "conscience" and "conscious," "affect" and "effect," "flout" and "flaunt," "loose" and "lose," "lead" and "led," "read" and "red," "border" and "boarder," or "populace" and "populous." Some grammar-check programs will highlight such problematic words, but these programs require the writer to make the correct choice. Keeping a good stylebook or grammar guide on your desk is the best way to make distinctions among similar words. Again, the writer or editor must catch the error, even though a spell-checker lives within the computer.

COMPOUND WORDS. Some compound words, such as "speedboat" and "bookkeeper," will pass spell-checkers as two words, even though they are correctly spelled as single words. The reason? The spell-checker recognizes the separate words—"speed," "boat," "book," and "keeper"—as valid entries, leaving the writer appearing not to know the correct spelling.

PROPER NAMES. As noted earlier, proper names—unlike most units of language—may be spelled any way an individual desires. The infinite variety of name spellings makes it standard for all names to be checked and double-checked, regardless of what spell-checking approves. Many names, such as Robin and Lily, are also common nouns listed in computer dictionaries. Often the correct spelling for the proper name is different from that offered by a spell-checker. For example, Robin may be "Robyn," and Lily may spell her name "Lillie." Double-check names in any document.

Both spell-checking and manual, word-by-word editing still are "berry much reek wired," as our earlier example stated. No machine can replace the complex decision making that an editor provides. In the information age, good writers and editors are even more essential to ensure accurate writing.

Grammar to the Rescue

Our world is fast-paced and fast-changing—hardly the kind of place you would expect to need something as tedious as a lesson on grammar. But today's communicator cannot afford to slow down audiences, and faulty grammar does just that.

Consider the reader who encounters "its" where "it's" should be. For a split second, the reader will pause and wonder about the error, the writer, and the publication. Sometimes the musing reader will stop reading entirely because of the slowdown or because of the reduced credibility or appeal of the flawed message.

People do not have to be grammar experts to stop and wonder about correctness. For example, any unusual use of "whom" or "who" may cause a reader to reflect rather than read on. "Now, what was it I learned about *whom*?" the reader muses, and the tempo of reading is lost.

Television viewers may cringe when the news announcer says, "The committee will reconvene their meeting tomorrow morning." They know a committee is referred to with an "its," not a "their." While they have paused to correct the sentence, they have lost the remainder of the announcer's message.

But My Grammar Is Good...

Most of us who pursue writing as a career consider ourselves to be language experts, and in general, our grammar and language use are far above average. Even educated people have problems, however. Evidence of grammar problems is found in mistakes made daily by adults in business letters, memos, and reports, as well as in newspapers and on the airways. An ad proclaims, "There's no down payment and no service charge!" To be grammatically correct, it should say, "There are no down payment and no service charge." A newsletter states, "Children will be grouped by age, irregardless of grade in school." There is no such word as "irregardless," which is simply an aberration of "regardless."

Educated, employed people regularly make grammar mistakes that other educated people will recognize. Writers need to learn what their most frequent grammar errors are and how to correct them. A first step in checking your grammar is to know what errors you are most likely to make.

Grammar Problems

Author Katherine C. McAdams, an associate professor at the University of Maryland, has developed "The Grammar Slammer," a workshop on grammar problems. It identifies five areas in which real-life errors are most likely to occur:

- Punctuation, especially commas, semicolons, colons, apostrophes, dashes, and hyphens.

- Subject and verb agreement.
- Correct pronoun choices that provide agreement and that avoid gender bias, such as "Each student has his or her book" rather than the more common and erroneous "Each student has their book."
- Correct sentence structures, especially when sentences use modifiers or require parallel structure.
- Word use—that is, using words (such as regardless) correctly; often this area involves spelling problems and confusing words that sound alike (such as "affect" and "effect" or "vain" and "vein").

This section follows the format of the Grammar Slammer workshop, giving a short lesson on each of the problem areas and following that lesson with some exercises. The approach is designed for writers who are bright, motivated, and capable of learning quickly.

The lessons provide a quick fix rather than an in–depth lesson. They are designed to refresh and renew rather than to reeducate. Going through the grammar lessons will help you identify your grammar deficiencies. You then can be on guard for your particular problems when writing and editing. You may find that you have many weaknesses in language skills and understanding. If so, you will want to study the books recommended at the end of this chapter or take a grammar course.

Test Yourself

To determine which areas you need to work on, take the following diagnostic quiz. Record your answers on a sheet of paper.

Grammar Slammer Diagnostic Quiz

The following sentences contain errors in grammar and punctuation. No sentence contains more than one error. Read each sentence. Circle the error, and in the margin note how the sentence should be written correctly. Sentence 1 is corrected for you as an example.

1. If past performance is any indication, Maryland should be considered a top challenger for the championship; having downed defending regional champion Duke twice in the regular season. (*Correction:* Use a comma in place of the semicolon because the second half of the sentence is not an independent clause.)

2. The list of candidates being considered as successors for the university chancellor have been trimmed to approximately 50 names, including four university officials.

3. The computer did not seem to be working today; it kept rejecting the operator's instructions.

4. The following afternoon, Wednesday, October 25, a Royal Indian Air Force DC-3 landed in the abandoned dirt strip of Srinagar Airport.

5. Traditionally, expected to be in control of their surroundings, the insecurity makes students uncomfortable in their new situation.

6. Franco's body will lay in state until services are held at the chapel.

7. Hopefully, the council will pass a new noise ordinance before the students return to campus in September.

8. Among those who attended services for Sloan were Ralph Fridgen, head football coach at Maryland; Maryanne Fox, chancellor at NCSU; Joab Thomas, former NCSU chancellor; and Paul Deitzel, former athletic director at LSU.

9. She predicted that neither McCain or Lott would receive the Republican nomination.

10. In its advertising, the Acme Company claims that they are in business only to do good works for the community.

11. Millie Rosefield, chair of the Rockland Historic Preservation Committee ran fifth in the Nov. 6 race for four council seats.

12. One of every five of the state's residents lives in the sort of poverty that drove Erskine Caldwell to write.

13. Three-fourths of the business district in Long Beach, N.C. was destroyed by Hurricane Hugo, which struck the coast in 1989.

14. Many a boy use to believe that he could acquire practically superhuman strength by eating the right cereal.

15. Jones said the parade would feature the homecoming queen, the marching band will play, a pep rally, and as many floats as possible.

16. Several people, all of them eager to give their opinions and all of them pressing forward to meet the governor, who was conducting interviews with voters in the area.

17. I like ice cream and cookies; I don't like cakes with icing.

18. Rosalie complained, and she had no heat.

19. Being a weight lifter, his muscles were well developed.

20. The alligator is hunted for their skin.

Several of the following words, are misspelled. Circle the misspelled words, and write the correct spelling for each in the space provided.

1. principal (of a school) _principle_
2. waiver (permission slip) _waver_
3. bore (a wild pig) _boar_
4. naval (belly button) _navel_
5. stationery (you write on it) _stationary_
6. role (a list) _roll_
7. roommate _roomate_
8. canvass (cloth) _canvas_
9. complement (flattering statement) _compliment_
10. cite (reference or footnote) _site_

Answers for the diagnostic quiz are included in Appendix B at the back of the book.

Grammar Problems Up Close

Examine the items you missed on the diagnostic quiz. You should have an idea of which grammar problems you need to review. The discussion of each problem is presented here and followed by exercises. Test your proficiency and move on. Record your answers on a sheet of paper. To check your work, look at the answers in Appendix B.

Problem 1: Punctuation

Perhaps no problem looms larger than that of punctuation. Few people actually know the rules and regulations of punctuation use. Most of us, much of the time, use the "feel good" school of punctuation, saying, "I just feel like I need a comma here" or "A semicolon just felt right."

Professional communicators must give up their "feel good" philosophy of punctuating. The first rule of punctuating professionally is this: **Do not punctuate unless you know a rule.** When you even think of adding a mark of punctuation, stop and think about whether it is justified by the rules in this chapter. If not, you probably don't need to punctuate at all.

If you find that you are punctuating excessively—that is, using more than three punctuation marks within any given sentence—it is probably time to rewrite that sentence. Sentences that require many punctuation marks, even if they are all correct, are usually too long and complex to be easily understood by readers. So another rule of punctuating professionally is: LESS IS MORE. Less punctuation leads to clearer, more readable copy. When in doubt, leave the comma out.

Commas

Literally hundreds of comma rules exist. But the nine listed here, distilled by high school English teacher Mary Penny in the 1940s, have been found over the years to take care of most everyday comma problems.

RULE 1. Use commas in compound sentences when clauses are separated by a conjunction such as "and," "but," "for," "nor," or "yet."

- She managed the restaurant, but he did the cooking.

Note: In such sentences, leaving out the conjunction leads to an error known as a *comma splice,* whereby a comma is left to do the work of joining two sentences: "She managed the restaurant, he did the cooking." Like weak splices in rope, commas are not strong enough for this task. A period or semicolon is needed to make a correct sentence:

- She managed the restaurant. He did the cooking.
- She managed the restaurant; he did the cooking.

RULE 2. Use commas to separate elements in a series. Such elements usually are adjectives, verbs, or nouns. *Note:* Journalism departs from traditional rules of punctuation by leaving the comma out before a conjunction in a series of elements. The text in this book follows the comma in a series rule, but the journalism examples do not—as you may have already noticed in reading this text.

English composition version:

- The tall, dark, handsome man hailed, lauded, and applauded Ben, George, Maude, and Rebecca.

Journalism version:

- The tall, dark, handsome man hailed, lauded and applauded Ben, George, Maude and Rebecca.

RULE 3. Use commas when attributing from quoted material. Commas set off words of attribution from the words of a one-sentence quotation unless a question mark or exclamation mark is preferred. Use them also in greetings:

- He said, "Hello." "Good-bye," she replied.

RULE 4. Commas follow introductory matter, such as after an introductory adverbial clause:

- When the team was forced to kick, the coach sent in his best players.

Commas also follow two or more introductory prepositional phrases:

- In the spring she returned to College Park. (no comma)
- In the spring of 1981, she returned to College Park. (comma needed because "in" and "of" are two prepositional phrases)

Also use a comma with a phrase that contains a verbal (i.e., a verb form used as a modifier):

- Singing as she worked, Mary answered the phone.
- Kicked by a horse, Don was more than stunned.
- To cure hiccups, drink from the far side of a glass.

RULE 5. Commas follow the salutation of a friendly letter and the complimentary close of any letter. Commas also follow capitalized elements, such as the complimentary close (e.g., Sincerely, Very truly yours), and a colon follows the salutation of a business letter:

- Dear Reese,
- Dear Dean Cleghorn:

RULE 6. Commas follow all items in a date or full address:

- July 16, 1962, is his date of birth.
- She has lived in Manteo, N.C., all her life.

RULE 7. Commas surround nonessential words or phrases:

- Well, we will just have to walk home.

Commas also set off appositives, which are words or phrases that rename a noun. Appositives amplify a subject:

- Betty Brown, his mother-in-law, has been married four times.

Also use a comma to set off nonessential modifying clauses and phrases:

- The president-elect, suffering from laryngitis, canceled his speech.

RULE 8. Commas surround words of direct address:

- Maria, please pass the butter.
- I can see, Fred, that you are lazy.

RULE 9. Commas indicate omitted verbs, usually expressed in another part of the sentence:

- Talent often is inherited; genius, never.

This rule is an old one and is rarely used today except in headlines. It would be rare to find a comma indicating an omitted verb in contemporary writing, but far from surprising to see such headlines as:

- Pilots Ask for Guns; Airlines, for Marshals
- Fridgen has much to gain this season; his team, even more

Semicolons and Colons

Miss Penny added three more rules to her list to take care of another widespread punctuation problem: the correct use of semicolons and colons. Miss Penny's rules 10 and 11 explain the two uses of the semicolon—the **only** two uses. Rule 12 explains the use of colons.

RULE 10. Semicolons connect two complete sentences if sentences have a related thought. Use of a semicolon usually creates a sense of drama:

- The brown-eyed, dark, and vivacious model, at age 25, seemed destined for quick success; on Dec. 11, 2001, her apparent destiny was altered.

RULE 11. Semicolons are used in a list separating items that require significant internal punctuation:

- He visited Richmond, Va.; Raleigh, N.C.; Greenville, S.C.; Birmingham, Ala.; and Baton Rouge, La.

RULE 12. Colons precede formal lists, illustrations, multisentence quotes, and enumerations:

- The following students received scholarships: Jim Johnson, Juanita Jones, Martha Taylor, Tiffany Eldridge, and Teri Sampson.
- He answered her with a parable: "A man once had six sons. Five of them...."
- Clinton listed the steps in his recovery program: First, to raise interest rates; second, to reduce spending....
- Do note use a colon after "include" or forms of "to be," such as "was" or "were."

Slammer for Commas, Semicolons, and Colons

Now, using Miss Penny's list of 12 rules as your reference, complete the following exercise. *Remember:* The most important rule is that you **do not** punctuate unless you know a rule. Defend each mark of punctuation that you use by citing one of the Penny rules on a sheet of paper.

Rule or Rules

1. Although we watched the Super Bowl we don't know who won.
2. John Blimpo an egocentric man dropped his hat in the fruit salad.
3. Guitars have six strings basses four.
4. The tall dark handsome man listed his hobbies as reading fishing painting and writing.
5. To Whom It May Concern

   The spelling and grammar test will be given on March 2 3 and 4 1991 in Room 502 of the Journalism Building.

   Grammatically yours

   J. School Dean

6. Dad go ahead and send the money now.
7. The women's basketball team was down by four points at halftime however they came back to crush their opponents.
8. Congress passed the bill but the debate took several weeks.
9. Well just be in by daybreak.
10. Her blind date was a real disappointment he talked loudly and constantly about his pet snake.
11. She was elected on Nov. 3 1972 in Baltimore Md. the city of her birth to serve as mayor.
12. She named her courses for the fall semester journalism English political science history and French.

Check your exercise by looking at the answers in Appendix B. Then go on to tackle some other troublesome marks of punctuation.

Hyphens and Dashes

Remember that hyphens and dashes, although often confused, are different.

The hyphen differs from a dash in both use and appearance. The hyphen is shorter (- as opposed to —), and it comes, without additional spaces, between two words that are combined to express some new concept, such as polka-dot and part-time. Hyphens are useful joiners that bring some creativity to language.

Rather than joining phrases, dashes are useful in separating them—usually where that separation can be heard. Dashes are sometimes used to replace commas to ensure that a pause is audible and even dramatic (e.g., "Although charming, he was—on the other hand—a thief").

Here is a list of guidelines for using hyphens and dashes correctly:

1. Never use a hyphen after a word ending in "ly."
   - The newly elected president stepped to the podium.

2. Use a hyphen to connect two or more related modifying words that do not function independently.
   - Kim always ordered the blue-plate special.
   - Todd dreaded any face-to-face confrontations.

3. The dash is a punctuation mark that one "hears." It is a noticeable pause. Choose a dash instead of a comma so that the audience can "hear" the pause.

4. Dashes work where commas would also work. The only difference is that the dash adds drama—and an audible break in the text. Because dashes may substitute for commas, they are used to set off nonessential material.
   - The murderer was—if you can believe it—a priest.

5. Too many dashes in any text may be distracting and even irritating to readers. Limit dashes to only the most dramatic of pauses. In most cases, such as this example, commas will suffice.
   - She is—as most of you know—a punctuation expert.
   - She is, as most of you know, a punctuation expert.

Other marks of punctuation, especially apostrophes, can be troublesome. Correct use may vary from time to time and publication to publication. Always check your stylebook, and keep a current grammar reference book handy.

Problem 2: Subject and Verb Agreement

Few writers make obvious errors in subject and verb agreement, such as "I is interested in cars" or "The class know it's time to go to lunch." But most people struggle with the following subject–verb agreement problems:

1. Collective subjects can be confusing. Some nouns that appear to be plural—such as "Girl Scouts," "checkers," and "economics"—are treated as singular units.
   - The Girl Scouts is a fine organization.

- Checkers is an ancient game.
- Economics is a difficult subject.

Some collective subjects, however, have Latinate endings and remain plural, although spoken language tends to make them singular, such as "media" and "alumni." In formal writing, these plurals require plural verbs.

- The media have raised the issue of the senator's competency.

2. The pronouns "each," "either," "neither," "anyone," "everyone," and "anybody" are always singular, regardless of what follows them in a phrase. Take, for example, this sentence:

- Either of the girls is an excellent choice for president.

The phrase "of the girls" does not change the singular number of the true subject of this sentence: the pronoun "either." Following are some other examples of correct usage.

- Neither has my vote.
- Either is fine with me.
- Each has an excellent option.
- Anyone is capable of helping the homeless.
- Everyone is fond of Jerry.

3. A fraction or percentage of a whole is considered a singular subject.

- Three-quarters of the pie is gone.
- Sixty-seven percent of the voters is needed to withhold a veto.

4. Compound subjects, in which two or more nouns function as the subject of a sentence, can lead to agreement problems. To solve such problems, substitute a single pronoun, such as "they" or "it," for the sentence's subject or subjects.

For example, transform this problem sentence: "The students and the teacher is/are waiting for the bus." By substituting, the subject becomes "they": They are waiting for the bus. Some other examples are:

- The opening number and the grand finale thrill the audience. (they thrill)
- There are no down payment and no service charge. (they are not there)

5. When subjects are structured with either/or and neither/nor, use the verb that corresponds to the subject closest to it, as in the following cases:

- Either the leader or the scouts pitch the tent.
- Either the scouts or the leader pitches the tent.

Slammer for Subject–Verb Agreement

Check your knowledge of subject–verb agreement by taking the following quiz. On a separate sheet of paper, write the verb that agrees.

1. He did say he would look at the sheet of names, which includes/include the owners of two apartment buildings.
2. Their number and influence appears/appear greatest in West Germany.
3. Experience in the backfield and the line gives/give the coach a good feeling on the eve of any opening game.
4. A first offense for having fewer than 25 cartons of untaxed cigarettes results/result in a $500 fine.
5. Before you make a final judgment on this student's story, consider the time and effort that has/have gone into it.
6. Who does the teaching? Full professors. But so does/do associates, assistants, and instructors.
7. She said they would visit Peaks of Otter, which is/are near Lynchburg, Va.
8. The news media is/are calling for a peace treaty that is fair to everyone.
9. The United Mine Workers exhibit/exhibits solidarity during strikes.
10. There is/are 10 million bricks in this building.
11. The president said that students today are too job-oriented and neglect the broader areas of study that constitutes/constitute a true education.
12. Five fire companies fought the blaze, which the firefighters said was/were the longest this year.
13. Each of the 100 people believes/believe in God.
14. It is/are the boats, not the swimmers, that stir up the dirt in the lake.

15. The editor told the staff there was a shortage of money for the news-room, a shortage she said she would explain to the board of directors, which decides/decide all matters on the budget.
16. One of my classmates typifies/typify student apathy.
17. Drinking beer and sleeping is/are the most important things in my life.
18. Dillon said he has insurance for everything except the buildings, which is/are owned by Thomas F. Williams.
19. Approximately 51 percent of the U.S. population is/are female.
20. There is/are only one way to beat taxes.
21. Neither the professor nor her two assistants teaches/teach this course in a style students like.
22. Each student is/are responsible for getting the work done on time.
23. All students considers/consider that an imposition.
24. The General Assembly and the governor disagrees/disagree on the solution.

Check your answers against those in Appendix B.

Problem 3: Correct Use of Pronouns

Pronouns are little words—"he," "she," "you," "they," "I," "it"—that stand for proper nouns. Look at this sentence:

- International Trucking is hiring 20 new drivers because it is expand-ing in the Southeast.

In this sentence, the word "it" is used to substitute for International Trucking. Pronouns help in avoiding needless repetition in language by do-ing the work of the larger nouns, which are called *antecedents.* In the previous example, "International Trucking" is the antecedent for the pronoun "it."

Pronouns must agree with their antecedents, as in the following examples:

- Marianne said she (Marianne) would never color her (Marianne's) hair.
- Baltimore became a model city after it successfully restored the water-front.
- Journalism is a popular major, and now it prepares students for many careers.

Following are guidelines to ensure correct pronoun choices:

1. Watch for collective subjects—groups that are treated as single units—and use the correct pronoun.
   - The committee gave its report.
   - The United Mine Workers gave out a list of its legislative goals.

2. When using singular pronouns, use singular verbs.
   - Each of the rose bushes was at its peak.
   - Everyone in the audience rose to his or her feet and chanted.

3. Use correct pronouns to handle issues of sexism in language. The generic person is no longer "he."
   - Each of the students had his or her book.
   - The students had their books.

4. Be attentive to stray phrases or clauses that come between pronouns and antecedents and cause agreement problems.
   - He presented the list of candidates being considered for the office and told the committee members to choose from it. (antecedent agreement)
   - The list of candidates for the position has been trimmed. (subject-verb agreement)

5. Use reflexive pronouns only when a subject is doing something to herself or himself or themselves.
   - Jan introduced herself to the new chancellor.
   - Henry never could forgive himself.
   - The relatives had the chalet to themselves.

Slammer for Pronouns

To ensure agreement of pronoun and antecedent, write the appropriate pronoun for each of the following sentences. Use a piece of paper to record your answers.

1. Each student had (his or her/their) assignment completed before class.
2. General Foods plans to change (its/their) approach to marketing baked goods.
3. Larry introduced me and (him/himself) to the governor.

4. The jury took (their/its) deliberations seriously.
5. The board of directors set a date for (their/its) annual retreat.
6. The Redskins (is/are) my favorite team.
7. Neither the Terps nor the Crimson Tide (was/were) having a winning season.
8. Neither of the teams (was/were) victorious.
9. The alumni voted to charge $1 an issue for (their/its) magazine.
10. Any of the three finalists (is/are) an excellent choice.
11. The six-member committee voted to reverse (its/their) decision.
12. The librarian's collection fascinated him, and he asked to borrow from (her/it).
13. The media (is/are) ignoring Perot's speeches.
14. Each of the students could handle the job by (himself or herself/themselves).
15. Everyone in the audience rose to (his or her/their) feet for the ovation.

Check your work against the answers in Appendix B, and prepare to tackle the biggest pronoun problem of all: the *who/whom* dilemma.

WHO AND WHOM. The word "whom" has all but disappeared from spoken English, so it is little wonder that few of us know how to use it correctly. Even though usage is changing, writers of published materials still need to know the rules that govern the distinction between "who" and "whom":

1. "Who" is a substitute for subjects referring to "he," "we," or "she," or the nominative pronoun. *or "they"*

   • Who saw the meteor?

   The statement, "He saw the meteor," as a question becomes, "Who saw the meteor?" "Who" is substituted for the subject "he." Relative clauses work the same way when "who" is substituted for a subject. In the sentence, "He questioned the man who saw the meteor," "who" substitutes for the subject of the clause, "He saw the meteor." This is confusing because the entire clause serves as an object of the verb questioned. But the function of the clause does not change the role of a pronoun; in this sentence, the role of "who" is as the subject of the verb "saw."

2. "Whom" is a substitute for objective pronouns, such as "him," "her," or "them."

   - Whom did he question for hours?

   The statement, "He questioned her for hours," as a question becomes, "Whom did he question for hours?" "Whom" is substituted for "her" as the object of the verb "questioned." Substitution works the same way in relative clauses. In the sentence, "Marcella was the one whom he questioned for hours," "whom" substitutes for the object "her" in the clause, "He questioned her for hours." Again, it is the role of the pronoun within its subject–verb structure that determines whether it is the subject or the object and therefore *who* or *whom*.

THAT AND WHICH. Another fine distinction between pronouns is the difference between "that" and "which." Again, the spoken language no longer follows strict rules regarding these subordinate conjunctions, but careful writers need to observe the following guidelines:

1. "That" is a restrictive pronoun, indicating that the information it precedes is essential for correct understanding of the sentence.

   - Dogs prefer bones that improve their dental health.

   The use of "that" tells us that dogs prefer only this specific kind of bone.

2. "Which" precedes nonessential material; therefore, it typically appears with commas (the ones used to set off nonessential information).

   - Dogs prefer bones, which improve their dental health.

   The use of "which" tells us that all bones improve dogs' teeth.

3. "That" and "which" are not interchangeable. As you can see in the example sentences, the meaning of the sentence is affected when the comma is added in the second sentence and "that" becomes "which." In the first sentence, dogs like only bones that are good for them; in the second, dogs like bones better than other things, and bones just happen to be good for dental health. The second sentence is far more logical.

Slammer for Who/Whom and That/Which

On a sheet of paper, write the appropriate pronoun in the following sentences:

1. Alvin, (who/whom) everyone adored, absconded with the family fortune.
2. Betty, (who/whom) was the apple of his eye, followed him to Mexico.
3. The FBI agents (who/whom) Alvin had avoided for several months finally arrested him.
4. Veronica, Alvin's sister, (who/whom) needed the money desperately, refused to post bond.
5. Alvin, (who's/whose) health was delicate, wasted away in prison.

Select the appropriate pronoun, then note the proper punctuation as needed in the following sentences:

1. Betty bought a gun (that/which) was on sale and set out to free Alvin.
2. She headed north from Mexico in a car (that/which) had more than 130,000 miles showing on its odometer.
3. The car (that/which) had New Jersey license plates was quickly spotted by police in Texas.
4. The Texans (that/which/who/whom) spoke in a slow drawl told her she was wanted in New Jersey for conspiring with Alvin.
5. She pulled out the gun (that/which) she had in her glove compartment and started shooting.
6. The police officer (that/which/who/whom) was standing closest to her car died after he was struck by a bullet.
7. Other officers took Betty's gun (that/which) now was empty of bullets.
8. They also arrested Betty and placed her in a jail (that/which) overlooked the Rio Grande.

Check your answers against those in Appendix B and move on to the next grammar problem.

Problem 4: Sentence Structure

Aside from fragments and run-on sentences, two other categories cause most adult problems with sentence structure: faulty parallelism and modifier placement.

Journalists often struggle with giving sentences parallel structure—that is, making sure that series or lists of phrases are parallel in form. Rather than, "He enjoys reading and to go skiing," use the parallel form, saying, "He enjoys reading and skiing." Writers must always remember to check lists within sentences as well as bulleted lists to see that phrases are stated in parallel form, as shown in these examples:

- Marvelene listed steps in planning a successful party: sending invitations early, greeting guests personally, and supplying abundant food and drink. (parallel gerunds: sending, greeting, supplying)

- A successful host always is sure

  To send invitations early,
  To greet guests personally, and
  To supply abundant food and drink. (infinitives are parallel)

Other sentence errors may occur when modifiers are placed incorrectly and give readers an inaccurate, sometimes humorous, picture, as for example, in these sentences:

Wrong: Swinging from an overhead wire, we saw a kite.
Better: We saw a kite swinging from an overhead wire.

Wrong: When wheeled into the operating room, the nurse placed a mask over my face.
Better: The nurse placed a mask over my face after I was wheeled into the operating room.

Wrong: We saw a herd of sheep on the way to our hotel.
Better: On the way to our hotel, we saw a herd of sheep.

To solve modifier placement problems, place modifying clauses and phrases closest to what they modify.

Slammer for Modifiers

Rewrite these sentences to correct misplaced modifiers. Some sentences are correct as written.

1. The waiter served ice cream in glass bowls which started melting immediately.

2. The Simpsons gave a toy robot with flashing eyes to one of their sons.
3. We saw a herd of sheep on the way to our hotel.
4. Most people have strawberry shortcake topped with mounds of whipped cream.
5. The house is one of the oldest in Rockville, where Mrs. Rooks taught ballet.
6. Flying at an altitude of several thousand feet, the paratroopers could see for miles.
7. I could not convince the child to stop running into the street without yelling.
8. After the first act of the play, Brooke's performance improves, the critic said.
9. While watching the ball game, Sue's horse ran away.
10. The museum director showed me a spider with the orange diamond on its belly.
11. The bank approves loans to reliable individuals of any size.
12. After being wheeled into the operating room, the nurse placed a mask over my face.
13. Riding in a glass-bottom boat, we saw thousands of colorful fish.
14. Aunt Helen asked us before we left to call on her.
15. Do it yourself: Make up a sentence suffering from modifier malady. Then correct it.

Check your work against the answers in Appendix B, and prepare for the final grammar problem: word usage.

Problem 5: Word Usage

English is a language enriched by words borrowed from other languages, resulting in a rich vocabulary—but also, in many cases, in unorthodox spelling and idiosyncratic usage. It makes little sense to have both "affect" and "effect" in the same language, functioning so similarly but not identically. And why do we distinguish between "pore" and "pour," or "flair" and "flare"? Who cares?

Careful writers have to care because subtle usage errors can cause big misunderstandings. In addition, correct usage leads to credibility; readers have confidence in error-free reading.

The number of troublesome words in daily use is so great that no attempt is made to list them all here. Instead, we have included as Appendix A

Professor Thom Lieb's Abused Word List, a catalogue of usage problems that most often plague writers. Get acquainted with the Abused Words List by working on the following exercise.

Slammer for Abused Words

Use Appendix A to help identify correct usage for each of the following troublesome words.

Hopefully
Affect *versus* effect
Less *versus* fewer
Lie *versus* lay
Sit *versus* set
Comprise *versus* compose

Watching Style

Part of good editing is ensuring consistency throughout writing. Using a consistent style guarantees that a certain pattern in word usage, titles, punctuation, abbreviations, grammar, and spelling persists. If IBM means International Business Machines in the first sentence of a television broadcast, it will mean the same thing later on. If Dr. means doctor on the first page of the newspaper, it will not mean "Drive" as part of someone's address on the obituary page. Consistent usage builds credibility and reduces chances of audience confusion.

Many media organizations follow a style that guarantees consistency. Most newspapers and public relations firms follow the style found in *The Associated Press Stylebook and Briefing on Media Law.* Others, including the *Washington Post* and the *New York Times,* have their own style manuals. Many universities and publishing houses use *The Chicago Manual of Style* or the style manual of the Modern Language Association.

The text in this book uses a style that differs from the Associated Press style, so you will notice discrepancies between usage in the text and in examples and exercises, such as 7:00 P.M. or 7 p.m.

No one is ever expected to memorize stylebooks, but writers and editors must be familiar with their content. When a question arises, they need to know where to find the answer. Writers will find that certain rules are used so often that they become second nature. For example, most writers become familiar with the capitalization rule for titles: Professional titles are capitalized before a person's name but never after a name. Here's an example, "University President Bill Sandler said classes would end early Tuesday because of the threat of a blizzard." After his name, the title would read: "Bill Sandler, university president, said...."

Basic Style Rules

The most broadly accepted style rules for professional communicators are those set out by the *Associated Press Stylebook,* which is periodically updated.

Titles

Long titles should go after an individual's name. William McCorkle's name is not lost if a short title is used before it, such as "University President William McCorkle." But his name would be hard to find if his title were "University Associate Vice Chancellor for Student Affairs and Services." When an individual has a long title, put the title after the name: "William McCorkle, university associate vice chancellor for student affairs and services."

When titles precede names, they are generally capitalized. After names, they are not.

Most titles are always written out. The only time some are abbreviated is when they precede a name. *The Associated Press Stylebook* indicates which titles can be abbreviated. For example, "governor" may be shortened to "Gov. Sheila Aycock" and "lieutenant governor" as "Lt. Gov. James Ramsey." Titles that are never abbreviated include "president," "attorney general," "professor," and "superintendent." Most military titles can be abbreviated.

Stand-alone titles are always written out, and they are never abbreviated or capitalized. Examples are "The vice president said he would turn over the files to the Justice Department" and "the pope will visit the United States in May." Note that "vice president" is not hyphenated.

Capitalization

The general rule is to capitalize proper nouns that refer to a person, place, or thing. Examples include "Sacramento is the capital of California" and "Mayor Harmon Bowles agreed to lead the town's Independence Day parade."

Abbreviations

Abbreviate only what your style manual permits. Abbreviate states' names when they are used with the name of a town or city; otherwise, write them out. Note that the Associated Press does not use postal abbreviations in text, except when the complete address is used with a zip code, as in "124 E. Main St., Lakeland, FL 33801." In other instances the Associated Press uses the following abbreviations: Ala., Ariz., Ark., Calif., Colo., Conn., Del., Fla., Ga., Ill., Ind., Kan., Ky., La., Md., Mass., Mich., Minn., Miss., Mo., Mont., Neb., Nev., N.H., N.J., N.M., N.Y., N.C., N.D., Okla., Ore., Pa., R.I., S.C., S.D., Tenn., Vt., Va., Wash., W.Va., Wis., and Wyo. Eight states' names are never abbreviated: Alaska, Hawaii, Idaho, Iowa, Maine, Ohio, Texas, and Utah. You can abbreviate months when they are used with a specific date: "Nov. 12, 1948." Write out "November 1948," however. Never abbreviate March, April, May, June, or July.

Don't abbreviate the days of the week or the words "assistant" and "association."

The Associated Press allows some abbreviations to be used on first reference because people are familiar with them, such as FBI, CIA, UFO, and IBM. But that does not mean to use only the abbreviation. The context of the story may require that the full title be used. On second reference, use the abbreviation or substitute words such as "the bureau," "the agency," "the object," or "the company."

Acronyms

Acronyms are abbreviations that can be pronounced as words, such as "AIDS" for "acquired immune deficiency syndrome" or "UNESCO" for "United Nations Educational, Scientific and Cultural Organization." See style manuals for the correct first and second references for acronyms, just as with other abbreviations.

Numbers

The general rule is to write out numbers zero through nine and use numerals for numbers 10 and higher. Always spell out numbers at the beginning of a sentence, however. In writing numbers above 999,999, write out the words "million" and "billion" rather than using all those zeroes. For example: "To clear the site, the construction crew moved 1.2 million cubic yards of dirt" and "Congressional aides discovered the budget would require an additional $1.4 billion in revenues."

The Associated Press lists two dozen or so exceptions to the rule, but the main ones are these:

Age. Always use a numeral for age: "She has a 3-year-old daughter and an 85-year-old mother."

Percent. Always use a numeral: "He estimated 9 percent of employees are truly satisfied with their jobs."

Time. Always use a numeral: "The guests will arrive at 9 p.m."

Dates. Again, use numerals: "He was born Jan. 3, 1926."

Temperatures. Use numerals for all temperatures except zero: "The weather service predicted the coldest weather in 15 years for the weekend, noting that temperatures would drop to 2 to 3 degrees below zero."

Dimensions. Always write height and weight as numerals: "The average height of the team's basketball players is 6 feet 4 inches." "The record-breaking carrot weighed 5 pounds."

Money. Write dollars and cents as numerals: "The price of an egg is about 10¢." "Hemming the dress will cost $9."

Copyediting Symbols

When you send your writing to a higher level for editing, you may get back a printed copy with editing marks on it. Following are some of the common editing symbols.

Paragraph mark	¶ The president met with House leaders about his proposed budget.
Capitalization	Police Sgt. william T. cassidy
Lowercase	The teacher picked 15 Apples.
Delete letter, word	She gave them to the students.

She gave them to ~~to~~ the students.

Delete punctuation   "Are you going?," she asked.

Transpose letters   She adrdessed 2,345 invitations.

Transpose words   The robber a had gun.

Insert punctuation   Marcia her sister, is a pianist.

Insert letters, words   Marian chose cho^p sticks for eating.

                            Marian _chose_ chopsticks for eating.

Add a space   Four players are needed for bridge.

Write out   The meeting will be (Tues.) night.

Abbreviate   (Governor) Rex Casey died today.

Copyediting Symbols in Practice

Look at the following sample from a church bulletin to see how it was edited
by proper use of copyediting symbols:

At a meeting last month, The Longview Church board

of deacons decided it wo^u ld hire an (asst.) director of

special projects.

The church has focussed much efforts of its on

programs for the hom^e less and neeedy, said the Rev. paul

Jacobs. The activities are more then he can can handle

along iwth his ministerial duties, he said.

Applications can be sent to the Church before

September 1.

Slammer for Style

Check your ability to apply the rules you have learned so far. On a separate sheet of paper, copyedit the following sentences according to Associated Press style. Also check for any grammar, spelling, or punctuation errors. Use proper copyediting symbols to save time.

1. Lieutenant Governor Stanley Greene was stripped of his powers by the N.C. Senate.
2. William Williams, Dean of the Graduate School of Journalism, will speak to students about graduation requirements on Wed. afternoon.
3. The students are expected to begin the test at 9:00 A.M. Tuesday.
4. The President lives at 1600 Pennsylvania Avenue, but his mail is delivered to the U.S. Post Office on Twenty-second Street.
5. The state Senate is expected to enact a bill to require polio vaccinations for children under the age of two.
6. The airport in Medford, Oregon was closed yesterday after an Alaskan airlines jet made an emergency landing on the runway.
7. The Atty. Gen. has a B.A. in history from American University.
8. The then-Soviet block countries sponsored the Friendship Games rather than attend the 1984 olympics in Los Angeles.
9. The city and county used thirteen busses to transport the children to the July Fourth picnic.
10. Water freezes at 0 degrees Centigrade.
11. Three houses on Sims street were destroyed by the fire, which began at 112 Sims Street.
12. Following the Federal Reserve action, three banks announced a one percent increase in the prime rate, putting it at six percent.
13. Longtime Senator Jesse A. Helms (R–North Carolina) used to be city editor of The Raleigh Times.

14. John L. Harris, 48 years old, of 1632 Winding Way Road was charged Tuesday with cocaine possession.
15. The champion wrestler measured six feet six inches tall and won 4/5 of his fights.
16. Army Sergeant Willie York was charged with misappropriating $1,000,000 dollars in construction equipment.
17. Hurricane Diana, blowing from the East, caused millions of dollars in damages to the east coast of the United States.
18. Colonel Max Shaw, who has served as a national guardsman for more than twenty years, is Ed's commanding officer.
19. Ability with a frisbee is not a valid measure of IQ.
20. We heard the kickoff announced over the radio at the Laundromat.
21. The stockings were hanged by the chimney with care, in hopes that Kirs Kringle soon would be there.
22. Travelling the 30 miles, or 60 kilometers, to Kansas City, we got 32 miles per gallon in our new minivan.
23. The five-year-old boy got on the wrong bus and was missing for 2 hours.
24. Sarah sold two hundred and two boxes of Girl Scout cookies to her neighbors on Sweetbriar Pkwy. and Pantego Ave.

Math for Journalists

All professional communicators must be able to handle routine computations such as adding, subtracting, multiplying, dividing, figuring ratios and percentages, and rounding off numbers. Such simple calculations are routinely used in daily journalism, and any error would make a story inaccurate.

Professor Phil Meyer at the University of North Carolina at Chapel Hill tells mass communication students that if they chose the field because they thought they could escape math, they were wrong. Basic math is necessary.

Here's a typical example of statistical writing that misses the mark: An advertisement tells audiences that computer prices have dropped 200 percent. That news would appeal to someone shopping for a new computer. But what's wrong here? When the price drops 100 percent, the item is free. Below 100 percent means stores are paying customers to take away computers. The writer needs a few quick lessons on math.

Here's another example of a writer in need of math skills: A news story reports that police chased a suspect for 90 minutes from Town X to Town Y, a distance of 300 miles. Possible? Hardly. The cars would be traveling 200 miles an hour to cover that distance in 90 minutes. Something is wrong with the information unless the cars were literally flying.

Basic Math

These types of errors show up continually in writing, usually because writers are careless. But a reader somewhere is going to see the error and doubt the writer's and the medium's credibility. Mass communicators need to know some simple math, or at the very least, they need to recognize when data are misrepresented and find someone who can do correct calculations.

Percent

A lead reports that the president's popularity dropped from 85 to 75 percent, a decrease of 10 percent. Correct? No. The decrease is 10 percentage points, but not 10 percent. That's the first lesson to learn in writing about percent. If you subtract 75 percent from 85 percent, you get a 10 percentage point difference. To calculate the percent difference, you need to find the difference and divide that by the base or original figure: $\% = d/b$ (i.e., percent = difference/base). Here, that would be 10/85, a change of 12 percent. It works the same way with increases. If the popularity goes up from 70 percent to 80 percent, the difference is 10 percentage points, which yields 70/10, or a 14 percent increase.

For another example, let's look at a financial story on company revenues. Suppose that Midland Trucking Company had revenues last fiscal year of $535,000 and revenues this year of $635,000. The difference is $100,000. If you follow the formula d/b = percent difference, you would divide $100,000 by $535,000. The percent change is 18.6 percent, or rounded off, 19 percent.

If you made an error and divided the difference by the new amount of $635,000, you would get a percent increase of 16 percent, a significant difference from 19 percent—and one that could affect stockholders' perception of company management. The writer for the company's annual report must be careful in calculating numbers that could influence investments or stockholder confidence.

Rates

Often, writers will state numbers as a rate—1 in 10 or 3 in 100—so that complicated figures are easier to understand. For example, a writer finds a health department report saying that 0.0021 percent of teens aged 13 to 19 in the county became pregnant last year. The writer decides to translate the percent into a figure that people can visualize.

One way to calculate the rate is to multiply the percent figure by 100 or 1,000 so that decimals no longer appear. In this case, multiplying 0.0021 × 1,000 gives a rate of 2.1 per thousand. Rates can be stated by hundreds, thousands, tens of thousands, and on up. More clearly stated, the rate of teen pregnancy is 2.1 per 1,000, or about 2 teens out of every 1,000 teens aged 13 to 19 living in the county got pregnant last year.

Probability

Writers need to have an appreciation for probability theory and an understanding of the likelihood that a predicted event will actually occur. If there is a 40 percent chance of rain, how likely is it that we will get wet? Should we write or broadcast the news that rain is on the way? We hear probability each time we listen to a weather report. But if the probability of rain is 40 percent, it's important to remember that there's also a 60 percent probability that the weather will be fine.

Writers often make errors when they combine one probability with another, such as, "The football coach predicts a 50 percent chance of thunderstorms and a 50 percent chance the game could be delayed." Does that mean a 100 percent chance the game will be delayed? No. To calculate the probability in this case, you must multiply one probability with another. The probability of thunderstorms and a game postponement is .5 × .5 = .25, or a 25 percent chance both will occur.

Reporting Poll Data

Many numbers are reported in poll stories every day in the media. An article notes that the president has an 83 percent approval rating. What does 83 percent mean to the average reader or listener? Translated, the 83 percent means that more than 8 of 10 people (remember your percentage calculations from earlier in this section) approve of his performance—and also that 2 of every 10 do not. You can break that down even further to say simply that 4 out of

5 (divide 8 and 10 by 2 to bring to their lowest common denominator) people approve of the president.

When reporting poll data, it is important to make the statistics as clear and understandable as possible. Readers need to grasp what the numbers mean. To report poll numbers correctly, writers must be able to read the charts to determine what the poll figures mean. The following table presents poll results, divided into categories by income. These responses came from people who were queried at the Rockland Mall about whether they support Proposition Y, a proposal for a new city entertainment tax:

	Yes	*No*	*Total*
Earn less than $50,000 a year			
Count	148	152	300
Percent	49.3%	50.7%	100%
Percent of total	26%	27%	
Earn $50,001 or more a year			
Count	159	109	268
Percent	59.2%	40.8%	100%
Percent of total	28%	19%	

A writer notes that almost 50 percent of respondents who earn under $50,000 a year support Proposition Y on the ballot. He or she can even translate that 49.3 number to one out of two people interviewed and still be fairly accurate.

But then the writer notes that 59 percent of respondents earn more than $50,000 and support Proposition Y. Is the writer correct? No. The 59 percent figure represents what percentage of those people who earn that amount of money favor the proposition. The total number of people who earn $50,000 a year or more is 159 plus 109 or 268. Of the 268 people in that income bracket, 59 percent favor the proposition.

To find out the percentage who actually earn $50,000 a year or more, you have to go back to the actual counts and recalculate from there. If you add all the counts in each box, you will find 568 respondents to the survey. To find out how many earn more than $50,000 a year, divide difference by base, or 268 divided by 568, or 47 percent of those surveyed earn more money—much less than 59 percent.

It is extremely important when reading poll results to be sure you read the information correctly and that you calculate differences correctly. Also, be sure to translate your information to tangible language.

Margin of Error

A necessary part of poll reporting is reporting margin of error. In a poll on the safety of the nation, 87 percent report feeling safe, "plus or minus 3 percent." That "plus or minus" figure is the margin of error.

In simple terms, the error figure, usually from 1 to 5 percent, represents the accuracy of the poll results. Researchers know that in any survey they must allow room for error. Common sense and statistics tell us that the more respondents who are polled, the more accurately the poll results reflect the opinions of the public at large. Statistically, once the number of people polled reaches a certain level, the margin of error doesn't change or improve much. With groups of several hundred respondents, margin of error stays around plus or minus 3 percent, even if hundreds of people are added to the response group. If careful sampling methods are used, the "plus or minus 3 percent" accuracy of the poll results will allow researchers to interview 1,200 U.S. residents and then estimate what 280 million people believe.

Most pollsters strive for a margin of error around 3 percent. Let's see how that works.

A poll says that 45 percent of Americans believe the tax burden is too great on middle-income people. Another 42 percent believe it is just about right, and 13 percent have no opinion. The pollster reports a plus or minus 3 percent margin of error. Here's how the results look in chart form:

Reported results (with error = + or – 3%)

Too heavy	45%
Just about right	42%
No opinion	13%

The margin of error indicates that the 45 percent who believe the tax burden is too great may, in reality, be 42 percent (minus 3 percent). Or it may be as high as 48 percent (plus 3 percent). Likewise, for those who think the tax burden is just about right, the range in reality could be as much as 45 percent to as little as 39 percent. So it's likely that neither group can claim a clear majority! With such close percentages, a writer cannot say: "Most Americans said they think the tax burden on the middle class is too heavy." It would be more accurate to report that many Americans believe that the tax burden is fairly distributed.

The Associated Press Stylebook has a separate entry for polls and surveys and lists the items that should be included in any poll story. This entry discusses margin of error and urges writers to take care, especially when reporting that one candidate is leading another. According to the stylebook, only when the difference between the candidates is more than twice the margin of error can you say one candidate is leading. The same rule applies to the tax burden survey results presented here: The difference between the two groups is 3 percentage points, not the 6 required to be twice the margin of error of plus or minus 3 percent. So it's clear that in the case of individual opinions about tax burdens—and in many political poll results as well—a writer would have to say that opinion is just about even.

Tips

Many schools and departments of journalism and mass communication are requiring their students to have basic competencies in math. At the University of North Carolina at Chapel Hill, faculty members in the School of Journalism and Mass Communication have debated adding a math competency requirement for journalism and mass communication majors.

Students who want to test their skills can find a math test online at www.unc.edu/~pmeyer/carstat/. Professor Phil Meyer and Associate Professor Bill Cloud at UNC–Chapel Hill produced the test, which has been subsequently modified. *USA Today* has been a partner with UNC–Chapel Hill in developing a math certification program for journalists. The online test is part of that effort.

In its discussion of numbers, *The Associated Press Stylebook,* recommends rounding numbers. That means that readers have little use for such numbers as $1,463,729. In this case, the writer needs to round the number; AP says to round to two decimal places, which would convert the number to $1.46 million. Rounding numbers makes it easier for readers to digest numbers and helps avoid inaccuracies.

The Associated Press Stylebook has other entries that relate to numbers, such as those on decimals, fractions, percentages, median, average, norm, and the metric system. Another section explains business terms. All these are necessary entries that can help writers when math is an issue, as is often the case in communications professions.

Slammer for Math

The following exercises will test your basic math skills. Please use a calculator. Answers are found in Appendix C.

1. The jury has 13 members. There are 4 members who are women. There are 2 African American jurors and only 1 of them is a man. There also is 1 Hispanic American man on the jury. (Round percentages to the nearest tenth.)

   a. What is the ratio of men to women on the jury?
   b. What percentage of the jury is female?
   c. What percentage of Hispanic American men makes up the jury?
   d. What percentage of African American men makes up the jury?

2. The town manager tells the town council that he is proposing that the town build a new recreation center. The center would be 15,000 square feet. He has an estimate that the cost to build would be $85 per square foot plus an additional $25 per square foot for furnishings.

   a. What is the cost to build the center?
   b. What is the cost to furnish the center?
   c. What is the total cost for building and furnishing the center?
   d. Round the total cost to the nearest $100,000.

3. A local advertising company is sponsoring a communitywide yard sale in a local middle school parking lot. Each booth space is equivalent to two parking spaces. Each parking space measures 12 feet by 8 feet. The parking lot has 240 spaces.

   a. What is the square footage of one booth?
   b. How many booths can the advertising company rent?
   c. At $30 a booth, how much revenue will the company earn?
   d. You decide to rent two booths to get rid of your old furniture. How much space do you get?

4. Sarah Lamb owns a house valued for tax purposes at $175,000. Rockland, the town she lives in, has a tax rate of 85 cents per $100

valuation. The Rockland City Council is proposing to raise the tax rate by 3 cents for next year.

a. How much in taxes did Sarah pay this year?
b. How much will she pay under the proposed tax rate?
c. What percentage increase will that be in her tax bill?
d. If her property increases in value 5 percent by next year, how much will her tax bill be under the proposed tax rate?

5. Look at the following chart about support for three candidates for mayor of Rockland.

	Smith	*Small*	*Tucker*
Female			
Count	107	137	31
Percentage	38.9%	49.7%	11.4%
Male			
Count	192	137	23
Percentage	54.4%	39.0%	6.5%

a. How many respondents were women?
b. What percentage of the total respondents were women?
c. What percentage of the total respondents favored Tucker?
d. What percentage of the total respondents favored Small?

6. Christine wants to go to the State Fair Friday night. Her mother said there is a 50 percent probability that she will be able to take Christine to the fair. But Christine's band director said there is a 75 percent change that he will schedule band practice on Friday night. What is the probability that Christine will actually get to the fair?

7. Jonathan works 40 hours a week at a local hardware store. He earns $6.50 an hour. The manager said he will give Jonathan a 25-cent per hour pay raise. How much will Jonathan earn a week with the raise?

a. $240
b. $10
c. $270
d. $260

8. Mr. Tennyson is teaching his class how to convert to the metric system. If the average weight for the class members is 135 pounds, what is that in kilograms? (*Note:* 0.454 kilograms is equal to one pound.)

a. 61.29
b. 50.3

c. 792
d. 297
e. 74.2

SUGGESTED READINGS

Theodore M. Bernstein, *Dos, Don'ts and Maybes of the English Language*. New York: The Times Book Co., 1977.

John Bremner, *Words on Words*. New York: Columbia University Press, 1980.

E. L. Callihan, *Grammar for Journalists,* 3rd ed. Radnor, PA: Chilton Co., 1979.

Claire Kehrwald Cook, *Line by Line: How to Improve Your Own Writing*. Boston: Houghton Mifflin, 1985.

Norm Goldstein, ed., *The Associated Press Stylebook 2001 and Briefing on Media Law*. New York: The Associated Press, 2001.

Lauren Kessler and Duncan McDonald, *When Words Collide*. Belmont, CA: Wadsworth, 1992.

Purdue University's Online Writing Lab. Available: http://owl.english.purdue.edu/handouts/grammar/index.html.

William Strunk, Jr., and E. B. White, *The Elements of Style,* 3rd ed. New York: Macmillan, 1979.

Kathleen Woodruff Wickham, *Math Tools for Journalists*. Oak Park, IL: Marion Street Press, January 2002.

REFERENCES

Katherine C. McAdams, *The Grammar Slammer*. College of Journalism, University of Maryland, 1991.

Mary Penny, Class handouts, Needham Broughton High School, Raleigh, NC, 1974.

Web site of Professor Phil Meyer, University of North Carolina at Chapel Hill, at www.unc.edu/~pmeyer.carstat.

3

Guidelines for Good Writing

For years, writing coaches at newspapers and magazines have worked to distill a set of qualities in writing that will catch and hold readers. Many people, such as Roy Peter Clark at the Poynter Institute in St. Petersburg, Florida, have spent a great deal of their professional careers analyzing the qualities of good writing. Authors such as William Zinsser, best known for his book *On Writing Well,* offer advice on how to strengthen and improve prose. Even communication researchers, charged with finding out what makes publications sell, have considered what qualities are valued in messages.

The research shows that the most effective writing is simple and forceful; that is, it says it straight without flourishes and pomp.

In this chapter, you will learn

- Four essential qualities in writing: accuracy, clarity, completeness, and fairness,
- Five broad rules for good writing,
- Specific tips to improve writing, and
- Editing steps to improve writing.

Watchwords of Writing

No message will succeed if it does not have four essential qualities: accuracy, clarity, completeness, and fairness. We know from the discussion of audiences in Chapter 1 that they can be fickle; once they are lost, they may not return. Writing that is accurate, clear, complete, and fair has a better chance of holding audiences, particularly those who may be clicking through a web site or leafing through a brochure.

Accuracy ensures the credibility of all writing. When the audience catches a misspelled name or an erroneous date, it doubts the accuracy of the information that follows. An audience that cannot trust a communicator will abandon him or her.

Clarity means the writer uses language that an audience understands. Simple language is preferred over complicated words. Jargon and technical language are avoided. The message comes through.

Completeness answers an audience's questions. A message that is complete satisfies the audience and does so quickly.

Fairness occurs when the writer has used a variety of sources to keep an article from being one-sided. The writer has excised any editorial opinion and has been as objective as possible.

Let's look at each element more closely.

Accuracy

Good communication of any kind always contains accurate information. Accuracy is comforting to audiences, who want to depend on information. Errors can occur at any stage in writing: gathering information through research and interviewing, transcribing notes, calculating figures, and creating the copy (when typos can occur). To ensure accuracy, writers must use good information-gathering techniques. They must obtain information only from reliable sources, then check and recheck it against other sources. Chuck Stone, syndicated columnist and university professor, notes, "If your mother says she loves you, check it out." If you find a discrepancy or an error and you don't have time to check it, follow the adage, "When in doubt, leave it out."

We are all prone to committing errors sometimes. Just because a well-known person recites a fact or the fact is found in a computer database does not mean it is correct. The potentate may be in error, and human beings type information into databases. Name spellings, middle initials, street numbers, birth dates—seemingly trivial details—become of monumental importance once they become part of a message. Such details may be accurate in notes but then may be transcribed erroneously into copy.

If messages are wrong, people are misled. Writers and audiences rarely forget the mishap when a name is misspelled or an address is wrong. Inaccuracies in messages lead to distrust among audiences—and they can lead to libel suits. Once audience members are misled by a source, they have difficulty trusting it again.

When the media covered the terrorist attacks on the World Trade Center and the Pentagon in September 2001, they noted repeatedly that they were reporting information as it developed. But such disclaimers did little to change the impact of erroneous information. Early reports noted as many as 800 people had died at the Pentagon. Final numbers were slightly under 200. Another story said rescuers found five fire fighters alive in a sport utility vehicle under the Trade Center rubble. In truth, only two were found. Deadlines and competition can lead to inaccurate reporting.

Clarity

A message will have impact if it is clear and straightforward so that everyone in its audience can understand it. "Send a check for $75 by February 1 if you want to ski with the Seniors Club in February" makes the requirement clear. The writing is direct and uses simple, to-the-point language.

A message needs to be so clear that no misunderstanding or confusion can possibly result. A university-wide e-mail note about a memorial service for a popular librarian who died described the church as "the Baptist Church on Michigan Avenue near Howard University." Unfortunately, more than one church fit that description. Because the message was unclear, several people missed the memorial service, a one-time event.

Completeness

Useful messages also are complete, giving sufficient information for real understanding and guidance. A news story that leaves out an important fact can be misleading and even harmful.

When Reagan National Airport reopened October 4, 2001, after the September 11 terrorist attacks, reporters had to include information on why the airport had been closed. The story would have been incomplete if reporters had not also noted why it remained closed well beyond the dates when other airports reopened: because of its close proximity to the Pentagon and other buildings in the U.S. capital.

Fairness

Messages will be more believable if audiences sense that the stories are fair. Readers or viewers will turn away from reports that they feel are skewed or not balanced.

For a story to be fair or balanced, it must have a variety of sources. That doesn't mean that every story must present each side of an issue in the same detail and the same number of words. Such balance is not possible in most writing. A reporter may not be able to get in touch with sources on one side of an issue, but in the story, the reporter should let readers know that he or she tried.

Writers must be careful in the language they use so that audiences don't ascribe any specific leaning or viewpoint to the story. Language should be neutral. Quotes can be inflammatory or weighty—but such language needs to be reserved to quotes attributed to specific sources, not to the writer.

Keys to Good Writing

Researchers, language professionals, and experienced writers agree on five basic tenets of good writing: (1) use short sentences, (2) use short words, (3) eliminate wordiness, (4) avoid jargon, and (5) come to the point quickly. Anyone can apply the rules while writing and editing.

Good Writing Uses Short Sentences

Most readability experts argue that regardless of age, education, or economic status, people prefer and understand writing that uses short sentences. Human beings have little patience with long, complicated sentences that tax their brain power. Of course, not all sentences should be short; readers would be bored, so sentence length should vary. A short sentence can have impact. A long, complex sentence can set up an idea for the audience or create a mood, and a short sentence can follow immediately, almost as a punch line. Get the point?

A study at the American Press Institute showed that reader understanding drops off dramatically if sentences exceed 20 words, and comprehension continues to drop as sentences grow longer. Only about 1 of 20 people studied could clearly comprehend 50-word sentences, a common length in newspapers and in academic writing.

Short-term memory rarely exceeds 15 seconds, which may not be enough time to read one of the many 50-word sentences in traditional magazines and newspapers. Consider this lead:

> The head of the federal agency that runs Medicare predicted yesterday that "several hundred thousand" elderly Americans will be dropped from private health plans this winter, despite the Bush administration's efforts to lighten the regulatory burdens on HMOs and coax them to keep taking Medicare patients.

By the time many readers have reached the end of that 50-word sentence, they may have forgotten the beginning!

The English language is based on a pattern of simple, subject–verb–object constructions. Most are short. Because people learn and use English this way in everyday life, they prefer this pattern in messages.

Readers would be more likely to warm up to a straightforward approach to the plight of elderly citizens who need health insurance, such as:

> Several hundred thousand elderly Americans are expected to be dropped this winter from private health plans, particularly HMOs, continuing the trend of plans to quit taking Medicare patients.
>
> The head of the federal agency that runs Medicare predicted yesterday that the private health plans will cut back, despite the Bush administration's efforts to lighten the regulatory burdens on HMOs and coax them to keep taking Medicare patients.

Journalism Professor Fred Fedler of the University of Central Florida says that simplicity makes stories more interesting and forceful. He cites as an example a prize-winning story by World War II journalist Ernie Pyle; the average sentence length was 10.6 words.

Good Writing Uses Short Words

Perhaps your high school English teacher praised you for using "penurious" rather than "stingy," or "inebriated" rather than "drunk." Then you were expanding your vocabulary, but now your audience will thank you for choosing the simpler word.

Just as they do with long sentences, readers and listeners become tired and discouraged when they face too many complex words—usually those exceeding three syllables. To be sure, you can use commonly known, longer words such as "responsibility," "establishment," "participate," and "governmental." Be sure, however, that the longer words are a better choice than a shorter version, such as "duty," "founding," "join in," or "federal" or "state."

When writing, select the simplest word possible to convey the meaning. For example, in a police story, avoid saying that the two men had an "altercation." Use the word "fight." Instead of "finalize," choose a word such as "conclude" or "finish." Rather than "exasperate," use "annoy" or "bother." Instead of "terminating" this paragraph, we will "end" it.

Good Writing Eliminates Wordiness

"You can almost detect a wordy sentence by looking at it—at least if you can recognize weak verbs, ponderous nouns, and strings of prepositional phrases," Claire Kehrwald Cook writes in her book *Line by Line: How to Improve Your Own Writing.* Her advice gives writers clues about where to find wordiness and where to improve sentence structure.

Author William Zinsser notes that the secret to good writing is to strip every sentence to its cleanest components. Writers must detach themselves from the information and chisel it to the bare essentials. Writers must throw out extra words and phrases—even extra sentences and paragraphs. Remember this adage: "Two words are never as good as one." Consider the simple word "new." When used in the following sentence, it is unnecessary: "Crews expect the new building to be completed within two months." All buildings under construction are new. Leave the word out.

Audiences can find the facts only when excess is trimmed. Sparse writing is more professional, more informative, more objective, and more likely to be read. Writer Stanley Elkin (quoted in Saltzman's *If You Can Talk, You Can Write*) describes the process of eliminating excess in writing: "[It's] a kind of whittling, a honing to the bone, until you finally get whatever the hell you're looking for. It's an exercise in sculpture, chipping away at the rock until you find the nose."

Wordy writing is likely to be redundant or repetitious. No writer needs to say that a fire "completely destroyed" a downtown block; if it was destroyed, the destruction was complete. This classic often appears: "Jones is currently the manager of consumer services." "Is" means "now," and "now" means "currently." Kill the word "currently." Think about other phrases such as "past history," "acres of land," "4 P.M. in the afternoon," "at 12 midnight," "dead body," and "totally incomprehensible."

In seeking wordiness, look specifically for unnecessary adjectives and qualifiers. For example, a project cannot be the "most" unique. "Unique" means one of a kind. Qualifiers such as "very," "truly," and "really" can generally be cut without damage to copy.

Sometimes a statement or entire paragraph that repeats a speaker's direct quotes can be deleted.

> Jones said he was delighted that the school would receive $40,000 to use for purchasing audiovisual equipment materials for the library.
>
> "I am just delighted that we will have the $40,000 to buy audiovisual equipment for the library," Jones said.

Delete the first paragraph. It does more than serve as a transition to the direct quote—it steals it.

As in art, too much embellishment in writing only detracts and distracts. Consider the effectiveness of the following message before and after its extra words are deleted:

> Ninety-two years ago, the Tung Wah Dispensary attempted to cure the ailments and afflictions of the San Francisco Chinatown community from its humble outpost at 828 Sacramento Street. When the institution realized that its cramped quarters were counterproductive to the logistics of health care, it expanded its services and relocated to 835 Jackson Street, eventually being renamed the Chinese Hospital.

Simplified, the history looks like this:

```
Ninety-two years ago, the Tung Wah Dispensary treated
sickness in San Francisco's Chinatown from its humble
outpost at 828 Sacramento Street. Cramped quarters and
expanded services led to a new location at 835 Jackson
Street, the building that eventually was named the Chinese
Hospital.
```

Without its embellishments—"ailments and afflictions," "institution," and "counterproductive"—this message is much more readable and just as informative.

Good Writing Avoids Jargon or Technical Language

In our high-tech society, so much jargon exists that it is difficult to tell what is jargon and what is plain English. Few people recall that "input" and "output" originated in computer jargon. The same is true of the terms "bottom line" and "in the red." These familiar terms are still questionable in good writing.

Examples of jargon abound in everyday life. Parents received an annual report from the elementary school. In listing the objectives for the year, the report stated

```
Objective Three: The mean score for the kindergarten
program will increase from 5.1 to 5.4 as measured
by the FPG Assessment Report. The lead teacher for
developmentally appropriate practice coordinated the
efforts of our kindergarten teachers to enable our
program to meet this objective.
```

For parents, what does this say? Not much. What is a mean score? What is the FPG Assessment Report? What is developmentally appropriate practice? When people see or hear such words, they stop. Confusion sets in. Parents just want to know how their children are doing in school.

Why Is Jargon Such a No-No?

Jargon should be avoided for several reasons. First, it makes too many assumptions about audiences. Technical language reserves a message for insiders: those who are familiar with the lingo. "Outsiders" who could benefit from the information may be put off. For example, an art exhibit notice that contains artistic jargon may scare away potential visitors to the gallery. Technical terms may create a feeling that the gallery is reserved for an elite group. As a result, an audience may feel excluded or perceive the message as exclusive. For the same reason, it is also wise to avoid foreign words and phrases in published writing—unless those words are commonly used, such as *voila*!

Second, jargon is precise only to the insiders who use it. Once again, consider the word "input," which may be anything from telephone conversations to cash contributions. A more specific term is better.

Third, jargon usually is ambiguous. The "bottom line" mentioned in a school newsletter may mean many things: expenditures, income, or both; parent satisfaction; student learning outcomes—or almost anything. Skilled writers avoid vagueness by avoiding jargon.

Of course, whether writers use jargon or technical language depends on the audience. If they are writing for a medical publication whose audience is nurses and doctors, the language can be more specific to that profession.

Too often, though, messages for general audiences or laypeople are filled with educational, legal, economic, or medical jargon. Some technical language because of its use has become more understood by the general public, such as "SAT" scores for "Scholastic Assessment Tests" and "AIDS" for "acquired immune deficiency syndrome." But language too often goes unexplained.

Another problem related to jargon is the use of institutional language: abstract terms and phrases that may communicate well in a specific workplace or institution but that lose meaning for a general audience. For example, medical professionals use the term "treatment modalities." That terminology is nonspecific and lacks meaning and interest, even to a well-educated general audience. Treatment modalities should be named in terms an audience can understand: a series of shots, an antibiotic for 10 days, physical therapy for several months, and so on.

A professor wrote, "Shrinking and unstable sources of funding lead to short-term dislocations." What he meant was a lack of consistent and adequate funding interrupts research.

Many institutional words began as one part of speech and have been transformed into another. A teacher may ask parents "to conference" at 4 P.M.; the vice president may decide "to host" a reception. In good writing, parents will meet with teachers, and the vice president will greet guests at the reception.

It is easy to find words to substitute for institutional terms, and the simpler words are always more specific. Some general, ambiguous terms found frequently in workplaces are "input" and "facilitation." *Input* may mean discussion or suggestions; *facilitation* may be planning or sponsoring an event.

Good writers find out what is meant by such terms, and they substitute simpler language.

Some terms cannot be avoided, such as the nation's "gross national product (GNP)." Writers must explain such words adequately when they use them. As *The Associated Press Stylebook* explains it, "The gross national product is the total value at retail prices of all the goods and services produced by a nation's economy in a given time period."

Although jargon is conversational, it rarely is efficient in writing. When talking, you can be sure how much your audience knows about your topic; you can supplement messages with hand gestures, facial expressions, and other visual aids; and you can clarify or define confusing terms if your audience looks puzzled or asks questions.

But when you are writing, your text stands alone and must be absolutely clear. Your goal as a writer is to eliminate misunderstanding, and eliminating jargon and technical language is a giant step toward that goal.

Good Writing Comes to the Point Quickly

Chapter 4 will focus on the need for writers to come to the point quickly. Perhaps this is the most problematic of writing challenges. A writer may not want to come to the point because the point is unpleasant: A company has lost money or laid off employees. A popular program has been discontinued. But audiences see through attempts to delay bad news, and they interpret them as sneaky ways to hide information. However unwelcome the message, direct communication conveys a feeling of openness and honesty.

Some writers fail to come to the point because they are in "writer's mode," self-indulgently crafting a long introduction to the main points rather than getting to those points. Readers of nonfiction are after information rather than art, and they consider the most direct messages to be the greatest masterpieces.

Still other writers have trouble coming to the point because they do not know what the point is. Critical thinking—deciding on the main goal in communicating—precedes every writing task. To come to the point, writers must know their audiences and analyze information carefully enough to know the point that audiences will want to know.

Writer and filmmaker Nora Ephron tells a story about her high school journalism teacher. In one lesson, he taught his class to recognize main points by telling them their faculty members would be attending a major conference the next day. He asked them to write a news story about it.

In the students' articles, the introductory paragraphs summarized the facts: All teachers would travel to a nearby city and hear famous speakers. After collecting the papers, the teacher threw them away and told the students, "The point is that there will be no school tomorrow."

Ephron says she never forgot the point:

> *It was an electrifying moment. So that's it, I realized. It's about the point. The classic newspaper lead of who-what-when-where-how and why is utterly meaningless if you haven't figured out the significance of the facts. What is the point? What does it mean? He planted those questions in my head. And for the first year he taught me journalism, every day was like the first; every set of facts had a point buried in it if we looked hard enough. He turned the class into a gorgeous intellectual exercise, and he gave me enthusiasm for the profession I never lost. Also, of course, he taught me something that works just as well in life as it does in journalism.*

These rules of good writing may be familiar to you already. But a little redundancy and repetition are like a drill to set indelibly in writers' minds the importance of copy that says it straight. Experienced writers know that in simplicity lies beauty and power.

Words

Three of the five good writing tenets just given—short words, avoidance of wordiness, and avoidance of jargon—focus on words, the basic unit of any oral or written message. A good writer needs knowledge of language, a good vocabulary, and the sense to know when a word is inappropriate or unnecessary.

The Power of Little Words

Most of the little words in our language come from the original language that was spoken in England before Roman and French invaders added their vocabulary to the mix. The English common folk retained their own words for everyday things, and they borrowed from Latin and French only when they had to.

As a result, the things nearest and dearest to us still are called by their original English names: home, fire, food, and mother, for example. And it is these words to which English-speaking people still respond emotionally. The word "home" has much stronger emotional appeal than the cooler, more technical word "domicile," which is borrowed from Latin. Likewise, "food" sounds good; "nutrients," a Latin-based word, is another matter.

How Little Words Are Successful

Professor and writing coach Carl Sessions Stepp says that people respond to small words because they usually are "first-degree" words, or words that are immediately understood. Everyone has a single, readily available mental picture of "home," along with a host of meanings and feelings associated with that mental picture. But few people can respond so completely to "domicile." The writer who uses "mother" taps the audience's rich reserves of emotion and information.

Stepp points out that larger, multisyllabic words, many of which have origins in other languages, are "second-degree" words. Such words are abstract rather than concrete. They produce no immediate images in the minds of readers or listeners and are often ambiguous when other information is given. Take, for example, the word "nutrition." Does it mean food substances, or measures of vitamins and minerals? It is a second-degree word because the audience needs more information for full understanding.

Consider other second-degree words, such as "facility" and "output." Compare them with these first-degree words: "school" and "grades."

Stepp argues that writers are more likely to appeal to audiences if they choose first-degree words and avoid second-degree words. In writing, we deal with many second-degree words that are part of science, technology, education, and almost every other field. Writers need to remember to define such words in first-degree terms whenever possible, as in this sentence:

```
Nutrition—the kinds of foods patients eat every day—is
the topic of a workshop for nurses at Sibley Hospital on
Saturday.
```

Little words are more heart-warming and more easily understood. They also save space, time, and the reader's energy. They are more readable. And audiences respond to readable copy with overall approval, giving high marks to writers and to the entire publication.

Look at the Associated Press article about a Dallas drug bust that follows. The language could not be much simpler. Most fifth-graders could read the story with very little trouble.

Crime, Fear, Poverty All Part of Life in America

Young Woman's Eyes Reflect Despair of Violent Nation

BY JULIA PRODIS

Associated Press

DALLAS—Her eyes are the color of earth, and as vacant as the lot next door.

She's sitting on a concrete step holding a baby that's not hers. Her 16-year-old friend is lying face down on the sizzling sidewalk beside her, his arms arched awkwardly behind him, his hands cuffed in plastic police ties. A girlfriend is similarly contorted at her feet.

"What's your name?" a police-woman asks this hot August day in Dallas.

In a low, slow whisper, she answers, "Latasha."

"La-what?"

"La-Tasha," the thin, moonfaced 19-year-old says with slightly more effort, her blank gaze never looking higher than the holster holding the officer's 9 mm semiautomatic.

Minutes ago, eight muscular members of the Dallas drug enforcement squad, wearing black boots and bulletproof vests, had stormed the faded yellow bungalow behind her. It took two heaves of "the slammer" to break down the door, blocked only by an empty bookcase.

Shrieks from inside, then blurs of motion as the young man bolted out the rear and the woman ran toward the back fence. Latasha Smith never said a word, and the baby didn't cry.

She has the dull look of someone who had seen this rerun too many times. Her look of despair, so deep it turns everything gray, is the same look that flattens the faces of the young and hopeless in poor, violent American neighborhoods everywhere.

Neighborhoods where crack heads fear friends and neighbors more than the cops. Where homes are so filthy detectives can't pick up evidence without something crawling on it. Where neighbors scatter when someone screams for help.

For Americans who say crime is their gravest concern, these calloused Latashas and their criminal friends stir angry fear. But for Latasha, it's just another day.

The baby with cocoa skin and wavy brown hair spits up on Latasha's chest as she rocks negligibly back and forth. Indifferently, she wipes his face with her droopy white tank top.

"Who's payin' for that baby?" the policewoman asks.

"It ain't MY baby," she retorts.

"It's my baby," says the 16-year-old boy, squirming awkwardly on the sidewalk. As he strains to lift his head to speak, the pebbles clinging to his cheek dribble to the ground.

Latasha tells the officer she has three children of her own and she's on welfare. She quit the last job she had washing dishes because she didn't like it. Her children are scattered with relatives and friends today.

"Did you grow up like this baby is growing up?" the reporter asks.

"My daddy shot my momma dead when I was 2." She speaks flatly, like a kid bored with homework. She was raised by her grandfather.

She doesn't explain why she is at this house that isn't hers holding somebody else's baby.

An undercover officer recently bought drugs at this house. The police had come back to clean it up and close it down—one of nearly 400 Dallas dope houses stormed this year.

After running background checks on the three, the sergeant in charge decides to arrest the handcuffed youths on drug charges and ticket Latasha for failing to appear in court after being cited for driving without insurance.

"Do you ever dream of a better life?" the reporter asks.

She shrugs.

She doesn't watch the van carry her two friends away. She just sits in front of the house with the For Rent sign and the broken door, holding someone else's baby, and stares blankly at the vacant lot next door.

Language can be a little grander and still be simple. In an analysis of the anthrax scare following the September 11, 2001, terrorist attack, writer R. W. Apple Jr. of the *New York Times* combined simple language to create clear images. Apple's column responded to Speaker J. Dennis Hastert's decision to dismiss the House of Representatives to allow checks for anthrax spores vis-à-vis the Senate's decision to continue working. Apple noted that while "a veneer of civility" existed in public, senators were criticizing the House's actions. "Veneer" denotes the thinness of the legislators' politeness. Later, he described "the dense crust of anxiety" that had consumed Washington since the attacks. "Dense crust" suggests a level of anxiety that is tough to cut through. In both instances, Apple reached for words that weren't usually associated with "civility" and "anxiety" but that say exactly what he means. Any writer should look for words that are simple, descriptive, and familiar to sharpen images for readers. Audiences can appreciate the craft that goes into such writing.

The Right Word

Wordsmiths such as the late Theodore Bernstein and the late John Bremner have long decried the lack of precision in language. Bremner lamented what he called "the surge of literary barbarism" in English usage. Both stressed the importance of knowing language and definitions. In his book *Words on Words,* Bremner wrote,

> *To love words, you must first know what they are. Yes, words are symbols of ideas. But many words have lives of their own. They have their own historical and etymological associations, their own romantic and environmental dalliances, their own sonic and visual delights.*

To language lovers like Bremner, writing is a love affair with language.

A careless writer describes a basketball player as "an intricate part of the team." Perhaps his footwork is intricate, but what the writer really meant to say was "an integral part of the team."

A letter from a university provost to a newspaper columnist thanked her for "the prospective" she gave to a local issue. The provost meant "perspective."

In a news story, a student quoted a professor as saying, "The meeting will be a great opportunity for faculty members to mingle with their piers." Professors overboard!

Language needs to be specific and correct. Television personality Archie Bunker often spouted malapropisms: words that didn't say what he meant. "Oriental" was "ornamental," and "distinguished" was "extinguished." We laughed. As writers, we do not want our audiences laughing at us—unless we mean for them to chuckle.

Similar Words

Words that sound alike are troublesome for writers. Among the most common homonyms are "principal" and "principle," "affect" and "effect," "its" and "it's." Such words are particularly troublesome today when writers depend heavily on computer spell-checkers. Few programs will know the difference between "naval" and "navel" or "stationary" and "stationery," as we indicated in Chapter 2. The resulting confusion can be misleading and embarrassing. Writers must be comfortable in reaching for a good dictionary or other reference book to check correct spelling and usage. Other references, such as those listed at the end of this chapter, are valuable for writers who are choosy about words. Refer to Chapter 2 for help with spelling in the computer age.

Writers should pay heed to synonyms. Many writers haul out the thesaurus when they are weary of using a word too often. But a synonym may not be specific. One editing teacher advises against using a thesaurus and prefers a dictionary. Remember that repetition of a word or words throughout a message is acceptable. Repetition can unify a message. For instance, use the word "bank" throughout a story about the opening of a financial institution's 78th branch bank. It unifies the release, and bank is more specific than facility.

Word Choice

While taking care with word usage, writers should strive to choose words that are universally accepted and understood. If they are unsure about a word or its use, they should consult a stylebook or a dictionary. *The Associated Press Stylebook,* for example, adds cautionary notes about how specific words included in its entries should be used. The note might warn that the word is offensive or derogatory. Dictionaries will include in the definition whether the word is below the normal standard for literate writing. Dictionaries also will indicate spellings of words and correct usage, as in the case of homonyms.

If a dictionary or a stylebook warns against usage of a word, as profanity perhaps, writers should use it only if they have a compelling reason. They may also have to explain in a note at the beginning of the article or the broadcast that the message contains offensive language. Using profanities and vulgarities is discussed more fully in Chapter 9 on quotations and attribution.

Sentences

Sentences should be complete. Each must have a subject and a verb and must state one complete idea, thought, or meaning. Granted, some writers use short but incomplete sentences for emphasis, such as "The day he left was cold and in the dead of winter. January 22, to be exact." Sentence fragments or stray phrases generally have little place in straight writing, and beginning writers should avoid using them.

This is a fragment: "January 22, to be exact."

This is a sentence: "The day he left was cold and in the dead of winter."

This is a sentence: "That day was January 22, to be exact."

Sentence Types

Grammarians define different types of sentences on the basis of structure.

- A simple sentence is one independent or main clause. It can have more than one subject and verb, object, and modifying phrase.

  Five people died Wednesday in a skiing accident in France.

  Six seniors and two juniors are on the University's debate team.

- A compound sentence has two or more simple sentences that may be joined by a conjunction such as "and" or "but" or by punctuation such as a semicolon.

  Fire destroyed a historic landmark in downtown Midland Tuesday, but the owners said they will rebuild the bookstore on the site.

  Semi-colon
  Many people have changed their diets to cut out high-fat foods; others have ignored warnings that a high-fat diet can cause heart disease.

- A complex sentence has at least one independent or main clause and other clauses that are dependent on the main clause.

  When the school board meets Monday night, it will vote on a controversial multicultural plan that some elementary school students' parents fear will focus on sexual orientation as well as on ethnic diversity.

[handwritten: 40 words↓ (too long)]

- A compound-complex sentence is a compound sentence with at least two independent clauses and one or more dependent clauses.

[handwritten: 3 ideas]

```
The Democratic candidate for lieutenant governor has
raised almost $600,000 for his campaign, which has been
hard fought against the Republican incumbent, and he
expects supporters to contribute even more after he
completes a three-day tour across the state.
```

[handwritten: better off 2 simple sentences.]

Vary Sentence Types

Good writers use a variety of sentence types, but they prefer the simple sentence. A good guideline is to use many simple sentences and to use compound sentences formed from short simple sentences.

Writers use complex sentences because of the need for attribution, amplification, and identification. But they work hard to avoid compound-complex sentences, saving them to express ideas that are difficult to state any other way.

Nahal Toosi of the *Milwaukee Journal-Sentinel* used primarily simple sentences in the following lead and included a complex sentence in the third paragraph for variety.

> WEST ALLIS—Ian Rotten's forehead is ground meat.
> Bruises and scars cover his arms. Blood streams down his face and over his swollen body.
> As fans yell for more, the wrestler is hoisted by his nemesis, Hardcore Craig, and dropped into a wooden case topped with glass and filled with barbed wire.
> Rotten is literally stuck.
> "Get me out of here!" he screams.*

Studies show that people of all ages and levels of education prefer simple sentences, in which subjects come before verbs and verbs before the remainder of the sentence. A series of simple sentences relaxes your readers or listeners and prepares them to encounter something more complex when it occurs in your text, as it inevitably will.

*© June 10, 2001 Journal Sentinel Inc., reproduced with permission.

Look at the sentence variety in the following story by Alison Delsite of *The Patriot-News* in Harrisburg, Pa. She uses a mix of complex sentences and simple sentences. Paragraph 5 is one complex sentence. But in the next paragraph a series of short, simple sentences carries the action.

Life–Saving Tickets Win Fame, But No Fortune

BY ALISON DELSITE

The Patriot-News

Patrick Gayle's lottery tickets weren't losers after all.

Not only did they help deflect a bullet and possibly save the Harrisburg man's life, they brought him a few days of fame and, maybe, a little extra cash.

Gayle was interviewed on CNN. Crews from TV's "Hard Copy" taped a segment outside the Allison Hill convenience store where he was shot.

He was interviewed for publications nationwide, including *The National Enquirer* and a lottery magazine in Florida. He did radio shows. "I told them, 'I feel blessed,'" Gayle says.

On April 23, Gayle was walking into a Regina Street store to play the Daily Number when he was struck by a bullet during a shooting that police say was a continuation of the long-standing Allison Hill-Uptown rivalry.

The bullet was deflected by a cigarette lighter and a wad of tickets in his shirt pocket. The lighter shattered. The tickets were tattered. The shirt had a hole in it. He wasn't injured.

The *Patriot-News* story about the shooting made the Associated Press' wire. Since then Gayle's phone has been ringing.

Edward Meyer, vice president for exhibits at Ripley's Believe It or Not, said Ripley's intends to do a cartoon on Gayle and hopes to purchase his tickets. For now, they are evidence, in the custody of Harrisburg police.

Meyer wouldn't say how much Ripley's would pay. "Probably a couple hundred dollars. Stories like this are right up our alley," he said. "We'll make it worth his while, but not make him rich." Gayle, a forklift driver, said he spends $40 a day on the lottery.

Meanwhile, the phone in Patrick Gaylor's home in Swatara Twp. also has been ringing.

It seems callers—including ones from TV's Montel Williams and

Maury Povich shows—unable to find Gayle's number, have called Gaylor's instead.

"They ask, 'Are you the person who was shot and saved by a pack of lottery tickets?'" said Gaylor. "No," he laughs. "But I hope he makes a lot of money off it anyway."

Reprinted with permission of *The Patriot-News.*

Common Sentence Errors

In constructing sentences, some writers forget the rule of parallel structure. In writing, all parts of any list or series must be parallel—that is, if the first element in the list starts with a noun, all others must be nouns as well. For example, the structure of this sentence is not parallel:

```
Previous legislative agendas included the Family

Preservation Act, child protective services, and

extending to school boards the right to ban corporal

punishment.
```

[handwritten: ? → switch from nah to verb]

Nouns in the list, "act" and "services," are not parallel with the verb form "extending." The sentence should be rewritten to read

```
Previous legislative agendas included the Family

Preservation Act, child protective services, and the right

of school boards to ban corporal punishment.
```

When writers start with a specific verb form, such as an infinitive with "to," they must keep the same format. The structure of the following sentence is not parallel:

```
The banquet is an occasion to reward corporations for

"family friendly" policies and recognizing volunteers and

the media.
```

[handwritten: ? to recognize]

It should be rewritten to read

```
The banquet is an occasion to reward corporations for
"family friendly" policies and to recognize volunteers.
```

Another common sentence error is the incorrect placement of modifying phrases or clauses. Such misplaced elements can lead to humorous and misleading sentences, such as the following:

```
After wheeling me into the operating room, a mask was
placed over my face.

The bank makes low-interest loans to individuals of any
size.

Mrs. Rogers was arrested shortly after 3 p.m. at the home
where the couple lived without incident.
```

Once spotted, modifier problems are easy to repair. Good writers train themselves to check modifier placement: Did the mask really wheel me into the operating room? Does the bank make loans based on height and weight? Did the couple really live in the house without incident? The questions can be cleared up by quick rewriting:

```
After I was wheeled into the operating room, a mask was
placed over my face.

The bank makes low-interest loans of any size to
individuals.

Mrs. Rogers was arrested without incident shortly after
3 p.m. at the home where the couple lived.
```

A good sentence can never be interpreted to mean more than one thing. Linguists say it has a "single reading"—meaning that the reader never needs to go back and read it again to understand it. If the reader goes back, it should be to savor the quality of the writing. Good writing aims for a single reading, so that readers move unobstructed through messages to meaning.

Paragraphs—Short Paragraphs

Words become sentences, and sentences become paragraphs. English composition books devote entire chapters to the topic of writing good paragraphs. When writers are concerned with transmitting information quickly, their ideas about paragraphing change. A paragraph is a whole presentation or argument on a topic in an essay for an English composition or literature class, whereas in mass communication, a paragraph is a single fact, thought, or "sound byte." That single thought or idea may take several sentences to explain. In newswriting, paragraphs are often short to break up blocks of gray copy. Journalists talk about "graphs," a shortened version of "paragraphs." One thought or idea is in a graph, and graphs are one sentence on occasion.

Effective use of three graphs of varying lengths is shown in this sports story by *USA Today* writer Chuck Johnson:

> Some major league players are in line to get rich quick over the next 10 days.
>
> The filing period for salary arbitration runs today through Jan. 14. A total of 113 players are eligible. Salary figures will be exchanged Jan. 18, and arbiters will hear cases Feb. 1–20.
>
> Atlanta, Montreal, St. Louis and Kansas City, with eight players each, have the most eligible to file.

Newspaper and magazine writers start a new graph to signal a new fact or a change of speaker—and sometimes just to give the reader a break. Readers appreciate white space in a publication, and frequent "graffing," as it is called, gives such visual relief by making space—literal and figurative—between ideas.

New Speaker Equals New Paragraph

One of the most useful functions of frequent graffing is that it effectively signals a change of speakers. Notice how Associated Press writer Ashley Grant moves smoothly from one quote to another, just by starting new graphs and giving background in between. The story focused on the four winners in Powerball.

> The Kentucky winner, David Edwards, 46, who lives outside Ashland, said he was recently laid off from his fiber optics job, needs back surgery and had no idea what he was going to do once his unemployment benefits ran out.
> "A lot of people work hard and a lot of people are out of work. And you dream you want a better life, and playing this lottery has done that for me," Edwards said.
> He bought $8 worth of tickets—seven for himself and one for his fiancee—at a convenience store just 90 minutes before the drawing.
> "I said, 'Help me Lord. I know it might not be right of me to ask you this, but can you just let me win this?'" he said.★

With quotations, the short bursts provided by one-sentence graphs add a lively, conversational air to newswriting and hold the audience's attention. "New speaker, new graph" is a writer's rule that can add clarity to all writing.

Most writing can benefit from shorter paragraphs. Bite-sized paragraphs may not be appropriate in all settings, but leaner paragraphs tend to streamline messages of all kinds and to save time and space, the most precious resources in any mass medium.

Where We Are

For many beginning writers, thinking about rules stymies them from the start. But let's summarize what we have said so far about good writing.

1. Good writing uses short sentences.
2. Good writing uses short words.
3. Good writing eliminates wordiness.
4. Good writing clears away redundancy, jargon, and institutional language.
5. Good writing comes to the point quickly.

★Reprinted with permission of The Associated Press.

6. Good writing has a mix of sentence types.
7. Good writing has short paragraphs.

When listed, the rules seem more manageable.

The Way to Clearer Writing

Writing often moves from the general to the specific, and this chapter is following such a path. At the outset, we discussed broad principles of accuracy, clarity, completeness, and fairness. We then looked at the basic tenets of good writing and the components of any piece of writing: words, sentences, and paragraphs.

Now for the specifics. Additional guidelines can help you say it straight. Keep the guidelines in mind as you write, but do not be so tied to them that you stop after every sentence to analyze whether it meets the standards of good writing. Go ahead and write, then go back and apply the guidelines in editing.

Write the First Draft as You Would Say It

Writing coach Robert Gunning said writers should write the way they talk. He argued that all writing would improve if people simply talked and wrote down what they said. Gunning was onto a great idea: First drafts are most effective when a writer puts down on paper what he or she would tell someone about a topic. Most people talk in subject–verb–object order that is easy to understand. The result is text that is conversational, uses simple language, and is easy to revise into a well-organized written message.

Colorful Description

Author Tom Wolfe made his fiction writing career by writing the way he talked. In his speech to the American Society of Newspaper Editors, Wolfe noted the phenomenon of the "trophy" wife, what the successful chief executive officer believes he deserves as a perk. He described the courtship ritual, adding his characteristic style, this way:

> ...*the sight out on the discotheque floor of the 57-year-old CEO with his trophy wife-to-be. He's wearing his hard-finished worsted navy blue chalk-striped suit. He's wearing his medium spread-collar white shirt...and he's wearing his hair combed back over his ears in little sloops known as the 57th Street biggie look. His*

trophy wife-to-be, his lemon tart, is out there, and she's wearing a pair of Everlast boxing trunks. She's got on a man's strap style undershirt. She's got a hairdo that looks as if a Snapper lawnmower's gone over her head....

  And he's beaming at her with red eyes through these walnut shell eyelids....
He's desperately trying to do the robot or the eel or the sadomacho until the onset of dawn, saline depletion, or myocardial infarction—or whichever comes first.
And after all, why shouldn't he? Because what are Mom and the Cutlass Sierra and Buddy and Sis up against a love like this? That first night on the disco floor, she wore a pair of boxing trunks while leather punks and painted lulus, African queens and sado Zulus paid her court. I grow old, the 1990s way. Deaf but from a Max Q octophonic beat. Stroked out but on my own two feet. Disco macho for you, my new cookie.

Don't Begin at the Beginning

After seeing a four-car collision, the typical observer arrives home and blurts out, "I saw an incredible wreck on Highway 501. Four cars collided; all the drivers were injured, and one car burned." Only then will the observer back up and give background: "I was in the left lane, coming home from the mall," and so on.

  Like urgent conversation, writing needs to jump straight to the point, then fill the reader in—just as we will discuss in Chapter 4 on writing leads. This technique gives writing a conversational tone and at the same time gets to the ever-so-important point of the message.

  Starting with salient facts is a natural way to tell about important information. Unfortunately, it is a form that most people forget after years of reading stories and writing essays, both of which usually start with formal introductions. If your goal is to say it straight, say it—your main point—soon in your message. Suspenseful beginnings work best in drama.

Writing and Editing: Two Compatible Tasks

When you spill out your conversational first draft, write it without stopping to edit. Mixing writing and editing wastes time and effort. If you edit as you go (and most amateurs do), you may fuss over a sentence that you eventually eliminate. At the very least, you will interrupt your own thought processes and conversational flow. So write first. If you pause to ponder sentence structure or information, that's okay. But do not wander or stray from the effort.

Some beginning writers lack the confidence to sit down and write. But author Joel Saltzman points out that we all are more competent wordsmiths than we think:

When you're talking, odds are that 98 percent of the time you don't even think about grammar. You're doing fine and it's just not an issue.... I am suggesting that you don't worry about it right now; because the more you worry about grammar, the less you're going to write.

After you finish your outpouring of prose, let the copy cool by taking a short break before you begin to edit. This separates the writing and editing processes and allows you to see your copy in a different way. If you edit or rewrite immediately after your draft is finished, you will read what you think you wrote rather than what is actually on the page. More about the editing process is covered later in this chapter.

Stick with Subject–Verb Order

Most human languages prefer to place subjects before verbs, and English is no exception. Curious people want to know who did something, then what they did (and to whom or what). Keep these audience interests and preferences in mind when you write. Subject–verb–object order generally gives the sentence action.

```
A man wearing a stocking mask robbed the university dining
hall late Tuesday night and locked the dining services
manager in a closet.

A massive earthquake registering 6.8 on the Richter scale
rocked Japan early Tuesday morning.
```

Readers get confused if subjects and verbs are scrambled, regardless of how artistic the result may be.

```
Came he swiftly to her bower?
```

Not in the information age.

Choose Active Verbs

Verbs are action words, but not all verbs are active. Some show no action at all, such as the verb "to be" in all its forms (is, am, are, was, were, be, being). Such verbs are less interesting and harder to picture than active verbs.

Writers prefer active verbs because they contain more information and sensory detail. "He was president" is vague compared with "He dominated the country as president." Good writing is filled with active verbs that evoke images in the mind of the reader or listener.

```
Lightner whacked the ball with such force that it sailed
over the outfield wall—his first home run of the season.

Babies cried, children clamored, balls thunked into holes,
tickets ching-ching-chinged into eager hands, the noise
competing against the Chuck E. Cheese theme song in the
background.
```

Choose the Active Voice

When writers use active verbs, they write in active voice.

"Lightner whacked the ball." The subject, Lightner, performs the action. The object, the ball, receives action. This sentence format is called *active voice,* and it is the natural order of English. "A man wearing a stocking mask robbed the university dining hall" carries more action than "the university dining hall was robbed by a man."

Every now and then, a sentence has no obvious subject and must be written in another format, called the passive voice. Take, for example, this sentence: "The law was changed several years ago." It is in passive voice. The recipient of the action, the law, has been moved into the subject position—probably because a long legislative process kept the writer from isolating a single person or session responsible for changing the law.

Research shows that people prefer active sentences over passive ones. The sentence "Congress passed the bill" is easier to read and comprehend than its passive equivalent, "The bill was passed by Congress." Skilled writers prefer the active voice and use passive sentences only when necessary. In our example about Lightner, a passive structure would hardly have the same impact: "The ball was whacked by Lightner."

Sometimes writers use passive sentences for emphasis: "The anticrime bill was passed by Congress." Here the writer wants to focus on the provisions of the bill rather than on congressional action and writes the lead accordingly.

Generally Put Time Elements after the Verb

Because verbs are stimulating to readers, they should come before less interesting elements. Audiences need to know when something happened, but they can wait to find out. The time element, a necessary but often dull part of a message, can be relegated to a place after the verb. Some writers prefer to put it immediately after the verb. Here are a few examples:

> Former Mayor Barry Anderson was married Tuesday morning in a small private ceremony.

> Grant applications requesting up to $100,000 for research on learning disabilities may be submitted through June 15 to the National Institutes of Health.

Sometimes, however, the time element carries importance and needs to go elsewhere—even first in the sentence.

> Wednesday a 14-year-old youth collected $125,000 that he found in a paper bag a year ago. The money was never claimed.

In the above example, the beginning and end of the sentence set up the time span: On Wednesday the youth cashed in after waiting a year.

> Beginning this weekend the city planetarium will offer extra weekend shows to expand its offerings for people who work and school children.

Right away, people know that an event is coming soon.

Be Specific Rather than General

Always give the most specific information you can. Significant details enlighten and delight readers and pack information into a few words. Instead of saying that actress Helen Hunt went shopping, tell what she bought: cosmetics. What kind? Inquiring minds want to know! Instead of saying that a reporter had a messy desk, try

```
On his desk Howard had a can of unsharpened pencils and two
potted ferns, both of them dead.
```

Watch out for words that have almost a generic quality, such as "facility." Be specific: bank, gymnasium, recreation center, high school. Use the specific noun.

Author Tom Wolfe has a marvelous talent for combining simple words into run-on, colorful, entertaining description, as you saw in the excerpt from his "trophy" wife speech to the American Society of Newspaper Editors.

Appeal to the Senses

An audience, whether it is reading or listening, still can use the full range of senses as it absorbs information. That means writers must pay attention to their senses when gathering information. Writers can report the facts or describe the scene without being subjective—a fear that many beginning writers have and that keeps them from being descriptive in their writing.

Writing that appeals to the senses—that creates mental pictures, aromas, and sensations—is more memorable and more appealing; it transports the audience to the scene of the message. Once captured, the audience is likely to remain in the writer's world long enough to get the message.

Through writing that appeals to all the senses, *Milwaukee Journal-Sentinel* reporter Nahal Toosi brings readers inside the Knights of Columbus Hall where fans gather to cheer and aid their favorite contenders.

> *The blood is real. So is much of the pain. So are the tacks, staples, barbed wire, wood and whatever else the hard-core wrestlers use to hurt one another....*
>
> *In a hall known more for wedding receptions than wrestling matches, nothing is sacred. Young women in tight pants and old men in plaid shirts shout obscenities together. Twentysomethings wearing Gothic makeup drink beer alongside ag-*

ing jocks. Old ladies sell hot dogs and hamburgers in the back; young security guards keep order in the front.

"Faggot! Faggot!" fans yell as two sweaty men in tights roll over one another. When a woman in the show stands at ringside, flaunting expensive breasts in a black bikini top, men yell: "Puppies! Puppies!" She loves it.

Most of the seats are arranged in two sets of rows between the ring and the main entrance. On one side of the ring, the announcer, along with DeSpirito and a few others, sit at a wooden table with an old bell.

Before and after matches, sometimes even during them, wrestlers use a microphone to incite the crowd, propel a story line or promote a future match. Audience members who are singled out—called an "ugly rat" for instance—have reached a new level of notoriety.

There are so many repeat customers that the fans become part of the show in their own right. DeSpirito's ideal fan is someone like Rita Segerson, 22, a cashier who lives in Milwaukee and never misses a Mid American show. She even provides some weapons for the hard-core wrestlers.

At a recent show, she and her friends brought in a bunch of long fluorescent light bulbs strategically tied to some wood. The device and other homemade implements go into a big can; wrestlers can pick one to use if they wish.

"It's fun; it's stress-relieving," Segerson said. "You can scream at the top of your lungs!"★

The reader sees and hears the crowd and senses how men and women throw themselves into the event. The smells range from sweat to hot dogs and hamburgers, the sounds from bodies crunching to fans screaming.

One need not be a feature writer to use sensory appeal. It works well in everyday forms of communication, such as directions to the company picnic. Instead of "turn right two blocks after the fork in the road and proceed to 1511," how about:

```
Look for a grove of tall pines two blocks after the fork in
the road; turn right and go to the red mailbox marked 1511.
You'll smell pungent smoke from Marvin's famous barbequed
ribs.
```

With such sensory appeal, it's doubtful that anyone will get lost.

★ © June 10, 2001 Journal Sentinel Inc., reproduced with permission.

Use Statistics Sparingly and Powerfully

We live in an era when numbers make powerful messages: A basketball arena will cost $121 million. A pharmaceutical company will lay off 1,600 workers.

Audiences become insensitive if they are bombarded by alarming numbers, regardless of how striking those numbers may be. Statistics of any kind should be delivered one at a time in good writing. Never let two numbers touch in written copy; avoid putting numbers close to one another except in direct comparisons:

> Women work 88 hours per week doing home and workplace
> chores, whereas men work about 60.

Another good rule of thumb is to limit yourself to no more than three numbers in any one paragraph to avoid overwhelming your reader or listener. In a business story, for example, numbers can be confusing, so spread them out and keep them simple.

> Comair, Delta's Connection carrier, will add four more
> routes next month out of its hub in Cincinnati.
>
> The new service will increase Comair's cities to 95. The
> carrier will operate 664 flights a day.
>
> In continued expansion, Comair plans to serve 99 cities
> with more than 750 daily flights within the next six
> months.

Professor Philip Meyer, who has been a consultant at *USA Today*, suggests that in any statistical report one or two numbers stand out as being crucial. The important numbers should appear early in your message, and others may be summarized in lists or tables outside the written text.

Translate Statistics into Everyday, Tangible Terms

People have little intuitive understanding of large numbers. The citizen who learns that a sports arena is to cost $121 million is left with many questions:

Is that a good price for an arena? How many new schools would that buy? How much will my county taxes increase?

Good writers provide an understanding of big numbers in several ways. One way is to compare one number with another:

```
The $121 million price tag compares with the $58.2 million
cost of an arena built in 1989 in Springfield.
```

Another way to present numbers is to give them in terms the average person deals with each day. Few of us can visualize $121 million, but many people can understand a 3.5 percent tax increase to fund the stadium.

The clearest way to present costs is to use an individual citizen as an example:

```
A person owning a home with a tax value of $154,000 will
pay about $200 more each year in taxes to finance the
arena.
```

Such writing allows the audience to understand personal gains or losses that may be obscured in reports of large numbers.

Double-Check Your Math

Many writers jokingly say they went into communications because they could not do math. But any writer needs to use numbers and must be sure they are correct. Errors can be embarrassing.

In a news story about salary increases at city hall, a reporter looked at the current year's salary for the city attorney: $65,000. The proposed salary for the next fiscal year was $69,000. The city attorney would get a 5 percent pay increase, she wrote. The actual increase was 6 percent. The reporter erroneously divided the difference of $4,000 by the new salary rather than the current salary. Other city employees were upset that the city attorney was getting 5 percent compared with their 2 percent. When the real difference eventually was published, the unhappiness grew. (And the city attorney expressed his anger that the figures were published at all, forgetting that the salaries of public officials are public record.)

When in Doubt, Leave It Out

Unless you are able to check the accuracy of a number, spelling, or surprising fact, leave it out or hold publication until you can check it. Accuracy is linked, in the minds of audience members, with quality—with media quality and writer quality. Your reputation is riding on what you write.

Some errors are painful to people in the community. A university magazine noted offhandedly that a famous scientist had discovered a new kind of plant. His research assistant, who in fact had made the discovery and received credit for it in scientific journals, called the reporter to correct the error. Few people will ever see a small correction notice, but people such as the offended research assistant will remember the slight for years.

Multiple copies of a mistake are always embarrassing, whether in an office memo or a front-page story. Such mistakes also may lead to legal problems. Chapter 8 discusses libel.

Rewrite Long Introductory Phrases

Audiences are eager to get to the point, and long introductory phrases slow them down. Long phrases also interrupt the subject–verb–object pattern that readers and listeners prefer.

Avoid:

```
Because the Redskins had been waiting all season for a
victory, several players refused to be interviewed.
```

Prefer:

```
Several Redskins players refused to be interviewed after
waiting all season for a victory.
```

Eliminate Long Strings of Prepositional Phrases

Any group of two or more prepositional phrases makes a sentence seem to meander rather than flow. Too many prepositional phrases strung together within a sentence are undesirable but easy to fix. Prepositional phrases are among the movable parts of any sentence; they also may be placed in new (short) sentences.

Avoid:

```
The school's marching band will appear in a series of
performances on three consecutive Tuesday afternoons on
the athletic field near the gymnasium on the school campus
beginning this Tuesday.
```

Prefer:

```
The school's marching band will present a series of Tuesday
afternoon performances beginning this week. The band will
play on the athletic field near the gymnasium.
```

Look for unnecessary prepositional phrases everywhere in writing. Take

```
Marilyn Jacobs, one of the writers of the letter, said the
group wants action immediately.
```

and edit it to read:

```
Marilyn Jacobs, who helped write the letter, said the group
wants action immediately.
```

Avoid Making Everything Look IMPORTANT

Some writers like to add emphasis by underlining text or by using capital letters, exclamation marks, bold type, and even quotation marks. Frequent use of such elements detracts from professional polish. Once in a while, everyone needs to add emphasis. Save it for when it *really* counts. In some messages, such as e-mail, emphasis can be interpreted as anger, exasperation, and even sarcasm.

Avoid a message that looks like this sentence:

```
If you don't get your information sheet in today, you WON'T
be in the new directory AT ALL.
```

Try:

```
If you don't get your information sheet in today, you won't
be in the new directory.
```

Clear Out Euphemisms

Most of us were taught to use euphemisms in polite conversation—to say "expecting" rather than "pregnant," "plump" rather than "fat," and "passed away" rather than "died." In fact, we like euphemisms because they are handy substitutes for embarrassing words. In media, straight talk is preferred.

Avoid:

```
The guard said that two residents of the correctional
facility had gone to "their just reward."
```

Prefer:

```
The guard said that two prisoners had died.
```

Using the straightforward words "prisoners" and "died" instead of the longer euphemisms keeps the sentence short and the reading easy.

Good writing requires specific information. Most euphemisms are designed to be imprecise—to mislead or give false comfort. Never forget that "protective reactions strikes" are "bombings" and that "peacekeeper missiles" are "nuclear warheads." Both terms came into vogue with the politically correct language. Politically correct terms generally are longer and less accurate than the synonyms they replace. For example, a drunk is a "person of differing sobriety," and a loser is an "individual with temporarily unmet objectives." Writers have to draw the line between what is acceptable taste and what is a surrender to faddish writing. Those who are not in the politically correct circle may wonder what on earth the writer is saying. Once euphemisms are removed, the meaning is clear and timeless.

Keep Writing Readable

Readability is defined most simply as the level of difficulty of a given message. Readable, or high-readability, writing is easy to understand. Several ways to measure readability have been found, most of which are based on (1) sentence length and (2) concentration or number of multisyllable words.

One common readability measure is the Fog Index, developed in the 1940s by Robert Gunning for United Press International wire service. Despite its age, the Fog Index is still used as a measure of readability. To compute a Fog Index, (1) calculate the average number of words per sentence in a given message and (2) count the number of difficult words, or those with three syllables or more, in a 100-word sample from the message. Add these two figures together and multiply by 0.4.

The resulting number—the Fog Index for the writing in question—corresponds to the number of years of education a reader would need to read and understand the copy. For example, a publication with an average of 22 words per sentence and 15 difficult words in the 100-word sample would have a Fog Index of 14.8. That means its readers would require some college education to read the piece comfortably.

Let's see how that works on the first four paragraphs of the Nahal Toosi story about Mid-Atlantic wrestling. Thirteen sentences have 165 words, or an average of 12.7 words per sentence. Words with three syllables or more in the first 100 words number 10. Add 12.7 to 10 and multiply by 0.4; the answer is 9.1. The Toosi piece has fairly high readability because of fairly short sentences on average. Only 10 of 100 words have three or more syllables, so her preference for simple words keeps the readability between middle school and high school. The *Journal-Sentinel* has a broad audience, so the writing level is consistent with its audience.

Most readability experts agree that clear writing is geared to the eleventh- and twelfth-grade levels. Even people with a great deal more education seem to be most comfortable reading at this level. Journalism Professor Fred Fedler notes that most wire service copy is written at about the tenth-grade level. Many grammar-check software packages have readability measures that automatically tell writers the readability of any piece.

The *Wall Street Journal's* Fog Index routinely falls into the eleventh- to twelfth-grade range, despite the complicated nature of financial reporting. A clever marketing strategy is operating here: Dow Jones knows that to make business reports palatable, they must be readable.

Be Aware of Misinterpretations

As writers edit their copy, they need to be aware of all possible interpretations of what has been written. They need to know an audience's language tastes for effective communication. Language choices can alter meaning for the reader or put a different slant on a message—often a slant that the writer never intended. Sometimes the results are comical, such as a ship was "birthed" instead of "berthed" at a nearby naval station, or a mother who wants "piece of mind." Think about the sentence, "Donations may be given by church members of any size." The size of the donations, not of church members, is the issue.

A prepositional phrase in the wrong place can change the meaning, as in "Lacey Smith died of a head wound at Memorial Hospital at 4 P.M. Wednesday." What the writer meant was that Lacey Smith died Wednesday afternoon at Memorial Hospital after suffering a head wound. Smith had the head wound before arriving at the hospital; Smith was not wounded by hospital personnel. "The thief was muscular with a round face about 5 feet 3 inches tall." How tall was the thief's face?

Watch Out for Language Trends

Writers should avoid popular trends in writing. As we noted earlier in the discussion of avoiding euphemisms, the politically correct movement substituted a myriad of words and phrases for ones that had been part of common language. In many cases, the new language is wordy and less precise.

The use of such "pop" language excludes segments of the audience that may not be cued to the lingo. Certainly language evolves. Each time a new edition of *Webster's* dictionary comes out, new words are included. Many of us can remember when "ain't" was not in the dictionary. Dictionaries list and define words that are common in the English language, but a dictionary is just one of many sources writers use.

One trend that has caused extreme pain to language experts is the conversion of nouns to verbs. Host has become "to host," and conference has become "to conference." With computer use increasing, the media use soon will be standard. Many computer terms already are accepted usage, but some writers still cringe when they hear words such as "input."

Another trend that offends many writers is the addition of "-ize" to create new words: "prioritize," "finalize," "maximize," "accessorize." Again, although the words have found their way into everyday usage, language professionals try to find better and more accurate verbs.

Editing, Editing, Editing

Good writing depends on good editing. Many student or beginning writers assume that a writing job is finished once they get a message down on paper. Already in this chapter, you have learned some guidelines or tips on how to improve your copy. Those guidelines can be applied in the editing process. No writer, no matter how long he or she has practiced the craft, can remember all the rules while writing the first—or even second or third—draft.

Between the first draft and the finished product comes polishing and editing. The first draft should be as good as you can create it. Editing will refine and improve that first edit. Editing is essential. North Carolina novelist and English professor Doris Betts tells students, "Handing in your first draft is like passing around your spittle"—in other words, unprofessional and offensive.

As a writer, you are responsible for editing and revising your own work, even if you work on a newspaper staff or in a large corporate communications office where others will edit your work. You are the originator, the one who must shape and streamline the initial draft. The draft must be clear, fair, accurate, and complete when it leaves your hands.

An editor can catch inconsistencies and grammatical errors and can ask questions to make the draft more complete. But he or she may not know enough about the subject to find all inaccuracies or may be harried because of a deadline and not have time to correct all flaws. Eventually, you may be an executive who must communicate policies to staff members, or you may be the sole information specialist within a nonprofit organization. No one else is likely to fix your writing and improve it.

As you gain experience as a writer, you also will be asked to revise the work of others. You may be promoted to an editing position or solicited by others who know less than you do about good writing skills.

Editing is hard work, and it is time consuming. It can be creative and satisfying. But, in any case, it has to be done. Editing is a crucial stage in the writing process.

William Strunk wrote *The Elements of Style,* a brief but pointed book on how to improve writing. Much of the material is still pertinent more than almost 80 years after it was written. Strunk's student, E. B. White, remembered the book from class and in 1935 had it published. White, who wrote the foreword, never forgot the advice of his mentor. He once told an interviewer that he rewrote essays as many as 14 times before they were published. He spent 3 years writing the popular children's book, *Charlotte's Web,* and almost 12 years writing *Stuart Little.*

Anyone who reads *The Elements of Style* can see that each word is carefully selected to say just what Strunk and White mean: There's no fat and no redundancy. Despite its age, the little book's wisdom and guidelines are invaluable to anyone who wants to be a serious, competent writer and editor.

The Steps of Editing

Writers should consider editing as a process. Specific tasks allow writers-turned-editors to be focused and thorough in the editing process. Of course, writer-editors approach a 6-inch story quite differently from a 40-inch feature. Sometimes, on first reading, an editor will decide the story needs substantial revisions; other times, only minor changes will be needed. That decision comes in the first step of the editing process and will determine how much time needs to be devoted to editing.

Writers who use computers should learn to edit at the computer screen. They may not have time to print out a draft and edit on paper. Editing on screen saves times and allows the writer to use computer tools, such as a spell-checker, to help in the editing process.

Editing follows basic steps: content, accuracy, language, and final read-through.

• The first step is to check for content. Read the written piece from start to finish to get the sense of what has been written. You may fix any minor errors, but at this point, determine whether substantial or minor changes are needed. Underline sections and note questions that need attention.

- You may determine that more research and rewriting is required. That reworking should come before moving to the next step.

- Once the content is okay, writers and editors must check for accuracy, an intense, time-consuming job. In a professional office, writers have help from editors or fact-checkers. But regardless of who helps, writers ultimately are responsible for the accuracy of their work.

- Next, review language. Are words simple, clear, and direct? Are sentences active and easy to read? Is the message free of grammar and spelling errors and bias? Remember that jargon and institutional language are rampant. This step is also when you tighten writing. If an article needs to be shortened, writers often can do that by substituting one word for a phrase, eliminating redundancies, and reducing long titles or numbers of prepositional phrases. Such fine-tuning improves writing and keeps complete paragraphs intact.

- After the revisions are completed, read the story again. Check carefully any sections that have been changed. Often, writers make new errors when they revise. The last stage is a final read-though for overall quality and reader appeal. This stage is what some people equate with the term *editing*. It is the final cosmetic once-over where the writer-editor is pleased with the story. If the writer-editor is not satisfied, then the editing steps should be repeated.

If you have been editing on the computer screen, you should do one final step: Consult the computer's spelling checker. It will catch spelling errors and also flag repeated words and missing spaces. Such errors are often overlooked.

Some writers may question the sequence in editing. But the reasoning is quite simple: It is efficient. If reviewing for language came first, sentences that had been fine-tuned could be deleted during later content editing. It's far better that the sentences go first. More important, the most critical tasks are done first in case the writer-editor runs out of time. For example, it is more important to write a compelling lead than to smooth out a transition. And it is more important for the piece to be complete and accurate than free of spelling errors.

Note: Editors should be flexible as they edit. If they see a problem that needs to be fixed, regardless of the stage, they should address it then. Editors who wait may forget to make the repair.

A Closer Look

The steps of editing have been outlined only to show why editing and revision are necessary. Let's look at what each step does.

READING THE COPY. Read through the entire piece uninterruptedly as if you were a consumer who had never heard of the subject. This is usually a step most writers skip; yet it is critical for them to step back and see the message as a whole, as audiences will see it.

"But why should I read my own writing before I start to make changes?" a student writer may question. "I collected the information. I wrote it. I know what's there." Within that statement lies the danger. Because a writer may be so familiar with a topic and its components, he or she may overlook whether the meaning is clear to someone new to the subject.

In the first step, the ideal scenario is to put away a piece of writing for a few days and come back to it. Then you can look at it with a fresh eye: with the eye of an editor rather than the eye of a writer. But you may not have that luxury. If you are pressed for time, get up, walk around, have a snack, and get some fresh air. Then return to your writing. You will see it from a new perspective.

Read aloud to slow down and to hear what you have actually written—not what you think is there. The most common errors detected by reading aloud are awkward language, inadequate explanations that confuse the meaning, and too much prose on a particular topic.

As you read and detect weaknesses, you can make simple notes in the margin, such as "fix," "delete," or "explain." You will find, after your first reading, that you are eager to get on with improving your writing.

EXAMINING STRUCTURE. If your piece needs substantial revisions, you may need to consider again the audience and ask, Does the message attract audience attention and meet audience needs? Does the lead adequately set up the article? Are all the points raised in the lead answered in subsequent paragraphs? Is the lead itself interesting and written in a way to attract an audience into the message?

The lead, as you will learn in Chapter 4, gives the audience specific cues about the substance of the message. To maintain your credibility with your audience, you do not want to promise a certain message in your lead and then not deliver it.

To hold the audience with the message, a writer must look at the overall organization and ask

• Is the message developed logically? Do facts follow in a clear sequence?

• Is the transition from one point to another effective? Each paragraph should be tied to the previous one.

• Are paragraphs organized so that each contains one thought or idea? Readers will be confused if too many thoughts are packaged into one paragraph. Start a new paragraph—basically a unit of organization—with each new quote or each new idea.

• Are there statements or sentences that stop you because they are out of context?

• Do all the quotes add to the message? Would it be better to paraphrase or omit some?

Again, the answers to these questions may require rewriting.

To determine if you need more information, ask

• Is the message up to date? Are the latest statistics used? For example, a television news story on accidental deaths attributed to alchohol must have this year's figures on reported cases, not figures from two years ago, or even last year. Your audience wants to know how serious the situation is today. If those numbers aren't available, you need to say so, and why.

• Are any questions raised that aren't answered? Each message must be complete. A news release that says a company is privately held must define what privately held means. A message that is written and not aired may need some description so readers can mentally picture the action.

The answers to the questions in this step of editing are guidelines for how much reporting and rewriting must be done so that copy is complete and flows smoothly and logically.

CHECKING FOR ACCURACY. No aspect of writing is more important than accuracy. Remember the professor's often quip, "If your mother says she loves you, check it out." Employees may ridicule an executive who includes inaccurate information in memos. Readers turn away from publications and advertisements where they repeatedly find errors. Students lose faith in text-books when they uncover wrong data.

The bottom line is trust: If your audience doesn't trust the validity of any part of your message, it will question the accuracy of the entire message. Once it loses trust, the audience will be less willing to believe in future com-munications from you and may move to other media, never to return.

Research has shown that even one error in a newspaper can cause read-ers to doubt the rest of the paper and to have less faith in the reporter's abil-ities. Accuracy, therefore, can build or break your reputation, not just the reputation of the medium that carries the message.

Steps to Ensure Accuracy

• Let your copy cool before checking for accuracy. Take a break for a few minutes so you can approach it with a clear mind. If you read it imme-diately, questionable material may not stand out.

• Check name spellings. Review your notes. Double-check with the researcher or another writer. Use a telephone book, city directory, or other printed reference. Correct names are essential to avoid confusion—and even legal trouble—when people have the same or similar names. For example, in writing about a nightclub singer named Delsie Harper, a reporter inadvert-ently left off the D, and the newspaper immediately got a call from a church deacon named Elsie Harper.

• Use reputable sources to confirm information. For example, the city budget director will have more knowledge on changes in the next fiscal year budget than will an anonymous city employee who calls a newspaper to complain.

• Make sure quotes that contain opinion or outrageous claims are attrib-uted, such as this one: "Women get what they deserve," a self-proclaimed an-tifeminist said today. The quote has some credibility with the attribution but would have more if the antifeminist were named.

• If quotes are libelous—that is, damaging to a person's reputation—either make sure they can be defended or cut them. A person's barroom allegation about his next-door neighbor's drug use is not protected by law and should never be published. You may quote a witness's remark in a trial, however, because what occurs in court proceedings is protected. See more about libel in Chapter 8.

• Question statistics. For example, a story reports that the president received positive approval from "more than half" of the nation. The actual statistic was 53 percent. The margin of error, or accuracy of the poll, was plus or minus 3 percent. Adding 3 percent to 53 percent means as many as 56 percent of the country support the president. But subtracting 3 percent from 53 percent also means that as little as 50 percent of the nation approve of him. And 50 percent is not more than half. More about math is in Chapter 2.

• Recalculate percentages. Your boss may tell you that the company CEO will get only a 7.6 percent pay increase. Check it. A raise from $150,000 to $172,500 is a 15 percent pay increase, not 7.6 percent. The inaccuracy would hardly make other employees confident in the public relations department and its message.

• On technical subjects, when there is doubt about an explanation, call an expert source and read your material to that person for comment.

Getting information right is also important because inaccuracies are audience-stoppers. When radio listeners hear statistics that they question, they puzzle over the error and no longer hear what you have to say. The best-constructed message framed in the finest form means nothing if your information is wrong or even confusing.

What if you cannot check a fact? Enlist someone else, such as a reference librarian, to verify what is in question. If you cannot verify information and you are working on a deadline, leave it out. If the information is vital to the message and it can't be checked, the message will have to wait. Never publish information if you have doubts about its accuracy. Remember the example about the World Trade Center and Pentagon earlier in the chapter.

USING CLEAR LANGUAGE. Editing is hard. It means giving up words. Student writers may have been rewarded for using polysyllabic words found on high school vocabulary lists, or they may have written at length to fill an English requirement for a term paper. Early in life, writers develop a bad habit of writing long. Such writers have a difficult time determining what words to cut to keep prose tight, to the point, and clear.

Consider these questions:

- Is the copy clear and easy to read?
- Are words simple, direct, and easy to understand?
- Are jargon and institutional language eliminated?
- Is redundancy gone?
- Are sentences short and to the point?

This step includes spelling, grammar, and punctuation. In the technological age, many writers use computers that have spelling and grammar checking systems. Few spelling programs adequately check troublesome homonyms, such as "affect" and "effect," "red" and "read," "naval" and "navel," "stationary" and "stationery," "trustee" and "trusty," "lead" and "led," and so on. Chapter 2 contains a guide to spelling in the computer age.

Just as you have to check spelling, you have to review grammar. Chapter 2 discusses common grammar problems; consult the reference books listed at the end of that chapter for additional help.

Writers must be on the lookout for jargon. Such language should be replaced immediately with clearer terms, so that, for example, "organizational inputs" become "suggestions from parent groups" and "facilitation of new methodologies" becomes "trying a new survey."

In this step of editing, you also need to pay careful attention to word choice. Remember: The right word enhances audience understanding and willingness to pay attention, whether the message is read or heard. "Let your conscious be your guide," may not affect listeners. And some readers might not even notice the confused choice of conscious for conscience. Those who do notice will not be impressed. If necessary, review the discussion of word usage earlier in this chapter.

If you need to shorten your article, do so by looking at phrases, groups of words, titles, and word usage for shorter ways to state the same idea. Here is where you can apply what you learned in this chapter. For example, the statement, "He decided to take part in the debate," could be rewritten: "He participated in the debate." Or, "The banners that were blue and white fluttered in the breeze" could be changed to "The blue and white banners fluttered in the breeze."

GIVING THE PIECE THE LAST ONCE-OVER. Read the entire piece again. At this point, no major reworking should be needed. Check, however, for any editing errors that may have crept in during earlier steps. The final reading is the last check to make sure that prior editing has produced a message that is complete, accurate, comprehensible, pertinent, and interesting. This is the time to congratulate yourself.

Now you may send your copy to your editor or to a corporate executive for review, if you are in an organization or business. If you are an advertising copywriter, the message will go to the account executive and then to the client. In print media, the story will go to an editor and in broadcast, to a news director. If you are a high school principal, your memo may be reviewed by the school system's superintendent before it is sent to parents. If you are a student, the article is turned in to a professor or instructor.

But do not think that turning in your piece ends the editing process. The copy may come back for another round of editing and changes before publication.

Putting the Rules in Practice

With your knowledge of guidelines for good writing and steps to editing, read the following newspaper story:

> A Grove City–area woman has been accused of rigging her ex-husband's washing machine in hopes of torching him and his trailer for the insurance money.
>
> State police at Mercer last week arrested Valerie Norine Lagun, claiming the 43-year-old had hoped to kill a semidisabled Thomas Lagun in May when he turned on his washer. She was charged with attempted murder, attempted arson and recklessly endangering another person.
>
> Free on $10,000 bond, Mrs. Lagun is again living with her 57-year-old ex-husband at her home at 458 Blacktown Road, Pine Township, detective Robert Lewis said Tuesday.
>
> "They're still using the washing machine," Lewis said.
>
> According to court papers at District Justice Larry Silvis' Worth Township office, Mrs. Lagun told police she conspired with another man in the plot. She agreed to pay him half of the $5,000 from Lagun's life insurance policy and $10,000 from their renter's insurance.
>
> Police didn't name the man—described as an acquaintance of Mrs. Lagun—because he hasn't been charged, Lewis said. Police know of his

whereabouts but are still gathering evidence in hopes of charging him, Lewis said.

According to court papers:

Mrs. Lagun told police she took the man to Lagun's trailer at 169 Jamison Road, Worth Township, after dark.

Once inside, the man wired three bottles containing gasoline to the washing machine. A flip of the washer's switch should have ignited the fire.

"It could've exploded and probably killed him if it blew up. The potential was there," Lewis said.

Lagun discovered the gasoline after an electrical breaker tripped when he attempted to use the machine, according to court papers. He reported the incident to police, and Mrs. Lagun confessed July 24.

She told police she was surprised the explosive didn't work, but happy that her ex-husband wasn't killed, according to court papers.

Mrs. Lagun has a preliminary hearing at 1 P.M. Jan. 8 before Silvis.★

The story has compelling interest: potential death, oddity in alleged method of killing someone, human interest because the ex-husband and wife are still living together despite the charges, and the twist about the washing machine.

Consider this rewrite that includes most of the original information. But it is rewritten to apply good writing rules and reorganized in a format to pull readers through the story and reward them at the end:

A Grove City–area woman has been accused of rigging her ex-husband's washing machine to explode, killing him and destroying his trailer so she could collect the insurance money. But that's not where the story ends.

Valerie Norine Lagun, 43, was arrested last week by police who claim she had hoped to kill semidisabled Thomas Lagun in May when he turned on his washer. She was charged with attempted murder, attempted arson and recklessly endangering another person.

Mrs. Lagun is free on $10,000 bond and has a preliminary hearing at 1 P.M. Jan. 8 before District Justice Larry Silvis.

According to court papers, Mrs. Lagun told police she conspired with another man and agreed to pay him half of the $5,000 from Lagun's life insurance policy and $10,00 from their renter's insurance.

★Reprinted with permission of The Sharon Herald Co.

The man—described as an acquaintance of Mrs. Lagun—hasn't been charged, detective Robert Lewis said Tuesday. Police know of his whereabouts but are still gathering evidence and hope to charge him.

Mrs. Lagun told police she took the man to Lagun's trailer at 169 Jamison Road, Worth Township, after dark. The man wired three bottles containing gasoline to the washing machine. A flip of the washer's switch should have ignited the fire, according to court papers.

Lagun discovered the gasoline after an electrical breaker tripped when he attempted to use the machine, according to court papers. He reported the incident to police, and Mrs. Lagun confessed July 24.

"It could've exploded and probably killed him if it blew up. The potential was there," Lewis said.

Mrs. Lagun told police she was surprised the explosive didn't work, but happy that her ex-husband wasn't killed, according to court papers.

Despite the charges, Mrs. Lagun is again living with her 57-year-old ex-husband at her home at 458 Blacktown Road, Pine Township.

And, noted detective Lewis, "They're still using the washing machine."

The following exercises will require you to apply the guidelines in this chapter. When you have completed them, take a message you constructed during the last week and rewrite it to be clearer and simpler.

Wrap-Up

Now you should have the tools and guidelines for good writing planted in your head. In any writing text, authors debate the order of topics—writing first then editing or the editing discussion before writing. In this book, we decided to make our audience—you—aware of good writing guidelines before you put pencil to paper or hand to keyboard. We wanted you to think about short words and paragraphs as you write. We also wanted you to accept editing as a major component of writing, not an afterthought. Your first draft doesn't have to be the polished version. With editing as part of the writing process, you have the chance to review your writing once or even many times. Having a plan for editing, or certain steps to follow, makes the editing process more complete and efficient.

An excellent resource for books to improve writing is the Poynter Institute for Media Studies web site at www.poynter.org. The bookstore offers materials by the institute's staff and others to guide writers in using language and writing powerful messages. The web site also gives writers background information on current media issues.

In Chapter 4, we move to writing itself and the critical thinking skills needed to craft a message—regardless of format. And as you are crafting that message, the guidelines and tools for good writing should be part of your work.

EXERCISES

1. Change the words used incorrectly in the following sentences:

   - The perspective [prospective] budget for the coming year will include raises for the city's fire fighters.
   - An incoming ice storm will effect [affect] whether we can drive to work tomorrow.
   - The state historical society will reenact signing the state constitution in the Capital. [capita]
   - The country's navel [naval] force has been reduced.
   - His desire for money is his principle [principal] guiding force in business.
   - The coach said the team ignored his advise [advice] to make it a passing game.
   - Jiminy Cricket said Pinocchio should let his conscious [conscience] be his guide.
   - The engineer eliminated the High Road sight [site] because it sloped too much.
   - Returning the stolen car to its owner is the best decision.
   - The most affective [effective] writing follows good writing principals. [principles]

2. Edit the following sentences to make them shorter and to the point:

   - In order to expedite the delivery, the company will add a third delivery truck for its routes [or] on Monday.
   - We will have pizza for dinner whether or not you choose to come.
   - She is presently employed as the assistant to the president, but she expects to make a decision whether or not to change jobs by the end of the year. [but she may change jobs by the end of the year]

- ~~If they are willing to pay the difference between the economy pack and the family pack, customers will learn that~~ the family pack will save them more money ~~in the long run.~~
- Students voted Thursday ~~to conduct a poll~~ to determine the status of living conditions in dormitories.
- Clarendon Park residents will march Saturday to protest the city council's decision to annex the neighborhood over residents' objections.
- If the school maintains lines of communication and makes the alumni feel as if they are still a part of the school ~~even though they have already graduated,~~ the school should have no problem reaching its fund-raising goal.
- The residents ~~of the neighborhood~~ said they would petition the city council to reconsider ~~again~~ the decision to allow beer sales before 11 A.M. on Sunday ~~morning, which would be against the wishes of many church-going citizens.~~
- Fifteen scholarship winners, ~~who were chosen because of their high academic achievement,~~ will be given $15,000 ~~in scholarship money~~ to use at the college of their choice ~~after they graduate from high school.~~
- Child-care experts disagree over whether or not children should be spanked as part of a parent's disciplinary techniques or whether or not putting children in a time-out away from activities is punishment enough.

3. Edit the following to <u>eliminate redundancy</u>:

- Susan is ~~currently~~ director of marketing sales.
- He <u>served</u> as ~~past~~ president of the Rotary club.
- The elementary school will need twenty-five acres ~~of land~~ for a multipurpose building, playground, and ball fields.
- Fire ~~completely~~ destroyed the town hall in ~~the month of~~ June.
- The ~~future~~ outlook for the economy indicates interest rates may rise ~~slightly.~~
- The circus will be at 3 ~~P.M. Sunday afternoon~~ and 7 P.M. Sunday ~~night.~~
- ~~Due to the fact that more than~~ two-thirds of the people did not respond, the picnic will be canceled.
- She climbed ~~up~~ the tree in order to get a better look at the defendant.
- John ~~went on to say~~ that any student's effort should be recognized.
- The Broadway show will close down six months after it ~~first~~ began.

4. Read the following story. Edit it. Make a list of questions for any missing information that would require more research. Follow Associated Press style, and use proper spelling and grammar. Watch out for redundancies. The audience is readers of the campus newspaper.

> All of the faculty members from the School of Journalism and Mass Communication will be attending on Thursday of this week a regional meeting of the Association for Education in Journalism and Mass Communication in Greensboro.
>
> The meeting will commence at 10 a.m. in the morning and conclude at 2 p.m. in the afternoon following a noon luncheon.
>
> In the morning, sessions will offer journalism educators the opportunity to have discussions on current issues addressing journalism and mass communication.
>
> At a luncheon program, professor Walter Blayless will be speaking on the topic of cigarette advertising and the effect on the nation's young people of today.
>
> The meeting sponsored by AEJMC is exemplary of the several regional meetings the organization holds across the country each year. The annual meeting is always held in August each year at different locations around the country.

Compare your editing steps to the following:

- First, you learned that the faculty members would be at a meeting on Thursday, the focus of the article.
- Second, you considered the lead. You might have wondered, What will happen to classes if all the faculty members are gone on a weekday? More research and interviewing would need to be done. The research might require you to write a new lead geared for the student audience. It would say

> Students in the School of Journalism and Mass
> Communication will not have class Thursday because
> faculty members will attend a professional meeting in
> Greensboro.

- Next, you would check for accuracy. You would check the spelling of Walter Blayless and the organization. You would also double-check to make sure that the meeting is in Greensboro. Then would come the most involved part. The first draft is wordy. Phrases such as 10 A.M. in the morning and 2 P.M. in the afternoon would be shortened to 10 A.M. and 2 P.M. Blayless will be speaking on the topic of cigarette advertising could be tightened to Blayless will speak on cigarette advertising. The final reading would be for overall quality.
- Your edited copy might look something like this:

> Students in the School of Journalism and Mass Communica-
> tion will not have class Thursday because faculty members
> will attend a professional meeting in Greensboro.
>
> A regional meeting of the Association for Education in
> Journalism and Mass Communication will begin at 10 a.m.
> and end at 2 p.m.
>
> Educators will discuss issues in journalism and mass
> communication during the morning sessions.
>
> The luncheon speaker, Professor Walter Blayless, will
> talk about cigarette advertising and its effect on youth.
>
> AEJMC has several regional meetings each year. The
> annual meeting is in August in different U.S. cities.

REFERENCES

R. W. Apple Jr., "Sense of Unease Grips Anthrax Preoccupied Washington," *New York Times,* September 18, 2001.

Henry Beard and Christopher Cerf, *The Official Politically Correct Dictionary and Hand-book.* New York: Villard Books, 1992.

Theodore M. Bernstein, *Dos, Don'ts and Maybes of the English Language.* New York: The Times Book Co., 1977.

John Bremner, *Words on Words.* New York: Columbia University Press, 1980.

E. L. Callihan, *Grammar for Journalists.* Radnor, PA: Chilton Book Company, 1979.

Clair Kehrwald Cook, *Line by Line. How to Improve Your Own Writing.* Boston: Houghton Mifflin, 1985.

Nora Ephron, "Writers' Workshop," video series produced by South Carolina Educational Television, 1980.

Fred Fedler, *Reporting for the Print Media.* New York: Harcourt Brace Jovanovich, 1989.

Norm Goldstein, ed., *The Associated Press Stylebook 2001 and Briefing on Media Law.* New York: The Associated Press, 2001.

Robert Gunning, *The Technique of Clear Writing.* New York: McGraw-Hill, 1954.

Lauren Kessler and Duncan McDonald, *When Words Collide.* Belmont, CA: Wadsworth, 1992.

Ernie Pyle, *Here Is Your War.* New York: Pocket Books, 1945.

Joel Saltzman, *If You Can Talk, You Can Write.* New York: Ballantine Books, 1993.

Carl Sessions Stepp, excerpt from videotape, "Taking Charge of Your Local Paper," National Rural Electric Cooperatives Association, Washington, DC, March 1993.

William Strunk, Jr., and E. B. White, *The Elements of Style,* 3rd ed. New York: Macmillan, 1979.

Tom Wolfe, excerpt from transcribed speech to American Society of Newspaper Editors, Washington, DC, April 1990.

William Zinsser, *On Writing Well.* New York: Harper & Row, 1976.

4

Getting to the Point

When the president of a university spoke at her installation ceremony, she discussed the broad issue of improving undergraduate education and specific points to achieve that goal. Media wrote the story from different angles. The student newspaper focused on greater rigor in classroom teaching. A television station with a broad viewing audience began its report with her call for accountability to state legislators. A business publication examined her challenge for a more aggressive investment policy to increase the school's endowment. The university's alumni publication looked at the outcome: the continued strength of the university's reputation and the value of its degree. A donor newsletter picked up her request for additional funds for scholarships and teaching-excellence awards.

Writers who are familiar with their audiences know what information will be relevant and appealing. Writers must alert audiences to messages that are important. They know what will attract the attention of the individual who juggles time for job, home, spouse, children, hobbies, and friends.

Messages must therefore hook the audience. The hook must be set in the first few sentences or paragraphs, called the *lead* of the message. That is when writers must show the relevance of the message and attract, entertain, and inform. That is when readers or listeners will decide whether the message is compelling, entertaining, or informative enough to warrant attention. Why toil over constructing messages that do not hook or reach audiences?

This chapter will discuss lead writing, specifically

- The role of audiences,
- Elements in lead writing,

- News values, and
- Types of leads.

What's the Point?

To hook a particular audience, writers must know why they are writing. It sounds simple enough. But many people regard writing as an artistic endeavor, not as a craft. They avoid thinking about the substance of what they are going to say. These writers sit down to write with a broad purpose or goal in mind, such as informing an audience about government waste. They haven't figured out the main point of the specific message, an essential element in hooking the audience.

Determining the point requires critical thinking. Writers must look at the components of the message and weigh each as it pertains to audiences. They must lay out the facts and evaluate their importance and relevance. The steps are part of the stages of writing discussed in Chapter 1.

What does a rural community need to know about issues in a state legislative session? How about a professional association of school board members? These two audiences will need different hooks for the same event. As writers consider information and audiences, they get closer to the point of the message, establishing where they want to start.

Getting to the point is like eating an artichoke: As you peel off the outer leaves and examine them, you get closer to the real heart of your search. You may toss out heavy, less interesting leaves. Closer to the center, you will find more succulent, flavorful leaves worthy of attention. And finally, you unveil the heart.

Finding the heart, or kernel of your story, is essential to writing. Along the way, writers will discover facts and pieces that relate to the main point, surrounding and supporting it like the artichoke's tasty leaves. Other pieces may be discarded. But the examining process must be completed first.

Consider the advertising copywriter who says, "I want to write an ad that will get more business for my client." He or she is still handling the whole artichoke—a big and unworkable problem. Thinking and planning—a stage of writing—will help in moving from the broad idea of producing an ad to the more specific task of communicating the client's specific benefit. The writer will get to the point.

If the client makes hand lotion, the advertiser's point may be beautiful hands or healthier skin or convenient packaging. If the client owns a tax service, the point may be customer peace of mind and the accountant's knowledge of tax laws. Once that benefit—the point—has been identified, the writer's job is to select precise words that will emphasize that point and grab a consumer's attention. And once writers have established where to start, they will know the direction to go.

In crafting messages, writers focus on the point, the hook, the lead, and the copy.

> The **point** is crucial information that justifies creating a message in the first place: A bill is passed. New funds are available. A road is closed.

> The **hook** is an enticing opening phrase or sentence that draws audiences into a message.

> The **lead** is the opening few sentences of a media message. Typically, it contains the hook and the point.

> The **copy** is the entire body of a media message, including a lead and all supporting information, such as new facts, background, quotes, and statistics.

In the Beginning Comes the Lead

In journalism the first sentences or paragraphs of a story are called a *lead*. The lead has a heavy responsibility. It is the bait to hook the reader. By educating, entertaining, or enlightening, it stimulates the reader to pay attention. The lead shows relevance and is relevant to the audience. It also entraps. A publisher once wrote that a lead must be provocative, vigorous, and even at times startling to the reader.

Every piece of writing has a beginning or opening statement; every piece of writing has a lead. Long-time syndicated columnist James J. Kilpatrick once wrote

> *The lead is vital to any writing, whether one is writing a novel, a short story, a book review, a term paper, a newspaper editorial, or a homily to be read in church on Sunday morning.*

A lead needs to establish relevance for readers:

```
If you are getting ready for the school year, just remember
malls can become crowded with back-to-school shoppers and
supplies may run out.
```

The lead contains the stimulus for reading, sets out the message's relevance, and gives the reader the most important information first. As the stimulus, the lead entertains, enlightens, and educates. As it sets out the relevance, it whets the reader's appetite to stay with the message. In giving the most important information first, the lead ensures that the reader gets the point quickly.

By digesting the most important information first, audiences know the essential details after the first few paragraphs. They are informed. They have the information they need because the writer hooked them and got to the point right away. They can stick with the story or even move to other messages.

The lead must also set up the story. After reading or hearing the lead, audiences should know the main points of the message that follows. If not, the lead has misled them, and the writer's credibility is damaged. How does a writer know whether the lead sets up the story? When the story is complete, a writer must consider the main points in the body of the message and ensure that they are noted in the lead. The lead sets up the story; the story backs up the lead. For example, a story reports a robbery at the campus dining hall and includes details about the robber locking the dining hall manager in a closet. That fact should be noted in the lead, along with the information that the robbery occurred and how much money was taken.

Journalists, primarily print journalists, have recognized for decades that getting to the point is essential to attract and retain readers. Media writers have found that they immediately must set out the critical aspects of the message for their readers, listeners, consumers, or other audience members. Writing a lead has become a crucial assignment for any writer in the information age.

Leads and Audience

Different audiences will react differently to leads. That makes sense. The audience of a local newspaper expects writing and prose that differs from what readers of a campus newspaper want. In a campus newspaper, leads will be focused to a university audience and its interests. The local newspaper has to attract an audience that includes students and university staff as well as people with no connection to the campus. The local newspaper may consider the language in a campus newspaper inappropriate for its audience.

Writers, whether for newspapers, online sites, or magazines, have to structure their leads and stories to suit their audiences. Consider the following two leads that appeared in the online editions of the *New York Times* and the *Miami Herald* on September 12, 2001:

> In what appeared to be parallel attacks on quintessential symbols of American financial and military power, airplanes slammed into both towers of the World Trade Center in Manhattan and, less than an hour later, into the Pentagon, outside Washington. (*New York Times*)

> In a catastrophic, full-scale terrorist attack on the United States, hijackers seized two American Airlines jetliners this morning, crashed them into New York City's World Trade Center and leveled both 110-story towers. Thousands were feared dead. (*Miami Herald*)

The *Times'* lead is 39 words; the *Herald's* is 38. Interestingly, both used fairly long introductory clauses, but the *New York Times'* clause is longer than the *Herald's*. Both had complex sentences—often a result of writers producing complex stories under stressful conditions. Both used vivid verbs— "slammed," "crashed," "leveled"—but the *Herald* used a series of three verbs while the *Times* used only one. The *Herald* used a short sentence at the end of the first graph to tackle the question of deaths.

The writing styles, although similar, also differ, particularly the choice of language. The *Herald's* language is much simpler and has fewer polysyllabic words. Each lead works for that particular newspaper's audience.

How to Get Started

To construct a lead, writers must know their information thoroughly. They must evaluate the information, using their judgment and experience to determine what is most relevant to their audience. As a prewriting activity, some writers go through their notes and add priority numbers next to information.

Before writing the lead that tells readers that it's about time to get ready for school, the writer listed information to be included: School starts soon, retailers advertise heavily for back-to-school items, malls and other stores can become crowded as people wait to the last minute, and supplies may dwindle.

Next to each fact the writer put a number corresponding to its importance to the audience. In writing the lead, the writer determined that the audience did not need to know the specific date that school started or how many students would be attending school in the county. Priority number 1 is that school will start soon and readers can avoid the crush and rush if they plan ahead. The writer sets out the main part of the story—getting ready for the school year—to warn the audience and the relevance—the audience can be overcome by crowds at malls and then find few choices.

Writers can avoid the actual numbering of facts through another approach. They can simply ask, "What must my audience know?" and then list three to five things in order of importance. In the case of back to school, the list would be something like this one:

1. It's almost time to start school.
2. If people want to avoid crowds, they need to shop now.
3. If people want to find items and have a choice, they need to shop now.

The main point would become the lead. Other main points would be fashioned into the rest of the copy. Writers have created in essence the format many journalists use—the inverted pyramid—that ranks information in descending order of importance. That format is discussed in Chapter 5.

Writers who struggle with ranking information and its relevance should remember that most people want to know the personal angle first. It all comes down to the audience's automatic question, "How does this message affect me?" The audience immediately looks for the explanation.

Sometimes stories or messages don't have that simple, personal component. Then writers must look beyond the "what about me?" question or relevance rule to other factors that make some pieces of information more important than others. Such factors are also guides to the selection of information for the lead. Those elements are called *news elements* and *news values* and are discussed next in this chapter.

News Elements

Certain elements are of interest in all writing. Journalists over the years have spelled out the elements that must appear in news stories: *who, what, when, where, how,* and *why.* That list is a basic starting point for any writer in determining what will go first.

These news components can form a question: "Who did what to whom, how, when, where, and why?" Every letter, news story, news release, or advertisement will answer this question.

Why are these elements important? Because people are most interested in other people, who they are, what they say and do, where they live and work, what happens to them, why they make certain choices, and how they deal with those choices. They are interested in conflict, competition, and achievements. People want to know about other people who overcome adversity, who are defeated, and who do the unusual. Look at this example:

> A Hollywood, Fla., man and woman exchanged wedding vows at 1,300 feet as they plummeted to earth hand-in-hand under silver parachutes five miles west of here Wednesday afternoon.
>
> Grace Mason and John Kempner met while skydiving at a local club and decided it would be the most significant way to start their married life together.

The elements are there:

Who: Grace and John

What: Got married

When: Wednesday

Where: Near Hollywood, Fla.

How: By parachutes

Why: Because they wanted to start married life in a manner meaningful to their courtship and to them

The two-paragraph lead summarizes what happened. Readers can decide whether they want to read further to learn more about Grace and John. The author has also set it up so that after reading two paragraphs, the reader knows the most important information and can turn to another message.

Where to Put Who *and* What

Putting all the elements in the first sentence can result in long, convoluted sentences. Consider the following lead and its clearer rewrite:

> Sam Atwood, an associate professor of political science at the University, told students in a speech Thursday in MacPherson Hall that they should be more concerned about world events that more and more directly affect their lives and their future.

Rewritten:

Students should be concerned about world events that more and more directly affect their lives and their future, an associate professor of political science at the University said Thursday.

Rather than the professor's complete name, a descriptive phrase or identifying label can be used to describe him in the first sentence. The location of the speech and why he was giving it can be included in a subsequent paragraph.

Writers must decide which elements deserve emphasis and are most relevant before they write a lead. All elements will be included somewhere in the story. As a general rule, *who* and *what* will be in the first sentence. So will *where* and *when* because they take up little space. This formula also follows the natural order of the English language: subject, verb, object. *Who, what, when,* and *where* set up an active structure: A masked man robbed the university dining hall of $3,000 Wednesday night and locked the dining hall manager in a closet. *How* and *why* can be included in the first sentence if they are unusual. A full explanation usually will require several sentences or paragraphs.

Consider this lead from the *Los Angeles Times* that focuses on who, what, when, and where.

JERUSALEM—Palestinians and Israeli peace advocates mourned the death Thursday of Faisal Husseini, a prominent leader of the Palestine Liberation Organization who was the scion of a near-legendary family and an early advocate of compromising with Israel.

Again, the elements are there:

Who: Palestinians and Israeli peace advocates
What: Mourned the death of Faisal Husseini
When: Thursday
Where: Jerusalem

A Closer Look at the Elements

Let's define the lead elements and what role they play in the copy.

Who defines the person carrying out the action or affected by the story. *Who* may not be a specific name, such as Grace or John, but rather an identification or label. For example, a news release may say in the first sentence that two marketing employees have been promoted and in the second sentence give their names and titles. But if the president is retiring, his name will be given first because it has recognition among company employees and in the community, as in the following:

> Charles Southwick, chief executive officer of Englewood Mills who began his career as a bookkeeper, will retire April 1 after 42 years with the company.

The *who* is Charles Southwick, specifically named because of the role he plays in the local business community. *What* represents the action: will retire. Usually *what* can be simply stated in a verb. Consider this news lead:

> A Richmond, Va., man died Wednesday when he lost control of his car and it crashed into a bridge railing on Interstate 95 South.

The verb "died" tells *what*. Similarly, in a letter to a high school's alumni, the verb tells *what:*

> Southeast High School's PTA is asking alumni to donate money to put at least two computers in every classroom by the end of the year.

What in the example is asking alumni for money.

When tells the audience the timeliness of the event being reported or the time frame of specific actions. Often it is one word. In most writing, *when* will go after the verb because the time element rarely is the most interesting information. Few leads begin with *when*. In the car accident example above, "Wednesday" tells when the accident occurred. In the lead on the alumni letter, the time frame is less specific. But an alumnus reading the letter will know that the goal for installing the computers is December 31 of that year, so contributions should be made between receipt of the letter and well before December 31.

When can also be used to set up a longer time frame, as in this *Washington Post* lead:

> Maryland Gov. Parris N. Glendening pardoned John Snowden yesterday, more than 80 years after the African American ice wagon worker

was convicted of murdering a pregnant white woman, and hanged despite lingering doubts about his guilt.

"Yesterday" tells when Glendening gave the pardon and "80 years" notes when Snowden was convicted and hanged.

Where gives the reader the geographic context of the story. In many cases that will pique audience interest because readers want to know about events that affect them. The closer the story is to the reader's backyard, the greater the interest will be.

Wire service and other stories in newspapers often start with *where* by using a *dateline,* the name of the city in capital letters, to let readers know immediately where the event occurred.

> BEIJING—Elated Chinese sang and cheered after learning that Beijing was selected on the second ballot as the site for the 2008 Summer Olympics.

In stories without a dateline, the exact location would be the first word or words in the lead only when it offers some unusual aspect to the story. Usually the *where* is tucked elsewhere into the lead.

> A slice of history awaits you at the Tastee Diner in Silver Spring.

How expands on the *what* aspect. Look at the following lead from the *Washington Post.*

> A man was killed and his body crushed yesterday when a dumpster he and a woman companion were sleeping in was emptied into a trash compactor in the Hampshire Knolls section of Northeast Washington. The woman was seriously injured.

The lead tells *who, what, when,* and *where* but also talks about *how:* how the man died.

Why gives the audience the reason a decision or a change was made or is pending or the cause of an event. In the Richmond accident example, the audience knows why the man died: because he lost control of the car. In the alumni letter, alumni are asked to give money. Why? So the school can buy computers.

To reiterate: *how* and *why* will go in the first sentence or lead if there is some unusual aspect or if they are essential to understanding the message.

> Yelling to police that he would never be taken alive, a Washington fugitive raced his motorcycle through a police roadblock near Springfield and was shot to death by law enforcement officers Thursday.

Why and *how* the man drove through the roadblock are immediately clear to the reader.

Watch Out for Too Much

Sometimes all elements fit concisely into a lead, as in the example about the Washington fugitive. But because all elements do not have to be in every first sentence, a writer can set up the point of the story using a few elements in the first sentence and explain the other elements in later paragraphs.

Consider this lead:

> A major housing development that preservationists believed had died last year has been resurrected by developers who say local planning officials are much more receptive to the revised version.

Are *who, what, when, where, how,* and *why* all answered in this first sentence? No.

Who: Developers
What: Are resurrecting a housing development plan
When: Implied now, but not stated
Where: Implied in the county, but not specifically stated
How: Not stated
Why: Because planning officials seem more receptive

The second paragraph of the story gives more explanation of *what* has happened, *when,* and *how.*

> Jonathan Gardner, one of the developers of the project, said a revised plan was submitted to the county planning board earlier this week. Developers resubmitted the plan after conversations last month indicated certain revisions could erase planning officials' objections.

The third paragraph answers *where* and gives more information, and the fourth paragraph moves into the controversy.

> The revised plan uses the same 300-acre site in southeast Granger County but has 46 fewer houses and relocates the swim and tennis club. Developers expect a public hearing to be set next month.
>
> Preservationists have vowed to fight the renewed development efforts. They say the issues haven't changed despite what they call minor modifications in the original plan.

The first sentence, or the first paragraph, stands as the lead to the story. The other elements, particularly how developers decided to resubmit the plan and what changes were made, are later components of the article. The lead would have been quite complex if the writer had tried to include all the elements there.

The first four paragraphs answer readers' initial questions—*who, what, when, where, why,* and *how*—and set up the rest of the story.

A lead attracts readers to the story because it has other elements—beyond *who, what, when, where, how,* and *why*—that must be considered when the writer is structuring the first sentence. These other elements are called news values.

News Values

In structuring leads, writers are also guided by what journalists traditionally have called *news values,* or aspects of an event that make it worth knowing about. We can also define news values as qualities that are of interest to people or are satisfying in some way. These values or qualities carry over into any writing.

The traditional news values that journalism professors teach and that become second nature to reporters are prominence, timeliness, proximity, impact, magnitude, conflict, oddity, and emotional impact. News values are important in any media writing because they guide writers in identifying and listing crucial information. Let's look at each of the news values and how they affect lead writing. Several are closely allied to the elements *who, what, when, where, how,* and *why* discussed earlier in this chapter.

Prominence

When the main character or characters in your story are well known, that is a signal to put those names in the lead. When President George Bush, for example, chokes on a pretzel and faints, the incident is major news. The routine becomes news, such as the marriage of Jennifer Anniston and Brad Pitt. Entertainment Wire listed their marriage as the biggest television news of the year.

People who are related to famous people are lead-worthy. Prominence extends even to pets, such as the extensive coverage of former President Clinton's pets, Sox and Buddy.

Timeliness

One adage in journalism is that old news ain't news. People want to know what is happening as soon as it happens. They want newness in the news. They want to know information they didn't know yesterday. They want timely, up-to-date news and depend increasingly on television, radio, and online services as initial sources of news information. Therefore, *when* an event happened is almost always in the first sentence of a story so that people will have a context for that event.

> The governor will honor five National Merit Scholarship winners from the state in a special ceremony at the Governor's Mansion Friday afternoon.

> BALTIMORE—Government regulators told Johns Hopkins University on Monday that the school may resume medical research on humans, four days after the regulators halted such studies because of the death of a volunteer.

Proximity

People are most interested about news that happens close to them. Audiences easily identify with stories with a geographic proximity—that is, those that occur in their own community, town, county, or state. They like to read stories about their neighbors' successes and even defeats.

Audiences are also interested in what happens to people from their communities in other locations. For example, people in Cleveland would want to know about an airplane crash in Washington State that kills residents from their city. A Cleveland newspaper might run this lead:

> SEATTLE, Wash.—Two Cleveland businessmen were among 19 people killed early this morning when a jet struck a radio tower just outside Seattle.

The lead emphasizes Cleveland's loss while telling that the plane crash occurred. Writers call this *localizing a message,* or putting the local angle on a story that originated miles away, so that audiences can see how the message relates to them and their community.

News reports may also have an emotional or nonspatial proximity, whereby readers identify with a certain group of people. People who have suffered heart attacks are interested in articles about how other heart-attack victims have coped. People who live in a college town may be more inclined to read about stories originating from other cities with campuses, even if the cities are far away. Basketball fans anywhere could relate to the following *Detroit News* lead about the pressure on a new coach to turn around the Detroit Pistons's record.

> AUBURN HILLS—The culture around the Detroit Pistons over the last decade has been one of prolonged futility. One playoff series victory since 1991. A 140-156 record the last four seasons. Six coaching changes in nine years.
> It has been a decade marked by false starts and frustrating finishes.

Impact

Audiences always want to know how they will be affected, whether by a road closing while a sewer line is being laid or by a sale at the local supermarket. Reporters often hear people ask, "But how does this affect me? What does this have to do with me?" High in any message should be an explanation of how an event affects individuals' daily lives or why they should be concerned.

When possible, the impact should be translated into tangible terms. For example, a water and sewer rate increase approved by the Little Rock Town Council Tuesday night will mean that the average resident will pay $3.52 a month more for service, bringing the average monthly bill to $31.96.

The impact of a hurricane is stated in terms of how people are affected: Thousands of residents are without electricity and hundreds of houses damaged. Consider impact in this lead from the *Baltimore Sun*:

> Civil defense sirens wailed and major highways into Baltimore were closed after a freight train hauling hazardous chemicals caught fire yesterday afternoon in a century-old railroad tunnel under Howard Street, shutting down much of the city's downtown.

Impact can be positive, such as the federal government mailing millions of refund checks:

> The federal government has begun mailing refund checks to U.S. taxpayers, part of President Bush's plans to put money in the hands of consumers.
> The impact on taxpayers is a few hundred extra dollars that the president hopes recipients will spend and as a result fuel a flagging economy.

Magnitude

Some folks like to distinguish between impact and magnitude in defining news values. *Magnitude* is defined as the size of the event. Death, injury, or loss of property are all elements of magnitude that attract audience attention. Large amounts of money, such as lottery winnings, as well as disasters, such as hurricanes, carry magnitude and are always big news. When a typhoon rips through the Philippines, the amount of damage inflicted and the speed of the winds are the magnitude of the storm. In an earthquake, the magnitude is the reading on the Richter scale.

Consider this lead, which has magnitude and an understood impact:

> Tuesday morning 54 school buses will drive more than 1,000 miles as they pick up 2,500 school children for the first day of classes this year.

The magnitude is represented in part by the 2,500 students, the 1,000 miles traveled, and the 54 school buses. The understood impact of the first day of school is much broader, affecting any household in the county that has school-age children, or an employee of the school system, or an early morning commuter.

Conflict

Most news reports contain some kind of conflict: contract disputes with striking workers, continuing struggles in Northern Ireland and in the Middle East, the battles between neighbors in rezoning issues, or a grievance filed by an employee against a supervisor. People like to read about conflict. The extent of the conflict, either its size or its duration, will determine whether conflict is included in the lead of the message.

Conflict permeates the news. For example, doctors and medical ethicists debated the use of fertility drugs and selective abortion of fetuses in multiple pregnancies after an Iowa woman gave birth to septuplets. Major conflict held the nation's attention in the 2000 presidential race when the outcome was undecided for days. Many newspapers wrote about the conflict, like this lead from the *Boston Globe*:

> Al Gore and George W. Bush waged a seesaw battle for the presidency last night in the closest race in decades, as the vice president picked up battlegrounds ranging from Pennsylvania to California and Bush won a string of states across the nation.

The conflict escalated as questions arose over ballots and the battle moved to the United States Supreme Court, as reflected in this lead from the *Hartford Courant*:

> A sharply divided United States Supreme Court shut down dozens of Florida recounts Saturday as it set itself up to hear a case that could finally decide the presidency.

Oddity

Editors often encourage writers to look for oddity or some unusual twist to a story, such as a police officer who responds to the accident call and discovers that one of the injured people is his son. When a meteor shower caused bright lights in the sky and even shaking as the meteors exploded, many alarmed people in the Northeast called police and emergency personnel. Their panic and an explanation of the lights and noise made the news. When Timothy McVeigh was executed in June 2001 for the Oklahoma City bombing, he became the first federal prisoner in almost 40 years to be put to death. That unusual aspect led the news:

> TERRE HAUTE, Ind.—When convicted terrorist Timothy McVeigh is put to death by lethal injection Monday, he will be the first federal prisoner to be executed in 37 years.

Whenever a writer is working on a message that has an element of oddity about it, care must be taken to ensure that people are not portrayed as freakish or unnatural. For example, a story on the largest baby born in the county in 30 years may not need to be written at all.

Emotional Impact

Writers are recognizing more and more that people like stories that affect them emotionally and that have emotional impact. This news value also is called *human interest* and *universal appeal*. It is the quality that draws audiences to children, young people, and pets.

Think about your own interests. In looking at a page of a company newsletter, the photo of children and balloons at the company picnic will probably have more appeal than the picture of the president presenting a $5,000 check to the local PTA president.

Consider a story, with accompanying photographs, of children at a petting zoo:

> The animals came by twosy, twosy, twosy—goats, sheep, ducks and a wallaroo.
> And there were Jim and Angie, the monkeys; Goldie and Scarlett, the macaws; and Ralph, the chimpanzee.

People also like stories tied to love and romance. The article about a couple who both are line workers for a local utility company has great appeal. Including that aspect in the lead will attract readers.

Death and injury are also events that convey emotional impact. They are important elements in stories and generally should be in the first paragraph, as in this example:

> PENSACOLA—An 8-year-old boy nearly killed in attack by a bull shark remained in critical condition at a local hospital after doctors reattached his severed arm.

Remember the Audience

In applying news values, writers must think about what is important to their audience. Knowing the audience determines the lead and also affects how the writer will rank information. For example, a college community audience hears the mayor speak in a lecture series. What he says looks like this in the college newspaper's lead:

> Students play a vital role in boosting the town's economy when they shop at downtown businesses, Mayor Leo Ryan said Wednesday.

The primary audience for the college newspaper is students.

What the mayor said has a different focus for the lead in the town's general-circulation newspaper:

> Town and college administrators need to develop a joint long-range plan that will address growth, particularly along the campus perimeter, during the next 20 years, Mayor Leo Ryan said Wednesday night.

A general-interest audience, primarily made up of town residents, would be more interested in what the mayor said that affected them directly.

News with a local angle also will have more appeal to audiences. Think of interest in concentric circles: People are interested first in what happens in their neighborhoods, then their towns, their counties, their states, their countries, the world. Leads should be written to focus on the local angle, such as:

> If you are planning to drive to Ocean City for the weekend, avoid Maryland Highway 113 near Dagsboro where highway crews are working and traffic is slowed to one lane.

Sorting It Out

At this point you are educated about the elements of a lead, but you still may be unclear about what goes first. That sorting process is learned best through practice.

Let's walk through the process.

You are a writer in a bank's corporate communications department. In three months, the company will open a fitness center for employees. The center will be in the old YMCA building next door to corporate headquarters.

You are to write a news release for the local newspaper. You have collected the needed information. Your list of elements looks like this.

Who: Amana Savings and Loan
What: Will open a fitness center

Where: Next door to corporate headquarters in the old YMCA
When: In three months
Why: To improve employee health and to provide a benefit to employees
How: By renovating the old YMCA

Now make a list of news values as they relate to the story. Ask whether each applies and if so, how.

Prominence: No

Timeliness: Yes; within three months

Proximity: Yes; in downtown

Impact: Yes; the renovation will mean local jobs and other economic benefits to the town. It will affect the lives of the company's 450 employees and the townspeople who have been wondering what will happen to the old YMCA.

Magnitude: Yes; the acquisition and renovation will cost the company almost $1 million.

Conflict: None internally. Shareholders approved the expenditure at the annual meeting. None externally. Town residents want the building saved.

Audience: Townspeople

Emotional impact: Could be for people who remember using the old YMCA

In writing the lead for the news release, you as the writer must consider the newspaper's audience—the townspeople—and ask, "What will they want to know first?" The answer is the timeliness of the renovation. The renovation is new news.

A first draft of the lead might read like this:

```
Amana Savings and Loan will spend $1 million to renovate
the vacant YMCA downtown on Sycamore Street to create an
employee fitness center that will open within three months.
```

Here you have answered *who, what, when,* and *where.* You also have addressed the magnitude of the project.

The second paragraph will answer *why* and *how,* and the third paragraph will explain impact.

```
The bank will renovate the old YMCA building to provide a
convenient way for employees to remain physically fit, said
employee manager Kay Barnes. The bank will use the existing
layout and install new equipment and furnishings.
    The project will mean additional jobs during the
renovation and later when the center opens, Barnes noted.
```

General Rules for Leads

No matter what type of lead you choose to write, all leads have common features.

Leads should be short. As a guide, some writers use no more than 30 words. Many wire service stories have leads no longer than 20 words in the first sentence or paragraph. This *USA Today* lead sets up the story in 17 words:

> NBA teams can officially begin signing free agents today, but don't look for a lot of surprises.

Or consider this even shorter seven-word lead from an analysis piece by R. W. Apple Jr. in the *New York Times*:

> —Anthrax is not contagious, but fear is.

Leads should be concise and to the point. Writers must eliminate unnecessary words. Look at the following lead and see what has been eliminated in the rewrite and how the focus has changed:

> A local day care center was broken into Wednesday night and property vandalized, toys overturned and a pet rabbit, named Ray, killed with a broom.

Rewritten:

> Vandals broke into a local day care center Wednesday night, killed the center's pet rabbit with a broom, overturned toys and damaged property.

Words in the lead should be precise and in the general vocabulary. The words in the following Associated Press lead are precise and show the impact:

> LAND O'LAKES, Fla.—When 3-year-old Mikey Spoul took his father's car for a joyride last month and explained "I go zoom," the act grabbed national attention and even became fodder for late-night show monologue jokes.
> But nobody's laughing now. Mikey torched his bedroom curtains with a cigarette lighter and burned down his family's home, authorities said.

Leads should use active verbs. Consider the verbs in the lead example above: "grabbed," "torched," and "burned down," or the verbs in this lead:

> A Forest City man smashed the glass door on a laundromat washing machine and yanked a 3-year-old child from the swirling waters Saturday morning.

Leads should be simple sentences, not rambling, convoluted sentences. No one wants to work too hard at understanding most communication. The writer has lost if the "huh?" factor enters in. That's when a person has to stop and reread a lead to understand what the writer is saying.

Compare the simple lead about the Forest City man in the laundromat with this more convoluted lead:

> Under a handgun-control plan, announced by state and county grass-roots organizations Monday, a person who sells a handgun to an unlicensed customer would be liable to a victim for three times his losses if that handgun is used to commit a crime.

Apply what you have learned about leads so far to untangle this report on controlling handguns. What's the point? Some grass-roots organizations have come up with an idea for making handgun salespeople more responsible for crime. What does the audience have to know? How about this lead:

> If a local citizens group gets its way, people who sell guns will help pay for the lives and property lost in handgun crimes.

Writers base the structure of their leads on the type of story and the audience. Some information, such as police reports, lend themselves to summary leads. Other material works better in a descriptive or anecdotal lead. The next section looks at leads and where each works best.

Summary Leads

The most common lead format is a summary lead that tells or summarizes the most important information:

> Four Northern High School students have received National Merit Scholarships.

> To reduce attrition, Telstar Corp. will build an on-site day care center that will enroll 125 children of its employees in May.

> The Republican Party is increasing its membership in Maryland, a state that Democrats once confidently claimed.

The summary lead serves the audience who skims newspaper stories, online articles, company newsletters, or handouts from school; who listens with one ear to radio news reports and one ear to the kids in the backseat of the car; or who casually tunes into the morning television news while getting dressed. Because of the crowded field of communication today, summary leads are used often to give people information quickly.

Summary leads are useful. They can be the introduction of a letter, the hook of an online story, the beginning of a news release, or the headline of a broadcast story.

Beyond One Paragraph

Although most summary leads consist of one sentence or one paragraph, they may be longer to provide adequate information and context. Leads must be clear and easy to understand.

Look at this lead from the *News & Observer* in Raleigh, North Carolina:

> On the big Monopoly board of radioactive waste disposal, Chem-Nuclear Systems Inc. seemed to have passed "go" last month.

That's when the company submitted a license application for its proposed radioactive waste repository in southwest Wake County and was expecting to receive a $2 million bonus from a state authority.

But the company might have skipped a few spaces. After thumbing through Chem-Nuclear's license application, the N.C. Division of Radiation Protection has determined that the 6,000-page document doesn't include at least 13 key pieces of information.

The writer sets up a complicated subject through a clever use of the familiar Monopoly game. Readers know in the third paragraph that there is a problem, a potential conflict. They are hit with an "oh, my" thought: How could a 6,000-page document leave out anything? Also note the use of the verb "thumbed." The verb gives the sense of scanning the hefty document, and it makes readers curious to know whether a closer look would reveal more missing pieces.

A writer in a company's corporate communications department needs to tell employees about payroll changes. She must do so in a way that is informative, pertinent, and clear.

Long Branch Entertainment employees will see in their paychecks next month some changes that represent good news and bad news.

The good news is the company's across-the-board 3 percent pay raise.

The bad news is each employee with a family plan will pay $30.16 more a month in health insurance premiums and employees with individual plans $16.32 more a month.

The three-paragraph summary lead contains information essential to employees: how the company's health insurance plan will change and how much their raises will be. The writer wanted employees to know right away that they were about to be hit in the pocketbook and why. Employees who want to know more about how and why the changes occurred will continue to read the message.

Multiple-Element Leads

The Long Branch lead on health care also illustrates how a writer presents more than one aspect to a message. Often, a lead has multiple elements or more than one point it must convey to readers. A *multiple-element lead* summarizes information for readers and sets up what will be covered in the rest of the copy. It presents a challenge to the writer, who must be wary of complex or convoluted sentences. The best approach is to rank the elements, put the most important in the first sentence, and then create a second or third paragraph to present the other points.

> A group of university students has presented a list of concerns to Chancellor Paula Walls, asking foremost that the university allow 24-hour visitation in dormitories.
> The letter, hand-delivered to Walls on Wednesday, also asks the administration to name more minority students to campus-wide committees, to recruit minority faculty members, and to put a ceiling on student fees.

From this lead, readers have the most important information first: the list of demands and the high-priority demand. And they know the content and structure of the message. For writers, the lead sets up how to organize the story: in order of the points listed in the lead.

Delayed-Identification Leads

Another type of summary lead is the *delayed-identification lead*. When an individual or individuals in a news story carry no prominence, their proper names are not given in the first paragraph. Rather, they are identified by a generic label: "An Orange County woman died when…" or "A Lockwood High School student has been named a National Merit Scholarship winner.…" Immediately, in the next paragraph, the individual is named. If more than one person is in the lead or first paragraph, the individuals are renamed in that order in the next paragraph. Consider this:

> An Orange County woman was arrested Tuesday night after police found two emaciated dogs tied to a tree in her backyard.
> Sara Louise McDaniel, 54, of 546 Calumet Drive, Lewisville, was charged with two counts of animal cruelty. Police took the dogs, Bruno and Trixie, to the county animal shelter for treatment.

Sometimes you need to delay identification even for famous people:

> President Bush's chief economic adviser predicted a U.S. recession after reviewing predictions for growth in the third quarter.

Lawrence Lindsey said in a speech to a national management symposium in Washington that although predictions are hard to make, he expected even less growth in the fourth quarter of the year. A recession is defined as two quarters of negative growth.

Other Lead Formats

Although the summary lead is the most useful, writers sometimes find other lead formats better suited to the kind of message they need to send. Some types of leads, such as anecdotal or descriptive, are popular in newspapers and magazines today. They can be risky because they don't hook readers soon enough. They must therefore be well written to entice readers to stay long enough to find out what the message is about.

In general, when using other lead formats, make sure you get to the point by the fourth paragraph. Otherwise, you may lose your reader. If you are writing for a newspaper, the story may have jumped to another page before the reader ever gets to the point.

Let's evaluate some types of alternative leads.

Affective Leads

Many newspapers have developed a lead style that focuses on people. A story about a big social, health, or economic problem can lead with one person to illustrate how individuals are affected. The lead makes readers feel the abstract on an interpersonal and even emotional level. The abstract then becomes real.

For example, using stem cells from umbilical cords has generated great controversy in the medical community. In this *Seattle Times* story, reporter Warren King uses a 9-year-old girl as an example of people who benefit from the treatment. Savannah Jantsch is used as an illustration throughout the story.

She reads voraciously. She adores animals, especially her cat Oreo. She plays, swims and laughs with her sister, Sydney, and a happy gaggle of friends. Yet five years ago, Savannah Jantsch's parents feared she would not last more than a few months.

Struggling with leukemia and a rare blood disorder, Savannah became one of the early recipients of stem cells from the umbilical-cord blood of a newborn. Infused in her body, the cells soon built an entirely new blood-cell system for the Bellingham girl, now a bright-eyed 9-year-old.

"It's a resource that has given our daughter a whole new life," her father, Jeff Jantsch, said last week. "It's like she's been two different people with different lifestyles and a different existence."

Savannah Jantsch is living proof of the healing power of stem cells, one of the basic building blocks of human tissue and the focus of so many headlines in recent weeks.

Eleven days ago, President Bush announced support for limited funding of research on embryonic stem cells, bridging a controversy over the ethics of tampering with the earliest stage of human development, the embryo. In an attempt to balance scientific progress with sometimes competing moral values, he approved federal funding only for research on cells already taken from embryos; no new embryos could be destroyed.★

The basic story is tied to President Bush's announcement, but King chose to put a human element into the story through Savannah Jantsch. The story goes on to explain stem cell research and its controversies.

The key to using the affective lead is to keep it short and get to the point right away. Writers must quickly reveal the social or economic issue the message is about. And they must use the individual throughout the story.

Anecdotal Leads

Writers can use anecdotal leads to put a human element into their messages, just as when they use an affective lead. Anecdotal leads are often longer than affective leads, but they tell a story and have a plot. Although they, too, delay the point of the message, they set up complex problems and their effects on individuals. Writers must use the anecdotal example throughout the story, not solely as a hook that is dropped after the lead.

Consider this lead in the *Philadelphia Inquirer* by Pulitzer Prize–winning writer David Zucchino:

> —Someone is knocking, quite gently, at the door.
>
> "Who?" asks the gatekeeper of a shooting gallery near Cambria Street, where a man with a syringe tucked behind his ear is mixing heroin with water in a bottle cap.

★Copyright August 20, 2001 Seattle Times Company. Used with permission.

A woman's voice answers, "Angela!"

The gatekeeper lifts a wooden barricade and the door swings open. A slender woman named Angela and her wild-haired friend Maureen bound through the breezeway, smiling and waving, intent on getting high. They have just spent $10 each at Fourth and Cambria Streets for two blue glassine bags of "Mercedes" heroin.

Soon needles are in the women's arms and heroin is coursing through their veins. Their heads droop and their eyes glaze and they are at peace. A few hours will pass before they must again shoplift to raise the cash to buy the drugs that lure them back to Cambria Street.

The daily journey of this pair of heroin addicts from their homes in New Jersey to a shooting gallery in North Philadelphia is a shopping trip. It is an expedition made thousands of times a year by thousands of drug customers, whose cash lubricates the economy of a place some narcotics officers call the Badlands.

The illegal drug trade pumps at least $250 million in cash a year into a three-square-mile swath of North Philadelphia anchored by the Badlands, the Drug Enforcement Administration estimates.*

Zucchino uses two women and how their lives are affected by drugs. The simple writing and description are compelling and pull the reader further into the story. The anecdote stands alone: the first seven graphs form a story that is complete.

Descriptive Leads

Like an anecdotal lead, a descriptive lead puts emotion or a human element into a message. It sets the scene for the reader. Consider the *Herald-Sun* lead into this story:

DURHAM—A crowd of curious children and adults gathered on the lawn and street in front of an apartment complex at 1108 Drew Street as homicide investigators began their work once again Saturday afternoon.

At the top of the stairs, the body of a man in his late 20s lay half inside an apartment, blood pooling beneath his head, a baseball cap still

*Reprinted with permission of *The Philadelphia Inquirer.*

clenched tightly in his hand. Blood streaks ran down the glass of the open door.

But before officers could finish snapping photos and questioning witnesses, shots rang out from across the road on North Hyde Park Street.

Toddlers screamed and the crowd ducked for cover behind patrol cars as several men ran out of an apartment, guns blazing as they fired at random. Someone yelled, "Get the kids out of the street!" as people fled inside, slamming doors.

The gun-wielding men jumped in a car and sped toward Alston Avenue, scattering people caught in the street as they left.

Subsequent paragraphs identified who was killed and gives details of the shooting.

In the following descriptive lead from the *Seattle Times,* a human element is ascribed to a machine. Writer Lisa Heyamoto has taken a subject that affects Seattle residents—drilling under Queen Anne Hill—and presented it in a readable, interesting manner.

She weighs 305 tons, is 27 feet long and creeps forward in four-foot intervals, her teeth gnashing through clay and rocks like corn nuts in a blender.

You can call her Cassandra, and she's been burrowing her way 150 feet beneath Queen Anne Hill all summer.

Cassandra isn't a Tolkien-esque subterranean monster. She's basically a drill—a giant one—carving a tunnel beneath Seattle that will store storm-water runoff until it can be treated and piped into Puget Sound.★

Question Leads

Question leads should be avoided. They are rarely successful. In most cases, they are the lazy writer's way out, and they turn off audiences. In almost every case, they give the audience the option to turn elsewhere.

```
Who will pay to build nuclear power plants?
```

★Copyright August 20, 2001 Seattle Times Company. Used with permission.

The reader might say, "Not me, and I don't care who pays." Think of another angle such as

```
The average electric consumer will end up paying the cost
for building nuclear power plants, a local watchdog group
stated today.
```

Occasionally a question lead can work, as in this one from the *Arkansas Democrat Gazette:*

> What's a prairie dog worth?
> Two to six years, Little Rock police say.

The reader at first mentally guesses a dollar figure, but then is surprised immediately that the correct answer is a prison term. The reader is hooked into the story on prairie dog-napping.

Quotation Leads

Such leads should be used sparingly because rarely does someone sum an entire speech or premise for a decision in one simple quotation. A quotation can be used if it is short, is relevant to the rest of the message, and does not need any explanation. It must be clear within itself. Look at this newsletter lead:

> "Taking advantage of the different opportunities available in the Scholars program is what made a difference in my academic career," said a University of Maryland senior who will attend Georgetown Law School next year.

The lead here is empty and nonspecific. The lead fails to point out that the senior is a semifinalist for a Rhodes scholarship, is the Student Government Association vice president, and was an intern at the FBI. A stronger lead would have focused on his accomplishments and linked them to his involvement in the Scholars program:

> Randy Cates, a senior at the University of Maryland, is a semifinalist for a Rhodes scholarship, one of the most prestigious international

academic awards; an FBI intern; and vice president of the student government association.

He is also a College Park Scholar, and he says that award "is what made a difference in my academic career."

A partial quotation is used effectively in this example from the Associated Press:

Smoking and drug use among U.S. teenagers are increasing after a decade of decline, a study showed Monday, and its author warned that "the stage is set for a potential resurgence of cocaine and crack use."

Direct Address Leads

The direct address lead talks straight to the reader or consumer. It usually gives advice or has a "hey, you" aspect to it.

If you haven't had your car inspected this month, you need to do it soon. The fee for state-required inspections will double July 1.

Wake up. You have only two weeks until April 15, the deadline for filing your taxes.

Staccato Leads

A series of single words identifies a staccato lead. It can be used for news, feature stories, or almost any kind of message.

Popcorn. Peanuts. Candy.
All those good things you buy at the movies will cost you more in local theaters starting Sunday.

Fair. Knowledgeable. Decisive. Accessible. Caring.
Those were some of the attributes that members of a selection committee used to describe Bill Burston, whom they recently endorsed as the new director of the 350-employee Housekeeping Services at UNC–Chapel Hill.

Choosing a Lead Type

In many cases the information will dictate the type of lead. A crime story, for example, generally will use a summary lead. A story on a city council meeting will need a multiple-element lead to cover the council's different actions. Lack of prominence will dictate a delayed-identification lead. But sometimes a writer must ponder and decide which lead will set up the story best. Look at this Associated Press lead about a 911 operator:

> NEW YORK—"You want the police to your house because your mother didn't come home?"
>
> It's nearly 7 P.M. on a Wednesday in the weeks before Christmas and somewhere in New York City, two scared young girls watch the clock, more frightened by the minute. They call 911 and reach Ivey Bruce.
>
> Her voice is soothing and steady. "OK, what apartment are you in? And what's the telephone number? And how old are you and your sister?"
>
> As she speaks Bruce types on a battered gray computer. The figures 10 and 11 appear on her screen, then "HOME ALONE." Another tap of a key speeds the girls' telephonic SOS to a police dispatcher in a nearby room.
>
> Bruce, a 45-year-old mother of two sons, nods as if to reassure the unseen child and then tells her police will be there soon.
>
> Like a novel half read, a mystery never solved, this story has no end for Bruce. After 14 years on the job, she knows that's as it must be.
>
> It's only suppertime in New York, and by the end of her 3:30 P.M. to 11:30 P.M. shift, this 911 operator will have heard accounts of panic and terror by the score.

The writer chose a long, anecdotal lead to set up a story about 911 operators. The story specifically follows one operator, Ivey Bruce, before it gives information about 911 services. By focusing on one typical call, the writer lets readers know how a 911 operator reacts to a call and interacts with the caller. The writer could have written a lead that said

> NEW YORK—The hectic and gargantuan New York City 911 service will field more than 10 million calls this year.

The system represents a lifeline found in 89 percent of the country. The operation rests largely with the 911 operators, who answer scores of accounts of panic and terror during their shifts.

Which lead works? The one with the human element will draw more people into the story than one that tosses out numbers. The faces behind the digits set up the story, and readers know by the end of the second paragraph that the key elements are 911, operators, Ivey Bruce, and calls.

Does It Work?

Once you have written a lead, scrutinize it, keeping in mind the guidelines in the leads checklist at the end of the chapter. Consider this lead from a daily newspaper:

> Ten-month-old Betssie Martinez-Oidor's fever soared to 105 degrees Monday. Her mother, Isabel Oidor, called York Hospital. Oidor and her husband, Gabriel Martinez, told a Spanish interpreter they had never seen their baby this ill.
> "They both got scared," interpreter Carmen Bones said. She told them to bring the baby to the hospital. They stayed until late Monday so the baby could be observed because of her fever. Betssie also had a runny nose, mild cough, and little appetite for her formula.★

As the reader, what do you think the story is about? The lead says that the baby is ill with a high fever. Is the story about the effects of fevers on infants? No. See how far you have to read before you know what the story is really about.

> Periodic doses of Tylenol® helped bring the fever down to 100.6 degrees by the time they returned Tuesday for a follow-up exam by Dr. Mary Barnes in the Mother/Child Clinic.
> Applying her stethoscope to the baby's back and chest, Barnes ruled out bronchitis and pneumonia.
> "I think the baby has the flu and an ear infection," Barnes said. "It's out there. There's so much of it around."
> "Maybe she got it through me," the baby's father said to Barnes in Spanish.

★Reprinted courtesy of *York Daily Record*.

Betssie's parents have been ill with flu-like symptoms. They're far from alone. Pennsylvania is one of about 20 states experiencing an earlier-than-usual start to the flu season. The state's physician general, Dr. Wanda Filer, issued a statement that some flu cases of a Type A strain known as A/Nanchang have been confirmed in residents of several counties.

By paragraph 9, the story is clear: Pennsylvania is having a flu epidemic. All the discussion about the baby's illness makes readers wonder about fevers, immunizations, colds, or perhaps care for children. The example of the sick baby could be used, but readers need to know sooner what the actual topic is. Consider the rewrite:

Ten-month-old Betssie Martinez-Oidor's fever soared to 105 degrees Monday, scaring her parents who took her to the hospital. Betssie has the flu. She is among the latest and youngest victims of this year's flu season. Pennsylvania is one of about 20 states experiencing an earlier-than-usual start to the flu season.

Then the writer can proceed with quotes from the parents and other details of the flu, its symptoms, and treatment.

Leads Should Do the Job

Remember to read through your stories carefully and ensure that your leads are honest: that they have set up for the reader what the story covers. Review the following checklist. Readers will be disappointed if they believe that a story is about one topic and discover that it is about another. Writers will lose credibility if they make false promises in their leads.

You can become a good lead writer, whatever the copy, by focusing on what is important to your audience, learning the guidelines of good writing, and reading good leads that are specific and present information accurately, clearly, and concisely. Look for such leads in everything you read.

Leads Checklist
Essential Lead Elements

1. I have looked at the facts and decided which are the most important.
2. My initial sentence is simple and complete.

3. My lead is accurate.
4. My lead is relevant to my audience.
5. My lead comes to the point, is well edited, and makes sense.
6. I have used understandable, fresh words and strong, active verbs.
7. My lead sets up the story.

Desirable Elements

1. I have emphasized the latest information.
2. I have included unusual aspects of the message.
3. If possible, I have used a local angle to show how the information relates to readers.
4. I have kept my lead short and readable—no longer than 30 words.
5. My lead attracts the audience's attention.
6. My lead summarizes the message.

Exercises

1. Read the following lead. Identify the elements and the news values present:

A third elementary school in Orange County will be delayed for a year because school officials have asked architects to revise the plans to include more space for computer labs, the school board chairman announced Monday.

The school will be a model for schools across the state and will take about 14 months to build.

Elements

Who:

What:

When:

Where:

Why:

How:

News Values (identify only those present; not all will be)
Conflict:
Timeliness:
Proximity:
Prominence:
Magnitude:
Impact:
Audience:
Oddity:
Emotion:

2. Read the following lead. Identify the elements and the news values present:

> Two fishermen whose boat capsized in the Atlantic Ocean were rescued Sunday after spending 24 hours floating in life preservers.
> George Blackburn and Brian Livengood, both of Wilmington, Del., went fishing off the coast early Saturday. Their boat capsized about 2 p.m. that day after a fire burned a hole in their boat. The Coast Guard rescued them about noon.

Elements
Who:
What:
When:
Where:
Why:
How:

News Values (identify only those present; not all will be)
Conflict:
Timeliness:
Proximity:
Prominence:

Magnitude:

Impact:

Audience:

Oddity:

Emotion:

3. Read the following lead. Identify the elements and the news values present:

> WASHINGTON—Hospital leaders told members of Congress Tuesday that reductions in Medicare and Medicaid could have great impact on the people they care for.
>
> The federal budget calls for $115 billion less for Medicare and $21.6 billion less for Medicaid. More than 1,000 hospitals across the country depend heavily on the two federal programs for about two-thirds of their annual revenues.

Elements

Who:

What:

When:

Where:

Why:

How:

News Values (identify only those present; not all will be)

Conflict:

Timeliness:

Proximity:

Prominence:

Magnitude:

Impact:

Audience:

Oddity:

Emotion:

4. Read the following lead. Identify the elements and the news values present:

> The Rockland Town Council approved a 3-cent property tax rate increase for the coming fiscal year budget and more programs to assist in low-incoming housing.
>
> The tax rate increase means a person who owns a home valued at $100,000 will pay $30 more a year.

Elements

Who:

What:

When:

Where:

Why:

How:

News Values (identify only those present; not all will be)

Conflict:

Timeliness:

Proximity:

Prominence:

Magnitude:

Impact:

Audience:

Oddity:

Emotion:

5. You are a reporter for the *Rockland Chronicle*. Write leads for the following information. List for each exercise *who, what, when, where, how,* and *why.* You may want to list the news values to help you determine what information should go into the lead. Think about the local audience. Write just the lead, not the entire story, for each.

   • A Rockland Community College student died yesterday. He was working at a construction site at Town Hall. The construction company he worked for was building an addition to the Town Hall. He was dead on arrival at Rockland Hospital. He died when scaffolding he was standing on collapsed and he fell three stories to the ground. One of the cables holding the scaffolding broke and he slipped off the scaffolding. A board from the scaffolding, which came apart, fell on his head as he lay on the ground. He worked part time for the construction company while he was in school.

- The Natural Resources Defense Council had a news conference today in Washington. The NRDC is a national environmental lobbying group. It said that smog is getting worse in metropolitan areas across the country and is reaching the stage of "a public health emergency." The group also said that the government is seriously understating the problem. Smog is the polluted air that irritates eyes and lungs and causes long-term health problems. The Council said unsafe levels of smog occur in many large cities twice as often as the federal Environmental Protection Agency says it does.

- Early this morning before the Rockland Community Day Care Center opened, vandals overturned toys, tore apart a plastic playhouse, and ripped down swings outside. Someone killed the center's pet rabbit. The center has had several other break-ins where people stole TVs and VCRs, but no damage this extensive. Nothing was taken in this break-in. The center has 50 children and 10 staff.

- The Rockland Planetarium has regularly scheduled programs at 7 P.M. and 8 P.M. on weekdays and 10 A.M. Saturdays. This weekend, the planetarium will expand its offerings to the afternoon. "Sam, Space Cat" will be at 1 P.M. and 3 P.M. on Saturday and Sunday. The film "Beyond the Earth" will be shown at 2 P.M. each day. The planetarium director said the additional showings will allow more people, particularly those who work during the week, to see the special offerings.

- Workforce.com, a local company in the Rockland Research Park, employs 85 people. Company officials have announced a restructuring that will layoff 60 employees and that they hope will allow them to save the company. Profits have dropped 40 percent in the last six months. Workforce.com was founded five years ago. It is an online employment company that had targeted a national clientele, but company officials said the number of clients did not reach expectations.

5

Beyond the Lead
Writing the Message

Once writers have fashioned the lead, they face the task of organizing the rest of the message. They must decide what will come after the first sentences or paragraphs that hook the audience. The ranking decisions discussed in Chapter 4 that help them write the lead are invaluable in helping them develop the body of the message. Again, with audience needs and interests in mind, the writer outlines how the message will evolve.

As mentioned in Chapter 4, journalists have traditionally used the inverted pyramid form of writing to get to the point quickly and to set priorities for basic news stories. The principle behind the inverted pyramid style—to order information according to its value to the audience—is valuable in much writing today, whether it is for ad copy, online writing, e-mail messages, Web pages, news stories, or newsletter or magazine articles. The process of ordering information for the inverted pyramid involves critical thinking, an important skill for writers.

Different styles of writing may be more suitable for other audiences or for a particular medium. Students will find various organizational styles in print publications: newspapers, magazines, company newsletters, and so on. If you find yourself reading a story from start to end, clip it, and study it to identify the elements that pulled you into and through the message. Save it. Some day you may want to adopt the style for a piece of your own.

This chapter discusses

- The inverted pyramid form of writing,
- News peg and nut graph,

- Other organizational styles, and
- How to unify writing.

The Inverted Pyramid

Leads must get to the point quickly, and messages must provide important information right behind the lead. Newspaper editors have recognized that need for decades. Henry A. Stokes, as an assistant managing editor for projects at the *Commercial Appeal* in Memphis, Tennessee, once wrote in a staff memo that reporters had to ensure stories attracted reader attention.

Stokes told staff writers that they were to "tell the news in an identifiable, functional format that guarantees the reader will receive the best information we can provide, written in a way that the reader can quickly and easily understand."

As a result, the newspaper adopted the four-paragraph rule: Tell the essential message in the first four paragraphs of the story. Details that could be cut would follow.

The format that Stokes advocated was the inverted pyramid style of writing, long a standard in journalism. With the inverted pyramid, information in a message is organized in descending order of importance. The most important and compelling information comes first and is followed by information of lesser value. The inverted pyramid has had a resurgence of popularity because of online publishing, which requires that important information be stated immediately.

To be successful at using the inverted pyramid, writers must be able to evaluate and rank information, and they must know what is most important to their audiences. This simple model shows how the inverted pyramid works:

Lead summarizes information. Next few paragraphs back up lead.

Next section provides background and additional important information.

Next section has information of lesser importance about the topics introduced in the lead.

Final section contains least important information, which could be cut.

In the inverted pyramid, the lead paragraph or paragraphs summarize the most important news values and elements and hook the audience. The next paragraph or paragraphs usually give additional crucial information that won't fit into the lead. Background information comes next. From there, subsequent paragraphs develop the topics presented in the lead, introduce other important information, expand the significance of the information, and give details.

Each section will vary in length, depending on what the writer has introduced in the lead and whether he or she is building the message with quotations. A local government reporter may devote four or five paragraphs to dialogue from a meeting before moving on to other city council actions set forth in the lead paragraph.

The inverted pyramid format helps a writer organize information logically, whether the topic is a single subject or has multiple subjects or elements. If the writer plans to develop several issues in the message, the summary multiple-element lead would set up the organization in the following way:

> The Rockland City Council voted unanimously Tuesday night to renew the city manager's contract for three years with a raise each year and to annex 325 acres south of Lewisville and Maxton roads.

Through the inverted pyramid, the writer sets up the order of importance in the lead and how the message will be organized. The most important item is the city manager's contract, which includes a pay raise. Because no one objected to the annexation of acreage, it carries less importance because it is not controversial. It can be discussed second. The important point, the action of annexation, is contained in the lead. The rest of the story follows the lead like this:

> In discussing City Manager Larry Morgan's new contract, council members agreed that Morgan had done an exemplary job in his six years as manager.
>
> "We couldn't find anyone better," said Council Member Dick Haynes, who made the motion to give Morgan a 10 percent pay raise in the first year of the contract and 5 percent in the second and third years.
>
> "We have maintained quality town services with only modest tax increases while Larry has been here," added Council Member Loretta Manson.

The council voted to annex the Heather Hills subdivision following a public hearing in which no one objected to the annexation plan. Residents who spoke said they wanted to come under the town's water and sewer services and to gain improved fire and police protection.

The inverted pyramid is more than just an organizational tool. It has been identified traditionally as a writing style that uses simple words, short sentences, and one idea to a paragraph. It also represents critical thinking: it forces writers to evaluate information and rank it in order of importance. Some critics have said that the inverted pyramid puts pressure on reporters to craft an attention-getting, information-packed lead, leaving them little time to follow through with a well-organized message. To be successful, writers must do both: write a compelling lead and organize a story logically. In reality, time constraints or deadline pressure may interfere with both functions.

Why Use the Inverted Pyramid for Media Writing?

Newspapers traditionally have used the inverted pyramid format for two primary reasons: to give readers the most critical material quickly so they can move to other stories if they wish and to allow a story to be cut easily from the bottom, leaving important information intact at the top of the story.

Many beginning writers question why they should follow the inverted pyramid style of writing when they plan careers in public relations, advertising, or marketing. They object to what they see as a rigid way of writing or formula writing—a basic format devoid of creativity.

At first glance, the objections seem valid. But as students use the inverted pyramid, they will discover plenty of opportunities for description and for their own style to develop. And they will learn that critical thinking goes along with the inverted pyramid style. They will also learn that their audiences expect upfront delivery of essential information and that critical thinking goes along with the inverted pyramid style. For the inverted pyramid, writers must gather information, list or rank information, write a draft, and rewrite, as outlined in Chapter 1.

John Sweeney, professor in the School of Journalism and Mass Communication at the University of North Carolina at Chapel Hill, teaches advertising courses. He advises all students, no matter what their major, on the value of learning the inverted pyramid structure.

"Before you can develop your own style, you have to master the basics," he tells introductory writing students. "You have to be taught to be meticulous. To say it succinctly, concisely, precisely. You have to be able to distill information, whether it's a 30-second spot or a piece of newswriting or an ad distilled from a 100-page document on product data.

"Writing also has to have access: Anyone can read it and understand it," Sweeney advises. "You have to focus on what's key, get to the heart of the matter, and put the issue in perspective."

Online journalism calls for renewed interest in and use of the inverted pyramid as a news-telling standard. Online journalists know that as much information as possible needs to be seen on the home page, or the first page of a web site. Thus, news items appear only as leads or briefs on the home page, offering links to full stories. An online editor has to copy only an article's lead for the front page. If the lead is well written, it will serve as a compelling link to the rest of the story.

Online journalism uses news briefs, rather than full stories, to attract readers because research shows that readers presented with full stories often click away. Holding audiences is a priority in online journalism. In this new medium, the old standard for direct communication, the inverted pyramid, aids writers in conveying information quickly and succinctly. All media writers must recognize the logic of using the inverted pyramid in an age when busy consumers are bombarded with messages.

The Inverted Pyramid for Other Media

Research supports the belief that the inverted pyramid retains value today, when the majority of messages are becoming shorter and more direct. Consider broadcast messages, which usually begin with a short, catchy headline to grab the viewer's attention and then summarize the main points. Because broadcast news stories are short, it is imperative for TV and radio reporters to fit in as many compelling facts as possible in the few seconds allotted. The inverted pyramid allows for the speedy, information-rich writing that broadcast demands.

Corporate communication offices and nonprofit agencies, whether they are staffed by professionals or volunteers, more and more follow the traditional inverted pyramid style. It puts their agenda where readers and editors can see it. Even advertising depends on the inverted pyramid style, communicating to consumers in an abbreviated way a product's qualities and the reasons for buying it. On Web sites, as in brochures and magazines, brevity is essential: Every word and second cost the client money.

The inverted pyramid can fit most kinds of media writing and other kinds of writing in the real world—even the garden club's minutes. Although it works best in shorter pieces, it can be adapted for longer, more complex pieces, many of which use the inverted pyramid format early and then other organizational patterns later. For example, nondeadline pieces, such as feature stories and documentaries, attract readers best by getting to the point and summarizing first. Simple pyramiding in nondeadline writing can attract readers by creating a mood, setting the stage for more detailed information, or providing a memorable image.

The first two paragraphs of a story written in inverted pyramid style can serve the online editor who needs compelling information for readers. Like many other online sites, Detnews.com uses headlines from its homepage as a guide to story topics. The lead then entices readers to view complete stories. Readers get the latest information quickly, as in this example:

```
While it is clear the Sept. 11 terrorist attacks sent
the U.S. economy spiraling into recession, the impact on
Michigan is likely to be even more severe because of the
state's already weakened condition and heavy reliance on
manufacturing.
```

Readers may then click on the headline to read the complete story.

Organizing a Story

The basic work of organizing a message in inverted pyramid style is done when you use the steps outlined in Chapter 4 for writing leads. The writer first identifies news values and the elements to structure a lead. News values and elements introduced in the lead will be developed in greater detail within the message. The writer will use the remaining news values and elements in subsequent paragraphs based on ranking information that is important to audiences.

For example, a news value, such as oddity, may be referred to in a lead but must be developed fully later in the message. Remember the lead in Chapter 4 on the couple who got married as they were skydiving? Although readers have the basics from the lead about how the wedding happened, they may want more information about why skydiving was important to that particular couple. The body of the message answers that question.

A Hollywood, Fla., man and woman exchanged wedding vows at 1,300 feet as they plummeted to earth hand-in-hand under silver parachutes five miles west of here Wednesday afternoon.

Grace Mason and John Kempner met while skydiving at a local club and decided it would be the most significant way to start their married life together.

"Skydiving brought us together," said Grace Mason Kempner after the ceremony. "It seemed to be the appropriate way to tie the knot."

She learned to skydive while a student at Dade Community College. Her husband was a paratrooper in the Army. They have known each other two years and have been jumping partners for the last six months.

Each wore a silver jumpsuit, but the bride carried a nosegay of white satin roses.

It's important here to note a difference between paragraphs in an essay for an English composition or literature class and paragraphs in even long forms of media writing. In an essay or composition, a paragraph can be a whole presentation or argument on a topic. But in mass communication, a paragraph is identified as a single unit of timely information. It is a solitary fact, thought, or "sound bite" from the larger message. When a writer is concerned with transmitting information quickly, his or her ideas about paragraphing change.

As mentioned in Chapter 3, journalists rarely use the word "paragraph." In the newsroom, a paragraph is a "graph." This abbreviated word symbolizes the abbreviated form that paragraphs take in news stories. A graph generally will have several sentences, but on occasion it may be one sentence long and transmit a single news element or news value.

Applying News Elements and News Values

Let's consider a message about the community theater in a town called Rockland. You are to write a news story about auditions for an upcoming production. The elements *who, what, when, where, how,* and *why* can be easily listed:

Who: Rockland Theater

What: Will have auditions for the play "West Side Story"

When: 7–9 P.M. Monday and Tuesday

Where: The theater at 211 W. Sycamore St.

How: People will read a piece of their own choosing, then one impromptu piece from the director

Why: So the play can be produced

Look at the news values we discussed in Chapter 4 and determine which ones apply here. The magnitude of the production and the timeliness of the pending auditions are relevant; news values such as conflict, oddity, and impact may not exist. Prominence is a factor if the lead role will be held by a well-known stage actress and local residents will have the chance to act with her.

You might write this lead:

```
Local residents can audition 7 to 9 p.m. Monday and Tuesday
for parts in the Rockland Community Theater's upcoming
production of "West Side Story" with film star Christina
Ricci.
```

The lead identifies the elements *who, what,* and *when,* as well as the news value of prominence. To handle the overflow from the lead, you must add a second paragraph to answer *where* and to show impact:

```
Auditions will be at the theater at 211 W. Sycamore St. and
led by Director Neal Folger. He is looking for 16 local actors.
```

Anyone interested in auditioning has the basic information from the first two paragraphs. In subsequent paragraphs you will expand on the lead, noting that the production also will require a 30-member chorus and explaining what people will have to do during the audition.

You would continue the story:

```
Local residents wishing to audition must prepare a song and
a part to read, said Folger. Each audition is not to exceed
five minutes.
```

```
People interested in being in a 30-member chorus need
prepare only a song not to exceed three minutes. They will
audition with the music director, Carole Banner.
```

You have determined that the audience would be most interested in the requirements for auditioning and how to audition. If aspiring actors could not meet the requirements, they would have no need to read further.

Those who are potential actors would want to know more about the selection process and when rehearsals would start. In the final paragraphs, you would state

```
"We will let people know by Friday if they are selected,"
Folger said. "Rehearsals will start the next week."
     The community theater produces six shows each year.
One in the fall and one in the spring have professional
actors.
     "Having professional talent promotes the theater and
makes the acting experience much more exciting for our
local talent," Folger said. "We have had wonderful success
in the past, and we expect the same for 'West Side Story.'"
```

In the last paragraph, you would use the director's quote to wrap up the message and look to the future.

Breaking It Up

Let's look at the story and see how the information was ordered and why.

```
Local residents can audition
7 to 9 p.m. Monday and Tuesday
for parts in the Rockland
Community Theater's upcoming
production of "West Side
Story" with film star Chris-
tina Ricci.
```

The lead tells *who* can do *what when* and *why*. It also includes the news value prominence of Christina Ricci, which might attract some people to audition.

Auditions will be at the theater at 211 W. Sycamore St. and led by Director Neal Folger. He is looking for 16 local actors. Local residents wishing to audition must prepare a song and a part to read, said Folger. Each audition is not to exceed five minutes.

People interested in being in a 30-member chorus need prepare only a song not to exceed three minutes. They will audition with the music director, Carole Banner.

"We will let people know by Friday if they are selected," Folger said. "Rehearsals will start the next week."

The community theater produces six shows each year. One in the fall and one in the spring have professional actors.

"Having professional talent promotes the theater and makes the acting experience much more exciting for our local talent," Folger said. "We have had wonderful success in the past, and we expect the same for 'West Side Story.'"

Graph 2 expands the first graph by telling where folks can audition and what is required during the auditions for the major roles.

Graph 3 continues to expand the information, giving details about auditions for lesser roles.

Graph 4 moves to the next step after auditions: when people will be notified and when rehearsal begins.

Graph 5 provides background on the theater and its productions.

Graph 6 is a follow-up quote to graph 5. A quote also makes a good ending.

Another Approach: The Second-Day Story

In the story just given, you have followed a traditional inverted pyramid format to announce the auditions. The story represents what could be called a first-day story. In looking at newspaper clips about the Little Theater, you believe another story is warranted. So you decide to do what is called a second-day story that gives new information and also includes background from the first-day story.

The lead and message might go something like this:

When Rockland Community Theater Director Neal Folger starts auditions for "West Side Story" starring Christina Ricci, most board of directors members will be crossing their fingers for a smooth year.

The board hired Folger, the former director of the River Road Theater in Danville, a year ago, and soon the theater was embroiled in controversy. Last year's season opener of "Grease" showed nudity when three performers dropped their pants as part of a song on mooning. This year's season opens Oct. 15.

"We felt we went through a wringer right off the bat last year," Board Member Mary Tyson said today. "Although some people like Neal's productions, most people in our community prefer more traditional entertainment. Nudity just has no place on our stage."

Board Member Justin Fellows said the board hoped for a successful season with less turmoil than the previous year.

"We think Neal is quite talented, but we are just a community theater, and we want fun, not indignation," he said.

Folger said he was surprised at the reaction to "Grease."

"I certainly learned what this community will accept on stage," he said. "This year we intend to produce shows that keep people fairly well covered."

Fellows added the board hoped Folger's appealing season
lineup will attract a substantial audience to the Rockland
Theater.

The director will have auditions for "West Side Story"
from 7 to 9 p.m. Monday and Tuesday at the theater at 211
W. Sycamore St. Folger is looking for 16 actors who will
play opposite film star Christina Ricci in the season's
opener.

Local residents wishing to audition for the major roles
must prepare a song and a part to read, said Folger. Each
audition is not to exceed five minutes.

People interested in being in a 30-member chorus need
prepare only a song not to exceed three minutes. They will
audition with the music director, Carole Banner.

People will be notified by Friday if they have been
chosen, Folger said, and rehearsals will begin next
week.

For the second-day story, you opted to put controversy in the lead. The
second graph gives readers background on how the controversy occurred.
The lead notes conflict, so readers expect to read comments from both sides,
which you include. In graphs 3 through 8 come the quotes from Tyson, Fellows, and even Folger that balance the story. Readers interested in auditioning will continue to read the message to find out information about the
auditions, which are mentioned in the lead. The specific times are included
in graph 9, and audition information is in graphs 10 and 11.

Again as the writer, you followed the inverted pyramid style of writing,
ranking the material in a way that is important to your audience. You set
up the lead about auditions and controversy. The need for answers to the
controversy will come first, followed by information on the auditions—
information that has been reported.

When Jessie Arbogast, age 8, of Ocean Springs, Miss., was attacked by a
200-pound shark, the story resulted in many days' coverage: the day of the
attack, the bravery of his uncle who killed the shark and pulled the boy's arm

out, surgery on that arm, concern about liver failure, and the doctors' belief that he had not suffered brain damage. The story also attracted attention because of its oddity and the seriousness.

While doctors monitored Jessie's progress, so did the local press. The *Pensacola Journal-News* ran a daily Jessie Arbogast update on its Web site, pensacolanewsjournal.com.

Getting There

Communicators first must be able to master the traditional before they can be avant-garde. Mastering the inverted pyramid style of writing gives any student journalist or communicator the basic plan for writing messages that focus on what is important and emotionally compelling for the audience. The style organizes information so that it is accessible, appealing, simply stated, and easy to understand.

On the practical level, mastering the inverted pyramid style also means throwing out the clutter that plagues most beginning writers. It means writing and rewriting and cutting unnecessary words to make the message cleaner and clearer.

Many writers abhor such admonitions to cut and tighten. They wonder how their writing will have any style or be differentiated from anyone else's. For routine assignments, it won't. But details and quotes, such as those in the article about the Rockland Community Theater's upcoming season, can be added to make messages more appealing—as long as the message still remains uncluttered.

News Peg and Nut Graph

Newspaper reporters talk about the *news peg* when developing stories. The peg, just like a peg on the wall where you hang a coat, is what a writer hangs the story on. It is the reason for writing the message. In our Rockland theater examples, the news peg in the first-day story is the auditions; in the second-day story, it is the residents' concern and hope for a smooth season.

Every piece of writing—whether it appears in print, is aired, or is shared—has a news peg. Writers, no matter what their skill or medium, have a reason for composing a message. That reason is spelled out in the *nut graph:*

the paragraph that defines the point the writer is making. The rest of the message expands and clarifies the singular idea in the nut graph.

The nut graph should be in the first four to five paragraphs, and sometimes it is more than one paragraph. Writers who put the nut graph any lower risk losing audiences who want to know the point of the message quickly. In some cases, the lead serves as the nut graph, particularly if it is a summary lead. Audiences who get a summary up front know why the story was written. When writers use anecdotal or descriptive leads, as described in Chapter 4, they must summarize and focus the message for audiences after drawing them in. In longer pieces, such as those described in the following section on other organizational styles, the nut graph becomes more crucial.

A story may have a descriptive lead, but it still needs the nut graph within the first few paragraphs. Look for the nut graph in this lead from the *Baltimore Sun*:

GRAND CANYON, Ariz.—Number 33 made a wide, sweeping turn and gently glided to a stop by a juniper on the sun-baked talus cliff, immediately drawing a crowd of excited spectators.

She had velvet black feathers, piercing ruby-red eyes, a pink bare head—and breath powerful enough to stop a freight train.

But beauty is in the eye of the beholder and these visitors to Bright Angel Lodge in the national park were entranced by the close sight of one of the world's rarest birds—a California condor.

Fourteen years ago, there were none in the wild and only a couple of dozen condors carefully nurtured by zoo curators. Through a costly and disputed captive-breeding program, nearly 60 of the broad-winged creatures—one of the world's largest flying birds—now soar through the skies of Arizona and California. Another 120 or so are being raised in captivity in California and Idaho as a very endangered species.

With its white-splashed black wings spanning nearly 10 feet, the California condor easily rides the uplifting thermals of the desert canyon, soaring as far as 150 miles in a day and as fast as 55 mph.

It is a sight that cheers the millions of people who come to the Grand Canyon each year and the wildlife officials who battled to pluck these giant vultures from their last natural habitat for captive breeding to save them from certain extinction.

Since 1982, more than $30 million in public and private funds has been spent to bring back the condor. The ultimate success is still uncertain, as these young, captive-bred birds attempt to resettle their ancient territories and produce wild-bred offspring.★

After a descriptive lead, the nut graph comes in graph 3, where readers learn about the program responsible for releasing almost five dozen condors into the wild. More information to support the nut graph comes in graph 6. Remember the stem cell research affective lead example in Chapter 3? Warren King's story is repeated here. Note where he puts the nut graph:

> She reads voraciously. She adores animals, especially her cat Oreo. She plays, swims and laughs with her sister, Sydney, and a happy gaggle of friends. Yet five years ago, Savannah Jantsch's parents feared she would not last more than a few months.
>
> Struggling with leukemia and a rare blood disorder, Savannah became one of the early recipients of stem cells from the umbilical-cord blood of a newborn. Infused in her body, the cells soon built an entirely new blood-cell system for the Bellingham girl, now a bright-eyed 9-year-old.
>
> "It's a resource that has given our daughter a whole new life," her father, Jeff Jantsch, said last week. "It's like she's been two different people with different lifestyles and a different existence."
>
> Savannah Jantsch is living proof of the healing power of stem cells, one of the basic building blocks of human tissue and the focus of so many headlines in recent weeks.
>
> Eleven days ago, President Bush announced support for limited funding of research on embryonic stem cells, bridging a controversy over the ethics of tampering with the earliest stage of human development, the embryo. In an attempt to balance scientific progress with sometimes competing moral values, he approved federal funding only for research on cells already taken from embryos; no new embryos could be destroyed.†

The nut graph in the Warren King story comes in graph 5 in the discussion about President Bush's support of limited funding of research on embryonic stem cells.

★By Michael K. Burns, *The Baltimore Sun*. Used by permission.

†Copyright August 20, 2001 Seattle Times Company. Used with permission.

Find the nut graph and news peg in the following story from *Newsday.*

This Tragedy Could Have Been Avoided

BY BOB GLAUBER

Newsday, Inc.

There were many warning signs in the last 48 hours of Korey Stringer's life. On Monday, the Minnesota Vikings' 335-pound offensive tackle sat out an afternoon workout after complaining of extreme fatigue.

On Tuesday, he returned to workouts held in 90-degree heat and continued practicing even after throwing up three times and summoning the team's training staff. By the time practice had ended, Stringer was showing other symptoms of heatstroke, such as fatigue and rapid breathing.

Within a matter of hours, Stringer was dead at age 27. His heart failed at 1:50 a.m. yesterday morning at Immanuel St. Joseph's Hospital near the team's training facility at Mankato (Minn.) State University. He is the first player in NFL history to die of heatstroke.

"We have lost a brother, teammate and friend," Vikings coach Dennis Green said during an emotional news conference yesterday morning.

"Korey meant so much for us because he always had that smile on his face. We are grieving. We are shocked," Vikings wide receiver Cris Carter said. "We knew it was critical. We knew the facts. We never thought he would die, but that wasn't the case here." Stringer is survived by his wife, Kelci, and a 3-year-old son, Kodie Drew. Funeral arrangements have not been made.

After completing Tuesday's morning practice session, Stringer walked to an air-conditioned shelter, where he complained of shortness of breath. Vikings trainers immediately attended to him, and an ambulance arrived within five minutes, according to team officials. When he got to the hospital, Stringer was unconscious and had a core body temperature of 108 degrees. Heatstroke is defined as a core body temperature in excess of 105 degrees.

Stringer gradually experienced multi-organ system failure throughout the day and night and was attended to by multiple medical specialists, yet never regained consciousness.

Stringer began having a problem with heat exhaustion during Monday morning's practice session, according to the team's head trainer, Chuck Barta. Stringer was treated for heat-related stress at the time, but was cleared to resume practice on Tuesday.

Neither Barta nor any Vikings medical personnel was available for comment yesterday about why Stringer was allowed to return to practice so quickly. Doctors were scheduled to speak at yesterday's news briefing, but no medical people attended. The team has not released any more details of Stringer's medical situation at the request of his family. A team official said yesterday afternoon that a medical update may be provided tomorrow.

NFL players routinely practice twice a day in extreme heat and humidity, but heatstroke is extremely rare, according to Giants trainer Ronnie Barnes.

"There's a fair amount of heat exhaustion, and that's why we're always taking precautions to give water, sports drinks, to replace fluids and electrolytes that are lost when players sweat," Barnes said. "Heat exhaustion is the first stage of a very deadly illness. But the fact is that 99 percent of the time, it's heat exhaustion, and replacement of fluids will help the problem. What's tragic is that you can go right from heat exhaustion to heatstroke very quickly."

The Jets team physician, Dr. Elliot Pellman, president of the NFL Physicians Society and a member of the NFL Safety and Rules Committee, said the sport's medical people are extremely sensitive to watching for signs of heat exhaustion or heatstroke.

"We take it very seriously," he said. "Despite the fact that the tragedy emphasizes the need for vigilance, we were already extremely vigilant." NFL commissioner Paul Tagliabue said the league's medical personnel have been sensitive to the issue of preventing heat-related problems, but indicated that the issue may need to be revisited.

"We will now ensure that our clubs again review their policies and procedures in this area," Tagliabue said.

Players and coaches around the league reacted in stunned disbelief at Stringer's death. Several teams held moments of silence in honor of Stringer. "We lost one of our own," said Baltimore Ravens coach Brian Billick, a former Vikings assistant. "And when I say one of our own, I mean one of the NFL family. Korey was one of God's gentle people. It's always a tragedy when you lose somebody young like that."

Jets head coach Herman Edwards gathered the team before yesterday morning's practice to tell them about Stringer's death.

"I brought the team out there to make them understand that you're not in control of your life. God is," Edwards said. "The NFL does a great job doing the best they can to prevent this from happening. When one of them happens, it's like an airplane going down. You never think it's going to happen."

In the Korey Stringer story, the third graph tells us he died—and that his death is the first in the NFL from heat stroke.

Other Organizational Styles

Although the inverted pyramid works for much writing, you may find other formats that are better for a particular message because of the event being reported. Some formats use the inverted pyramid format to introduce material, then move into another organizational pattern.

Chronological Format

In some cases, making the decision about how to organize a message is easy. Chronology—telling events in the same order in which they occurred—often can meet audience needs. A news story about a bank robbery, for example, would have a summary lead telling that the robbery occurred, where, and when. Then events would be revealed chronologically. The writer would organize the rest of the story by using time elements, as in the following article:

> A masked woman robbed the First Guaranty Savings and Loan on Main Street shortly after 9 a.m. today and escaped into a thickly wooded area nearby. Police have made no arrests.
>
> The robbery occurred when the woman entered the bank and approached a teller. She handed her a note asking for money and saying she had a gun in the sleeve of her sweatshirt.
>
> Although the teller did not actually see a gun, she gave the woman an undisclosed amount of cash. The woman put the money into a purple sack, ran from the Savings and Loan, and disappeared in the woods behind the bank's parking lot.
>
> At 6 p.m., police were still looking for the suspect, who was described as a white woman in her mid-20s. She weighs about 150 pounds and stands about 5 feet 6 inches. She has shoulder-length blonde hair. She wore a purple

```
sweatsuit and had pulled a stocking as a mask over her
face. Bank employees could not describe her facial
features.
```

Here, the lead, or the first paragraph, states *who* did *what where* and *when* and the latest information. Graph 2 shows how events unfolded. The last time element tells readers the status of the investigation at the newspaper's deadline.

While some messages can be developed chronologically, organization generally is not that simple. Not all messages involve action that evolves over time. For example, a high school principal writing in the school newsletter cannot use chronology to inform teachers about changes in ordering classroom supplies. Although teachers may be interested in the events that led up to the changes, they want to know the specific changes immediately. That is when another format, such as inverted pyramid, is needed.

Hourglass Format

Some writers have adapted chronological development to longer stories in what they call the *hourglass format* of writing. A summary lead followed by the inverted pyramid style gives readers the most important information in four to six paragraphs, allowing them to stop at the end of the inverted pyramid segment. Then the writer sets up more information with a simple statement by a source, such as: "Maynard described the events this way."

Beyond the transition statement, the message unfolds chronologically. Writers can use the style for many kinds of stories, such as telling of the search for a lost child, recounting a day in the life of a popular singer, or bringing out the details of a baseball game. Many stories on the disappearance of Washington intern Chandra Levy appeared in 2001. Writers used the inverted pyramid format up front, updating the story, then developed the message chronologically, using the hourglass format with details of her disappearance.

Electronic media writers often use the hourglass format. For example, a local television station aired a story about a crime that police had been unable to solve. After noting the latest information, the reporter said, "Here's how police have recreated the sequence of events." The details that followed were a chronological account of the crime. The story ended with the reporter showing the local telephone number for Crimestoppers.

Mapped Format

Assistant Professor Jacqueline Farnan and newspaper copyeditor David Hedley discussed another variation on the inverted pyramid style called the *mapped format*. They noted that the inverted pyramid becomes confusing for longer pieces, but they believed it serves as a way to introduce the most important elements of the message.

Mapped format is a technique to indicate points of interest within the message, just as a map includes highlights for its readers. The mapped format benefits topics that are of mild interest to readers, such as business and government. It also aids readers in finding information that is of particular interest to them in longer stories.

A mapped message is organized into sections. The first is the inverted pyramid lead. Subheads in a subject–verb–object sentence help readers, especially those who just scan stories, define categories of information. Readers can quickly find the segments of information that most benefit or appeal to them.

The mapped format can also help the writer organize. Let us assume you are writing a story on the cost of funerals and the alternatives to traditional burial. Your research finds categories of information: reasons why funerals are expensive, caskets and their costs, funeral home expenses, cost of burial plots, cost of cremation versus burial, memorial services, and how to cut costs. After drafting the lead, you can group categories of information under subheads, which help organize the story and readily identify parts of the story for readers.

Martin Merzer and Elinor Brecher of the *Miami Herald* were among many reporters who covered the terrorist attacks on the United States on September 11, 2001. You may remember the lead from their September 12 story shown in Chapter 4. They used a mapped format of subheads to guide readers through that initial story.

> In a catastrophic, full-scale terrorist attack on the United States, hijackers seized two American Airlines jetliners this morning, crashed them into New York City's World Trade Center and leveled both 110-story towers. Thousands were feared dead.
>
> Two United Airlines planes also crashed this morning, one in Pennsylvania, the other in a still-undisclosed location. A plane slammed into the Pentagon, collapsing one side of the five-sided structure. An explosion rocked the State Department in Washington.

The White House and the Capitol were evacuated. Military troops were deployed. Authorities sealed the borders with Mexico and Canada.

President Bush and all top national officials were reported safe this afternoon. In Florida at the beginning of the day, Bush left hastily and his plane landed at a secure military base in Louisiana.

"We will hunt down and punish those responsible for this cowardly act," he said in a 1:10 p.m. address. "We will do whatever is necessary to protect the American people."

"We Are at War"

Said Rep. Curt Weldon, R-Pa.: "We are at war, we are actually at war. This is a 21st Century war."

The American Airlines planes carried a total of 156 people and the United Airlines planes carried a total of 110 passengers, according to airline officials.

The toll of dead and injured were certain to rise—steeply.

"I have a sense it's a horrendous number of lives lost," said New York Mayor Rudolph Guiliani.

American Airlines identified the planes that crashed into the Trade Center as Flight 11, a Los Angeles-bound jet hijacked after takeoff from Boston with 92 people aboard, and Flight 77, which was seized while carrying 64 people from Washington to Los Angeles.

In Pennsylvania, United Airlines Flight 93, a Boeing 757 en route from Newark, N.J., to San Francisco, crashed about 80 miles southeast of Pittsburgh with 45 people aboard. United said another of its planes, Flight 175, a Boeing 767 bound from Boston to Los Angeles with 65 people on board, also crashed, but it did not say where.

Air Travel Shut Down

Military units—including an infantry regiment in Washington— were deployed. All air travel throughout the nation ceased and near chaos reigned at airports in Miami and Fort Lauderdale. Trading on Wall Street was suspended. The United Nations was evacuated.★

The rest of the story carries subheads that show people's emotions or describe the events: Show Strength, Massive Clouds, Can We Pray?, Second

★Reprinted with permission.

Pearl Harbor, and Bodies Falling. Readers can skim the story to the points that interest them.

Newspapers are not the only medium to use mapped formats. CNN News Online uses subheads in its full stories to break up text and to assist readers in finding information.

Numerical Format

A writer may organize a message numerically or by points. For example, a city council votes on three issues: water and sewer rates, a rezoning application, and the town manager's contract. The writer would list in the multiple-element lead the actions taken and the votes, thereby setting up the three points to be expanded, in that order, in the body of the story.

Writers covering a speech will often use a numeral or point-by-point format that follows the organizational structure of the speech. For example, a speaker discusses three major risk factors in heart disease. The writer notes the three risk factors in the lead: smoking, lack of exercise, and lack of a well-balanced diet. The points serve as transitions from the lead to the sections of the message. The reporter's story might read:

Cardiovascular disease is the No. 1 cause of death in the United States, but it can be reduced with lifestyle changes such as no smoking, regular exercise, and a well-balanced diet, the chairman of the American Heart Association's Wayne County chapter said Tuesday.

Gus Rivas said Americans should pay attention to the risk factors at an early age and get children to be aware of healthy lifestyles.

More than 3,000 children smoke their first cigarette every day. This number will translate into more adults who are at risk for cardiovascular disease.

"Children consume more than 947 million packs of cigarettes in this country," Rivas said. "More than 25 percent of high school students who smoke tried their first cigarette while in the sixth grade."

> Youngsters need to exercise, he noted. Studies show
> that today's youth do not get enough regular exercise.
>
> "Riding a bike, walking, even doing household chores
> can establish fitness patterns," Rivas said.
>
> A well-balanced diet low in fat is essential to reduce
> the risk of heart disease, Rivas said. About one out of
> four children is obese, and obese children are at a risk
> for obesity as adults.

The writer followed the lead, using the three points or risk factors as a way to organize and unify the story.

Brights

All short articles are not news. Some news stories can be written so that they become a *bright*—that is, a short news-feature no more than five paragraphs long and with a twist at the end. Consider the following bright that resulted from a routine police report of a missing man:

> PHOENIX—Tammy Plumb called police when her husband didn't return from a one-day hunting trip. Four days later, Jesse Plumb was found by an army of searchers—unharmed, but feeling sheepish about a tryst with another woman.
>
> Plumb might be billed $13,000 for the mountain search, which involved a helicopter, dogs and more than 40 deputies, sheriff's Sgt. John Kleinheinz said.
>
> Tammy Plumb has moved out.

Unifying Writing

Any story, memo, news release, or online message needs unity to be a coherent and complete piece. Each paragraph in a written piece must follow the preceding paragraph logically and build on previous information. Each section of the piece must fit the subject or theme. Unifying writing takes careful thought and planning, and it requires rewriting or reorganizing after a draft is done.

Transitions and repetition of certain words are ways to unify writing and to get readers from the beginning to the end. The first two or three paragraphs set up many of the unifying elements—for example, people, places, things, controversy, or chronology.

Repetition of Words

Some writers are uncomfortable repeating words in their writing. They pore over the thesaurus or dictionary, looking for synonyms that may not be as good as the word itself repeated. Repetition is okay; it offers unity in a message and gives readers familiarity. Repetition is also clearer; readers are not stopping to match synonyms and words.

The topic will determine the words repeated. A memo that covers changes in employee benefits should use the word "employee" throughout rather than switching from "worker" to "staff" to "professional." The same applies in writing about an organization; "organization" or the organization's name can be used throughout rather than "group," "agency," or "company."

Transitions

Transitions are cues for readers. They set up changes in location, time, and mood, and they keep readers from getting lost or confused.

A simple sentence or word may be needed as a logical bridge from one section of the message to the next. Any transition should wrap up the previous thought and introduce the next one.

> "We must continue our efforts to reduce teenage pregnancy, and our programs are aimed to do that," the governor said.
> While the governor defended his policies, others in state government cited lack of action on welfare issues for his dwindling popularity.

The second sentence indicates a shift from the governor's words to those of state government officials.

Most writers are accustomed to simple words or phrases as transitions. Look at some of the following words and phrases that give readers certain information about where a story is going:

A change in opinion: but, on the other hand, however

Clarification: in other words, for example, that is, to illustrate, to demonstrate, specifically, to clarify

Comparison: also, in comparison, like, similarly, on the same note, a related point

Contrast: but, in contrast, despite, on the contrary, unlike, yet, however, instead of

Expanded information: in addition, an additional, moreover, in other action, another, further, furthermore, too, as well as, also

A change in place: above, higher, beneath, nearby beside, between, across, after, around, below

Time: while, meanwhile, past, afterward, during, soon, next, subsequently, until then, future, before, at the same time

Look at how a few transitions work. In developing a story chronologically, time serves as a transition. Refer to the First Guaranty bank robbery story earlier in this chapter. The time elements pull the reader from shortly after 9 A.M., when the robbery occurred, until 6 P.M., when the woman still had not been caught. In other stories, time-oriented words and phrases could be "at the same time," "later that day," "Tuesday," and "last week."

A story about voter reaction on election day uses polling sites around town as geographic transitions: "Voters at Precinct 35 (Town Hall) said…," "Those voting at Precinct 15 (Main Street Presbyterian Church) said…," "Precinct 2 voters (Blackwell Elementary School) said…." Other geographical phrases would be "on the other side of town," "at his father's 25-acre farm," "next door," and "at the White House."

Tone to Unify a Message

Knowing audiences will help the writer determine what tone to set in organizing and writing a message. The tone or mood of a story can act as a unifying device. A PTA newsletter editor knows that her audience is busy, fast-moving, and distracted by children, work, day-to-day routine, and a deluge of media bits. She knows her audience is in need of quick information about kids and school. She must write lively copy with short, pithy sentences and paragraphs. Active parents need newsletter copy that looks like this:

```
Spring cleaning may leave you with trash and treasures.
Please donate them to Southview School's Trash and Treasure
sale! This year's sale is planned for May 9.
```

> Doris Tucker will begin receiving donations April 26
> at her home, 322 Dale Drive. For more information, call
> 499-2342.

In contrast, a newsletter for adults 50 years and older requires a more serious, thoughtful tone as well as some humor and nostalgia amid careful, complete news updates and obituaries of members. An article might begin in a personal way:

> On November 12, Seniors Together lost one of our great
> members and friends, Gladys McKenzie, who gave endlessly of
> her time to us and our organization. We share in the grief
> of her family but feel blessed that we had the chance to
> know Gladys.
>
> Gladys became such a part of our volunteers and
> outreach to our members who were homebound. She joined the
> organization eight years ago and always had a smile and
> willingness to put in the extra time where needed.

A writer's knowledge of audiences will determine the mood or tone that will best maintain interest and retain it throughout the message.

Quotations to Unify Stories

Quotations can be effective transitions throughout writing. They add liveliness and an emotional element, allow people to speak directly to readers and listeners, and help them feel more connected to personalities and events. They can supplement facts and add detail. News stories and news releases should have a good balance between direct and indirect quotes. Information on direct and indirect quotes, attribution, and punctuation of quotes is given in Chapter 9.

Look back to Chapter 3 and Nahal Toosi's quotes. She allows readers to get inside fans' heads through the quotes that she uses: "It's fun; it's stress-relieving," Segerson said. "You can scream at the top of your lungs!"

Quotations can refer to the lead and wrap up a piece, they can leave the reader looking to the future, or they can add a touch of humor. But sometimes writers have to be careful in using a quote at the end. If the story is cut from the bottom, readers should miss only a chuckle, not important information.

Unifying Devices in Practice

Let's go back and look at the second-day newspaper story on the Rockland Community Theater. What are the unifying devices? First, see what the lead set up.

—When Rockland Community Theater Director Neal Folger starts auditions for "West Side Story" starring Christina Ricci, most board of directors members will be crossing their fingers for a smooth year.

Broadly, the lead hints at a controversy and lets readers know that board members will be quoted. Words that are established for repetition are "theater," "board," "directors," "year," "Folger," "audition," "director," and "season."

The board hired Folger, the former director of the River Road Theater in Danville, a year ago, and soon the theater was embroiled in controversy. Last year's season opener of "Grease" showed nudity when three performers dropped their pants as part of a song on mooning. This year's season opens Oct. 15.

The second paragraph spells out a controversy and describes what occurred. Words repeated for unity are "board," "Folger," "director," "theater," and "season." We are also given a time element: last year and this year.

"We felt we went through a wringer right off the bat last year," Board Member Mary Tyson said today. "Although some people like Neal's productions, most people in our community prefer more traditional entertainment. Nudity just has no place on our stage."

Graph 3 uses a quotation from a board member. Readers expect to hear from at least one. The quote gives board members' feelings and why the nudity was a problem. Repeated are the themes of last year's controversy, nudity, and the director.

Board Member Justin Fellows said the board hoped for a successful season with less turmoil than the previous year.

Graph 4 introduces another speaker and reiterates last year's controversy and the upcoming season.

"We think Neal is quite talented, but we are just a community theater, and we want fun, not indignation," he said.

Graph 5 gives readers more information about the director and repeats the idea of a community that disapproves of nudity on stage.

Folger said he was surprised at the reaction to "Grease."

Graph 6 is a complete sentence and a new graph, which lets readers know that a change in speakers has occurred, and a defense is coming. It continues the unity through the words "Folger" and "Grease."

"I certainly learned what this community will accept on stage," he said. "We intend to produce shows that keep people fairly well covered."

Graph 7 repeats "community" and begins the transition from last season to the current season's offerings.

Fellows added the board hoped Folger's appealing season lineup will attract a substantial audience to the Rockland Theater.

The Fellows quote in graph 8 completes the transition from last year to the current year. It also repeats the words "Fellows," "board," "Folger," "season," and "theater."

The director will have auditions for "West Side Story" from 7 to 9 p.m. Monday and Tuesday at the theater at 211 W. Sycamore St. Folger is looking for 16 actors who will play opposite film star Christina Ricci in the season's opener.

Graph 9 introduces the new information about the auditions. Again, the familiar words are there: "director," "audition," "theater," "Folger," and "season."

Local residents wishing to audition for the major roles must prepare a song and a part to read, said Folger. Each audition is not to exceed five minutes.

People interested in being in a 30-member chorus need prepare only a song not to exceed three minutes. They will audition with the music director, Carole Banner.

People will be notified by Friday if they have been chosen, Folger said, and rehearsals will begin next week.

Graphs 10, 11, and 12 are complete ideas about different aspects of the auditions. Graph 10 begins with information about the major roles, whereas graph 11 is about the lesser parts. Each uses words such as "audition," "Folger," "director," and "song" as unity. The last graph wraps up the story with an indirect quote that looks to the future.

News versus Feature

Students may wonder where the feature story fits in the discussion of print formats. Most articles printed today are news-features or features. Traditionally, writers have used one value to distinguish news from features: timeliness. Features have a timeless quality. They can be published any time and remain useful and entertaining. News, however, must be printed immediately. The death of a nationally known fashion designer is news; a story about fashions is a feature. In sum, news tells, a feature shows.

To the traditional distinction of timeliness writers must add another consideration: How much did the reader see? In other words, did the story take the reader to the scene? Did the writer make the reader feel that he or she was there? It has been said that journalism becomes literature when it tells the reader not just what happened but what it was like. Erik Lawson writes in *Isaac's Storm*, his book on the hurricane that struck Galveston in 1900:

```
The wind neatly sliced off the top floor of a bank,
leaving the rest of the building intact. It stripped slate
shingles from houses and turned them into scimitars that
disemboweled men where they stood. Atmospheric pressure
fell so low, a visiting British cotton official was sucked
```

```
from his apartment trailing a slipstream of screams from
his wife.
```

More than 100 years later, feature writing must still carry the visual impact. Because electronic media more and more have assumed the role of breaking news, newspapers and magazines have taken on a visual aspect seen in more description, analogies and metaphors, and explanation or analysis. The feature story's job is to flesh out the headline on television or radio and to provide the substance and follow-up—even with a news story of the magnitude of the Oklahoma City bombing. The *New York Times* page-one story's second paragraph described the sound and force of the explosion for readers this way: "It was like a battleship's battery of 16-inch guns opening fire."

At the heart of today's feature writing is what Gene Roberts, retired executive editor of the *Philadelphia Inquirer* and managing editor of the *New York Times,* expected of his writers. His expectations are aptly described in the text for the Eugene L. Roberts Prize awarded to qualifying students at the School of Journalism and Mass Communication at the University of North Carolina at Chapel Hill:

> The Eugene L. Roberts Prize is meant to encourage and is dedicated to the story of the untold event that oozes instead of breaks; to the story that reveals, not repeats; to the reporter who zigs instead of zags; to the truth as opposed to the facts; to the forest, not just the trees; to the story they'll be talking about in the coffee shop on Main Street; to the story that answers not just who, what, where, when and why, but also "So what?"; to efforts at portraying real life itself; to journalism that "wakes me up and makes me see"; to the revival of the disappearing storyteller.

Features today are stories—old-fashioned stories with a beginning, a middle, and an end. Unlike the inverted pyramid form that can be cut to fit space, working up from the end, the end of a feature story cannot be lopped off to accommodate space needs. The end is just as important as the beginning. A writer or editor cuts judiciously or "prunes the text" of a feature, if cuts are needed.

Writing the Feature

Writers use anecdotal and descriptive leads in feature stories before getting to the nut graph or the actual news. The example of the 911 operator in Chapter 3 shows how a feature approach can be adopted for a news story:

> NEW YORK—"You want the police to come to your house because your mother didn't come home?"
>
> It's nearly 7 p.m. on a Wednesday in the weeks before Christmas and somewhere in New York City, two scared young girls watch the clock, more frightened by the minute. They call 911 and reach Ivey Bruce.
>
> Her voice is soothing and steady. "OK, what apartment are you in? And what's the telephone number? And how old are you and your sister?"

The *Wall Street Journal* has utilized this approach to the point that it's often called the *Wall Street Journal* style. It takes the reader through the hard facts of the story—the background, analysis, and details that form the hard core of the story—but it focuses on an individual or a project or a family or, in the case of the following example, dogs:

> At a medical station bathed in flood-lights, four doctors prepared one of the emergency workers for the long day ahead. They taped his legs and fitted him with new boots. They offered him food and checked his eyes, because acrid smoke and dust would be clouding and burning them in the coming hours.
>
> But mostly, they kissed his snout, rubbed his belly and said things like, "What a good boy, Porkchop!"
>
> For a week, Porkchop, a one-year-old Australian shepherd with a blond coat and highlights, has been combing the steel knots of debris that were once part of the World Trade Center. In his time off, he cracks acorns, eats ants and watches the Animal Planet cable channel.

> In the past few days, he has been searching for signs of
> life and death among the ruins. He hasn't found survivors.
> But Porkchop has discovered so many human remains that his
> handler, Erick Robertson of Oakhurst, Calif., says he has
> lost count.

Now, we see the nut graph, as discussed earlier in the chapter:

> In what is believed to be the largest canine deployment
> ever, an estimated 350 specialty dogs are at the World
> Trade Center. Even cat people admire them. With names
> like Dutch, Tuff, Bigfoot, Sally, Max and Cowboy, they work
> 12-hour shifts tunneling through voids and teetering on
> unstable rubble to pick up the slightest whiff of life
> and death.

Other canine workers are introduced, such as "deep-chested Dober-man pinscher, Metrodobe Spicey's Sunny Boy, aka Sunny." Readers learn how the dogs are trained through "macabre products, such as 'Pseudo Corpse,' which mimic the smell of decomposed flesh." The reporter notes how the work affects the dogs through stress colitis and dust from tunneling through debris and describes the vets who work to keep the dogs in good health.

Then, the story comes full circle:

> After a bath rid him of the dust and grease on his head,
> Thunder headed for the rest area uptown, while Porkchop, in
> his orange booties, headed for the pile. The fur on their
> hocks swayed behind them as they trotted away. A vet shook
> her head and said, "Such good dogs."

Beyond the reporting the writer did for this story, he observed closely, listened well, and used details effectively.

How the writer elects to tell the story is also important. In the *Wall Street Journal* example, the writer used the dogs to tell one aspect of the search and recovery operations after the World Trade Center bombings in September 2001. The complete story is shown here.

Porkchop Is Among Hero Dogs Combing Trade Center Rubble

Trained to Sniff Out the Living and the Dead, Hundreds Gladly Work 12-Hour Shifts

BY JARED SANDBERG

Staff Reporter of the Wall Street Journal

At a medical station bathed in flood-lights, four doctors prepared one of the emergency workers for the long day ahead. They taped his legs and fitted him with new boots. They offered him food and checked his eyes, because acrid smoke and dust would be clouding and burning them in the coming hours.

But mostly, they kissed his snout, rubbed his belly and said things like, "What a good boy, Porkchop!"

For a week, Porkchop, a one-year-old Australian shepherd with a blond coat and highlights, has been combing the steel knots of debris that were once part of the World Trade Center. In his time off, he cracks acorns, eats ants and watches the Animal Planet cable channel.

In the past few days, he has been searching for signs of life and death among the ruins. He hasn't found survivors. But Porkchop has discovered so many human remains that his handler, Erick Robertson of Oakhurst, Calif., says he has lost count.

In what is believed to be the largest canine deployment ever, an estimated 350 specialty dogs are at the World Trade Center. Even cat people admire them. With names like Dutch, Tuff, Bigfoot, Sally, Max and Cowboy, they work 12-hour shifts tunneling through voids and teetering on unstable rubble to pick up the slightest whiff of life and death.

"If people are going to be found alive, the dogs are the ones to find them," says Barry Kellogg, who runs the Veterinary Medical Assistance Team, a part of the U.S. Public Health Service that treats animals in disasters.

Now that the effort is more recovery than rescue, the cadaver dogs, from as far as Europe, play a critical role in giving answers to the thousands of families of the missing. Families visiting the site seem to know that and produce pictures with hopes that handlers have seen the victims. To date, Porkchop has identified remains along with wallets and purses that have led to the identification of four people.

"Our primary mission is to get people out," says Michael Kidd, a 36-year-old member of Miami-Dade Fire Rescue, whose German Shepherd, Mizu, has gone on missions as far away as Turkey. "But what's important here is a sense of closure for the families."

Cadaver dogs get years of training with their handlers, who are typically members of fire departments or are emergency medical technicians. They must be unflustered in the face of screaming people and earth-moving equipment and physically capable of moving through confined spaces and even climbing ladders. Though many police department K-9 units have visited the site, the local urban search-and-rescue teams tend to have the most rigorously trained dogs, some of which meet standards of performance set by the Federal Emergency Management Agency.

They must learn new tricks that oppose their instincts. When a dog runs, it digs its claws into the ground. When the surface moves, a dog tends to jump off. But cadaver dogs learn to keep their feet spread without disturbing anything in their path. That's why many don't use the flood of dog booties donated to the site.

They learn to crouch, lowering their center of gravity, when rubble shifts beneath them, says Shirley Hammond, a 67-year-old canine search specialist from Palo Alto, Calif. Her deep-chested Doberman pinscher, Metrodobe Spicey's Sunny Boy, a k a Sunny, nudges her gesturing hand with his snout in search of stroking.

How do you teach a dog to find human remains? There are macabre products, such as "Pseudo Corpse," which mimic the smell of decomposed flesh. Other handlers use bodies and placentas donated to science. With a sense of smell thousands of times more sensitive than a human being's, dogs can pick up scents through concrete.

At the World Trade Center, the dogs work in teams in different sectors of the rubble. Structural engineers investigate areas to determine whether they can safely be explored. Hazardous-materials specialists, known as "Hazmat," look for pockets of jet fuel, diesel fuel, Freon and toner—to name a few. Then come the hounds. When they find remains, some will bark. Others are trained to lie down. Rescue specialists move in to seek out what the dogs have located.

To counter the cut pads, exposure to chemicals and dehydration, the public health service has deployed the Veterinary Assistance Medical Team, or VMAT. Working 12-hour shifts, those men and women and volunteer veterinarians staff a medical station in the middle of West Street, near Chambers Street, a few blocks north of the Trade Center ruins.

A 50-foot tent has a table of syringes, stations for ear cleaning and eye cleaning, cabinets of gauze and bandages, bags of intravenous solutions hanging from posts, Musher's Secret paw protection and enough toys, bones and biscuits to stock a pet shop. A sign hanging inside reads, "Emergency Horns. 1 Horn = Silence. 3 Blasts = Evacuate."

Last Saturday night was quiet. As vets changed shifts at 11 p.m., no dog showed up for hours. Then Cara, a two-year-old Beauceron herding dog, arrived. She had just tunneled through a 40-foot space with a camera strapped to her. Her handler wanted her nails filed and salve for her eyes. Vets checked her and found her to be dehydrated and recommended that she get fluids when she got off her shift. She returned to "the pile" in a small vehicle 10 minutes later.

For the next three hours, only volunteers pushing shopping carts strolled by, offering up food, flags and Dr. Scholl's shoe inserts. Every few minutes, huge twisted beams glided by on flatbed trucks. A few minutes after 2 a.m., an ambulance with a massive police escort including motorcycles headed north with the remains of a police officer. Two more elaborate escorts made the same trip, one at 3:25 a.m. and another three hours and 10 minutes later.

At 5:01, the next patient rolled in—a German Shepherd working as a patrol dog for the New York City Police Department. Dwyer, his ears pointing behind him, was suffering from diarrhea and was still skittish from being nipped on the rump by another dog. Mitch Biederman, a volunteer vet, said Dwyer suffered from stress colitis. Another vet gave him a physical and dispensed an antibiotic.

At 6 o'clock, a shift change took place, and with the Con Edison and Verizon telephone workers streaming northward, the dogs arrived. First was Kinsey, a black Labrador retriever who wagged her body more than her tail. The vet took her temperature and cleaned her up. She grabbed a braided chew toy as her handler noted that there is the scent of decaying flesh "everywhere. It's overwhelming."

Cholo, a German Shepherd, came in next. Like most of the specialty dogs, he is part of an urban search-and-rescue crew, this one from Texas. But he searches for survivors, not cadavers. And he didn't find anybody on his shift, said Bert Withers, the search manager. To avoid depressing the dogs after a disappointing day, some handlers will hide and let their dogs find them. The only thing upsetting Cholo now was the shower he was about to get—from a hose and bucket hooked up to a make-shift tripod. From the look in his eyes, a bath was a betrayal.

Last on the scene was Thunder, a six-year-old golden retriever who is part of the Puget Sound, Wash., Urban Search and Rescue. Thunder, too, got a medical exam. He has been tunneling in through the rubble. "He's stressed out that he can't be on the pile more," says his handler, Kent Olson.

After a bath rid him of the dust and grease on his head, Thunder headed for the rest area uptown, while Porkchop, in his orange booties, headed for the pile. The fur on their hocks swayed behind them as they trotted away. A vet shook her head and said, "Such good dogs."

Reprinted by permission.

Writers are often looking for a fresh way to portray a subject that is covered time and time again. At the retirement of a living-legend baseball star, a writer assigned to the story with a horde of other reporters noticed the star's wife standing several feet behind him, and to the side. The writer told the story through her reaction to the tributes being offered to her husband and his farewell words. At a routine story of children going off to camp, a writer noticed that one child's parents had a hard time saying goodbye; they'd kiss the child, send him off toward the bus, then call him back...again...and again...and again. The writer told the story through that family.

Students will find that they use news and feature formats in whatever career they choose in print journalism. Newspaper reporters, magazine writers, freelance writers, newsletter editors, novelists, columnists, and others rely on the organizational styles discussed here to produce messages.

Writing formats change. Newspaper reporters, for example, have adopted more narrative styles of writing, using anecdotal and descriptive approaches. Some editors believe that style will attract more readers; others say the style will pass. Time will be the test of whether new formats attract and retain audiences.

But no matter what style or format they use, and whatever medium they work for, print journalists follow the same writing process outlined in Chapter 1. Some, such as magazine writers, have time to put their work aside before editing. Newspaper reporters who work under deadline pressure, however, find that they compress the stages. They may have little time for extensive rewriting and editing. Those tasks may fall to others in the newsroom, such as metro editors and copy editors, with whom writers share their work. In any case, the written piece proceeds through those stages before it is published for audiences.

Moving on with Writing

Throughout the text, the need for good writing skills will be stressed over and over. But basic skills aren't enough. All writers, regardless of which medium will publish their work, must be accurate in gathering and printing information. Editors at all levels can improve their copy, but no editor will know whether the information is correct. The reporter must accept the burden of accuracy. Failure to check and double-check facts can result in libel suits for newspapers and destroyed credibility for writers. Once a writer has ruined his or her reputation, it may be impossible to regain believability.

Writing is a series of choices—choice of language, pertinent facts, introductions, organizational pattern, tone, quotes, and topics—and all need to be made in an informed way, based on what writers know about their audiences.

Books and other writers can give you tips on how to organize your writing. The best way to learn is to apply the techniques through your own efforts. Do not let organization just happen. Remember the stages of writing. Make an outline. Consciously apply a certain organizational style to your writing. Let someone else read your piece to see whether it makes sense.

Good organization helps you reach your audience. Return to the Associated Press story on pages 72–73 in Chapter 3. The reporter uses all the strengths of simple writing, repetition for unity, and quotations as transitions to pull readers through an emotionally compelling story that could have been just another routine drug bust story. The following chapters will guide you further in knowing your audience and writing for it.

EXERCISES

1. You are a reporter for the *Rockland Chronicle*. You have picked up the following police report—written last night—from the Town Police

Department. Write a message with a summary lead, then develop the message in chronological order.

Report: Tony's Restaurant Robbery

Investigating Officer: Sgt. Rodney Carter

At 10 p.m. a robbery at Tony's Restaurant was reported. Owner Tony Hardy said that he was working late preparing the payroll when a man wearing a stocking mask entered the back door of the kitchen at about 8:40.

Hardy said that the man told him to go into the office and open up the safe. Hardy took almost $3,000 out of the safe and put it into a blue, waterproof sack.

The restaurant closes at 9 p.m. Hardy said he thought the robber knew he was there alone, but that he didn't think the robber was a Rockland resident.

Hardy said he got a good look at the man: a stocky white man, about 5'6", and round-faced. He estimated the man's age to be 24. Hardy said the man's shoulders were so broad that he might have been a weight lifter. Hardy suggested that if the thief wanted to lock him up somewhere, the storage closet off the kitchen was as good a place as any. The thief agreed and locked him up there. The thief wrapped a clothes hanger around the door. He told Hardy he had a partner, and that Hardy wouldn't live to see his family and relatives if he came out of the closet before 15 minutes had passed.

Hardy said he waited the 15 minutes even though he didn't believe the story about the partner, or at least a partner who would be stupid enough to hang around for 15 minutes. He had no trouble getting out and then called the Rockland Police.

We have some leads on the suspect and the investigation is continuing.

2. From the following information, write a summary lead for the *Rockland Chronicle* that focuses on *who, what, when,* and *where* plus human interest. Then develop the message in hourglass format.

From the Rockland police chief, Ralph Robinson, you learn the following:

Two sisters were playing at a Laundromat about 5 p.m. yesterday. The girls are the daughters of Nancy and Phillip Childs of Rockland.

The girls were with their aunt, Janice Childs. The 3-year-old, Jennifer, climbed into one of the washing machines. Her sister, Elizabeth, 7, closed the door. The machine started filling up with water. When she realized the washer was running, Elizabeth ran to get her aunt. Ms. Childs tried to open the washer door but could not, because the washers are equipped with automatic locks on the doors.

Robinson said the girl was trapped in the washer for more than five minutes before she was rescued. He said a customer had put coins into the machine before the little girl crawled inside, but the customer hadn't used the machine because he thought it wasn't working.

On the telephone you talk to Paul Hecker of 601 Arbor Drive in Rockland. He was on his way home from work and stopped at the Glen Rock Shopping Center to buy groceries. He heard screams coming from the Glen Rock Laundry and Dry Cleaner. He ran inside the Laundromat to see what was going on. Ms. Childs ran up to him and asked him to save the child. She asked if he had any tools, so he ran back to his toolbox in the back of his truck and got a hammer. Hecker said he took the hammer back inside and smashed the glass in the washing machine door. He then reached in and pulled her out.

A Rockland Hospital spokesperson said Jennifer was admitted yesterday afternoon and was listed in good condition. Her parents could not be reached for comment.

3. You are a reporter for the *Rockland Chronicle*. You are to write a story from the following information. Focus on a summary lead with a local angle. Organize the story in inverted pyramid.

A group of 55 cyclists from the United States arrived in Ho Chi Minh City in Vietnam yesterday. They ended a 1,200-mile course through Vietnam. The trip took them 20 days. The course was fairly grueling through some of the country's mountainous areas as well as flat parts. The group camped and stayed in villages along the way.

The U.S. Cycling Federation, which arranged the tour, said it planned to organize another event next year. Officials said the tours are a way to allow U.S. residents to get a close-up look at the country and their people.

When the group arrived it was greeted by firecrackers, flower necklaces, and cold towels. Bob Lester, 33, of Rockland, was one of the cyclists on the trip. He said, "This trip was the most amazing thing I have ever done in my life. I would recommend the experience to anyone who can pedal a bike." The cyclists are expected to return to the United States in two weeks.

The tour was part of an effort to open up Vietnam to outsiders and to present a different picture of the country than people had come to expect from the Vietnam War.

Among the cyclists were seven Vietnam veterans and three Vietnamese-Americans, all from the United States. The 55 cyclists were from 23 states.

Several of the Americans said the journey had erased any doubts they might have held about Vietnam and its people.

4. You are to write a story for the next issue of the *Rockland Chronicle*. Write a summary lead, then organize the story point by point. Your audience is Rockland residents.

LuAnne Neal, director of public affairs for the state Department of Commerce, tells you today that the state is launching a three-part train safety program. The state has had its share of train crossing accidents, one recently in Rockland County where a man was injured when his car was hit at a crossing. The worst accident occurred five year ago when an engineer was killed and more than 350 people injured when a trail derailed after hitting a truck near Rockland.

First, the state is asking that state highway crews work in cooperation with the Department of Commerce to inspect train crossings in the state. Engineers who ride the trains will spend the next month noting intersections that don't have lights or warning signals that possibly might need them. Highway workers can do the same in their jobs.

Second, the state is compiling statistics on the most dangerous railroad crossings in the state, that is, the ones with the most accidents. That way officials will know where to focus state and federal monies in improving the most dangerous crossings.

Third, a public education program will caution drivers on crossing railroad intersections. Too many times an accident was caused because a driver tried to beat the train to the intersection. That kind of action endangers not only the driver but everyone on the train, whether it is a passenger train or a freight train. The state will put flyers at drivers' license offices and in license renewal tag offices around the state. The flyers will be distributed to all students taking drivers education. Notices will be sent to all people who are renewing their automobile or truck license tags.

REFERENCES

Jacqueline Farnan and David Hedley, "The Mapped Format: A Variation on the Inverted-Pyramid Appeals to Readers." Paper presented at the Association for Education in Journalism and Mass Communication Conference, Atlanta, GA, August 1993.

Fred Fedler, *Reporting for the Print Media*. New York: Harcourt Brace Jovanovich, 1989.

"Newswriting for the Commercial Appeal," produced by Lionel Linder, editor, and Colleen Conant, managing editor, 1989.

William Zinsser, *On Writing Well*. New York: Harper & Row, 1976.

6

Recognizing Bias
and Stereotypes

Understanding bias means considering your own background as well as the backgrounds of others. Many people believe they can write about other people without allowing any personal bias to creep into their stories, news spots, or news releases. But few people can step outside personal bias because most people are unaware of how ingrained their beliefs and attitudes can be. All of us have biases or preconceived notions about others. Bias is not just overt, as racial prejudice or political beliefs are. It is subtle. And it comes from who you are.

Consider your background. Did you come from a suburban middle-class home where you attended a school with little ethnic diversity? Did you speak a language other than English at home? What is your family's ethnic or racial background? Did you grow up in an urban ethnic neighborhood— Italian, African American, or Laotian?

Did you live in a subsidized housing project, in an inner city, or in a small town of 5,000 people or fewer? Maybe you grew up on a farm or ranch and your nearest neighbor was a half mile away. Did you attend private or public schools?

What is your gender? Do you or does someone in your family have a physical or mental disability? What is your religion? What political party do you claim?

All these aspects of your background and many others built your attitudes and beliefs. As a communicator you must become aware of your attitudes and beliefs to curb the bias that is still evident in many stories produced by the mass media today—and the bias that keeps many stories from appearing.

Bias often surfaces in stereotypes that show up in adjectives or nouns used to describe certain groups. People form stereotypes from their perceptions of individuals' or groups' behavior and from their experiences and those of friends and relatives. Think about the label in the sentence "Jane is a typical college student who wants to have a good time and study as little as possible." As a student you would not want people to ignore your full array of attributes and view you only as a lazy, party-animal student. The generalization is not fair to you or most other students. As a writer you must learn to confront such stereotypes and avoid perpetuating negative overgeneralizations about groups.

In this chapter, we will discuss

- How writers can begin to recognize bias,
- How bias in writing affects specific individuals and groups, and
- Specific tips on how to avoid bias in writing about individuals and groups.

The Bias Habit

Journalists' cultural values can affect their ability to be truly fair. Because of the way the brain processes information, people must categorize and label people and events. Walter Lippmann referred to this phenomenon in 1922:

> *The real environment is altogether too big, too complex and too fleeting for direct acquaintance. We are not equipped to deal with so much subtlety, so much variety, so many permutations and combinations. And although we have to act in that environment, we have to reconstruct it on a simpler model before we can manage it.*

The adaptive process means that people do not see as many perspectives as possible, or they develop a view that does not fit reality. Most important, in this adaptive process, people will select the information that confirms their attitudes and beliefs, according to journalism researchers H. Stocking and P. Gross, who add that people may not even be aware that they process information with a cognitive bias. They do not have to make a conscious effort to be biased; in fact, they may be trying to be unbiased, as journalists do in attempting objectivity.

It is important to remember that bias surfaces in many arenas. Adjectives and nouns are ascribed to people because of where they live, their political beliefs, their sexual orientation, and their religion. Bias attributes certain characteristics to women, men, people with disabilities, children, older people, and members of ethnic and racial groups. Labels are dangerous. They are offensive and usually imply inferiority. They do not describe individuals, nor do they apply to groups. Writers who do not think perpetuate negative stereotypes and myths.

All stereotypes do not necessarily appear negative, however. For example, a majority-culture stereotype is exhibited in several kinds of traditionally American stories such as cowboy stories, soap operas, or musicals where the heroes are usually depicted as tall, broad-shouldered, white, and handsome and where women most frequently play minor roles.

Another example of a positive stereotype is the "model minority" in the Asian-American community, where people are depicted as geniuses in music, math, and science. That generalization, although it seems complimentary, is not true and affects the majority of Asian Americans who might not have aptitudes in any of these fields.

Bias in Writing

Groups such as journalists construct a shared view of "reality" because of the similarities in the way they view the world. Timothy Crouse in his book, *The Boys on the Bus,* explained the close working relationship among political reporters on the campaign trail:

> *It was just these womblike conditions that gave rise to the notorious phenomenon called "pack journalism" (also known as "herd journalism" and "fuselage journalism"). A group of reporters were assigned to follow a single candidate for weeks or months at a time, like a pack of hounds sicked on a fox. Trapped on the same bus or plane, they ate, drank, gambled, and compared notes with the same bunch of colleagues week after week.*

As early as 1950, one famous study showed how wire editors relied on their own values to select the news. David Manning White reported that "as 'gatekeeper' the newspaper editor sees to it (even though he may never be consciously aware of it) that the community shall hear as a fact only those events which the newsman, as representative of his culture, believes to be true."

Almost half a century after the civil rights movement became a force in the United States, inequities based on race and ethnic background persist. Mass media have both helped and hindered the effort for equal rights in this country. On the one hand, they give voice to various social movements and allow the message of equality to reach a mass audience. On the other hand, they perpetuate misinformation and ignore a myriad of other ethnic groups.

Although the complexion of management is changing, most people who run the mass media are of Western European descent, and a large majority are male. They have little context, therefore, to help them know what it is like to be an African American, Native American, Asian American, Hispanic American, or other person of color in the United States. (Only about 7 percent of journalists nationwide are from these groups.) Too often, stories about those communities are reported with an outsider's perspective, resulting in misinformation or stereotypes. In other cases, the stories may not be reported; the group may be invisible to the journalist.

The issue of race and the media—both how the media cover race and the racial makeup of newsrooms—surfaced in the 1968 Kerner Commission Report. The report was commissioned by the Johnson administration after the Los Angeles riots. As part of the report, the committee looked at media and race. Ten years later, another study, *Window Dressing on the Set: Women and Minorities in Television: A Report of the United States Commission on Civil Rights*, noted the token roles played by women and minorities in TV news and sitcoms. The two are considered classic cases that started media managers looking at racial issues and prompted news organizations, such as the American Society of Newspaper Editors, to launch diversity committees.

Consider some of these overt problems of bias in coverage:

- The *Time* magazine cover that shaded football star O. J. Simpson's face so that his complexion was darker, conveying a sinister countenance.
- The rush to believe that even Muslims who were U.S. citizens were affiliated with the radical fringe accused of the World Trade Center and Pentagon attacks.

- The belief that teens with green hair and black leather jackets are drug users.
- The use of black or Hispanic women as the subject of photos about welfare when the majority of welfare recipients are white, not Hispanic.

The California Commission on the Status of African American Males produced in 1997 a 200-page report, "African American Males: The Struggle for Equality." One chapter looked at media portrayals of African American men. One author reported that news media generally equate African American men with aggressiveness, lawlessness, and violence. The entertainment media then builds its portrayals from news accounts. The study pointed out a common stereotype that African American men use drugs in disproportionate numbers. A U.S. Justice Department–sponsored survey showed, however, that 10.6 percent of white respondents said they had used cocaine in their lifetime, whereas only 6 percent of African American respondents said they had used the drug.

Breaking the Bias Habit

Today, writers and reporters are trying, through better awareness, to overcome their own biases in addition to their own biases in addition to cultural bias implanted in the news. But old habits die hard. A first step is for writers to be aware of their own biases and how easily biases can slip into communication. Take religion as an example. Our religious beliefs may contain opinions about others that we should not include in our writing, even though we firmly believe them. Some writers may have Biblical or "sacred text" attitudes and opinions about homosexuals, Jews, gentiles, African Americans, and women. In other words, religion may teach us things about those who don't believe as we do.

Another important way to break the bias habit is to know your own biases. You can check yourself by taking the Implicit Association Test, a University of Washington and Yale University test that measures biases regarding race, age, gender, and ethnicity. You can find it online at http://buster.cs.yale.edu/implicit.

What's important in the real world is that communicators do not convey these preconceived notions in their communication, even if they believe them.

Writers also must not fall into the habit of ascribing tired adjectives to certain groups, as noted earlier in the chapter. Writers unconsciously tend to write on traditional stereotyped templates, such as "rural-urban," "black-white," "rich-poor/tale of two cities," "old-young," or "rags to riches/Cinderella." Writers need original and accurate language to describe individuals.

Society itself is giving writers some help. Today a multicultural approach is being integrated into numerous aspects of society, from school textbooks to television advertisements. All types of cultures in the United States are gaining a voice. As someone disseminating information, you can learn to tap into these cultures for stories and diverse insights.

Media can have an impact in breaking the bias habit. As newsrooms become more diverse, the types of stories aired or printed will continue to become diverse. Reporters can describe people as individuals, not cast them in broad terms ascribed to a group. Reporters can also become circumspect when using language and learn what terminology individuals and groups prefer.

Many organizations have developed guidelines on language use. The minority professional journalism organizations also have web sites that may include examples of stereotyping or negative portrayals. For example, the Asian American Journalists Association posted on its web site after the terrorist attacks in September 2001 a reminder to media to cover the Arab American community responsibly and fairly. The site included links to help journalists become informed.

Students can become more familiar with groups, their goals, their membership, and current issues by accessing web sites, such as www.latinolink.com for the Hispanic American community; www.netnoir.com for African Americans; www.seniornet.org for seniors; www.thirdage.com for adults 50 years of age and older; and www.planetout.com for lesbians and gays. Most sites have links to related organizations. Others are listed in Figure 6.1.

Considering Specific Groups

John Mitrano, executive director of the National Organization of Italian Students and Educators, noted the following in a survey:

> *While there is usually a grain of truth to stereotypes, over time, these become no longer salient. With the twilight of ethnicity upon us in third and fourth generation*

FIGURE 6.1   *Helpful Web Sites with Cross-Links to Other Informative Sites*

---

http://newswatch.sfsu.edu/—A combined site for all four major associations of minority journalists and the National Lesbian and Gay Journalists Association. It includes a comprehensive *Style Guide* and updated essays on contemporary issues and topics on minorities and media.

http://www.unityjournalists.org/—The Unity Web site, self-described as "a strategic alliance of journalists of color acting as a force for positive change in the fast-changing global news industry." It includes a link to the *Detroit Free Press* publication: "100 Questions and Answers about Arab Americans: A Journalist's Guide": http://www.freep.com/jobspage/arabs/index.htm.

http://www.mosaicweb.com/index2.htm—A multicultural site that is constantly updated. It includes links to "Filipino-American," "Caribbean," "women," and "multicultural."

http://www.spj.org/diversity_profiling.asp—The Society of Professional Journalists's "Guidelines for Countering Racial, Ethnic and Religious Profiling."

> *families, new portrayals must be used to depict groups accurately. Television shows, movies, and advertisements must emphasize the qualities that we see ourselves as having. We must also become vocal and mobilized when we do not like the way we are portrayed.*

Many words and images applied to specific groups have historically negative and derogatory connotations. Writers must be aware of them and avoid them.

Racial and Ethnic Groups

Writers must avoid terminology that perpetuates beliefs that all members of any group look alike, talk alike, think alike, or belong to the same political party. Selecting language is the first step.

Some language, although it may seem biased, can be appropriate when used in a historical context or with cultural sensitivity, noted Pale Moon Rose, president of the American Indian Heritage Foundation. Terms such as *redskin* and *brave* are acceptable if used appropriately and in a historical context.

Linda Cook Roberts, who won an International Association of Business Communicators Gold Quill for an affirmative action communication program, years ago (see *Without Bias* in References) developed the following guidelines for writing about racial and ethnic groups. The guidelines still stand:

• Avoid presenting members of racial or ethnic groups as if they are all the same. Too often, for example, African American neighborhoods are presented as "drug-infested." This assigns a negative status to a whole people and their neighborhoods.

• Refrain from using descriptive words that strengthen racial or ethnic stereotypes. Consider this sentence from a *Washington Post* article on Washington, D.C., monuments:

And he chose an unusual man to help: Benjamin F. Banneker, a free black man who was a math whiz and self-taught in astronomy.

The word "unusual" clouds the sentence with a potential stereotype: the implication that African Americans are not helpful, are not intelligent in math, or are unable to learn astronomy on their own.

• Describe race or ethnic origin only when it is pertinent. In an article about Jessica James becoming the vice president of a local bank, it is not relevant to mention that her great-grandparents were born in slavery.

• Understand the problematic racial and ethnic undertones of some language. For example, the term "minority" is problematic in an international sense because people of color make up the majority of the world's population, and population changes in the United States mean that some ethnic groups are the majority in certain locations. Remember also that "minority" always refers to a group rather than to certain individuals; it is best to use the term "members of minority groups" rather than "minorities."

• Never use a patronizing focus or treat a member of an ethnic group as a token. Ivan Penn, a reporter for the *Baltimore Sun,* was the first African American to serve as editor-in-chief of the student newspaper, the *Diamondback,* at the University of Maryland. But he describes himself first as a reporter, as a University of Maryland alumnus, and as a former *Diamondback* editor.

• Integrate coverage of ethnic groups into all aspects of articles or broadcasts instead of doing periodic "special" editions.

• Look for a diversity of sources when writing. A Native American might be interviewed about political struggles instead of the meaning of a ceremonial dance.

Sexism

Women have risen to powerful jobs in both the public and the private sectors, but they have not gained enough power to transform their image in the media. Many writers thoughtlessly use language that treats women as inferior or that is demeaning or insulting. They are sometimes referred to as girls or mothers and are described by their physical attributes such as "attractive" or "brunette" or "shapely."

For example, when Carol Moseley Braun, an African American woman from Illinois, successfully ran for the U.S. Senate, a *Washington Post* feature referred to her in its lead as "a celebrity with a problem." It then revealed that her problem was having to find pantyhose at a hotel gift shop. A story about a male candidate probably would never focus on his troubles in buying an undershirt.

Such writing still appears. Consider media coverage of repeated allegations against former President Clinton about his sexual conduct. One of the female protagonists, Linda Tripp, who taped Monica Lewinsky, was described in a *Washington Post* article as "a divorced middle-aged mother who needed to keep the paychecks coming…." The implication by the writer was that Tripp was a woman who would do anything for money. Readers questioned the relevance of labeling her as divorced and middle-aged. The facts would have been better placed in a paragraph devoted to biographical information about Tripp.

At the same time, a *Chicago Tribune* writer described Clinton's secretary, Bettie Currie, solely as "typically wearing a crisp blazer and pearls, her hair pulled back into a chignon." What is a crisp blazer? Well ironed? And many people wondered what a "chignon" was. The manner in which Currie handled Clinton's appointments proved of more value to readers than a sketchy, imprecise physical description. Writers should use description when it is complete and adds to the understanding of an individual's personality. Feature writers must be especially careful when creating a mood. Often what looks like interesting detail may come across as sexism in disguise. Writers should guard against describing women in terms of their physical appearance and men in terms of wealth and power.

Beginning writers should also be aware that some other writers and editors are sensitive to the use of gender-specific nouns such as "chairman," "fireman," "stewardess," and "mailman." When possible, use "chairperson," "firefighter," "flight attendant," and "postal service worker" or "letter carrier." Writers should also know their publication's policy about courtesy titles. Many organizations have eliminated courtesy titles such as Mrs., Miss, and Ms. before women's names. The last name is used on second reference.

Sexual Orientation

Writers should also avoid perpetuating negative images based on sexual orientation. Gay and lesbian rights movements since the mid-1960s have worked diligently to recast gay and lesbian portrayals in society. Until the mid-1970s, most news stories that referred to gays and lesbians did so only in the context of police reports. Gay and lesbian issues have been addressed in the schools, in the workplace, and in the military. Despite increased coverage, some editors and reporters still produce stories that present homosexuality as deviant, and negative stereotypes continue.

Writers and broadcasters must be careful not to make value judgments when a source is gay or lesbian or when the subject deals with homosexuality. Saying, for example, that a source "confessed" to being gay communicates negative, secretive feelings about homosexuality that your openly gay source will resent.

A person's gender or sexual orientation should be ignored in a message unless it is relevant. People's sexual orientation may be part of the fabric of the message but should be woven in as part of who they are, not presented as their complete identity. For example, gays and lesbians are well-known actors and leaders in fields such as science, politics, and medicine.

Madeleine Blais of the *Washington Post* wrote a multidimensional profile of Jim Graham, the director of the Whitman-Walker Clinic in Washington for people with AIDS. The article described Graham's life and the clinic's life without making sexual orientation the focus. One paragraph described Graham's coming to grips with his alcoholism and his coming out to his wife. At an Alcoholics Anonymous meeting, Blais reported, "he told her that on the night before their wedding he had sex with a man who kept asking him if he knew what he was doing getting married. He wanted to ask her forgiveness." The reporter's work was done without bias.

Writers should never make assumptions about people's sexual orientation or people's sentiments toward gay and lesbian issues. Some people favor equality for all people. Remember that many people who are not gay or lesbian support gay and lesbian rights, just as many white people support civil rights for people of color.

Disabilities

Unless you or someone in your family has a physical or mental disability, as a writer you may tend to forget people with disabilities exist. Among the derogatory labels applied to disabled people are "crippled," "deformed," and "invalid." The Disabilities Committee of the American Society of Newspaper Editors noted a list of terms to avoid, including "special," which is seen as patronizing; "stricken with or suffers from" instead of "a person who has" a specific disability; "victim of" rather than "a person who has" AIDS or cerebral palsy.

Unlike other groups that receive discrimination because of social norms, people with disabilities face discrimination both from attitudes and from real barriers created by society's architectural and communication barriers. Maybe you have never seen a person who uses a wheelchair in your local grocery store because there is no curb cut in the sidewalk in front of the store or no ramp at the door of the store. Maybe you have had little interaction with a profoundly deaf person because you do not know where to find a Telecommunications Device for the Deaf (TDD), which would allow you to call the person on the phone.

Many people, including writers, forget that people with disabilities constitute a vital, and numerous, part of our society. Government estimates are that 18 percent of the U.S. population, about 48 million people, has some form of disability. Therefore, a significant number of today's audiences either have a disability or know someone who does. Yet, people with disabilities receive only sketchy news coverage or are rarely written about. Writers are missing readable, audience-enticing stories about civil rights violations, new technology, legislation, and changes in business practices. An enterprising reporter could mine such story topics indefinitely.

The late John Clogston, a journalism professor at the Northern Illinois University, said that writers often portray people with disabilities in one of three demeaning ways: They imply that people who have a disability are somehow less human than other people; they present them as medically defective or somehow deviant or different in society; or they go overboard in trying to portray them positively, thus making them superhuman or "super-crips," as Clogston called them.

Writers have a tendency to focus stories on the individual rather than the issues surrounding a disability, and they tend to wrap people with disabilities in pity and sympathy. Joe Shapiro, who covers social policy and disability issues for *U.S. News and World Report,* suggests that "instead of writing the sad story about the 10-year-old boy saving money to buy his mother an electric wheelchair, write the sad story of a health-care system that doesn't provide the funding to get the needed chair for that mother."

Writing about People with Disabilities

Lucille deView, syndicated columnist on aging for Knight-Ridder/*Tribune* and the writing coach for the *Orange County Register* in California, recommends the following tips for writing about people with disabilities:

- Let people with disabilities, not a friend or family member, speak for themselves in your writing.

- Recognize the individuality of all people.

- Look beyond the individual to the issue if possible. If someone who uses a wheelchair is also an athlete, you might ask about the accessibility of local gymnasiums, swimming pools, and outdoor sports facilities.

- Look beyond the person's disability and get a well-rounded view of his or her life. Having a disability is just one small aspect of who a person is. He may collect antique sheet music, or she may have been a police officer during the 1980s.

- Ask about language. Ask which terms they prefer for publication. Do not assume that because they use a term, it is acceptable to all. Someone may refer to himself or herself as a cripple, but this is a derogatory term and should not be used.

- Avoid assigning superhuman traits. People with disabilities participate fully in aspects of life: They have all types of jobs, and they have spouses and families. If they are athletes, it is because they enjoy physical activity. Find out about the societal barriers they may have faced in achieving their goals, just as you do in any interview.

- Mention a disability only if it is pertinent to the message. It is not relevant to mention that a business owner uses a wheelchair unless he or she is talking specifically about access issues or other disability-related issues.

Be careful about writing that someone succeeded "in spite of" a disability—a phrase often viewed by people with disabilities as extremely patronizing. Some writers may contend that a disability implies that individuals are not able, and if they succeed, then the news value of emotional impact and conflict are there to attract readers. Never assume that an accomplishment by a person with a disability is unusual.

At one time, leaders' disabilities often were not a visible part of reporting. When the late Sen. John East ran for election in North Carolina, all photographs showed him sitting. Few voters realized that he used a wheelchair. President Franklin D. Roosevelt conducted business from a wheelchair, and controversy arose when one panel in the FDR Memorial in Washington, D.C., put him seated in a wheelchair. A Kennedy family book and documentary film footage released several decades after his death showed President John F. Kennedy unable to lift his children or to bend deeply.

In general, people specializing in coverage of disability issues recommend two easy rules in writing about people with disabilities. First, avoid clichés and clichéd constructions. Use value-neutral terms—that is, words that do not stereotype. Avoid saying that someone is confined. The person gets out of the wheelchair to sleep and to bathe. To that individual, the wheelchair is liberating. It is more accurate to say the individual uses a wheelchair. Second, never inject pity or a condescending tone into copy.

Ageism

Older people may also face stigmatization by society, and the mass media play a role in that process. In some instances, older people are labeled as forgetful, senile, rigid, meddlesome, childlike, feeble, fragile, frail, gray, inactive, withered, or doddering. Such adjectives may describe older people at some point in their lives or may be medically appropriate. But if such words are used indiscriminately, they demean older people and perpetuate inaccurate stereotypes. With the repeal of mandatory retirement, older people continue to work into their 70s and even 80s if they choose. They do most things that younger people do.

Consider an example from a *Texas Monthly* profile on then Texas Governor Ann Richards. The story was written because of rumors that she might one day run for president. At the outset, appearance stereotypes were broken: Richards was pictured on the cover in a white leather outfit sitting on a motorcycle.

The article presented the 58-year-old governor, who is also a grandmother, in a multidimensional way—not as an older woman who happens to be governor but as an effective, dynamic governor who happens to be an older woman. Her bouffant white hair is a sign of age and a symbol of her political personality. Her hairstyle, which was popular in the 1950s, successfully contrasts with her liberal feminist beliefs. Her age is relevant only as a part of who she is.

Lucille deView suggests that writers avoid these myths about older people:

• Older people can participate in a variety of activities, so do not adopt a "gee whiz" attitude toward their abilities. Most people over the age of 50 continue the physical activities they enjoyed when younger, whether swimming, hiking, or playing tennis.

• Older people should be seen as individuals, not as members of a senior age group in which people are believed to have the same interests and abilities. Older people's interests are just as varied as those of individuals in other groups.

• Older people are not stereotyped in appearance. They dress in numerous fashions, and not all older people have physical problems or even gray hair.

• Age does not mean loneliness or loss of sexual interest. One study showed that 74 percent of older men and 35 percent of older women live with spouses. Another 23 percent of older women live with relatives or unrelated people, and 7 percent of older men do the same, according to Mary Spencer's *Truth about Aging: Guidelines for Publishers.* Although more people 65 years of age and older are living alone, they often choose that path for more independence.

DeView says that writers should focus on realistic presentations of older people. Some older people have no financial problems, whereas others struggle financially during their later life. Not all older people have ill health or are unable to cope with poor health. Although 45 percent of older people have serious medical conditions, they may not severely limit their participation in society. Only about 5 percent of older people live in nursing homes.

Children also should not be portrayed in an unpleasant light. Not all children are immature, naive, whining, sneaky, dishonest, or lazy. Children mature and develop at different paces. Some are responsible, creative, athletically gifted, loving, aggravating, and mean. Each must be considered individually and be allowed to ascribe traits to himself or herself, as did one 5-foot teenager, who described herself as being "vertically challenged."

Overcoming Bias in Writing

Even after a discussion of bias such as the one in this chapter, traces of insensitivity can still creep into writing. You need to be constantly aware of your own background and attitudes to understand when and how bias might surface in writing, to recognize it, and to exorcise it.

Writers, reporters, and broadcasters today must be trained to avoid the flaws of their predecessors in the mass media. They must learn to question their own beliefs and assumptions to understand better the diverse ethnic groups within society.

Today's writers, through better awareness, are trying to overcome cultural bias by sifting through information and presenting the least stereotypical and biased picture possible. Messages—from school textbooks to television advertisements—use a multicultural approach that presents all kinds of people. But despite education, old biases die hard for many, and every time a bias is confirmed by a writer, it is strengthened for readers.

Beginning and even experienced writers sometimes pass along stereotypes, such as the dizzy blonde or dishonest politician, because they think people like and understand such shorthand portrayals, just as they like cartoons. Therein lies the danger. Because mass media professionals present distinctive images of people and groups, they can determine how consumers view people and groups who are not like themselves. Thus, writers must work responsibly in disseminating information rather than misinformation.

Make sure that what you write or broadcast does not perpetuate negative stereotypes. Stereotypes communicate inaccurate information and can undermine the quality of your work. Sensing stereotypes and avoiding them is a critical step on the path to better writing.

EXERCISES

1. Describe yourself culturally and ethnically. List any physical disabilities or other pertinent differences. Make a list of words or phrases, both negative and positive, that you have seen used in reference to your special traits. Compare your list with those of others in your class, and compile a directory of words you should avoid when writing, and why. Explain the connotation of each word. Make a list of acceptable words or phrases.

2. What is the ethnic makeup of your college or university? The town or city where your school is located? Do a five-day content analysis of your local or student newspaper. Count the number of stories each day in the news, sports, and features sections. Count the number that focus on an ethnic group or an issue related to an ethnic group. At the end of the five days, calculate what percentage of the newspaper's stories related to ethnic groups. Do the percentages match the groups' makeup in the university's or town's population? Was coverage positive, negative, or neutral? What types of stories do you believe are missing?

3. Do a similar content analysis of the evening news broadcast, locally and for a national network. Count the total stories and the number concerning ethnic groups. Give your impressions about whether the general coverage was positive, negative, or neutral.

4. You have the opportunity to interview the incoming student government president, a son of two Laotian refugees. List five objective questions you could use to begin the interview, then list two effective questions you could ask to determine his experiences with cultural differences in the United States.

5. Examine your local or student newspaper. Find examples of stories about various ethnic communities or societal groups that do a good job of unbiased writing. Bring examples to class to share and indicate why the stories could be models for writing.

REFERENCES

A. Arluke and J. Levin, "Second Childhood." *Public Communication Review* 1:2, 1992.

"Communities Inc. First to Link Special Internet Audiences Online," CNN Custom News, Dec. 10, 1997. Available at: http://www.cnn.com.

Timothy Crouse. *The Boys on the Bus.* New York: Random House, 1993.

Lucille deView, "Regardless of Age: Toward communication sensitive to older people and children," in *Without Bias: A Guidebook for Nondiscriminatory Communication.* New York: John Wiley & Sons, 1982.

"Focus on Racism in the Media." *Extra!* July/August, 1992.

Jan Jarbue, "Ann's Plans." *Texas Monthly,* July 1992.

M. Johnson and S. Elkins, *Reporting on Disability, Approaches and Issues.* Louisville, KY: Advocado Press, 1989.

Gretchen Kell, "Media Is Much to Blame for Negative Stereotypes about African American Men, Says UC Berkeley Journalism Professor," Online news release. University of California at Berkeley, June 1997.

Walter Lippmann, *Public Opinion.* New York: Harcourt, Brace and Co., 1922.

Eric Newton, *The Open Newspaper.* A Maynard Institute Workbook. San Francisco, Robert C. Maynard Institute for Journalism Education, 1994.

J. Pickens, ed., *Without Bias.* New York: John Wiley and Sons, 1982.

President's Committee on the Employment of People with Disabilities, *Statistical Report: The Status of People with Disabilities.* Washington, DC: U.S. Department of Labor, 1994.

Reporting and Writing about People with Disabilities, 5th ed. (Brochure). Lawrence, KS: Research and Training Center on Independent Living, University of Kansas, 1996.

Pale Moon Rose and John Mitrano, Comments. In *Surveys of Ethnic and Racial Groups,* by Jan Johnson Elliott, associate professor, University of North Carolina at Chapel Hill, Fall 1993.

Mary Spencer, *Truth about Aging: Guidelines for Publishers.* Washington, DC: National Retired Teachers Association and American Association of Retired Persons, 1979.

H. Stocking and P. Gross, *How Do Journalists Think? A Proposal for the Study of Cognitive Bias in Newsmaking.* Bloomington, IN: Eric Clearinghouse on Reading and Communication Skills, 1989.

"The News Media and the Disorders," Chapter 15 of *Report of the National Advisory Commission on Civil Disorders,* Kerner Commission Report, 1968.

David Manning White, "The 'gatekeeper,'" *Journalism Quarterly,* Vol. 27, No. 3, Fall 1950, p. 383.

Window Dressing on the Set: Women and Minorities in Television: A Report of the United States Commission on Civil Rights. 1977.

Without Bias: A Guidebook for Nondiscriminatory Communication, International Association of Business Communicators, 1977.

"Women's Lifestyles: A Special Report," *Scripps Howard Editors Newsletter.* Cincinnati, OH: Scripps Howard Newspapers, Spring 1989.

7

Research and Observation

Writing begins with an idea. During a trip to the ocean, a writer is fascinated with the porpoises that periodically surface and roll as they travel offshore. She wants to write about porpoises. But she needs more information than just her observations to write a factual, accurate, complete, and entertaining article. She must learn more.

Gathering information is like detective work. As a sleuth, you start with a clue. Step by step you add pieces until you have enough information to reconstruct events and solve the case. As a writer, you add to your knowledge until you can create an accurate and complete summary of the topic.

Writers, like detectives, gather information from research, interviews, and observations. Also, like detectives, writers gather a broad array of information to ensure their searches are objective. Research allows writers to study what others have already found out. That information may be in books, magazines, letters, statistical abstracts, encyclopedias, data banks, or any number of other sources. Writers can access thousands of documents that have been stored online and in library retrieval systems.

Armed with facts retrieved in research, writers can interview expert and relevant sources to add personal comment on the topic. Personal reflections add context and interest to facts. Interviewing, quotes, and attribution are discussed in Chapter 9.

Writers also note their observations. Student writers are sometimes reluctant to include their impressions for fear they will appear too subjective. They must overcome that fear. In the porpoise story, the writer would be remiss not to describe the rolling action as the sleek, gray mammals break water a hundred yards off the beach. Audiences want to know what the animals look like and how thrilled the author is at seeing a school of several dozen porpoises dotting the waves as they surface for air.

In this chapter, you will learn

- How to develop search strategies that will mine library and online resources,
- Specific sources to consider,
- Plusses and minuses in online and other research, and
- How observation is a part of gathering information.

Getting Started in Research

Writers start out as generalists; they know a little about a lot of subjects. Some develop specialties or subject areas they prefer, whether they are newspaper or electronic media reporters, public relations practitioners, or advertising copy-writers. They may cover general assignment topics or report on special beats, such as business, medicine, sports, the environment, children's issues, government, religion, or the media.

Whether they are generalists or specialists, writers need to do research. A medical writer may know medical terminology, but if he wants to write about stem cell research, he must become knowledgeable about the topic. A government reporter must learn about the newly elected members of Congress before she goes to the opening session.

Writers need to find information that is accurate, relevant, and up-to-date. Time is their greatest enemy. Most writers have deadlines and have limited time to devote to research, particularly if they write for daily publications. So they need to find information quickly and efficiently.

Barbara Semonche, a former newspaper librarian, is the librarian at the School of Journalism and Mass Communication at the University of North Carolina at Chapel Hill. She has developed a dozen guides for students in the quest to find information. She notes

> *You can be certain of two things: either you will find useful information efficiently or you will not. You will find too much information or too little. Your success will depend, to a certain extent, upon the quality of your search strategies. The other part is finding the best reference sources.*

Developing a Strategy

To be successful in research, you need a strategy to find information. Once you have defined your topics, you must make a list of questions, identify obvious sources, conduct searches for additional sources, review those sources for additional leads, refine their questions, and then interview.

You are a medical reporter and want to write a story on childhood immunizations. You first list information you need to know, such as the following questions:

Initial Question List for Story on Childhood Immunizations

Who has to be immunized?

What are the state laws?

What shots do children have to have?

At what ages do children get which shots?

Are there any reactions to the shots?

How much do the shots cost at a doctor's office?

Can children get shots at public health clinics? How much do they cost?

Where are the clinics here? What are the hours for immunizations?

How many children register for school and aren't immunized?

Is this a problem locally?

Have any other diseases surfaced locally?

Why don't parents get their children immunized?

Additional Questions after Research

What are the risks to children who aren't immunized?

Do children ever die from immunizations?

What are the reactions parents can expect?

How many children in the state aren't immunized properly when they start school?

How many immunizations are given each year in the state? In our county?

What childhood diseases are appearing again?

How much of the cost of immunizations does the government pay?

Do we consider some diseases eradicated?

Thirty years ago children suffered from mumps, measles, and even polio. Now children can be protected against even chicken pox. Are we too complacent about a resurgence of diseases?

Are there any diseases left that children need to be protected from?

If a certain number of children are immunized, does that protect other children, as in the herd effect?

What factors prevent parents from having children immunized at the proper time?

What immunizations do college students need?

The obvious sources would be newspaper and journal indexes, articles and information at online health sites, pediatricians, and local health department and school officials. You would also interview experts and agency officials.

Eventually your source list grows to include state health officials, state statutes that stipulate which immunizations children must have to enter school, officials at the Centers for Disease Control, legislators who allocate funds for immunizations, parents, and even children. You refine your list of questions for each source and prepare to interview your sources.

Your search strategy is similar if you are writing a story for the alumni magazine on a graduate whose first novel has been published. She is an assistant professor at a college in another state. Before the interview, you need to find information on the author. The first part of the strategy is to start close to home: the university's alumni files and the yearbooks for the time the author was on campus. Perhaps her publisher's Web site contains biographical information on authors.

You then might consult general biographical reference books. Your alumna might be notable enough to be included in *Who's Who*. But you discover she's not. If you can find no accessible biographical history, you will have to rely on a strategy that includes interviewing former professors, roommates, colleagues, friends, and family members. You may have to call the English department where she teaches and have someone fax her curriculum vitae. You may have to consult newspaper indexes in her home state to find specific articles about her. If one source indicates an organization to which she belongs, you may need to look for references on that organization. Articles about the organization may include material about your up-and-coming author.

Basic Reference Sources

A multitude of references exist. Many are in libraries, and many are online—and some appear in both places. Traditional texts, such as *Romeo and Juliet* and *Bartlett's Familiar Quotations,* exist as searchable Web sites. Figure 7.1 lists some additional helpful Web sites. Whatever the form, writers always need general reference books, such as encyclopedias or the *World Almanac,* which is updated annually. Some reference books furnish interesting or unusual data, such as an *Acronyms, Initialisms and Abbreviations Dictionary,* which can clarify the meaning of the acronym M.A.S.H. *20th Century Day by Day* includes millennium celebrations around the world. More specific references include *Film Directions* and *Encyclopedia of the Middle Ages.* Or you may check quotes in publications such as *Familiar Quotations* or the words of a presidential speech on the White House Web site. *Standard and Poor's* lists officers of major corporations and their addresses and telephone numbers, which can lead to expert sources.

The best place to launch your research is the online catalogue of your college or university library. The online catalogues permit searching by key-words as do Web browsers that link users to relevant sites. Keyword searches greatly increase the ease and speed of getting useful results.

Today's researchers and writers use hundreds of sources and always must be sure sources are credible and updated. Listed here are some types of publications that writers traditionally have relied on for information. Remember: Most publications have Web sites.

BIOGRAPHICAL SOURCES. Such sources list information about well-known people. Some are specific, such as *Who's Who in American Politics.* The

FIGURE 7.1   *Helpful Web Sites*

United Nations information at www.unesco.org or www.un.org.

United Nations demographic information at www.un.org/depts/unsd/demog/.

U.S. population data at www.census.org.

U.S. government information at www.access.gpo.gov or www.whitehouse.com.

Congressional Quarterly at www.cq.com.

Standard and Poor's at www.standardpoor.com.

Investigative Reporters and Editors at www.ire.org.

Authors, quotations, facts, and other links at www.bartleby.com.

information will include birthdate, parents' names, education, career, awards and achievements, and family data. Among other biographical sources are *Who's Who, Webster's Biographical Dictionary, Current Biography, Contemporary Authors Autobiography Series,* and *Who's Who among Hispanic Americans.* More than 100 biographical dictionaries exist, each focusing on a special group or profession.

STATISTICAL INFORMATION. *Statistical Abstracts of the United States* is one of the most widely used reference books and is online. It provides information from the number of police officers in Albuquerque to the number of houses with indoor plumbing in Lincoln, Nebraska. Data are based on information collected by the federal government and other sources. *Census of Population of the United States* is published every 10 years after the U.S. Census is conducted. Census information also is available on CD-ROM and the Internet at www.census.gov. *Editor and Publisher Market Guide* contains data on cities, such as the number of shopping malls a city has and whether its water is fluoridated. Most states compile statistical books, particularly those dealing with vital statistics: births, deaths, marriages, and divorces. Writers can find information on states, counties, cities, and even sections within cities that is especially helpful if they are looking for the local angle on a story. For international information, writers can consult the *United Nations Demographic Yearbook.*

A word of caution: Because of delays in reporting year-end figures and in producing the copies, you may find the most recent information online.

POLITICAL AND GOVERNMENT INFORMATION. The *U.S. Government Manual* contains information on departments and agencies in the executive branch. *Congressional Quarterly* publishes a weekly report that catalogues the voting records of Congress and major political speeches. States annually publish manuals that contain information about branches of government and legislatures, summaries of the state history, the state constitution, and biographies of major state officials. Information on foreign governments and leaders can be found in reference books such as *The Politics, Cultures and Economies of the World* and *Current World Leaders.* Remember to check for online sites.

GEOGRAPHIC DATA. Writers may need to locate cities, towns, and countries. They can refer to local maps or the *Times Atlas of the World* and *Rand-McNally Commercial Atlas and Marketing Guide.* Online sites, such as mapquest.

com, will guide writers to locations and even give directions to get there. Writers can find up-to-date maps of continents and regions at sites such as World Sites Atlas at www.siteatlas.com.

BUSINESS INFORMATION. Writers may need data on a company or an industry, and students may need information on a potential employer. Today's competitive companies usually have extensive and interactive Web sites. Research on companies may also be found in annual reports, which are on file in many libraries. Comparative data on companies may be found in resources such as *Dun and Bradstreet, Standard and Poor's,* and Moody's *International Manuals.*

Writers should always remember basic sources such as telephone books, city directories, and maps. They should rely on assistance from reference librarians to direct them to current and complete indexes and other references. Many beginning writers waste time trying to find information on their own when they could do research much faster if they would ask for direction. Librarians can help writers with search strategies and key words that will expand their source list.

PROFESSIONAL SOURCES. In any search for information, writers should consider professional organizations as sources. Often those sources have links or references to other depositories of information. The professional sources can also provide updates on media issues, contact names, and historical background as well as serve as a means to verify facts.

Some mass communication sites worth checking are the Poynter Institute at www.poynter.org; the American Society of Newspaper Editors at www.asne.org; the Inter American Press Association at ww.sipiapa.org; Nieman Reports at www.harvard.edu; World Association of Newspapers at www.wan-pres.org; Public Relations Society of America at www.prsa.org; American Advertising Federation at www.aaf.org; Electronic Journalists Association at www.rtndac.org; Investigative Reporters and Editors at www.ire.org; and Society of Professional Journalists at www.spj.org. Also available are the organizations that serve particular interests, such as medical, legal, government workers, construction, architects, and on and on.

Pitfalls in Research

The hunt for information may be complex. Librarian Barbara Semonche warns that not all information is in a compact, convenient form. At the start of a search, students may discover people with the same name, such as William Perry. William Perry was a football player also known as "the Refrigerator." Another William Perry was secretary of defense under President Clinton.

Information may be dated. Some biographical reference material is not cumulative, and you may have to look in earlier editions or references that are not online. Students and other researchers must remember that not every reference includes every individual, and those that do may not have all the facts about an individual. Researchers must look at many sources to find complete information. Searching for information is rarely one-stop shopping. Using many sources helps uncover discrepancies and inconsistencies about information and also helps ensure that information is as accurate as possible.

Writers should look continually for other sources. The research game is a detective hunt. Names or sources mentioned in an article or in references can lead to nuggets of information elsewhere. The only constraints will be time and deadline pressure.

Government Sources

Local, state, and federal governments produce millions of pages of documents every year. Documents range from official findings, such as federal Food and Drug Administration studies, to county tax records and the disposition of local traffic cases. Most government documents are open and accessible to the public. Many are free by mail on request, and others are available at the city hall, at the county courthouse, at a regional federal repository, on the World Wide Web, or at the Library of Congress. They provide a wealth of information for writers and curious citizens.

Government officials and others have taken advantage of the information age to put reams of material online. Agencies maintain their own Web sites that provide history, facts about elected officials, agendas and minutes of meetings, and other relevant data (see Figure 7.2). Try THOMAS, a congressional online system; Congressional Record; congressional legislation digests; and directors of congressional members' e-mail. Even the White House has its own Web site featuring news releases of the day, speech transcripts, and access to the Cabinet members' agencies.

Public Records

Routine government documents are considered to be public. The documents have been created by government, which is supported by taxpayers' money. Researchers, writers, and anyone who wants the documents can request to see them or to have copies made. All states have laws that pertain to what is and what is not a public record. The general rule most journalists follow is that any document is considered to be a public record unless the agency or individual who has the document can cite the section of state statute or federal law that prevents its disclosure. If the agency cannot, it must relinquish the information.

FIGURE 7.2   *The Bush Administration Created FirstGov.gov as One of Many Federal Government Sites*

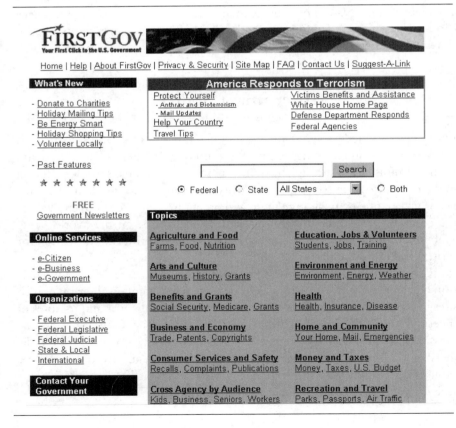

Media writers should know what the open records laws are for their particular state. State press associations can provide the law and its exceptions. Publications such as *The News Media and the Law,* published by the Reporters Committee for Freedom of the Press, can be consulted. The Electronic Frontier Foundation is a valuable resource and can be accessed via Internet.

Agencies can charge a reasonable fee for photocopying documents. Most states have regulations pertaining to computer storage of public documents and reasonable charges for making copies or providing access to computerized information. Some news organizations have the computer capability to tap directly into state databases, such as drivers' license records.

Freedom of Information Act

In 1966, the U.S. Congress passed the federal Freedom of Information Act (FOIA). The act became law in 1967 and has been amended four times. The law is much like state laws regarding public records. Anyone is allowed to make a written request for information from any federal agency, but not all information is available. The act provides broad exemptions, such as information relating to national defense or foreign policy, internal personnel rules and practices of an agency, personnel and medical files that would constitute an invasion of privacy, information compiled for law enforcement purposes, and geophysical information such as that related to well locations.

The media have worked continually to reduce the number of exemptions. Michael Gartner, former president of the American Society of Newspaper Editors, once lamented in a speech on national Freedom of Information Day that the name "Freedom of Information" implies that government is holding information hostage. He objected to many of the restrictions, particularly those that prevent publication of what the United States broadcasts to developing countries over the Voice of America.

The act sets out the procedure for requesting information, the time required for an agency to respond, appeals procedures, and fees. Individuals must pay the cost of photocopying the information but can request waiver of that cost if the release of the information is in the public interest.

Writers or individuals seeking information under the act may be frustrated. Delays can occur even when procedures are followed. The request must be specific and must be sent to the proper agency. When the information is uncovered, a reporter may receive sections or entire pages inked out to protect exempted information. The reporter pays the cost of photocopying all pages—even the blackened ones.

Freedom of Information Act searches can be time consuming and costly, but many journalists and researchers have used them to find information for fact-filled articles. For example, Jon Elliston, a staff writer for the *Independent Weekly* in Durham, N.C., used the FOIA in 2001 to obtain the Federal Bureau of Investigation's file on Charles Kuralt, the famed TV journalist who died in 1997. Elliston, who has used the FOIA extensively, requested documents on Kuralt out of curiosity, he says, but he didn't expect to find much. "I knew that the FBI compiled dossiers on many prominent reporters during the Cold War," Elliston says. "But I'm used to thinking of Kuralt as a mainstream and patriotic journalist, so I didn't think the bureau would been too concerned about him. Still, he did some famous reports on American underdogs, labor unions and migrant workers, for example, so I wondered if he caught the bureau's attention."

On April 4, 2001, Elliston wrote the FBI's FOIA office, requesting "all documents relating to Charles Kuralt, the deceased journalist." (Had Kuralt still been alive at the time of the request, Elliston would have been required to secure a privacy waiver from Kuralt to see his FBI records. No such waivers are required for the deceased.)

The FBI responded rapidly, in comparison to some FOIA requests, which can take years to complete. Five weeks later, the bureau mailed 10 pages of declassified documents to Elliston. Half of the papers, which dated from 1962 to 1965, were stamped "SECRET," and most had large sections blacked out by the FBI prior to release. Routing information on the papers indicated that all of them had crossed the desk of FBI Director J. Edgar Hoover.

Even with the heavy excisions, Elliston was able to use the papers to piece together a story about how the FBI had kept tabs on Kuralt's work. Hoover's men, the documents indicate, checked on Kuralt's credentials and loyalties after he filed reports from Cuba and other Cold War hotspots. In July 1962, a Cuban exile activist named Carlos Todd spoke before the Senate Subcommittee on Internal Security and accused Kuralt of broadcasting pro-Castro reports. These charges, it appears, are what generated the official paper trail; a month later, the FBI opened its file on Kuralt.

Though Kuralt was later exonerated in a report prepared by Senate staffers, the FBI continued to monitor some of the broadcaster's dispatches from Latin America. His reporting on the 1965 U.S. invasion of the Dominican Republic, for example, drew scrutiny from a high-ranking FBI official.

At times, Elliston says, the deletions in the documents led him to dead ends, but he found ways to fill in some of the blanks. By juxtaposing the FBI records with Kuralt's personal papers, which are on file at the University of North Carolina at Chapel Hill's Wilson Library, he was able to tell what Kuralt activities drew the FBI's attention at a given moment. Still, he knows he only got part of the story.

"The blacked out parts of these documents hide secrets that were put to paper almost 40 years ago," Elliston says. "I'm not convinced that the FBI is protecting national security by shielding so much of its Kuralt file from the public."

Seeking further disclosure of the documents, Elliston filed a FOIA appeal letter with the FBI in June 2001. "Since the events discussed in the documents occurred nearly four decades ago, and since the subject is deceased, surely additional portions of these documents can be disclosed without harming national security or the privacy of individuals," Elliston wrote.

Four months later, Elliston had yet to receive a reply. But he's hopeful that his appeal will prompt additional declassification. "I've seen this work before," he says. The appeals process is written into the FOIA law, and using it, researchers and reporters have often succeeded in gaining greater disclosures.

Online Research

Technology has changed the way writers collect, transmit, and share information. Distance is irrelevant. A public relations practitioner in Detroit can search the Web for background information on the success of drugs to treat acid reflux disease and fax it to a company official in Switzerland. A reporter can write a story on a laptop computer during a meeting and transmit it in a matter of seconds to the city desk 30 miles away. Photographs, maps, and other visuals in color, as well as text, can be e-mailed anywhere.

The major change in recent years has been the way information is stored. People who began writing careers in the mid-1980s and earlier have seen a phenomenal change in the way they seek information. In the "old days" before 1985, most searches for information centered on treks to libraries—newspaper, city or county, university—or wherever resource books were housed. People handled paper to get information.

Computers have allowed anyone who produces information to store it so that others can access it. This public storehouse of information within the Internet is commonly called the World Wide Web. More and more writers can call up information in a matter of seconds while sitting at computers in the office, at home, in the dorm, or in the library. Newspapers, books, magazines, library holdings, company profiles, and even job banks are online for writers who have Internet access. Electronic indexes and databases offer citations, abstracts, and even full text records.

As the Internet has developed, many databases have been made public on the World Wide Web. The lines are blurring between traditional databases, once accessed through library or university services and at a cost, and what is stored on the Web. The number of databases available online grows daily in number, diversity, and ease of access.

Recognizing the importance of online proficiency and the role of computers today, more and more universities are requiring students to have their own laptops and to take Internet courses. But the proliferation of online information has not made everyone a user and expert. Some people still are novices in the Internet world. Getting online remains difficult for many individuals because they cannot afford the cost of a computer. Although prices for Internet service providers have come down, consumers must pay to access the Internet.

Individuals get on line by subscribing to commercial services that allow them access to online services or to setup e-mail accounts. Subscribers pay a fee to secure logons and passwords to enter the systems. They also must pay for the service, generally a flat rate per month. Many people do avoid fees and even the cost of a computer, however, because they access the Internet at workplaces, libraries, or schools.

When people get online, they search for information, download data, photos, or text to their computers, send email, or chat. They use search engines or key words to find information on any topic. Web site addresses are displayed everywhere—in brochures, in advertisements, and on cereal boxes.

Most students entering college today are comfortable with computers and are eager to be online. They are accustomed to instant messaging as a means of communication. They do much of their research online. Even *The Associated Press Stylebook* recognizes the Internet as a staple of journalistic reporting and writing and includes a section on the Internet and terminology.

But as much as students and professional writers have come to depend on the Internet, they must still have some skepticism about what they find there. Anyone who uses the Internet needs to stay current on developments and regulation. With the proliferation of available information has some discussion of issues on privacy, legal uses, copyright, and ethics (discussed in detail in Chapter 8). A helpful publication is Nora Paul's *Computer Assisted Research* published by the Poynter Institute in St. Petersburg, Florida. Updates are available online.

Pitfalls of Online Research

As with any aspect of research, writers must be careful in selecting sources and in using material. Those cautionary words are even more important in regard to the Internet. The plus sides of online research are obvious, but some minuses to remember are:

• Information on the Internet is not necessarily accurate. It is difficult to tell if information is credible. Anyone can create a Web site and pose as knowledgeable on a topic. Writers must double-check the accuracy of what they find online.

• Internet sources may not be up to date. Although information may be accessed quickly, it may not be as current as a researcher would like. Lag times exist for adding information to databases. Check for dates when sites were last updated.

• Users have to wade through a lot of junk to find what they want. General search engines give researchers hundreds or even thousands of hits on a subject. Researchers need to be careful in crafting key words in their searches or should use specific topic search engines, such as www. webmed.com for medical information.

• Web sites come and go. Many dot.com companies are created then disbanded. People put up Web sites then pull them. Attribute and date any information that you find. When you go to look for it later, it may be gone.

• Online information may not be complete. Sites often have only summaries of analyzed data rather than the data that would allow researchers to do their own analyses.

• Much of what is on the Internet is not in an archive or stored any-where. Pages are up for a few hours then are gone. Some efforts are under-way to save and store online information because librarians believe that online pages, just like newspaper pages, chronicle history and should be kept. Newspapers and other media sites have archives, but to access them, you must subscribe.

• High demand may make it difficult to sign on, or the sites themselves may not have the software to accommodate many hits at one time. Some sys-tems may even have down time while they upgrade.

• What you find may not be clear. In their haste to get information on-line, people have little regard for the quality of writing or the content.

Despite all these warnings, the Internet is a valuable tool. And writers should remember that it is just a tool. Online researching may be the first choice, but it should not be the final stop. It is just one step in the research process.

What You Can't Find Online

Writers today must remember that online information is a recent pheno-menon. Most history is buried in letters, memos, newspapers, magazines, and other written material not catalogued in online databases. When writer Nadine Cohodas began researching her book, *Spinning Blues into Gold: The Chess Brothers and the Legendary Chess Records*, she went hunting. Her re-search included visits to the Chicago neighborhoods where brothers Phil and Leonard Chess had their offices and where the great blues singers performed.

Cohodas produced a book that brought information to readers they would not have gotten on their own. Finding the details required hours and hours of reading trade journals, such as *Billboard* and *Cash Box,* to understand the evolution of the record company; poring over Chicago newspapers; and scouring public records such as old liquor licenses to trace the brothers' busi-ness beginnings, city phone books and directories to confirm the relevant addresses, and the Federal Communications Commission archive for details about their radio stations. "You have to love the hunt," she said.

Every now and then Cohodas had her "eureka" moments when she found something that provided the telling detail for a piece of the story. For example, she needed information about the history of the Macomba Lounge, owned by the Chess brothers. She explains how she found it.

> *To find out what the Macomba Lounge had been, I photocopied about 30 pages of the Chicago Yellow Pages in the tavern listings, then read them one by one to find the same address. Lo and behold, the Congress Buffet showed up at 3905 S. Cottage. I used that name to request the liquor license for that venue so I could trace the history further.*
>
> *Meanwhile, I found the only ad anyone knows of for the Macomba Lounge by going through the now defunct* Chicago Bee *week by week in the first or second year Leonard and Phil were in the club and that's when I saw the ad—a sweet moment.*

The result of nearly three years' work was a fascinating account of two Polish immigrants who built a company promoting black singers such as Muddy Waters, Chuck Berry, Bo Diddley, and Etta James. *The New York Times Book Review* named it as one of the notable nonfiction books of 2000, and the book won the 2001 Blues Foundation Keeping the Blues Alive Award.

Observation

Observation is an old method of research that still is a key tool in gathering information. At the same time writers note what speakers are saying, they should be noticing how speakers deliver their remarks, how they move their bodies, what they are wearing, and how the crowd reacts to their comments. Such details are part of the reporting process.

Many students and inexperienced writers, however, are reluctant to include too many details. They fear that audiences will doubt their descriptions. They believe that using description borders on being subjective when, in fact, leaving out description may distort an event. For example, a story may reveal a speaker's eloquence and pointed remarks on U.S. trade with China, but the reporter may not include that only 22 people were seated in an auditorium that holds 550 people. Although the speaker may have been eloquent, the speech's title failed to attract a sizable audience.

Seeing Isn't Enough

Many people notice their surroundings or the events happening around them in one dimension. They see. Rarely do people consciously smell, taste, hear, or touch their environment. Even using only sight, most people miss much of what goes on. So do writers. They have not trained themselves to observe events that happen simultaneously. At the state fair, a writer may notice the lines in front of concessions but not see the child wailing for more cotton candy, the youth loaded with three bright green teddy bears, the overflowing garbage at a nearby trash can, and the cigarette hanging from the hawker's lips. The unobservant writer does not smell the odor of fried dough, taste the grease in the air near the ferris wheel, hear the ping-ping from the shooting gallery, or feel the slap of heat from the barbecue cookers.

To be skillful observers, writers must hone all their senses. To be complete and successful writers, they must describe scenes to absent audiences. Even when viewers see events on television, they still need the reporter's or news anchor's observations. When television covers the annual Thanksgiving Day parade in New York City, for example, reporters must identify floats and provide background on performers. Viewers need the information to understand what they are seeing.

General Observation

Many people exist on autopilot. They drive the same route to work, live in the same house or apartment for years, and work in the same office. They become less and less observant. What about you?

Any person or writer can hone observation skills. Try this experiment: Take a piece of paper. Describe what your roommate or friend wore to school or work today. Note colors and types of fabric, if possible. What did you eat for breakfast? Can you remember the smell as well as the taste? What about the color or feel? What sounds do you hear in this room? Can you name more than three?

Keep a notebook in your car, backpack, or pocket. Start recording what you see and hear in multidimensional ways. Although most people can note different sounds, it is harder to catch and record events happening simultaneously. The oft-told adage is that two people on a street corner would give two different accounts of an accident witnessed by both.

Think of ways to compare what you see with events or items that are common knowledge. When author Barbara Victor met Iraqi leader Saddam Hussein, she noted to a group of college students, "He looked like [singer] Tom Jones in an Yves St. Laurent jumpsuit." She could have said that he looked like a pop singer in a one-piece outfit, but the image would not have been the same.

How Observation Changes the Action

Often you need to take notes unobtrusively, especially when the act of note taking may change the behavior of an individual you are observing. Did the person across the aisle on the bus sit up straighter when she noticed you writing? Did your friend start picking up his clutter when you started taking notes about the room? Your presence can change the way events unfold.

When reporters cover a meeting, a rally, or a store opening, their presence affects how people behave. The town council members sit up straighter and look busy when the public access television channel is airing the meeting. Rally organizers look efficient and engaged when reporters approach. Store officials beam smiles of success on the first day of business.

The trick to accurate observing is to observe over time. Most people can maintain a facade for some time, but they cannot keep it up forever. You may have to observe for more than a few minutes. Despite the television cameras, the losing team's cheerleaders are hardly as media conscious at the end of a game as they were at the outset. Two hours into a meeting, the mayor may forget the unobtrusive camera and rail against the accusations of an unhappy citizen.

Participant Observation

Social scientists have long used observation by participants as a means of getting information about groups. They join a group as participants to observe individual behavior within a group and the individuals' interactions. Journalists also have adopted the practice, gaining admission and recording the interactions of the group. Such intrusion by journalists affects the way people interact. Over time, however, reporters become accepted, and other members may forget their role.

Because their presence does affect how members relate, some journalists have opted to become members of groups and not to identify themselves as reporters. In the 1890s, reporter Nellie Bly pretended to be a mental patient to get a true picture of how the insane were treated at Blackwells Island, New York's asylum for the mentally ill. Some have joined cults, followed the Hell's Angels, or gotten jobs in nursing homes. One reporter in her mid-20s enrolled in a Philadelphia high school to observe it firsthand—and was invited to the senior prom. Before resorting to undercover work, reporters and their editors must determine that a change of identity is the only way to get the story.

In either case, problems can arise when it is time to write. Reporters may feel a kinship to the group and have difficulty setting themselves apart. Journalists who become group members put their impartiality at risk in writing a story. Writers may become too emotional or too attached to sources and not be able to distance themselves. They also run the risk of not knowing completely whether their presence altered the group in any way. They can double-check their reactions and observations, however, by interviewing a balanced mix of sources. Reporters may also suffer complaints from group members who may feel betrayed when the article appears.

Nonverbal Communication

Although writers get the bulk of their information from sources and from interviewing, they can add details from nonverbal communication. Such cues come from the way people move or act when they say something. A politician may raise her eyebrows at a constituent's question. A child may shift his hands behind his back when leaving the kitchen. A teacher may frown while correcting student essays. Each action implies a thought or behavior to the observer. The politician may be surprised. The child may be guilty of swiping a cookie. The teacher may be unhappy about a good student's low grade.

When recording nonverbal cues, reporters must be careful. The same cue may carry different meanings for different observers. Furrowed eyebrows may indicate puzzlement or anger. Waving hands can mean agitation or enthusiasm. A smile may be sincere or forced. Generally, one action alone is not sufficient to indicate how an individual is feeling. The gestures must be catalogued in addition to words and other body movements. A reporter may have to go so far as to ask an individual what a particular posture meant. For example, pacing during an interview may not be a result of nervousness; the interviewee may suffer from restless legs syndrome, but no reporter could tell that simply by observing.

In addition, nonverbal actions may have different meanings across cultures. In some cultures or ethnic groups, individuals do not have eye contact while speaking. An ignorant or inexperienced reporter might be suspicious of such behavior, thereby including a cultural bias. When business leaders from the United States engage in negotiations with Japanese officials, they have to learn etiquette and protocol. For example, the Japanese consider it offensive to write on a business card, while in the United States, executives and others make notations or add home telephone numbers to business cards. The good reporter learns about cultural differences or asks questions to clarify behavior. Such sensitivity and awareness is essential to accurate reporting.

Dangers in Observation

John Salvi was charged with murdering two people and injuring five others in shootings at two abortion clinics in Boston. When Salvi was arraigned on weapons charges in conjunction with the shootings, Gary Tuchman of CNN gave a live report and description for audiences who were not in the courtroom. Tuchman described Salvi as wearing a blue blazer, white shirt, white socks, loafers, and nice pants. The description implied that Salvi had dressed conservatively and neatly. A print news account reported that Salvi was wearing "an ill-fitting blazer." The implication here contradicted the neat appearance of Tuchman's report. Which account was right? Audiences who heard and read the two accounts may have noticed the discrepancy and been puzzled. Or maybe it just added to their belief that you cannot trust the media to be right.

Tuchman also took his reported observation one step further. He noted to viewers that if they had a stereotype of someone who would be charged with committing murder, Salvi did not look like that stereotype—that is, Salvi did not look like someone who would commit murder. Viewers may have wondered: "What does the stereotypical murderer look like? Why didn't Tuchman give us a description of that stereotype?"

Observation plays a major role in writing, but we must be circumspect about the descriptions we use. As was discussed in Chapter 6 on bias, we as writers carry our prejudices and biases with us as we collect information and write. We must be careful. Think about Tuchman's reference to a stereotypical murderer. Can you describe one? Of course not. If murderers were readily identifiable, people who have been killed would have had some warning. But murderers vary in shape, size, age, gender, skin tone, hair color, and clothing preference. They do not all have greasy hair and shifty beady eyes and act furtively or in a suspicious manner.

The Importance of Accuracy

As we noted in the account just discussed, Tuchman's observations may have been distorted by his experiences. He may have a stereotypical idea of what a murderer looks like. Writers can bring biases to observation, just as they can to any aspect of reporting.

Just as you double-check facts, you should be circumspect about your observations. Take emotions into account. If you covered an antiabortion rally, you may have found your emotions surging if you are pro-choice. Despite your role as a journalist, your feelings may not be neutral. Your feelings may influence your description. Be aware.

To ensure accuracy, you should record impressions in your notebook at the scene or as soon as possible afterward. The longer you wait, the fewer details you will remember accurately. Memory fades over time.

Like other kinds of research, observation leads to a more complete message. Description that is simple, clear, fair, and complete also will aid accuracy. Writers should lay out description alongside other facts and allow audiences to judge for themselves. Audiences invariably will apply their own biases to the description and form their own opinions, but the writers' choice of words should not be the deciding factor.

EXERCISES

1. Gene Roberts, former *New York Times* managing editor and *Philadelphia Inquirer* editor, is coming to campus to give a lecture. Before the lecture, he will have a news conference, and you will attend for the campus newspaper. First, you need to find out more information. Using three biographical sources, answer the following questions. Cite the reference used. One reference should be online.
   a. When and where was Roberts born?
   b. Where did he go to college?
   c. What newspapers did he work for other than the *Times* and the *Inquirer?*
   d. Has he written any books? If so, list the titles.
   e. Has he won any awards? If so, list them.

2. Identify a reporter in your college community or in your hometown by reading bylines and articles in the respective paper. Call the reporter and

ask what sources he or she uses in researching stories. Note whether the reporter uses online sources to retrieve information. Find out how the reporter ensures accuracy in using sources. Share the information with your class.

3. You are the state desk researcher for the local newspaper. The state editor wants to do a story on parents who are charged with killing their children. In making the assignment to a reporter, the editor asks you to do an online search of national newspapers and magazines to find accounts of such crimes. Your task is to prepare a memo to the state editor that lists six references to substantial articles on parents who are charged with killing their children. The references need to be annotated; that is, they should be accompanied by explanatory notes as well as enough information to enable the reporter to find the articles.

4. Pick a place on campus or attend a town government meeting as an observer along with another student. Use your senses to take notes on what transpires outside the actions of passers-by or officials. Write a description of the meeting, using aspects such as the room, the mood, the speakers' attitudes, the officials' attitudes, the tone of the meeting, and how many people attended. Then compare your account with the other student's account. See what each of you chose to include and chose to ignore. Compare the ways you described aspects of the meeting. Then discuss what made your observations different.

REFERENCES

Nadine Cohodas, Using documents. Interview via e-mail, October 2001.

Jon Elliston, FOIA searching. Interview, October 2001.

Freedom of Information Act, 5 U.S.C. 552, 1966. Amended in 1974, 1986, 1996.

Michael Gartner, Speech in honor of national Freedom of Information Day. Washington, DC, National Press Club, March 1989.

Bruce D. Itule and Douglas A. Anderson, *News Writing and Reporting for Today's Media,* 3rd ed. New York: McGraw-Hill, 1994.

Margaret Jackson, *Selected Resources for Journalists.* Chapel Hill, NC: Business Administration/Social Sciences Department, Davis Library, University of North Carolina at Chapel Hill, 1989.

Lauren Kessler and Duncan McDonald, *Mastering the Message: Media Writing with Substance and Style.* Belmont, CA: Wadsworth, 1992.

Mary McGuire, Linda Stilborne, Melinda McAdams, and Laurel Hyatt, *The Internet Handbook for Writers, Researchers, and Journalists.* New York: Guilford Press, 1997.

Nora Paul, *Computer Assisted Research: A Guide to Tapping Online Information,* 4th ed. St. Petersburg, FL.: The Poynter Institute for Media Studies, 2001.

Randy Reddick and Elliot King, *The Online Journalist: Using the Internet and Other Electronic Resources.* Orlando, FL: Harcourt Brace College Publishers, 1995.

Chip Rowe, "A Journalist's Guide to the Internet." *American Journalism Review,* January 1995.

Barbara Semonche, Personal interview. Chapel Hill, N.C., School of Journalism and Mass Communication, University of North Carolina at Chapel Hill, 1995.

Leslie Walker, "Web-Page Collection Preserves the Online Response to Horror," *The Washington Post,* September 26, 2001.

8

Legal and Ethical Issues

A newspaper intern is fired after editors discover that he has plagiarized parts of several stories from other publications.

A major broadcast network is sued after it airs a story criticizing a grocery store chain's meat packaging. One problem is that two reporters who worked in a meat department didn't state on their job applications that they were members of the news media.

An actor sues a tabloid for libel after it reports she was drunk and disorderly in a Washington, D.C., restaurant. The magazine had not a single reliable source for the story.

A reporter writes a story about a company's alleged bad business practices, using information from executives' voice mails that he accessed without their permission. The newspaper recanted the story, paid a huge out-of-court settlement, and fired its reporter.

These scenarios may sound improbable, but each is true. Each story and the newsgathering methods used to produce it had consequences for the reporter and the media outlet that printed or aired the story. In gathering and using information, writers often face a mix of legal and ethical issues. Decisions are not always easy because laws and ethics constantly change.

In many cases, state and federal law aids reporters in their quest for information. For example, *shield laws* protect reporters from revealing their sources in court. *Libel laws* outline the conditions under which individuals can sue when they feel they have been falsely defamed. Although state laws protect citizens and public figures in regard to privacy, *implied consent* may protect a reporter who goes on private property to get a story. Many laws have been around for years and have evolved through the courts. Others, such as many shield laws, are more recent.

Over the last decade, the media law battlefront has moved from libel cases to disputes over how media gather information. Subjects of news coverage have sued the media for misrepresenting who they are or the type of story they are working on, for trespassing on private property, and for using hidden cameras or hidden tape recorders. Some media observers say that the methods represent unethical behavior by reporters, and some courts have begun to rule that such actions violate the law.

Other issues for writers in the information age have been plagiarism and copyright violations. Information gathering today via the Internet makes it easy to commandeer information and claim it as the writer's own work—whether unintentionally or purposefully. Sometimes the writer stores information and later inadvertently uses it without attributing the original source. In other cases, the material is stolen outright. In any case, the writer may have plagiarized and possibly infringed on another's copyright.

Copyright violations occur when writers use another's work and don't get permission. It is not sufficient simply to credit the original author, unless the material falls under a category known as fair use, explained later in the chapter.

In this chapter, you will learn

- What libel is,
- The issues of privacy and the relationship between sources and writers,
- The dangers of plagiarism and what constitutes copyrighted material,
- How ethics policies guide writers, and
- When writers cross the line in gathering information.

Libel

Writers can unknowingly or carelessly damage an individual's reputation. Even if a slip is unintentional, if the libel is in print or is aired, the writer can be sued, as can a newspaper, a television station, a church administration, or a nonprofit group.

Libel can occur in any writing: a news article, a news release, a public service announcement, annual reports, corporate financial statements, a television talk show, a student's Web site, or a church bulletin. If a news release is mailed but not published, the writer could still be sued for libel because dissemination of the falsity occurred. A radio or television station that broadcasts slander (oral defamation) or libelous statements can be sued under the state's libel laws.

Libel often occurs when people write about topics they do not really understand. Inexperienced reporters, student writers, and occasional writers are most at risk. Good data collection, complete identification, and good writing techniques can prevent many libel problems, however. Mass communication professors advise their students to be absolutely accurate, thorough, and scrupulously fair in what they write.

The legal system will protect writers who do a good job of investigating and who use many sources. Innocent mistakes made without negligence or actual malice are not libelous. The protection often will hold even if they write something that turns out to be false and defamatory.

A huge body of law exists on libel. Thousands of libel cases have been filed. Although most editors, writers, and copyeditors do not need to be lawyers, they do need to know the basics of libel law. A writer may be the only member of a nonprofit organization's communication staff; he or she needs to know what might cause trouble. Libel laws differ from state to state. For example, the statute of limitations, or time within which a person can file a libel suit, varies; it is usually from one to two years. Writers should be familiar with the libel laws in their states or in the states in which the material will be disseminated.

Elements of Libel

Writers who know about libel law do not have to be afraid to write negative information. If they know the essential elements of libel, they won't be chilled into self-censorship.

An individual—the person written about—has to prove six essential elements to win a libel case:

1. *Defamation.* The individual has to show that the information was defamatory or bad enough to cause him or her to be held up to ridicule or contempt.
2. *Identification.* The story clearly identified the individual by name, in a recognizable photo, or through description.
3. *Publication.* The memo was circulated, the story printed, the news release received, the report aired, or the message was read by just one

person outside the newsroom or the writer's workplace other than the person written about.

4. *Falsity.* The information published was not true. In a few cases, the burden of proof falls on the media, which attempt to prove the information was true.
5. *Harm or injury.* The individual has to show harm to his or her reputation or emotional well-being. Proof of monetary loss can increase the amount of money the media have to pay if they lose.
6. *Fault.* The individual has to prove that the newspaper, radio station, or other party was at fault in presenting the libel.

To win a case, most plaintiffs have to prove all six elements. On the sixth item, court decisions have set different criteria for private citizens and public figures.

In most cases, ordinary folks have to prove a standard of fault called *negligence* to win a libel suit. They must show that the writer failed to follow professional standards or acted unreasonably in carrying out his or her research and in writing.

Celebrities or people in power or politics have to go further in establishing fault. They must prove that the writer knew that the information was false or showed reckless disregard as to whether the information was true or false. That is called *actual malice.* That element came about through the 1964 *New York Times* v. *Sullivan* case, in which the United States Supreme Court ruled that a public official cannot recover damages for a defamatory falsehood relating to his or her official conduct unless he or she proves that the statement was made with actual malice. Actual malice is extremely difficult to prove and is the major hurdle for most plaintiffs.

Let's say you are writing a story about your town's mayor. During interviews, an unreliable source tells you that the mayor leaves town twice a year to meet his childhood sweetheart—not his wife—at a mountain cabin. If you were to write that bit of information without further investigation, you would be setting yourself up for a libel suit. Your reliance on a single, unreliable source would be reckless disregard for whether the information was true.

People are defamed, perhaps falsely, every day. Just think about the hundreds of police reports naming people who have been arrested. They can prove many of the six elements, such as publication, identification, and defamation. But would they win a libel suit? Rarely.

A Writer's Defenses in a Libel Suit

Within the legal system are defenses writers can use to protect themselves against a libel suit even if the person they wrote about can prove the elements listed earlier. The major defenses are these:

1. *Truth.* The writer can prove the information was substantially true through reliable witnesses and documentary evidence.

2. *Fair report or privilege.* Writers are protected when they report fairly and accurately material from official government proceedings or reports. That is one reason news media rely so heavily on government meetings and sessions. A witness can falsely accuse someone in court of committing murder, and you as a reporter can print the accusation. You are protected from a libel suit if the charges were made during a court session. Your reporting must be accurate, fair and balanced, attributed to the government meeting or record, and not motivated by spite or ill will.

3. *Wire service defense.* Some states have adopted what is known as the wire service defense. Newspapers and other media organizations are protected if they get a story from the wire services, such as the Associated Press, and reprint it. It would be impossible for writers to verify every fact that appeared in a wire service story. Wire service clients have to trust that the information sent to them is true.

4. *Statute of limitations.* Individuals cannot sue after a specific number of years has passed.

5. *Opinion defense.* The opinion defense protects two kinds of statements. Writers are protected if they are critiquing a performance or service as long as they give a general assessment that is incapable of being proved true or false. For example, a restaurant critic could write that the restaurant food is not good. The critic could not say that the chef stole the high-quality meats for his family, leaving lesser meats for the restaurant dishes—unless that were true, of course.

The opinion defense also protects what is known as hyperbole: wild exaggeration that no one would believe to be true. For example, in the 1980s, the federal courts said *Hustler* magazine had a First Amendment right to publish an outrageous insult directed at television evangelist Jerry Falwell.

Falwell had sued the magazine after it published a cartoon parody of Campari liqueur's "first time" advertising campaign. The cartoon depicted the Rev. Falwell as having his "first time"—his first sexual encounter—while drunk with his mother in an outhouse. The courts said no one would believe such an outrageous allegation, so the evangelist's reputation had not been damaged.

As a footnote, writers should know that they cannot be sued successfully for libel by the government—state, local, or federal. Writers can say that the federal government or some part of it is an overgrown, bumbling bureaucratic mess without fear of being sued. But they cannot write that the director of a particular agency has misspent government funds without getting into trouble.

How to Avoid Libel Suits

Writers do not want to be sued for libel even if they win. Libel suits are costly, time consuming, and emotionally draining. They can go on for years. People do win libel cases against media. For example, CapCities Communications lost a $11.5 million libel suit when one of its New York television stations incorrectly identified a restaurant owner as having ties with organized crime. In 1994, an attorney won a $24 million judgment against the *Philadelphia Inquirer,* which had reported he quashed a homicide investigation when he was an assistant district attorney because it involved the son of a police officer. The case took more than 10 years to conclude.

Ninety percent of libel cases filed never make it to court. Some are dropped, and some end up in out-of-court settlements, which cost media actual payouts and attorneys' fees. Libel suits are to be avoided.

Some recommendations:

- Don't write lies and publish them.
- Use credible, reliable, multiple sources.
- Recognize the importance of fairness.
- Be accurate.
- Be complete.

Also, be polite if someone complains about inaccuracy. One study showed that most people who sued decided to do so after they were treated rudely when they pointed out the mistake.

Corrections

Most publications have a policy on writing corrections when errors have been made. Some editors say that any correction should be as prominently displayed as the error; that is, if the error is in a front-page headline, then the correction needs to be large and on the front page, not buried on page 22.

Lawyers may caution against widespread use of corrections because they could be used as an admission of guilt: The correction states that the newspaper made a mistake. Others note that the correction can mitigate any punitive damages if the individual libeled chooses to sue. Media outlets may have a policy to run corrections in all cases because they believe they should correct their mistakes and not lie. In most cases, the correction includes only the correct title, statistic, address, or whatever was wrong and does not repeat the erroneous information.

Privacy

Reporters frequently face privacy dilemmas in their quest to gather and report the news. These dilemmas are both legal and ethical and provoke loud public protests when the public believes the media are trampling the privacy rights of individuals in the news.

Right of Privacy

The doctrine of the right to privacy has evolved to protect individuals and to give them the right to be let alone, particularly from unwarranted publicity. Decisions from lower courts up to the United States Supreme Court have involved individuals' right to privacy.

Privacy law varies considerably from state to state, and writers should know what constitutes invasion of privacy in their states or in the state where articles will be published or stories aired. Generally, however, there are three ways writers sometimes invade individuals' privacy while gathering and writing information.

First, a journalist might go on private property without permission to get a story. The writer then could be sued for intruding on the property owner's privacy. In such cases, the journalist is sued for his or her means of gathering information, not for the content of what he or she wrote. The writer could be sued successfully even if no story resulted.

Second, a writer might disclose private and embarrassing but true facts about an individual, who could claim the facts should not have been published. But winning that suit could be difficult for the person who sues, because courts are hesitant to punish the news media for publishing the truth. Also, if individuals become part of a newsworthy event, they forfeit their right to privacy. The courts have upheld the forfeiture even if the individual became part of the news event involuntarily. For example, a private citizen may become a hostage in a bank robbery and therefore is part of the news event.

Third, *The Associated Press Stylebook and Briefing on Media Law* notes that the news media "may be liable for invasion of privacy if the facts of a story are changed deliberately or recklessly, or 'fictionalized.'" These privacy cases closely resemble libel cases, and just as with libel considerations, writers must be careful to be accurate and thorough.

In some states, privacy law is so protective of the media that privacy is more of an ethical problem than a legal one. In dealing with the ethics of privacy, many media outlets have categories of individuals and treat them differently. Politicians and public officials are held to a higher standard of behavior in what journalists will or will not pursue. Some newsgathering is more aggressive, and less concern is given to privacy rights.

Media also hold to a high standard public figures who trade on their public image or who are briefly prominent in the news. Reporters may assume that a higher standard of behavior means officials have less privacy. Other people, the common folk if you will, garner more privacy from the media.

Public versus Private Property

Some privacy disputes hinge on whether the news took place on public or private property. For example, a Christmas parade on city streets is considered a public event in a public place, and reporters—whether print or broadcast—would have access to people viewing or participating in the parade. Furthermore, people in public places should expect their actions to be public—and those actions can be reported in the media legally. A grandmother who attends the parade and whose photo is printed in the local newspaper cannot sue successfully for invasion of privacy.

Courts consider people's homes to be the most private places, so reporters need to be especially cautions when they gather news in people's homes.

Places between private homes and the Christmas parade sometimes are more difficult to locate on the public/private property continuum. For example, it took several cases for the United States Supreme Court to determine that shopping malls are private property, even though they serve as the social hubs in many communities. Working reporters asked to leave shopping centers must do so, no matter what the news event.

In all court cases concerning privacy violations, consent might be a useful media defense. The best consent defense results when a reporter is invited onto private property or told explicitly that she or he has permission to be there. Next best is implied consent, which occurs when a property owner knows who the media are and doesn't ask them to leave. If a police officer tells the media it's okay to be on private property, the media may not be protected. The Supreme Court has ruled that police violate the Fourth Amendment rights of homeowners when they give permission.

At the same time, reporters must heed a police officer's order to leave property and can be charged with trespassing if they don't. Consider the Reporters Committee on Freedom of the Press's guidelines on access:

> *Regardless of whether news occurs on public or private property, if you ignore police orders regarding access you risk arrest and prosecution. Case law makes clear that police can limit media access when they believe such restrictions are needed for public safety or to prevent interference with an investigation, and that the First Amendment does not provide immunity from criminal sanctions for disobeying police orders.*

When to Publish or Not

Media often take criticism when they publish too much information. For example, critics charge that the public doesn't have a right to know the name of a crime victim, such as a rape victim. They contend that the public needs to know when and where such crimes occur, but not the victim's name or address.

Most newspapers do not publish names of rape victims. Some states have laws that allow police to withhold the names of any crime victim if they believe publication will put the person in danger or cause him or her more harm. Some media will publish or broadcast victims' names only with their permission. Others note that the names are part of public record, and that if a person is charged, the name of the victim or accuser should also be included.

Media also can get into trouble when they publish quotes that they believe are relevant but in reality are libelous. For example, a newspaper reporter is covering the trial of a woman charged with involuntary manslaughter in the death of her 6-month-old daughter. The reporter walks a litigious tightrope if he or she includes a family member's quote that implies the woman's guilt and that was said outside the courtroom. If the family member makes the comment as part of court testimony, the reporter is generally protected against a libel suit. But if the remark is said in a parking lot while the trial is underway, the reporter and his or her editor must be careful not to republish any libelous statement by the parking-lot source. If they do, they can be sued for libel.

Most newspapers follow the policy of publishing private information if it relates to or affects public officials' or public figures' public duties. For example, when Washington, D.C., intern Chandra Levy disappeared, attention eventually focused on the private life of Congressman Gary Condit. His relationship with Levy emerged, as did his relationships with other women outside his marriage. Many voters questioned Condit's judgment and even called for his resignation after learning more about his personal life. The media believed they had a responsibility to publish the personal information.

Copyright and Plagiarism

Copyright and plagiarism become concerns when writers take original work that they did not create and use it without permission. A *copyright* is a right granted to the creator of an original work to control copies and reproductions of his or her work, derivatives of his or her work, and the rights to perform and display his or her work. Others who want to use the creator's work—such as reproducing copyrighted photos on a personal Web site—must either receive permission in writing (and usually pay for that use) or agree to a license that specifies terms of the use, such as using a computer program.

Plagiarism is more an ethical issue; it occurs when a writer takes original material and claims it as his or her own. A writer can violate copyright law without plagiarizing, and a writer can plagiarize without violating laws. In both instances, however, the penalties can be severe.

Copyright: A Definition

Copyright is the legal ownership of a story, publication, book, song, online article—anything that is produced as original work and fixed in any tangible medium, such as a newspaper or CD-ROM. When a work is copyrighted, the owner has exclusive legal rights to its use. Anyone can copyright material by applying to the Copyright Office in the Library of Congress. Anyone can claim a working copyright as soon as a piece is created. But without registration, an individual cannot sue for copyright infringement. Generally, an individual has ownership of the work for his or her lifetime plus 70 years for work produced after January 1, 1978. For corporations, the time is longer: 95 years from publication or 120 years from creation, whichever is shorter.

People, such as authors or songwriters, copyright their work so that they can benefit solely from royalties or the money it earns. Newspaper companies copyright each issue of the newspaper, a series, or longer articles. Online sites are also copyrighted. Copyright is designed to encourage the creation of more works and to benefit the public. If authors are given exclusive rights to their works for a period of time, the assumption is that they will create more.

In most cases, anyone who wants to use any portion of copyrighted material has to get permission—and often must pay a fee to use the material. For example, a writer who is doing a book on authors of horror stories cannot quote extensively from author Stephen King's work without permission. An advertising copywriter who wants to use the music from an Andrew Lloyd Webber song must get permission. In both cases, the writers would probably pay a fee based on how much is used and in what context.

Some material can be used without permission or payment of fees. Anything produced by the federal government is considered public domain and can be used. If a private organization does a report for the government, however, that material might be copyrighted. Anything that is considered noncopyrighted material is okay to use: facts, ideas, procedures, processes, systems, methods of operation, and principles, to name a few. That means the fact that the United States was a British colony or the text of Einstein's theory of relativity can be used. But a historian's analysis of the British impact on the colonies or a researcher's interpretation of Einstein's work may be copyright protected.

The Copyright Act of 1976, section 107, allows for what is called *fair use* of copyrighted material for "criticism, comment, news reporting, teaching, scholarship, or research." Fair use of material is not an infringement of copyright and does not require the permission of the copyright holder. For example, a book reviewer who wants to quote from Stephen King's novel in his review would not have to get permission to use the excerpt.

The factors to consider for fair use are:

1. The purpose and character of the use, including whether such use is of a commercial nature or is for nonprofit educational purposes;
2. The nature of the copyrighted work;
3. The amount and substantiality of the portion used in relation to the copyrighted work as a whole; and
4. The effect of the use on the potential market for or value of the copyrighted work.

Translated, that means a writer—or a university professor—cannot use someone else's material to earn money for himself or herself or that detracts from the money-making potential of the copyrighted material. The individual also cannot use a major portion of the material. Some people follow a 5 percent rule; that is, no more than 5 percent of the copyrighted work can be used without permission. Some follow a 50-word rule. To avoid any question over how much is acceptable use, get permission or check out a copyright holder's stipulations. For example, some newspapers do not require permission to use 30 words or less of a story. You can find out through their permissions offices.

Getting into Trouble

With the development of the Internet and the proliferation of computers, more and more material, including software, is illegally copied. Copyright holders sue for copyright infringement and hope to collect monetary damages, including an amount for lost royalties.

Writers get into trouble with copyrights when they believe that the material they are using is fair use. Sometimes they believe they are not using a substantial part or that their use is somehow exempt for educational reasons. Or they believe that the work has been quoted so much that it has become part of the public domain and can be used. Some also erroneously assume that citing the author or source and giving credit protects against copyright suits.

If writers have questions about copyright infringement, they should consult an attorney familiar with copyright law. The discussion here is not to frighten students or media writers away from using material; however, all writers must be aware of laws and penalties for using others' work without proper credit or authorization.

Recent Copyright Conflicts

A major issue in copyrights in recent years has been the unauthorized copying of songs from compact disks or movies from video cassettes. Let's say a person buys a video and makes a copy for a friend, or a person burns a CD for a buddy. Artists who made money, or royalties, from the sale of their CDs and videos each time they were aired in public began suing to keep from losing income. One issue in this conflict is who owns the rights to a piece: the artist, the company that distributed the work, or the individual who bought a copy. Ownership is important in any litigation and also in determining lost revenue.

To address copyright infringement of digital media, Congress passed the Digital Millennium Copyright Act, signed into law in 1998. Among other items, the act amended the copyright law to provide limits on the liability of service providers, or sites that stored information online, from the conduct of their users who might violate copyrights. If service providers are aware of violations and do nothing, they, too, are liable.

Copyright will always be an issue for artists and creators who want to ensure that they receive credit for and earn income from the work that they produce. You as a writer must be aware of copyright laws and ensure that whatever material you use falls under fair use. If you are not sure, consult a lawyer—or find out who owns the copyright, secure permission, and pay any requested fees.

If the fee is expensive, then you will have to determine whether the material justifies the cost. Don't think you can get around use by paraphrasing and believing that will protect you. If the paraphrase can be readily identifiable as the author's words or if the work is substantially similar, you can get into trouble.

Plagiarism: A Definition

Plagiarism occurs when people take information, even information that is not copyrighted, and use it as their own without crediting the original source. With the growth of the Internet, plagiarism occurs more often, intentionally and unintentionally. Attribution of sources can help mitigate plagiarism but it is not always a protection against charges of plagiarizing.

An intern at the *San Jose Mercury News* was fired after editors found he had plagiarized articles from the *Washington Post* and other publications. A reporter for the *San Francisco Chronicle* saw similarities in articles the intern wrote and stories that appeared in the *Post*. When editors investigated, they found that information had been copied from other publications, too.

The *Indianapolis Star* and the *Indianapolis News* suspended their television columnist when editors discovered he had plagiarized a column by a TV writer at another newspaper. The columnist admitted he had lifted the column, which editors discovered before it was published.

A sports columnist for a college newspaper was fired after the editor learned that sections of his column were taken from a *Sport Illustrated* columnist's work. The editor wrote an open letter to the newspaper's readers to explain how the plagiarism occurred and the resulting action.

Students and novice reporters often get themselves in trouble by using information and not properly crediting the source. Sometimes the error occurs out of ignorance rather than deliberately stealing material and using it as their own. In other cases, reporters may take material because of pressures of meeting deadlines, the lack of ideas, or inadequate information through their own research.

Whatever the reason, the consequences are dire. The owners of copyrighted material can sue for copyright infringement. In most cases of plagiarism, however, writers who steal will be suspended or fired—and their credibility will be severely impaired.

How to Avoid Plagiarism

The easiest way to avoid plagiarism is to be honest. Honesty covers how reporters gather information, store it, and use it. When reporters are gathering material, they need to be meticulous in their note taking and in citations. If they download a story from the Internet, they must ensure that they have included the source and date. If they copy information from a book, newspaper, or magazine, they must include a citation. Noting sources completely is necessary for proper attribution—that is, giving the original source credit. Attribution is further discussed in Chapter 9.

If writers are working on a project that takes days or even months of investigation, they must be exceedingly careful when they return to notes they have not viewed in a while. When fashioning the story, they must be aware what notes were their own and what came from another source. Writers can use material as their own that is factual. Remember from the discussion earlier in the chapter that even material that is condensed, summarized, and rewritten from another source should be attributed, as should any material used verbatim.

Of course, you should never take another person's work and claim it as your own, regardless of deadline pressure. A professor in a reporting class became suspicious when a student turned in a final project story that was much better than her other work throughout the semester. A quick check on the Internet pulled up dozens of stories on the student's topic—and blocks of copy pulled from three or four articles. The student had submitted the work as her own and violated the university's honor code, punishable by suspension. The outcome proved more severe than the penalty of not writing the story at all.

Ethics in Gathering Information

What is ethical in writing? Just as in any profession, *ethics in journalism* is a set of moral choices about what writers should and should not do in gathering and disseminating information. Journalists' ethical decisions determine their behavior.

Communicators must behave ethically. In most cases you can't be sued for ethical violations. States don't have ethics laws, like libel laws. You can't go to jail for revealing the source of your story even after you promised you wouldn't, but you could be sued for breach of contract. You won't get disbarred like a lawyer or lose your license like a physician, but if you violate your code of ethics or that of your publication, you lose your credibility or your source—and possibly your job. The bottom line is your professional reputation.

When it comes to ethics, mass communicators are often criticized for the kinds of information they publish and for violating individuals' privacy, as discussed earlier in the chapter. They are criticized for failing to remain objective and for stepping over the line from reporting to commenting. They are criticized for violent or sexual content that appears on television or online sites. They are also criticized for the way they collect information, from stealing to deceiving to harassing unwilling sources.

Former newspaper editor and ABC News president Michael Gartner notes that communicators have an ethical responsibility in the age of technology. "Readers don't know what is fact or fiction, what is an enhanced photo, what is slanted or straight, or what is the docu in docudrama," he cautions. "What comes out of a computer can be just as biased as what comes from a pulpit."

Communicators must be just as careful with their language and how it is interpreted as they are with their newsgathering techniques. In some situations, writers have ethics policies to guide them; in other instances, they have to use gut instinct.

Ethics Policies

Most news organizations, advertising agencies, public relations firms, online sites, and other mass communication fields have ethics guidelines. Some policies come from parent companies, such as Gannett, which rewrote its ethics policy in 1999 and then conducted in-house training at its more than 80 newspapers and media outlets. Other media rely on professional organizations for guidance, such as the American Advertising Federation.

Most ethics policies establish an environment in which employees are to work. Some companies use ethics contracts, and employees agree to them when they are hired. Policies outline areas where ethical considerations arise, such as conflict of interest, confidentiality of sources, impartiality of reporting, accuracy, acceptance of gifts or honoraria, and community or political involvement. Policies may be extensive, such as Gannett's policy (accessed at gannett.org/) or they can be as short as one page.

In addition to written ethics policies as guides, journalists should have their own ethical standards. In some cases, reporters have to use what their gut says, rather than refer to the company policy. For example, an editor learns that the son of a popular, local minister has become an out-of-wedlock father. The editor wants you the reporter to write a story because the minister has attracted a large following because of his views on teen abstinence. What does your ethical compass say about pursuing this story?

Ethics in Newsgathering: Deception

In recent years, the media have been criticized more and more for using deception to get their information. Deception occurs in everything from posing as other people to using hidden cameras or tape recorders to gather news. When is deception acceptable? Most editors would agree to deception if the information cannot be obtained any other way. The information would have to be of such importance that knowingly deceiving sources is acceptable. And editors and lawyers would have to be part of the decision to resort to such newsgathering techniques.

Deceptive newsgathering is not new. One of the most well-known cases occurred in the late 1970s when the *Chicago Sun Times* set up a bar called the

Mirage. Reporters posed as bartenders and waiters and used hidden cameras and tape recorders to secure evidence that building inspectors, police officers, and other city officials were soliciting bribes to allow the bar to operate. The series won several awards and was nominated for a Pulitzer Prize, the highest award in journalism. The Pulitzer Prize board rejected the series, however, because it felt that the *Sun Times'* methods were deceptive and unethical.

Students in an advanced reporting class were investigating whether citizens treated homeless people differently from others on downtown streets. As part of the story, students approached residents and asked for directions. Some students were well-dressed and neat in appearance; others wore disheveled clothes and had not shaved or combed their hair. The students found significant differences in residents' demeanor and interaction toward students who were neat and those who were not. They incorporated the reactions into their stories.

Such investigation, sometimes called *participant observation* because reporters put themselves into the situation as participants, can produce information that adds to a story. However, reporters should not inject themselves into a situation in a way that could change the outcome of the story.

Deception was at the heart of the highly visible ABC/Food Lion case in 1992 in which ABC reporters applied for jobs at a Food Lion store to check out complaints about how Food Lion repackaged meats for sale. The reporters used false resumés that failed to include the fact that they were practicing journalists. They used hidden cameras to film their work that subsequently was aired on ABC's *Prime Time Live.*

The reports alleged that Food Lion workers repackaged outdated meats with newer meats and that they bleached meats, among other offenses. Food Lion executives sued, not for libel or falsity in the reports themselves, but for fraud, trespassing, and breach of loyalty. Initially, a North Carolina jury awarded Food Lion $5.5 million, but on appeal, the amount was cut to $2. Despite the ultimate reduction of any monetary settlement, reporters' credibility had been damaged and their ethical behavior hanged in the public eye.

The *San Jose Mercury News* fired a reporter who used his status as a graduate student at the University of Iowa to obtain information from the university archives and use it in a story. The article revealed that university researchers had used children from an orphanage in a project on stuttering—actually turning the children into stutterers. The archives are open only to students, staff, and faculty members, and anyone using the archives must sign a form that the use is for research only. The reporter got the information a month before he began his internship at the newspaper—and wrote on the form that he was a graduate student in psychology when he really was a student in journalism.

Such cases and the case study below show that the legal battlefield for media is shifting from concerns with individuals or companies suing for libel to concerns with methods used to gather information.

Ethics in Newsgathering: A Case Study

On May 3, 1998, the *Cincinnati Enquirer* published an 18-page special section on Chiquita Brands International Inc. The investigative news series in the Gannett-owned newspaper detailed alleged company abuses ranging from bribery to spraying unsafe chemicals at its banana plantations in Central America and the Caribbean. Two reporters—Michael Gallagher and Cameron McWhirter—produced most of the writing, which was reviewed by *Enquirer* editors and Gannett executives and lawyers before publication.

The editor's note that prefaced the series said some of the information had come from more than 2,000 voice mails supplied by a Chiquita executive—in addition to traditional methods of reporting: interviews, documents, and visits to banana plantations.

When the series broke, Chiquita officials reacted quickly. They claimed that Gallagher had illegally accessed the company's voice mail system. Within two months, the *Enquirer* fired Gallagher, ran a front-page story renouncing the series, and pulled the stories from all Gannett libraries. *Enquirer* employees were also not allowed to answer questions about the series, and Gannett wired Chiquita a reported $14 million as an out-of court settlement and to keep the company from suing.

The printed apology noted that the reporter—Gallagher—had assured editors he had obtained the information in an ethical and lawful manner. But it also noted that with the charges from Chiquita, the paper could not trust him.

After a special prosecutor was appointed for a grand jury investigation, the Hamilton County district attorney's office charged Gallagher. He eventually pleaded guilty to intercepting internal company communications. Throughout the investigation, Chiquita officials questioned the reporter's access to its private messages but not the content of the series.

Chiquita chief executive Carl Lindner ironically had owned the *Enquirer* until he sold it in 1975 and was at one time the second-largest holder of Gannett stock. Some observers believed that his one-time ties to the paper might have been leveraged in arranging a settlement.

The *Enquirer*/Chiquita fiasco created much debate in the media community about the *Enquirer*/Gannett capitulation to Chiquita in the front-page apology. It also brought to the forefront once again the discussion of how reporters obtain information. Generally, the courts have upheld reporters when they use material sources give to them, even if the material was stolen. When reporters steal the information, then they are subject to legal charges.

Some media observers felt the content of the stories outweighed the issue of the voice mail messages. The lingering question was just how Gallagher obtained the material. Did he hack into Chiquita executives' voice mail? Did a disgruntled employee give him an access code? It's hard to understand exactly what went wrong and why because the major players still aren't talking—but journalists still are.

The lesson for aspiring journalists is to be honest, ethical, and legal in information gathering. Methods should be unquestionable. Information should be accurate. Editors should always know a reporter's source and serve as backup in the event someone has doubts about a source's or the reporter's credibility. The *Enquirer* and Gannett seemed to have all their bases covered, including having news executives and lawyers review the content ahead of time. But the series that the *Enquirer* had hoped would be a Pulitzer Prize contender ended up costing Gannett more than money. It damaged the newspaper's reputation and crushed employee morale.

Other Newsgathering Dilemmas

Other ethical brouhahas arise in information gathering, particularly in discussions about whether a story warrants media attention. You suspect that a public official is having extramarital relations, so you stake out his house and discover that he spent the night in an apartment of a woman not his wife. Do you write the story? You learn that an antiabortion rights activist had an abortion as a 15-year-old. Do you include that information in a story when she leads an antiabortion protest?

Public officials' behavior has been the focus of many news stories since the *Miami Herald* staked out the apartment of Democratic presidential contender Gary Hart in Washington, D.C. The news media published photos of Hart with a woman, not his wife. Although Hart never admitted his relationship with model Donna Rice was sexual, he withdrew as a Democratic contender.

Former President Bill Clinton went through an impeachment trial on charges that he committed perjury and obstructed justice in denying that he had a relationship with intern Monica Lewinsky. California Sen. Gary Condit became the topic of media scrutiny when intern Chandra Levy disappeared and an investigation initiated by her parents revealed their relationship—and allegations by other women of relationships with Condit.

Is reporting such behavior unethical? Journalists would cry no; they are reporting the news. The public outcry comes when the stories report and re-report lurid and seemingly minor details of such relationships. Audiences become saturated. The answers to such publication issues have to be reached case by case, medium by medium. What one publication decides to print, another may refuse to include.

The Outcome

As noted earlier, when unflattering information is published about an individual or when companies question a reporter's methods in getting details, the media are attacked for violating someone's standards of ethical behavior. They have to justify their means and the importance of the information gathered.

Reporters should always consult their editors when they plan to use deception or any other method to get information. They should determine that they have exhausted all other means and that the benefit of going undercover outweighs any negative impact. When the stories are published, editors should be forthcoming in letting audiences know how the information was gathered and why such methods were used.

A good policy is to gather news in a manner that allows the public focus to go where it should—to the wrongdoing that you are reporting, advises Associate Professor Cathy Packer at the University of North Carolina at Chapel Hill. Unethical and illegal newsgathering techniques shift the public focus to the media, and the bad guys walk away looking like victims, she notes. Without circumspect decision making and honesty with audiences, any medium—and the reporter—will lose credibility. When credibility is lost, so are audiences.

EXERCISES

1. Can you use the following information in a story? Explain your reasoning and any defenses you could use if you were charged with libel.

   a. You are a doing a story on drug use in the county. A police source tells you that a certain spot on Main Street, a bench outside Walton's restaurant, is a known place for drug deals.

b. You are covering a case about a man who has been charged with involuntary manslaughter in a car accident that killed two teenagers. You do a search of prior convictions and find he has two for careless and reckless driving in another state.

c. A state senator who is running for reelection tells you that her opponent is a tax evader who has not paid any state income taxes in the last five years.

d. You are covering the performance of Alice Batar, a local resident who has begun a successful acting career. You have been assigned to write a review of her performance in the community theater's production of *Who's Afraid of Virginia Woolf?* Prior to the performance you overhear two people next to you talking about Batar's latest divorce and what one called "a really pathetic settlement on her part."

e. You are to write a story about the chancellor of your university. You interview a faculty member who says that the chancellor "runs off at the mouth and doesn't pay enough attention to faculty members' needs."

2. Write a two-page report on plagiarism, using at least three sources. Include a fellow classmate's views on plagiarism. Include at least one example other than what is in this chapter. Include your views on plagiarism as an ethical issue and what the consequences should be for a reporter who is found to have plagiarized material.

3. Go online and find the site for your hometown newspaper. See if you can find on the site the newspaper's code of ethics. If not, e-mail the editor and find out if the newspaper has a written code or can tell you how ethical behavior is conveyed to the staff. Bring in the code or information to share with class members.

4. Look at codes of ethics from various professional organizations such as the American Society of Newspaper Editors, the American Advertising Federation, Public Relations Society of America, and others. Compare the issues that each covers as ethical considerations.

5. Consider the following scenarios. Discuss in class how you would behave in each situation and whether you would use the information gathered.

a. You are a state legislative reporter. A number of legislators meet every Thursday night for dinner at a local restaurant. One of the legislators whom you cover on a regular basis invites you to come along one night. Do you go?

    b. You are interviewing the director of the local community theater for a story on the upcoming season. You are having lunch together at a local restaurant. At the end of the meal and interview, the director picks up the tab and goes to pay for both of you. Your portion of the bill is $6.50. What do you do?

    c. You suspect that a local real estate company is discriminating against Hispanic tenants when it comes to rental housing. Your editor suggests that you and another reporter, who is Hispanic, pose as a couple and try to rent a house from the company. What should you do?

    d. You cover the financial industry as a business reporter. At the end of an interview on mortgage rates, the banker says to contact him whenever you are ready to buy a house and he'll make sure you get a really good interest rate. Do you call him when you are mortgage hunting?

REFERENCES

"Appeals Court Sides with ABC in Food Lion Lawsuit," ABCNews.com, Oct. 20, 1999, at http://abcnews.go.com/sections/us/DailyNews/foodlion991020.html.

"California Paper Fires Intern for Plagiarism," *Publishers' Auxiliary,* Jan. 22, 2001, Vol. 147, No. 2, p. 20.

Mari-Frances Cline, *Copyright Infringement and Liability on the Information Superhighway.* Stetson University College of Law, paper for Computer Law class, Spring 1997.

Copyright Act of 1976, Section 107 at http://www.loc.gov/copyright/title17/.

Don Fost, "*Mercury News* Case Stirs Debate over Ethics of Deception," *San Francisco Chronicle,* Aug. 8, 2001.

Michael Gartner, keynote address, Association for Education in Journalism and Mass Communication, Washington, D.C., Aug. 5, 2001.

Norm Goldstein, ed., *The Associated Press Stylebook 2001 and Briefing on Media Law.* New York: The Associated Press, 2001.

Cathy Packer, lecture, School of Journalism and Mass Communication, Sept. 5, 2001.

Reporters Committee for Freedom of the Press, at www.rcfp.org.

Carole Rich, *Writing and Reporting the News.* New York: Wadsworth, 1997.

Nicholas Stein, "Banana Peel," *Columbia Journalism Review,* Sept./Oct. 1998 at www.cjr.org/year/98/5/chiquita.asp.

Joe Strupp, "TV Columnist Canned," *Editor and Publisher,* September 11, 1999, at http://www.archives.editorandpublisher.com.

9

Interviewing, Quotes, and Attribution

Asking questions and collecting answers—interviewing—is an essential skill for all media writers. Becoming a skilled interviewer takes practice; it is not something someone does naturally.

Most of us interview in a casual way when we are introduced to someone new. We ask questions: Where are you from? Are you a student? What year are you in school? What is your major? We hope to get responses that help us learn more about the person.

But if you are going to write about that individual, your questions have to be much more specific. You hardly have enough for a story to know that Mark Monroe is a junior from Lake Geneva, New York, majoring in computer science. You need more detailed information, perhaps his career objective and how he sees the role of computers in information retrieval.

So good interviewing is more than just carrying on a casual conversation. It takes skill, and it takes practice. This chapter will start you on the road to becoming a good interviewer.

In this chapter, you will learn

- How to prepare for an interview,
- How to conduct an interview,
- How to handle off-the-record information,
- How to use quotes, including quotes in speech stories, and
- The importance of accuracy, attribution, and punctuation in quotes.

Interviewing as a Challenge

Writers do interviews in different ways. The medium they work for, deadline pressures, the accessibility of sources, and people's willingness to talk affect how well a writer can plan and do interviews. Writers face challenges as they work diligently to reach as many sources as possible before a deadline. They become detectives as they figure out just whom they should interview and how. Like anyone else, writers feel nervous and even excited when they have the chance to interview a well-known newsmaker or celebrity. And they feel great satisfaction and accomplishment when a source answers their questions and gives them something extra.

When a train derailed in an old tunnel under Baltimore's downtown streets, reporters had to interview dozens of firefighters, government officials, train personnel, and others to create a factual account for the next day's edition of the *Baltimore Sun.*

Read the following story and see if you can identify how many sources were used. The byline on the story listed two lead writers and reporters, David Michael Ettlin and Del Quentin Wilber, but a tag credit line noted that an additional 20 reporters contributed to the story.

Train Fire, Toxic Cargo Shut City

DAVID MICHAEL ETTLIN AND DEL QUENTIN WILBER

Civil defense sirens wailed and major highways into Baltimore were closed after a freight train hauling hazardous chemicals caught fire yesterday afternoon in a century-old railroad tunnel under Howard Street, shutting down much of the city's downtown.

Choking black smoke spewed from both ends of the 1.7-mile Howard Street Tunnel, and fear of an explosion or toxic fumes from a cargo that included dangerous acids prompted authorities to ban pedestrians and vehicles within five blocks of its openings at Camden Yards and Mount Royal Station.

Problems were expected to continue today, complicated by a water main break above the tunnel at Howard and Lombard streets that flooded the roadway and nearby businesses, and had officials speculating on whether it was related to the train fire.

Firefighters were trying early today to reach the source of the fire deep in the tunnel, using thermal imaging devices. There was speculation that the train had derailed, but the cause of the fire was unknown.

The crisis began about 3:10 p.m., according to CSX railroad officials and the train's two-man crew, when an emergency air brake halted the train in mid-tunnel. Its conductor and engineer—the only known occupants of the northbound, 60-car train—said they were unable to repressurize the brakes. They thought initially that the smoke was exhaust from the diesel engines and set about uncoupling and driving them the last quarter of the way out of the tunnel.

By the time the Fire Department was notified at 4:15 p.m., black smoke was rising through manhole covers on Howard Street and the situation was falling out of control.

The Fire Department sounded five alarms in assembling 125 firefighters and equipment. As firefighters aimed water cannons from each end toward a blaze they could not see in the smoky blackness, activities above ground slowly came to a standstill. Drivers were trapped for hours on gridlocked streets, and people waited at curbs for buses halted on their rounds. The Metro subway was closed for an hour until inspectors were sure there was no smoke in the tubes, and light rail service was severed near its midpoint.

The second game of a day-night Orioles double-header was canceled, downtown stores closed, and the University of Baltimore's evening classes halted. The Coast Guard closed the Inner Harbor to boat traffic at 5 p.m.

The water main break about 6 p.m. knocked out electrical power to nearly 1,200 residences and businesses, reduced or cut off water pressure as far south as Port Covington and left part of Lombard Street under 2 feet of water.

Firefighters tried to reach the train from the southern end of the tunnel early but were forced back by what they thought were chemicals that made their skin burn. About a half-dozen firefighters wearing standard turnout gear went in with hoses, trying to reach the train about three-quarters of a mile away through smoke and intense heat, said Fire Department Lt. Jim Boyer. "They got within 300 yards of the derailment, but they felt the skin on their necks burning," he said, speculating that chemicals had reacted with perspiration. "You can't fight a fire from 300 yards.

"Any chemical situation, plus in an enclosed space like a tunnel, that's terrifying," said Boyer, a Baltimore firefighter for three decades. "I haven't seen anything like this since I did damage control in the Navy 30 years ago."

At least 22 people, including two firefighters with chest pains, were treated at area hospitals, most for respiratory or eye irritation, officials reported.

Many of the freight cars were carrying wood pulp and other

combustibles, but nine were carrying chemicals from North Carolina to New Jersey, including five tank cars full of acids.

Two were full of fluorosilicic acid, two of hydrochloric acid, and one of glacial acetic acid. Other substances on the train's manifest were ethylhexyl phthalate, propylene and tripropylene glycol.

Among the most dangerous was the fluorosalicic acid, a chemical that, diluted, protects children's teeth from cavities. In its concentrated form, it can cause severe burns to skin, lungs, nose and throat, with the effects often taking hours to appear.

Most of the other chemicals on the train were common ingredients used in manufacturing.

Typical of these modern multipurpose chemicals is propylene glycol, a compound used to de-ice airplanes and plumbing pipes, and also used as a solvent in food ingredients.

According to their "material safety data sheets"—standardized information from the manufacturers provided for guidance in accidents— these chemicals are mildly to moderately irritating to eyes, lungs and throat when they are inhaled, and can burn the skin.

"Acids are very soluble in water, so when you breathe them in, it's as if you're pouring the acid right into your body," said Dr. Jeffrey Hasday, head of the pulmonary and critical care medicine division at University of Maryland Medical Center.

The danger, said Bruce Anderson, director of the Maryland Poison Center, depends on the extent of exposure to the chemicals. But there was no evidence last night that any had leaked.

Hazardous materials experts from the Maryland Department of the Environment tested the air repeatedly at both ends of the tunnel.

"There's no acid content in the smoke," agency spokesman John Verrico reported last night, adding that tests showed a significant wood-ash content.

"In the testing we've been doing, we have not found any compounds of concern," he said. "It's smoke from a fire which is going to be irritating, but we're not finding any acid compounds, which is kind of a sigh of relief."

Train conductor Edward Brown, 52, of West Baltimore, and engineer Chad Cadden, 27, of Stewartstown, Pa., said they did not know what caused the automatic emergency brakes to activate.

"I don't really know what happened," Cadden said, recounting how the train stopped with the tandem locomotives three-quarters of the way through.

Robert Gould, a CSX spokesman, said: "We do not know if it is a derailment or not; we just do not know."

The National Transportation Safety Board said it is sending investigators today.

According to Gould, the crew saw that diesel fumes were building up and uncoupled the locomotives to move them out of the tunnel. But after completing that task and turning back to walk along the train, Gould said, "they recognized they had a problem and notified dispatchers."

Cadden said, "We knew something had happened, and we debated about going back. We had no idea it would be something like this. We didn't know it was something serious."

The city's old civil defense sirens, heard in tests at 1 p.m. every Monday, blared a danger warning about 5:45 p.m.—the first time since the system was installed in 1952 that it was not a drill, according to Public Works Department spokesman Kurt L. Kocher.

Public Works Director George L. Winfield said the point was to get people's attention—hoping they would check the news and get the word to close windows, stay indoors and out of the affected area.

But many people were caught downtown and could not get out. Outside Lexington Market, more than three dozen people spent hours waiting for buses. Many complained that buses bearing "Not in service" signs kept passing. They would race to line up, but the buses wouldn't stop.

"We can't get home," said Donna Delauder, who at 7:30 p.m., had been waiting 2 1/2 hours to catch a bus from work to her Cherry Hill home.

Mayor Martin O'Malley was returning from a political crab feast in Crisfield when he started getting calls that there was a problem, and said he closed roads into the city "to err on the side of caution" because of "an apparent derailment and for the potential for something worse."

"This has been pretty disruptive and there's more to come later on with possible road closures tomorrow," the mayor said last night. "We still don't know what we're dealing with. These things happen."

Police, some wearing cloth-face masks, blocked Conway Street from Camden Yards to the harbor.

All major highways and several smaller routes into Baltimore were closed, but by early today all had been reopened.

O'Malley said remaining concerns included "the structural integrity of Howard Street."

The mayor praised fire personnel: "I thought about how lucky we are to have brave firefighters who grab a hose and walk into a tunnel with smoke billowing out of it, not knowing how far they'll get before there might be an explosion."

Reporters contributing to the *Sun*'s coverage of the tunnel fire included: Liz Bowie, Julie Bykowicz, Tim Craig, Heather Dewar, John Eisenberg, Lisa Goldberg, Michael Himowitz, Richard Irwin, Michael James, Roch Kubatko, Howard Libit, Marcia Myers, Jon Morgan, William Patalon III, Michael Scarcella, Joe Strauss, Michael Stroh, Timothy B. Wheeler, and Jeff Zrebiec.

By David Michael Ettlin and Del Quentin Wilber, *The Baltimore Sun*. Used by permission.

The team of reporters had to cover all town services that were affected, such as transportation, fire, police, and public works. They included comments from officials as well as residents who were stranded downtown. Readers, who had seen accounts on television, expected to see more detail in the next edition of the *Sun* and to learn the continuing impact of the disaster. The report is an example of what newspapers can provide that audiences would not find in other media.

Research before Interviewing

The first step in interviewing, of course, is to know your topic. The second is to do research. Before any interview, you should have knowledge of your topic and the people you will interview. The general rule is not to go into an interview cold. You will have more success if your source quickly sees that you are prepared. Preparation shows that you are serious about the interview, and it flatters the source.

With deadline pressure, however, some journalists may find that they do not have time to do research before they have to be on site to cover an event. On some occasions you may go into an interview unprepared. Experienced writers or reporters will tell you that such an experience is uncomfortable and often embarrassing. No one wants to walk up to the newest Nobel Prize winner for medicine and ask, "Now just what was your work that caused you to win?" With the advantages of technology today, a reporter can be on his or her way to an interview while a researcher searches files for background information. The reporter can get data from the researcher and arrive somewhat prepared.

Writers—whether print or broadcast reporters, online journalists, freelancers, public relations practitioners, or advertising copywriters—look in their own files first for information, then move to the company's or community's library. They may find other articles or broadcasts about their topic, or they may consult research materials such as government sites. Some may access the Library of Congress. Specific tips on research are in Chapter 7.

In many cases, other people are the best sources of information. When U.S. Sen. Jesse Helms, a Republican from North Carolina, announced he would not seek reelection in 2002, media across the country reported the story. Helms would have served five terms as a senator. He had chaired the powerful Senate Foreign Relations Committee and had earned a reputation as "Senator No" because of his votes on major issues. In covering the story, reporters included quotes from dozens of Helms's supporters and detractors to get a picture of Helms's legacy in Congress. The interviews proved valuable in giving readers a complete picture of Helms, the politician.

Sometimes a national or local event may prompt the media to do an informal survey of people's opinions; for example, reporters may ask for residents' views on changes in Social Security or on plans to widen Main Street. Those stories require meaningful questions to get good quotes and complete identification of respondents. Such stories are a way to get readers or viewers into the newspaper or on radio or television. Media, as well as public officials, can uncover public sentiment.

Some opinion surveys are more formal. Polling firms spend millions of dollars each year interviewing voters about their favorite candidates and consumers about their favorite products and services. Marketers use the results to promote everything from a specific candidate to toothpaste. Their questions have to be worded carefully to avoid bias and to obtain relevant, pertinent, and accurate information. Such firms have professionals to draft questions and oversee interviews.

Getting the Interview

Once you have sufficient knowledge, you must determine whom it is you want to interview. For a story on credit card fraud, a local bank president might be a primary interview. But you must also talk to experts in the financial services industry, consumers, and whoever is knowledge about the subject. Some names may appear during research, and some may come as referrals in other interviews.

Setting Up the Interview

When you know who it is that you want to interview, you need to determine the best method of interviewing and make an appointment, whether the interview is by telephone or in person. Some interviews can be conducted by e-mail. Online questions and answers are fast and convenient, but remember that they have serious limitations. Like an Internet site, the source may not be known to the writer. The writer who interviews only online loses the candid spontaneity that comes with live interviews, as well as any sense of the source's surroundings and personal characteristics. A low chuckle or a timely grin are impossible to detect online.

In setting up any interview, you may have to go through a secretary or a public relations person who maintains the source's schedule, or you may be able to call the person directly.

Make sure that a source has firsthand information. If you are working on a story that requires expert opinion, for example, be sure that your source is an appropriate one. The primary surgeon for a lung transplant is a much better source than a hospital public information officer or a physician who assisted during the operation. People who have never been involved in a child abuse case and are just giving you secondhand or hearsay information are not good sources for a story on that subject. A few filter questions up front can eliminate unnecessary interviews: "I am looking for people who tried to break into the country-western music market. Did you ever sing professionally? Or perhaps prepare a demonstration tape for an agent?"

In setting up an interview, be sure to specify the amount of time you will need. Don't underestimate, or you will lack time to ask all your questions. Some people may be willing to be interviewed on the spot, so be ready with your questions. Others will want to set a specific time at a later date. Ask for more time than you will need.

Select a comfortable place for an interview. The source's terrain is best, as he or she is usually more relaxed in a familiar environment. The reporter also has the opportunity to observe personal items, such as family photographs or collected memorabilia, that can add to the story.

Avoid doing interviews during meals. People have difficulty talking while eating, and a discussion over who should pay for food—source or writer—can be uncomfortable. If the individual is from out of town and staying at the local hotel, you may choose to do an interview over coffee—a fairly inexpensive way of meeting and talking.

Dress appropriately for the interview. If you are interviewing the chief executive officer of a Fortune 500 company, wear a suit. If you are meeting a cotton grower in his fields, shuck the cashmere coat. And, if you are meeting with teenagers at the local hangout, jeans are okay.

What to Work out in Advance

Do not agree to pay for an interview. Only in very rare situations should you consider paying for information. The news organization may agree to pay because the source's information is newsworthy, but any payment should be worked out ahead of time and be consistent with company policy. If you are a freelancer, you should not agree to pay for information; publications may not buy your work if sources were lured by profit.

Before you start on your list of questions, work out arrangements if you plan to use a tape recorder. A tape recorder is advisable if you are planning an interview that is long or one that might contain controversial or important information. You might want a tape as a backup if you suspect a source might question your quotes in the printed article. Some people may feel uncomfortable with a tape recorder present, and they may need reassurance before you show up. One good way to have a source agree to be taped is to stress your need for accuracy in getting quotes right. Few people will argue.

If you are doing an interview by e-mail or telephone, establish a time period for questions and answers so that you will get responses by your deadline. You also might want to agree on a code word that the source will include at the end of responses so that you know the source answered the questions and not someone who had access—whether legally or illegally—to the e-mail account. Some writers use e-mail only as a follow-up to a telephone or face-to-face interview. Professors and professional media may prohibit e-mail interviews.

Some people will want to see a list of questions before they agree to an interview. Such a request can be honored if sources need to collect specific information, such as statistics. People who are not used to being interviewed may want some time to formulate responses. Or if you are getting an actuality to use in a broadcast, a source may want a few minutes to prepare a response. In many cases your deadline will determine whether you have the luxury of submitting questions and waiting for responses. In any case, don't give up the right to ask a question that is not on the list.

Some sources will ask if they can see the article before it is printed or listen to the tape before it is aired. Of course, if you are a public relations practitioner or an ad copy writer, your source—who may be your client—will have final approval. But in the news business, the answer is no. Deadline pressure generally precludes spending the time for a source to review the message. Sources can become editors, wanting to change more than what applies to them.

If a source insists on previewing the piece, check it out with an editor or producer. You may want to find someone else to interview. Be clear if the answer is no. One inexperienced reporter caused herself and her newspaper some unpleasantness because a source thought he would have the right to edit a story citing him before it was printed. The reporter did not flatly say no, and the source misunderstood, believing he could review the story in advance. When the story appeared, the source felt deceived.

Writing the Questions

Interviewers, no matter how skilled or practiced, should write a list of questions before an interview. The list can be typed and printed or scribbled on an envelope. The questions ensure that all important aspects are covered during an interview. A reporter can review the list before ending an interview to make sure all points were asked. Questions also serve to keep an interview on track. For example, a minister might divert an interview to a discussion of the writer's religious beliefs. The writer can refer to the list and remind the minister that she is there to interview him. The list can also fill in lags in the conversation.

Covering the Basics

Obviously, when you are planning questions, you want to ask the basics: who, what, when, where, how, and why. But you need to ask other questions to get more information and to make the message complete. One formula for interviewing is called GOSS, an acronym for *Goals-Obstacles-Solutions-Start,* devised by Professor LaRue Gilleland of the University of Nevada. It can be applied to many interviews and is based on the assumption that people have goals, that obstacles loom before goals, and that solutions can be found to obstacles. Talking about goals, obstacles, and solutions gives the source plenty to talk about. During the interview, you may discover that you need to "start"—to go back to the beginning of an event or topic to get a more complete understanding.

For example, you might interview a chemist who does research on polymers. Using GOSS, you would ask what are the goals of her research, the obstacles to discovering new uses, and the solutions to overcome the obstacles. "Start" would lead you to ask about the whole field of polymer research and what is happening in this particular laboratory compared with others.

Ken Metzler, author of *Creative Interviewing,* has suggested two more letters to Gilleland's GOSS: *E* for *evaluation* and *Y* for *why.* Evaluation suggests a need for an overall assessment of the situation—seeking meaning beyond the facts. To get such information, the writer asks for the source's interpretation: What does all this (polymers and research) mean to you? The *Y* is a reminder not to forget to ask why a situation has occurred.

Think about quantitative questions. How many times has the baseball star struck out? How many ounces of marijuana were confiscated, and what is its street value? How many tons of concrete are needed for the runway, and is that equal to filling the high school football stadium to the top row?

When formulating questions, think of the unusual aspects. Don't hesitate to include questions you and your audience would like answered. You might even ask friends or colleagues what questions they would include if given the chance.

Conducting an Interview

Always be punctual for an interview. Making a source wait is rude and may cost you the interview. Call to let the individual know if you will be late.

If you are interviewing a celebrity or high-ranking official, avoid having the air of a fan or worshiper and avoid appearing nervous or excited. Few people would be calm the first time they interviewed an Oscar winner or a country's head of state. Butterflies are to be expected, but you should show respect rather than adulation.

Getting Started

After you introduce yourself, start an interview with some questions that will set a relaxed mood. For example, if you are in the person's home, comment about trophies, collections, or decor. Show you are interested. Don't ask weighty questions right away.

If you are using a tape recorder, put it in an inconspicuous place. A source who is uncomfortable with the tape recorder may spend more time looking at it than at you. Make sure to use a tape that will cover the length of an interview. You don't want to waste time every 15 minutes checking to see whether the tape has run out.

Most states require that you notify people if they are being taped. If you are doing a telephone interview and plan to tape it, you must ask the individual's permission before you turn the recorder on. Rarely, if ever, will you need to hide a tape recorder in your briefcase or under your clothing.

Avoid starting an interview by asking people what they do or routine information. They will know that you haven't done your homework, and they could be insulted. You may need to verify information, however. A student who interviewed author Barbara Victor discovered in a biographical source that she was born in 1944. A question revealed that Victor actually was born a year later, in 1945.

Before beginning an interview, ask yourself the questions in the checklist shown in Figure 9.1.

Asking the Questions

Ask the easy questions first. That can allow the person to relax and feel comfortable in responses. How to ask the tough questions is covered in the next section.

Be straightforward and specific in questioning. Don't beat around the bush. "So, Mr. Rich, you have investments and your construction business. And you have inherited money from your uncle and aunt. And I imagine there are lots of people out there who are wondering how much you are worth." Of course, you can preface a question with a statement, but don't talk around a question—ask it. "Mr. Rich, you have investments and inheritance that have many people asking the question: Just how much you are worth?"

As you take notes, be sure to read back any quotes to ensure you have complete and accurate statements. Sometimes a person will talk quickly or start a sentence, stop midway, and begin again. You may need to repeat part of a quote and ask the speaker to confirm or clarify what he or she said.

Maintain control. Don't let the person lead you. Keeping an interview on track may be difficult for a student writer or inexperienced reporter.

FIGURE 9.1   *Checklist for Interviews*

- Have I researched thoroughly my subject and source?
- Have I selected the right people to interview?
- Have I set up the interview in a place conducive to the interviewee?
- Have I allotted adequate time?
- Have I worked out using a tape recorder? Is it in good working order?
- Have I written a thorough list of questions?
- Do I feel prepared and confident?

Someone who is accustomed to being interviewed may have an agenda or may have what seem to be the usual canned responses. A politician, for example, may ignore a question about changes in tax laws and answer instead about his or her plan for economic development. If the person digresses, wait until there is a suitable pause, then steer the person back to the subject. Use your list of questions as a reference. If you interrupt, you could be cutting off some valuable comments.

Avoid becoming interviewed. Try to keep yourself out of an interview. Often a person will throw questions at the interviewer. Be polite and firm and remember that you are there to do an interview, not to be interviewed.

Watch your body language. Avoid any behavior, such as nodding your head, that may subtly indicate you agree with comments. If the source believes you are sympathetic and empathetic, he or she may expect a positive story.

Maintain a friendly but professional distance. Do not become the source's friend. Writers who get too chummy with their sources can create tension when the article is published. The source may believe that the writer betrayed confidences.

Leave all preconceptions and misconceptions at home. You may be a single working journalist with no children, and your interview is with a stay-at-home mother with five children. Mask any feelings of envy of her domestic life or notions that her job is not as fulfilling as yours. Do not be antagonistic if you disagree with a person's philosophy. Some people will open up if they sense that you do not agree with them, however.

Listen to the source. Be aware of inconsistencies. Be willing to divert the conversation from the prescribed list of questions if you hear a tidbit that should be developed through another line of questioning. If you do not understand a response, ask for clarification. Remember: If you aren't clear about information, you'll never convey it clearly to audiences.

The Tough Questions

Save all embarrassing and controversial questions for the end of the interview, such as those dealing with a person's gambling debts or reports that a director has bipolar disorder. Of course, if a suitable occasion to ask such a question occurs during an interview, ask it. Be aware that you run the risk of having an interview terminated if you ask a particularly sensitive question. When asking these questions, be straightforward. If you act embarrassed, you will transmit that feeling and possibly not get a response.

Many times writers must interview people who have suffered trauma or witnessed a traumatic event. An individual may have endured years of repeated physical abuse, survived a plane crash, been a hostage in a domestic dispute, or been wounded. A person may have witnessed a friend's drowning, seen a fiery truck crash, or found a house full of diseased and starving animals.

Writers must understand that people who have suffered trauma or an atrocity recover from those events in different ways and at different times, depending on the particular trauma and their personalities. Judith Lewis Herman notes in her book, *Trauma and Recovery,* that part of the healing process is remembering and telling the event. People seeking quotes and information may find individuals who are quite willing to talk and others who refuse to be interviewed. Herman writes:

> *People who have survived atrocities often tell their stories in a highly emotional, contradictory, and fragmented manner which undermines their credibility.... It is difficult for an observer to remain clearheaded and calm, to see more than a few fragments of the picture at one time, to retain all the pieces, and to fit them together. It is even more difficult to find a language that conveys fully and persuasively what one has seen. Those who attempt to describe the atrocities that they have witnessed also risk their own credibility.*

Reporters must be aware of the psychological state of people who have just experienced a tragedy or atrocity. They should ask the questions but understand when they do not get complete or even accurate responses. Interviewing more than one source may be required to get a full picture of what actually happened. Reporters may have to come back later for follow-up interviews well after a traumatic event occurs.

Just as it is difficult to approach victims and witnesses, it is hard to interview victims' families. Again, reporters must try to ask the questions, but they must respect a person's right not to answer.

The media, particularly the electronic media, have drawn criticism for asking family members of victims "How do you feel?" only minutes or hours after a relative's death. Although some may view such questioning as aggressive, others regard it as heartless. In some instances, reporters might find that a family member is willing to talk and is helped by remembering the individual. Again, reporters must use judgment and good taste in what they include in their writing and how far they should go in trying to get information.

Interviewing during traumatic situations came before the public in a powerful way after the terrorist attacks on the World Trade Center and the Pentagon. The Dart Center for Journalism & Trauma at the University of Washington has an informative web site at uwdart@u.washington.edu that defines trauma, gives specific advice on interviewing trauma victims or witnesses, and outlines what clues reporters should recognize if they are adding to the stress through interviewing.

The fact that the person does not answer a tough question is often noteworthy in a story. A former foreign service diplomat who settled in a small town was arrested on charges of shoplifting. When he refused to answer reporters' questions after his trial, the reporter noted his refusal in the story. His silence supported statements that he was close-mouthed about his current life. But don't fail to ask a question in the expectation that a person might not answer it. You may be surprised and get a response.

Off-the-Record Information

In the middle of an interview, a public official says, "The following information needs to be off the record." Stop the official. Don't let him or her talk any longer. *Off the record* means you cannot use the information. As a writer you don't want information you cannot use. Politely refuse the information. Then you can proceed to clarify what the official means. People have different definitions of what off the record means: Don't use the information at all; use it but don't attribute it to me; or use it to ask questions of others, but I never said it.

As an interviewer you must remember that many people who have information want to share it but may not want to take responsibility for making it public. They will let you as the writer do it anonymously, or let you find someone else to confirm it and become the public source. Be careful. Audiences do not necessarily believe information that is attributed to "a source close to the president" or "a high-level State Department official."

Refusing to accept off-the-record information from a source may just get it for you. People who have juicy information usually feel important and want to show they know something you don't. Think about it. Has a friend told you some gossip about someone else and sworn you to secrecy? Within 24 hours had you shared it with someone else, despite your promise? Few secrets exist that are known only by one person. If you refuse off-the-record information that you cannot use, the source may open up.

Think about the Consequences

A final warning: Make sure you and the source are clear on how the information can be used before you accept it. If you agree to use the information but not the individual's name, you must comply. If you agree the tidbit is confidential, you must not publish it. You may want that person as a source again. If you act unethically and violate the agreement, you can write that person off your source list, and you may attract unflattering attention to yourself and your employer.

Consider the problems the *New York Times* encountered with off-the-record information. A *Times* reporter, Marian Burros, was one of five reporters invited to lunch at the White House when Hillary Clinton was first lady. Mrs. Clinton set up the luncheon to discuss her image problems with media representatives. The first lady's comments during the 2½-hour luncheon moved from on the record to off the record. A *Times* article on the luncheon included Mrs. Clinton's statement that she was politically "naive and dumb" in her health care proposals during her husband's first term. The White House, and even other reporters present at the lunch, claimed those particular comments were among the off-the-record statements. The *Times* defended its reporter.

Confusion would have been avoided if the entire conversation had been either on or off the record, rather than jumping around. The publication of off-the-record comments, such as Mrs. Clinton's, whether in good faith or in error, creates problems between sources and reporters. Sources may be more skeptical and guarded if they have to fear that comments shared in confidence will be attributed to them. Reporters may not have access to necessary background or off-the-record information because sources do not trust the media.

Note-Taking Tips for Interviews

Most people talk faster than an interviewer can write. If you have trouble keeping up, politely stop the source and ask for a moment to catch up on notes. You could preface it by saying, "I want to make sure I record this correctly, so I need a moment to complete your last comment." Few sources would respond, "I don't care if you get it right. I want to keep talking."

Be sure when you are writing comments that you get them completely rather than in bits and pieces that may not fit together when you write the article. Complete notes help you avoid taking quotes out of context or misinterpreting quotes later.

If you have a quote that is complete, put it within quotation marks in your notebook. Then you will know you have the speaker's exact words when you review your notes and are ready to write.

You may find it handy to flag your notes as you take them. Put a word or two in the margin to indicate where certain information occurs. For example, you may have a wide-ranging interview with the incoming Democrat speaker of the state legislature. "Welfare," "tax cuts," "power," and "education" would remind you where each topic was discussed.

At the end of an interview, take a few moments to review notes and questions to ensure that you have asked all your questions. Most sources won't mind waiting while you double-check. If a quote is not clear, ask the source to repeat it. "You said earlier, Mr. Speaker, that changing the rules will help the House pass legislation faster. Could you clarify the parliamentary procedure a little more?" You also might want to ask if you can telephone if any clarification is needed when you are producing the story.

After an Interview

Take time after you leave an interview to review your notes. Fill in any blanks that might appear confusing later. Note your feelings, the qualities of the source, any additional description, and other details while they are fresh in your mind. You may wish to transcribe your notes immediately to retain important details or impressions. If you store your notes on your computer, you can call them up easily when it is time to create the piece.

After an interview, you may want to write the person a thank-you note.

Selecting and Using Quotes

You have pages of notes from your interview. How do you determine which quotes to use? The same rules for using quotes from interviews apply to selecting quotes from speeches, presentations, or even published works. You want to select quotes that are vivid, show opinion, reflect the speaker's personality, support the speaker's thesis, and unify a piece of writing.

When to Use Quotes

In organizing material, writers have to decide whether to quote an individual, then whether to use that information in an indirect or direct quote.

Direct quotes give the exact words of the speaker. The quotation marks signify to readers "here's exactly what was said." Direct quotes are used for colorful statements, opinion, and emotions. Direct quotes can convey an individual's personality and manner of speaking. Here's one rule to follow: Use a direct quote if it is better than any paraphrase.

Direct quotes can be either complete quotes or partial quotes. Here is a complete direct quote:

> "We are not selective about whom we arrest," said Police Chief Martin Bray.

Or

> "The federal government spent millions of dollars to enact the 1986 Truth in Mileage Act, and now it has pulled $600,000 in funding to enforce it," said Charles Bradley, president of the National Odometer and Title Fraud Enforcement Association in Nashville, Tenn.

A partial direct quote would be written as

> Company President William Olsen said he would not discuss the reasoning behind the 3 percent pay increase for employees, noting only that "we have to consider many factors in our operating costs and employees' salaries and benefits are part of those factors."

Or even shorter, as in

> The coach said the player was "furious at the lack of compassion" exhibited by the fans when he made the error in the third inning.

Or

> The senator vowed "to use every last little bit" of his influence to block the bill increasing military spending.

Be careful not to switch person even in a partial quote—for example, switching from third person ("the senator") to the first person ("my influence") as in the following sentence:

> The senator vowed to "use every last little bit of my influence" to block the bill increasing military spending.

A grammatical sentence would use the words "his influence," but then the quote would be inaccurate. In such cases, rewrite, quoting only the phrase "to use every last little bit" as in the first example.

As a note, most writers avoid using what are called *orphan quotes*—that is, quotation marks used for emphasis on a single word.

> The special envoy said the cease-fire represented a "monumental" effort.

Why use quotations? "Monumental" is hardly an inflammatory phrase or an unusual adjective.

To Paraphrase or Not

Indirect quotes are used to summarize or paraphrase what individuals say, particularly if they have rambled about an issue or topic. They do not use a speaker's exact words and are not set off with quotation marks. Writers use indirect quotes to keep quotes relevant and precise.

Many writers find indirect quotes particularly valuable when speakers have digressed from the main topic or when they inject jokes or anecdotal material that cannot be used.

U.S. Secretary of Labor Elaine Chao followed in the tradition of previous Labor secretaries when she made her first pre-Labor Day address. As with many speeches, part of her comments needed to be paraphrased. Here is an excerpt from her speech:

> *Today, in many cases, unemployment often means a disconnect between the new jobs our economy is producing and the current skill levels of Americans in the workforce. The skills gap is too wide for many Americans, and often jobs created by the economy go begging because employers cannot find qualified workers. Job training and education are more important than ever—especially for workers in manufacturing jobs and those just starting out.*

The result in good media writing is the following single indirect quote:

> Chao said to avoid unemployment, workers need to learn new skills that will make them marketable for the jobs being created in today's economy.

Indirect quotes are valuable in providing a source's information. They are effective in balancing direct quotes within copy.

Correcting Speakers' Grammar and Other Slips

Reporters who covered a high-level state official quickly learned that the man was not a good speaker. He had a vernacular accent for that region of the state, used incorrect grammar, and stated goals that seemed out of reach. How to quote him?

Early in the official's tenure, most print journalists chose to paraphrase his remarks so they could clean up the grammar errors. Even in some of the direct quotes, the official sounded well schooled. But a few print journalists soon discovered that cleaning up the official's language was not good practice. Audiences who also watched local television broadcasts saw and heard the official as he really was. The image they read in the newspaper did not match.

Journalists are faced continually with deciding how to use quotes. If a speaker uses improper subject–verb agreement, should the writer correct it in a direct quote? How far should writers go in cleaning up quotes? In the case of the state official, print journalists figured out they had to be true to the quotes or else paraphrase. They could not dramatically clean up the quotes, put them in direct quotations, and tell audiences, "Here's exactly what the man said." He didn't.

The Associated Press Stylebook advises writers:

> *Never alter quotations even to correct minor grammatical errors or word usage. Casual minor tongue slips may be removed by using ellipses but even that should be done with extreme caution. If there is a question about a quote, either don't use it or ask the speaker to clarify.*

Are Profanities and Obscenities Acceptable?

The Associated Press Stylebook also advises writers not to use profanity, obscenities, or vulgarities unless they are part of direct quotations and there is a compelling reason for them. Writers are cautioned to warn editors of writing that contains such language. The language should be confined to a single paragraph so that it can be easily deleted. Writers should not modify profanity, such as changing "damn" to "darn." Editors may change the word to "d—" to indicate that profanity was used by the speaker but no compelling reason exists to spell it out in the story.

Writers need to check with their publications and media organizations to determine their particular rules on profanity, obscenities, and vulgarities. Some specialized publications and television shows include such language. Audiences who subscribe to or buy such publications or who view such programs are familiar with such language and either do not find it offensive or overlook it.

General Rules about Quotes

• Never make up a quote. Quotes must be accurate.

• Don't take a question that is answered "yes" or "no" and turn it into a direct quote. For example, if an interviewer asks a high school basketball coach if he believed many students bet on the outcome of games, and the coach answered, "No," the quotation in the newspaper should not read

> Coach Lyman Jones said, "I don't think many students bet on the outcome of our basketball games."

All you can really say is this: When asked whether he thought many students bet on the outcomes of games, Coach Lyman Jones replied, "No."

• Watch out for redundancies when setting up quotes. Use the direct quotes to expand.

Avoid:

> She said she was surprised at being chosen the school's outstanding senior. "I was so surprised when they called my name," Melissa said.

Prefer:

> Melissa said she was surprised when the principal called her name. "I couldn't move or react," she added. "I felt glued to my chair in shock."

• Set up situations before using the quote so that readers will have a context for quotes, as in the following Associated Press story:

> An exercise program supported by the federal government and the trucking industry is aimed at eliminating spare tires on the truckers.
> The goal is to make interstate drivers slimmer, healthier—and safer.

The Rolling Strong Gym has opened at a truck stop in North Little Rock, Ark., and others are planned elsewhere along Interstate 40. The president of the Richardson, Texas, health club company, as well as government and industry officials, are watching to see if the truckers will work out.

"It's been long overdue," said Paul Todorovich of Myrtle Beach, S.C., an independent driver. "I'm hoping it catches on and they flourish."

Transportation Department officials also hope so. "Research shows that drivers who are physically fit are safe drivers and that exercise is key to getting people into healthier lifestyles," said Transportation Secretary Rodney E. Slater in a statement endorsing the concept.

● Use "according to" only with printed or factual information. Do not use it as an attribution to a person.

Avoid:

The state's prison system is 3,456 inmates above the legally allowed level, according to the secretary of correction.

Prefer:

The state's prison system is 3,456 inmates above the legally allowed level, said the secretary of correction. According to prison documents, the level has been too high for the past seven years.

● Use attribution in the middle of a sentence only if it occurs at a natural break. Otherwise, put it at the beginning or the end so that you don't interrupt the flow of the person's statement.

Avoid:

"We can always," he said, "commission a new statue for the college commons."

Prefer:

"We can always commission a new statue for the college commons," he said.

Acceptable:

"The marine sciences lab is vital to the state's economy," he said, "and we must persuade the legislature to allocate more funds this year."

• Always use attribution for statements that use "hope," "feel," or "believes." You as a writer are not inside another person's head; you know how he or she feels, thinks, or believes because you were told.

> The district attorney said she believes the verdict fell short of what she expected the jury to do. She said she believes the community will be angered that Ammons was not found guilty of first-degree murder.

More on Attribution

Quotes, whether direct or indirect, must be attributed completely and adequately. Readers or listeners must know who is talking and who is making each statement. They need to know the proper sources of information. The general rule is that attribution should go at the beginning of each new quote or at the end of the first sentence, whether the quote is one sentence or more than one sentence.

If the quote goes on for several paragraphs, attribution usually is placed at least once in every paragraph, and most writers follow the rule of attribution somewhere in the first sentence. Some writers will omit attribution in a middle paragraph if they have several short paragraphs of quotes by the same speaker. The key is to ensure that readers know who is talking.

If paragraphs contain strong statements of opinion, however, the writer must use attribution for every sentence.

For many writers, particularly news writers, "said" is the attribution word of choice. "Said" carries no underlying connotation as to a speaker's emphasis or meaning; it is neutral. "Added" and "told" are also fairly neutral. Attribution words that contain subtle meanings include "emphasized," "stressed," "declared," "demanded," "ordered," "stated," "criticized," and "contended." Writers avoid many of these words.

Do not use words such as "smiled," "laughed," "grimaced," "chuckled," and so on as attribution words. They are descriptive words that tell how a person was behaving when she or he said something. Rather than writing "'Hello,' he smiled," use "he said with a smile." Phrases such as "she said, and frowned," "he said, and grimaced," and "she said, then laughed" are preferred.

When using attribution that includes a person's title, do not place the title between the person's name and the attribution verb.

Avoid:

The University will accept 3,475 freshmen for the incoming class, Polly Wilson, director of undergraduate admissions, said.

Prefer:

The University will accept 3,475 freshmen for the incoming class, said Polly Wilson, director of undergraduate admissions.

Punctuating Quotes

General punctuation rules are discussed in Chapter 2. Here are the basic rules for punctuating quotes:

• Attribution at the end of a quote—whether direct or indirect—must be set off with punctuation. In most cases, the punctuation will be a comma.

Fifteen barrels of sardines will be delivered Wednesday, he said.

"Fifteen stinking, dripping barrels of sardines will be delivered Wednesday," he said.

"Will you deliver the barrels of sardines before noon?" he asked.

• Attribution at the beginning of an indirect quote is not set off with punctuation.

He said 15 barrels of sardines will be delivered Wednesday.

• Attribution at the beginning of a direct quote requires punctuation. If the quote is only one sentence long, use a comma. If the quote is two or more sentences long, use a colon.

Johnson said, "We have spent three days examining the department's books and have found no evidence of impropriety."

Johnson said: "We have spent three days examining the department's books and have found no evidence of impropriety. We will recommend that no further action be taken."

- Quotations within a direct quote are set off with single quotation marks.

"He said, 'Go ahead and throw it away, just like you have done every game,' and he walked out and slammed the door," Smithers said.

"I think 'Sixth Sense' was a frightening movie," she said.

- Commas and periods go inside quotation marks in direct quotes.

"Fifteen stinking, dripping barrels of sardines will be delivered Wednesday," he said.

Matthews said, "This race should be the test of every man's and every woman's physical and mental stamina."

- When placing the attribution at the end of the first sentence in a direct quote, the attribution is closed with a period. It marks the end of a sentence.

Wrong:

"The new gymnasium is fantastic and humungous," said basketball player Brad Jones, "We're proud to play there. We really feel important playing our games now."

Right:

"The new gymnasium is fantastic and humungous," said basketball player Brad Jones. "We're proud to play there. We really feel important playing our games now."

- Question marks go inside or outside quotation marks depending on whether they are part of the quotation.

Mark said, "Are you asking me whether I cheated on the exam?"

One of Dionne Warwick's popular renditions included "Do You Know the Way to San Jose?"

- Consider what may be slightly confusing but correct punctuation here:

Sara asked Kate, "Have you ever seen the movie 'Gone With the Wind'?"

Here, the writer has a movie title that must be set off with quotation marks within a direct quote plus a question mark that is not part of the title.

- If the attribution breaks up a direct quote, it must be set off with commas and the quotation marks continued.

> "Go ahead and throw it away," said Smithers, "just like you have done every game."

- If a speaker is quoted for several continuing paragraphs, the quotation marks are closed only at the final paragraph. Each paragraph must open with quotation marks to indicate the person is still speaking.

> Resident John Loftis of Hollowell Road said, "We have been waiting two years for the southeast area to be annexed, and we are getting annoyed that the town council has further delayed a decision.
> "I have written and my neighbors have written all the council members to say we want town services and are willing to pay for them.
> "We just don't understand what the holdup is," Loftis said. "If a decision doesn't come after the next public hearing, I plan to picket city hall."

Not closing the quotation marks at the end of the first and second paragraphs tells the reader that Loftis has not finished talking. The quotation marks at the beginning of graphs two and three reopen the continuous quote from Loftis.

Covering Speeches

Covering speeches presents a challenge to note taking and organization. Taking notes during a speech is much more difficult than during an interview (discussed earlier in this chapter). In an interview, you can ask an interviewee to wait a few seconds while you fill in your notes. During a speech, you cannot stop the speaker; you have to keep up with what he or she is saying.

Taking notes during a speech, however, is somewhat like taking notes for a professor's lecture: You want to have as much material to study as possible, and you may have the opportunity to ask a clarifying question after the lecture is over. You may find that developing a shorthand is the easiest and fastest way to get complete notes.

Use times when the speaker is telling a joke or an anecdote to review your notes and to complete sentences. Put quotation marks around remarks that you know you can use as direct quotes. That helps when writing the stories.

Good note taking means listening carefully to what speakers say. Ears can deceive. Consider the following errors made when writers did not listen carefully and then did not think when writing the story.

> "Bureaucrats are never seizing in their efforts to keep information from the public," he said.

The speaker actually said "ceasing" not "seizing."

> "Having a big hearth has nothing to do with how big your wallet is," said Mrs. Bush.

She actually said "heart" not "hearth."

> "The creation of new toxic dumb sites has all but been eliminated," Browner said.

She really said "dump" not "dumb" sites.

> She saluted American industry, small business, schools, and American citizens for banning together to solve the country's environmental problems.

The speaker said "banding" not "banning."

> People in countries have "the need to create extinct, stable governments," he said.

What the speaker said was "distinct," not "extinct."

> Canada stepped outside its democratic laws to get the treaty written, she said.

The speaker actually said "diplomatic" not "democratic."

Sometimes writers hear the right word but misspell it. That damages their credibility and can be embarrassing. For example, one writer called a school's lecture series the "Wheel" lecture when it is named the Weil lecture.

Another referred to a river as the Noose River when it is spelled Neuse. Consider these:

> Investigators found millions of land mines sewn into the earth, Williams said.

The writer should have written "sown."

> "Our commitment cannot waiver," she said.

She said "waver."

> "Congress is trying to role back the progress of 25 years of environmental legislation."

It's "roll" not "role."

> "America should be neither a claste nor a classified society."

The speaker said "classed" not "claste."

> "Ronald Reagan was applicable with the press during his presidency."

The speaker said "affable."

> "After belaying a question about tithing, [Ronald] Reagan whispered to me, 'I should have taken your advice,'" journalist Helen Thomas said.

Thomas said "belaboring" a question.

> "The accident does not pose any immediate treat to nearby residents."

The writer made a typographical error. The speaker said "threat" not "treat."

Tips for Writing about Speeches

• When you start to write the story, always look for the theme. Ask yourself, What does the speaker want us to know? In one speech the theme

may be the importance of democracy, in another the value of higher education, and in yet another public service. It may be in the speech title, or the
speaker may deviate and pick out a pet subject on which to elaborate. The
theme will be a clue to the lead for your story. Generally, in the lead, a summary of what the speaker said will go first, and then attribution will end the
first sentence. An exception is made for a prominent speaker, such as the
president or a local government official. Then the name goes first.

- Rarely will the first paragraph be a direct quote. Few speakers summarize their comments in 20 words or less. The lead may use a partial quote.

- Write a lead that states what the speaker said. Use attribution verbs
such as "said" or "told."

- Do not write a label lead that simply identifies the topic or theme
of the speech. That means *do not* use attribution words such as "discussed,"
"talked about," "spoke about," or "expressed concern about." See the
difference:

Label lead:

Three members of the Broadcasting Board of Governors held a
panel discussion on the future of international broadsating on the university campus last Wednesday.

Summary lead:

U.S. government broadcasts to regions all over the world can
explain democratic values to people living in countries that have
repressive governments, according to a panel of experienced broadcasters and journalists who spoke at the university last Wednesday.

- Have a second graph that follows and supports the lead.

- Do not have a second graph that burdens readers with background on
the speakers. See the difference:

Graph 2:

The panelists were David Burke, chairman of the Broadcasting
Board; Evelyn Lieberman, director of Voice of America; and Kevin
Klose, director of the International Broadcasting Bureau, which over-
sees Voice of America, Radio and TV Marti, and Worldnet Television.

Better second graph to follow the summary lead:

"By providing news and public affairs broadcasting, we can help them establish stable democracies," said Kevin Klose, a panelist and director of the International Broadcasting Bureau, which oversees Voice of America, Radio and TV Marti, and Worldnet Television.

The third graph would note the other two panelists and the qualifications that speak to their credibility. You do not have to include a complete résumé. If the panel had a discussion title, it would be included in graph 3. Writers would also summarize here the topics covered, such as

The panelists primarily focused on the role of U.S. broadcasts since the fall of the Berlin Wall, but they also discussed new technology and how to bring their organizations into the twenty-first century.

• Have a balance of direct and indirect quotes.

• Look for a direct quote as a good way to end a story. Or end the story with more background about the speaker.

• Make sure your story has adequate attribution, even if you cover only one speaker.

Covering a Presidential Speech

When the president speaks, the media cover his remarks. President George W. Bush traveled to the Giant Forest Museum in Sequoia National Park, California, to set the stage for comments on the environment. Read the following transcript of his speech and see if you can find the lead. Remember: Information for the lead might not be found early in the president's remarks.

Thank you all very much. Gale, thank you very much. You're going to like working for Gale. She's a common-sense person who cares deeply about our national park system, and about our nation's environment. I picked a fine, fine person to lead this very important agency. And, Madam Secretary, thank you for traveling with me today.

Dick, thank you very much for your fine hospitality. It's a fantastic trip up to Moro Rock. I'm a survivor of the march up to Moro—(laughter)—led by Debbie Byrd, chief ranger. What a fantastic hike it was. It's a spectacular place. And it must be a joyous place to work. And for all of you who work on behalf of the people of the United States in the Park Service, I thank you very much for your service. (Applause.)

I'm so very pleased that three members of the United States Congress are here, three really fine public servants—Cal Dooley, Gary Condit, and George Radanovich. Thank you all so much for coming. (Applause.)

I, too, want to thank the board members of the Sequoia Fund, and the board members of the Sequoia Natural History Association. Thank you for working with these fine public stewards to make sure this park offers this beauty for every citizen who wants to come here.

Any day that you can take in sights like these is a great day. It has been a great day for me. *This place leaves each of us with a feeling of incredible humility. That's one reason why it's so important. In our daily lives we're surrounded by things of our own making—buildings and machines and goods we create ourselves. There's much to admire and appreciate in the works of man. But come here and you're reminded of a design that is not our own. Here we find a grandeur beyond our power to equal.* *

We're standing amongst the largest trees on Earth, and some of the very oldest. When the Mayflower *arrived on the eastern shore of this continent, the great sequoias were already here. When the seal was fixed on the Magna Carta, the great sequoias were already here. They were here when the Roman Empire fell, and they were here when the Roman Empire rose. And had Christ, Himself, stood on this spot, He would have been in the shade of this very tree.*

* *When men and women walk into a setting like this, we must walk with care. Of all the forces on Earth, only man is capable of cutting down a sequoia, and only man is capable of fully appreciating its beauty.* *

And, fortunately, more than a century ago, the government of the United States stayed the hand of all who would destroy this place and these trees. That decision, by President Benjamin Harrison, reflects an ethic of respect for the natural world that was once shared only by a few, but is now a basic commitment of American life. *Our duty is to use the land well, and sometimes, not to use it at all. This is our responsibility as citizens; but, more than that, it is our calling as stewards of the Earth. Good stewardship of the environment is not just a personal responsibility, it is a public value.* *Americans are united in the belief that we must preserve our natural heritage and safeguard the land around us.*

This belief is affirmed in our laws. With more than 80 million acres under protection, our national park system has set the standard for the world in preserving natural lands. We've given a reprieve to our national symbol, the bald eagle. Through cooperative efforts with wildlife biologists and private landowners, the condors are back in the wilds of California. Americans have come to understand that other creatures need the room to roam and places to live.

Other laws express this same commitment. Our lakes and rivers are much cleaner than they were 30 years ago. Firm limits on toxic emissions have greatly improved the quality of the air we breathe. And I'm proud that it was my dad's signature on the Clean Air Act amendments of 1990 that helped reduce acid rain and urban air pollutions.

Over the last three decades, nearly 3,000 hazardous waste facilities have been closed. We've made much progress in ridding our towns and cities of brown-fields, and even more progress will be made over the next several years. And the Environmental Protection Agency has begun or completed cleanups in more than 90 percent of the sites targeted under Superfund. This marks tremendous progress in protecting our nation's environment. It's not the doing of a single party or the branch of government, or a state or a community or a group, it's been the work of Presidents and Congresses and governors, as well as landowners, environmental-ists and local leaders. All have responded to the appeal of conscience and the clear wishes of the American people.

Today, I continue to speak about my conservation policies and the principles that will guide them. These policies reflect the vital role we each play as stewards of our lands, and the federal government's part as steward of nearly one-third of the American landmass. And they reflect that while we've made great progress, much more must be done to protect the environment.

In spite of the successes of the past 30 years, at times we've seen needless con-flict and policies that have done more harm than good. Today we must seek the best ways to achieve the common goal of leading to posterity a nation of fresh air, clean water, and natural beauty. These policies arise from the conviction that a healthy environment is national concern and requires an active national government.

At the same time, states and localities have their own responsibilities for the environment. They have their own authority, too. And usually they have a better grasp of the problem and what is needed to solve it. Washington has sometimes relied too much on threat and mandate from afar, when it should be encouraging innovation and high standards from the people closest to the land.

My administration will adopt a new spirit of respect and cooperation, because, in the end, that is the better way to protect the environment we all share—a new environmentalism for the 21st century. Citizens and private groups play a crucial role. Just as we share an ethic of stewardship, we must share in the work of stewardship. Our challenge is to work in partnership. We must protect the claims of nature while also protecting the legal rights of property owners. We will succeed not by antagonizing one another, but by inviting all to play a part in the solutions we seek.

For the federal government, good stewardship begins right here, in this and in the hundreds of other park areas across America. Washington has a very clear and direct responsibility for these lands. Yet many parks have gone years without receiving the kind of care and upkeep the American people expect. More than 287 million people now visit our national parks each year.

At the same time, however, many of our parks have gone neglected. So, today I'm announcing the National Parks Legacy Project. My administration will make a major investment in our national parks to preserve the legacy of protection for future generations. We will spend $5 billion over 5 years to clean up the backlog in maintenance, and make our parks more inviting and acceptable to all citizens.

We're the first administration to request full funding for our country's Land and Water Conservation Fund, to provide needed dollars to help local folks meet conservation concerns.

This park is a model to follow. The Park Service is nearing completion of a project to remove structures once thought necessary, but which now threaten to damage the roots of the sequoias. In my budget, I propose spending $1.5 billion to help complete this project. Working with the local community and the Sequoia Natural History Association, we will offer the young and old alike an opportunity to learn more about the wonders of nature.

In all our parks, we want visitors to feel welcome and to enjoy the experiences that nature and history have to offer. Future renovations will make this more possible by adding, for example, many more miles of carefully drawn hiking paths. Here again, Sequoia is a model, allowing for more visitors without destroying the very things that draw people here—the scenery, the quiet, the animals left unharmed in their natural habitat. And we will leave them that way.

Our parklands are home to thousands of species of flora and fauna. And as stewards of these lands, the federal government has the responsibility to protect and nurture them in their habitats and enhance the science that helps to protect biodiversity. For the next five years, we'll protect nearly 4,000 miles of river, and restore nearly 9,000 acres of parklands to their natural conditions. We have more than doubled the budget to help us better study our parks' natural resources, learn better ways to protect and restore them, and teach visitors about how they can help.

My administration will also pass new rules to help remove haze in many of America's national parks. Our national parks are for all to visit, and all Americans to enjoy. And we will continue our work to make these national treasures accessible to those with disabilities and to welcome people of all backgrounds. And to make sure that we're achieving our goals in these areas, I'm asking our park rangers to prepare stewardship plans for each park in America.

I'll also direct Secretary Norton to prepare an annual report, describing the condition of our parks, with recommendations of ways to improve them. Some fear that places like this are scenes from a passing world; they're not. They will be here as long as we're willing to show careful regard for the environment. This is a great responsibility. I strongly believe our country is equal to it.

America, itself, is just 225 years old—a momentous era, and yet so short a time in the life of the world. We cannot see into the centuries ahead, but we can be sure, in a place like this, that we're in the presence of enduring things. And it will be to our lasting credit if these works of God are still standing a thousand years from now. Thank you for having me. (Applause.)

President Bush used the majority of his speech to set up a historical perspective of parks and the beauty of nature. Toward the end, he noted that his administration will spend $5 billion over five years to fix up parks.

Following is how Robert Hillman wrote the speech for the *Dallas Morning News.* And also check out Hillman's attention to detail, such as the exact time length of the speech and other information that gives context. You may also notice that the *Morning News* uses courtesy titles as part of its style.

SEQUOIA NATIONAL PARK, Calif.—Standing beneath some of the largest and oldest trees on earth, President Bush on Wednesday detailed his $5 billion plan to fix up the national parks as a keystone of what he called a "a new environmentalism for the 21st century."

Much has been done during the last 30 years to clean up the nation's air and water and protect its natural majesty, Mr. Bush said, but there is much more to do.

"At times, we've seen needless conflict and policies that have done more harm than good," he said. "Washington has sometimes relied too much on threat and mandate from afar, when it should be encouraging innovation and high standards from the people closest to the land."

Under his vision of a "new environmentalism for the 21st century," Mr. Bush said he hoped to foster a "new spirit of respect and cooperation" as well as provide new funds to address lingering maintenance needs at the parks.

But in his 14-minute address under the towering Sequoia trees, Mr. Bush did not mention criticism by environmentalists, Democrats and others of his envi-

ronmental policies now and as governor of Texas. Indeed, on Wednesday, some conservationists said his $5 billion plan was not nearly enough.

During last year's presidential campaign, Democrat Al Gore and his supporters repeatedly blamed Mr. Bush for the heavy air pollution in Houston, portraying it as the dirtiest city in America, and attacked his proposal to explore for oil and gas in Alaska's Arctic National Wildlife Refuge.

In recent weeks, critics have complained of the president's lack of support for an international global warming treaty, his broken campaign pledge for tougher regulation of carbon dioxide emissions from power plants and his decision to roll back the standards for arsenic in drinking water. He also has been criticized for his support of logging in national forests.

On Wednesday, Mr. Bush sought to strike a balance between a better environment and a flourishing economy.

"We will succeed not by antagonizing one another, but by inviting all to play a part in the solutions we seek," he said. "My administration will adopt a new spirit of respect and cooperation because, in the end, that is the better way to protect the environment we all share."

"Good stewardship of the environment is not just a personal responsibility, it is a public value," he said. And "good stewardship begins right here" in Sequoia and the hundreds of other federal parks.

Under his National Parks Legacy Project, first outlined during the campaign, Mr. Bush is asking Congress for $5 billion over the next five years to clean up and fix up a lingering backlog of maintenance problems.

Mr. Bush also ordered an annual State of the Parks Report from Interior Secretary Gale Norton, who accompanied him Wednesday, and individual "stewardship plans" for improving each park and using it more efficiently.

"Washington has a very clear and direct responsibility for these lands," the president said, noting that more than 287 million people visit national parks each year. "My administration will make a major investment in our national parks to preserve the legacy of protection for future generations."

In addition to the $5 billion, Mr. Bush said he was proposing $3 million to support restoration of the Florida Everglades and other funds to reduce haze in the parks and add 5,200 miles of trails, among other initiatives.

The administration, however, is holding back on the purchase of more parkland.

"It's a question of whether we should pay our existing bills or go on a shopping spree," Ms. Norton said.

The National Parks Conservation Association called for more.

"Some things can't wait to be protected," said Courtney Cuff, the association's Pacific regional director.

Mr. Bush's $5 billion plan is a good start, she said, but a "little more balance" is needed.

His plan favors "brick-and-mortar projects and roads," she said, over other festering needs, such as improving air and water quality and providing better management of the park resources.

Leaving Los Angeles Tuesday afternoon, Mr. Bush took Air Force One to Fresno, hopped a helicopter for a short lift, then rode the last hour or so to Sequoia in a motorcade that stretched several city blocks.

After a night at the new Wuksachi Lodge, he was up early for a stop at the General Sherman Tree, billed as the "largest living thing on earth." He addressed park personnel and others beneath a canopy of giant Sequoias.

"They were here when the Roman Empire fell, and they were here when the Roman Empire rose," he said. "And had Christ himself stood on this spot, he would have been in the shade of this very tree." ★

A Parting Shot

Whether you are using quotes from an interview or a speech, remember the following:

• Be circumspect in your use of quotations. Just because you have a quote doesn't mean you have to use it.

• Look for variety in quotes when you are writing, and use a mix of indirect and direct quotes.

• Remember *The Associated Press Stylebook* rule about correcting quotations.

• If you are not sure about a quote, follow this rule: When in doubt, leave it out. Don't try to reconstruct it as a direct quote. And be sure you have the gist of the remarks if you convert the comments to an indirect quote.

• Develop tape recorder skills so that you can use one to assist in long or complicated interviews.

★Reprinted with permission of the *Dallas Morning News.*

EXERCISES

1. Interview a friend or classmate about social life on your campus. Consider using a tape recorder to practice taking notes and listening to the tape again to double-check accuracy. Take careful notes. Then list five quotes, with correct attribution, that you might use in a finished story about social life at your school. Focus on correct attribution and use of both indirect and direct quotes.

2. Identify a campus leader who has been in the news recently. Select a specific topic related to the leader's expertise. Set up an interview and prepare questions as outlined in the chapter. Take a tape recorder to record the interview. When the interview is over, transcribe the tape. While interviewing, take notes on the surroundings to add description. Write a story that focuses on the campus leader's view. Use a mix of direct and indirect quotes.

3. You are a reporter for the campus newspaper. Your editor has asked you to come up with a story based on money, specific to the campus. Ideas might be the cost of tuition or books, lack of enough financial aid, lack of funds to maintain classrooms, cost of getting settled in a job after graduation, increased student fees. Think of a story that would interest your audience: students. Stick to the campus for interviews. You must use more than one source. If the story relates to campus funding, you will need to talk to an administrator. You would also want to talk with a student who is affected. Be sure to have enough sources. After the interviews, write a story showing both sides of the issue.

4. Many publications reveal how average citizens feel about or react to an event. Editors will select a current topic and assign a reporter to get public reactions. Scan today's daily newspaper and select a current topic, such as an ongoing international conflict, national legislation, a campus issue, or another major event that students and staff would have read or heard about. Interview 10 people. Ask each one the same question. If you have to ask a question that is answered yes or no, you will need a follow-up "Why?" or your responses will be skimpy. Get each individual's name (check the spelling) and two other identifying labels: year in school, academic major, hometown, age, residence. Your attribution would look like this: Jane Smith, a senior chemistry major, or Alex Jones, 19, of

Whiteville. Write the story. The first paragraph should have a summary lead, giving the results of your informal poll, such as "Five of ten university students interviewed Thursday at the student union said they believed the presidency is a tough job that receives little credit, and not one student would want the job." The second paragraph gives the question: "The students were asked, 'What is your assessment of the job of president, and would you want the job?'" Then you can proceed with each person's response.

REFERENCES

John Brady, *The Craft of Interviewing.* Cincinnati: Writer's Digest, 1976.

Rene J. Cappon, *The Word: An Associated Press Guide to Good News Writing.* New York: Associated Press, 1991.

Norm Goldstein, ed. *The Associated Press Stylebook 2001 and Briefing on Media Law.* New York: Associated Press, 2001.

Judith Lewis Herman, *Trauma and Recovery.* New York: Basic Books, 1992.

Ken Metzler, *Creative Interviewing,* 2nd ed. Englewood Cliffs, NJ: Prentice-Hall, 1989.

10

Electronic Media

```
When you write for electronic
media, your copy will look like
this: A script format that
occupies half the width of the
page. But the content will
remain accurate, concise, and
complete, just as in any
writing you do.
```

Writing for the electronic media—radio and television—requires the basic writing skills discussed in earlier chapters. Broadcast messages must be concise, clear, and simple so that audiences can understand the information.

Even though most electronic messages are written before they are aired, broadcast writing differs in some respects from writing for print. Audiences tuning in to radio, for example, have to rely on their ears to get the message. Writing must be clear and specific. Writers have only one chance to catch audiences, who cannot go back and reread the lead.

In broadcast messages, writers and reporters must look past the written word for audio and visuals that enhance the message. A radio reporter can use an actuality or sound bite, such as a recorded interview or the sounds of traffic. But the actuality must attract audience attention and fit the report. Television reporters must combine writing with videotapes that include audio and live shots from the scene of an event. The writing must match the visuals and make the report come alive, appealing to the audience's senses.

In this chapter, you will learn

- The similarities and differences between print and electronic media writing;
- The essential qualities of electronic media writing;
- How to write for radio, television, and online; and
- The trend toward convergence.

Print and Electronic Media Writing

Similarities exist between good writing for print and electronic media. The media themselves—primarily radio and television—dictate some differences in format and approach for their particular audiences. Writers need copy that is readable and that can be heard.

Similarities

THE WRITING PROCESS. The skills learned in the writing process discussed in Chapter 1 apply to electronic media. Broadcast reporters start with an idea, do research and interviews, then produce copy that is well written and relevant to their audiences. The writing process stage of outlining is critical for electronic media writers, who must plan a story before they leave the scene of an event. They must have a variety of visual shots to illustrate their stories as well as an outline so they can get necessary audio, such as a quote from a county commissioner, or video, perhaps a shot of fire trucks, that will be needed to produce the final story package. Once in the editing lab, they usually don't have time to go back and shoot a visual for the 6 P.M. news.

NEWS VALUES. All mass communication writing has to have some news values from among those discussed in Chapter 4: prominence, timeliness, proximity, impact, magnitude, conflict, oddity, and emotional impact. Electronic media writing is no exception. Timeliness is the most critical news element for electronic media. Radio and television, because of their ability to broadcast live, can get information out to audiences as news events occur. Immediacy is the key. For a news clip to last throughout a 24-hour cycle, the event must be compelling. In radio and television, news that happened in the morning may be old in the afternoon, whereas newspapers can and do print yesterday's news. Conflict is another key news value for electronic journalism. Viewing conflict firsthand on television can make an audience remember a story for a lifetime.

CLEAR, CONCISE WRITING. The rules of using short sentences, active voice, and short words, avoiding jargon and technical language, cutting wordiness, and getting to the point quickly are particularly critical in broadcast writing. Broadcast stories are generally shorter than those in print. Whereas a print news story may use 120 words to tell an event, a broadcast report may have to condense the account to 15 seconds. Newscasters read about 10 words in 4 seconds; a 15-second broadcast story is about 35 words long. Every word counts, therefore, and language must be clear and precise. Few listeners will understand jargon or complicated language.

RESEARCH. Like print reporters, electronic reporters develop sources and do research and interviews. Research can be more difficult. Print reporters can access stories in library files or on computer databases fairly quickly. Electronic media reporters must review tapes to learn what the station may have covered before—a time-consuming process. Most electronic reporters do not accumulate clips and files they can readily consult. Television stations, for example, have file footage, but those archives are not as extensive as are newspaper libraries or morgues.

At some stations electronic media reporters must be generalists and cover a variety of topics, even within a single day. Many reporters are assigned to several beats. They may attend the governor's news conference in the morning and a fire the same afternoon. Radio reporters rarely have the opportunity to specialize in a particular area or beat, such as medicine, business, or local government. More and more television reporters, however, are assigned to specific areas such as politics, health, education, and others.

Differences

DEADLINES. Reporters for electronic media often work under tighter deadlines. Print reporters may have a 7:00 P.M. deadline for a morning newspaper, whereas a television reporter must have a story on the air at 5:00 P.M. The television reporter also may be producing several stories for that evening broadcast, perhaps two news briefs and one package that includes a standup, or appearance, by the reporter.

WRITING STRUCTURE. Because radio and television reports are shorter than print versions, they must be written to be understood the first time. They have only one chance to be heard. And they must make it through clutter. Most radio and television audiences are doing other things: driving the car, listening to children's voices, cooking dinner.

Electronic media reporters start a story with a headline to grab listener or viewer attention. Then they give a lead to the story, which generally sets up the context for the story. Next comes explanation. The wrap-up usually focuses on the possible effects. For television, the entire story may run an average 30 seconds; for radio, the report may be only 20 seconds.

In addition to writing the story for television and even radio, the reporter will have to write several advance headlines or teasers that anchors can use to promote an upcoming newscast. In a teaser, reporters give only enough information about a story to make viewers watch it later. For example, a story may need a teaser or lead-in during an afternoon newsbreak, plus another teaser or a lead-in just before the 6 P.M. news. Then a reporter must write a lead-in for anchors before being introduced. Finally, a reporter will give her own lead on the story. All are different, gradually adding information without revealing the entire story.

Electronic reporters may not use the inverted pyramid style of writing in structuring their stories. They may hold readers throughout and give a summary or wrap-up at the end.

STYLE. Electronic media writers adopt a more conversational style in writing their articles. Often the style is narrative and more like telling a story to listeners. For example, a reporter might use contractions in sentences. A more casual style still requires clear, concise writing.

FORMAT. Because electronic media require audio and/or visuals, the format for producing or typing stories differs from print format. Electronic and print journalists follow some of the same guidelines, such as double-spaced copy with one-inch margins, but electronic reports must add cues for audio and visual elements. Radio reports are typed across the page, just as print journalism stories are, but notes on what prerecorded elements will be inserted must appear between blocks of copy that will be read aloud.

In television reports, copy fills the right-hand side of the page; cues for the technical members of the crew appear in the left-hand column. Abbreviations, such as VO for voice-over when the announcer or reporter switches from the studio to the videotape, are indicated in the left-hand column.

Some broadcast journalists type their copy in all caps, but others prefer upper- and lower-case. (The broadcast writing in the rest of this chapter is set all caps to differentiate it from print formats.) Paragraphs are not split between pages, and each story is typed on a separate page. Specific style rules on how to use abbreviations, numbers, and attribution are explained later in the chapter.

COST. One point to remember is that electronic production—whether for an hour-long documentary or a 20-second news spot—is expensive and requires a team effort. Movies cost millions to produce; budgets for staff and equipment in television newsrooms are costly.

For example, print journalists can get by with collecting information in an 89¢ notebook with a 25¢ pencil. A television reporter's field unit—camera, battery pack, and lighting—costs $20,000 to $50,000. A news production van costs at minimum $100,000. Add satellite or microwave equipment, and the price tags start at $250,000. If the van is a top-of-the-line model, the cost can reach $500,000. Print journalists need computers and printing presses. Television reporters require editing equipment, studios, and satellite dishes. Radio reporters are on the economical end of electronic media production, requiring less in-house equipment to air their broadcasts.

The Differences in Practice

A radio reporter and a print journalist are rewriting wire service copy for their respective media. How would their leads look, based on the differences between broadcast and print writing? Let's see.

The print journalist writes:

ALBANY, N.Y.—New York Gov. George Pataki may fulfill a campaign promise today and sign legislation to create a death penalty.

The broadcast writer develops this lead:

NEW YORK'S GOVERNOR IS EXPECTED TO SIGN A DEATH PENALTY LAW TODAY.

The broadcast writer does not use a dateline, uses the present tense, avoids a complicated proper name, and establishes a context of death penalty legislation that can be explained later. Consider two other examples:

A survey reports that all women have similar concerns.

Women are most concerned about balancing home and job, health insurance, and stress, according to a survey released today.

Which is the broadcast lead? The first one is. It is short and uses attribution at the beginning to establish the source immediately. It also establishes a context for the story to follow.

Leads and Structure

No matter where an electronic journalist works, the need for clear concise writing is essential. Sabrina Smith Davis was a reporter for KOAT-TV in Albuquerque, New Mexico, the ABC affiliate. Davis began her career as a radio reporter then made the transition from radio to television. She summarized the need for good writing:

You have to be able to write. In radio, all audiences have is your voice and what they hear. As a reporter, you have to write the story colorfully and to visualize for audiences what they only can hear. If you can do that, you are ahead of the game. In television, good writing is also essential. So many people in television write in a boring way because they rely on visuals. Do this test: To see if the video matches, turn down the volume and just watch the video to see if you know what the story is about. As a viewer, you should have some idea. If you can write well and integrate visuals well, then you will do well as an electronic media journalist.

Writing for electronic media means writing for the ear: using short sentences, having speech that is more conversational, following a subject–verb–object sentence order, having copy that is clear and understandable, and putting smooth, clear transitions between thoughts. Let's look at producing broadcast copy, following these guidelines.

Broadcast Leads

A broadcast lead is short and gives basic information. It should be written in present or future tense to set the tone of breaking news. The lead may be catchy and even entertaining. It causes the audience to stop and listen to the story. As noted earlier, the lead generally establishes a context for the story. Specific information will follow.

THIRTEEN PEOPLE GET RICH IN INDIANA.

THE MAYOR WILL ANNOUNCE TOMORROW THAT NEW JOBS ARE COMING TO THE AREA.

The context is clear in each example. The first story will be about Powerball lottery winners. The second lead sets up audiences for a story on economics with information about how many and what kinds of jobs and the name of the company. In both instances, the leads are much shorter than in print.

Broadcast writers who cover continuing or recurring stories try to find leads that will pique audience attention and interest in just a few words.

UNION WORKERS PICKETING AT BALTIMORE HARBOR.

A SURPRISE WITNESS MAY TESTIFY BEFORE CONGRESS TODAY IN THE ENRON INVESTIGATION.

WHAT'S UP IN THE STOCK MARKET TODAY?

Broadcast Structure in the Message

Again, the structure of any electronic message must consider the audience's ear. The message must be clear and direct. Sentences are short and are written primarily in subject–verb–object order. Language must be simple. The writer develops the story using the three-part format: context, explanation, and effect. It sets out the context or the reason why the story is being written. It may focus on one news value or latest information—that is, timeliness. The second part is explanation, whereby listeners or viewers get more information, whether it is background, a historical perspective, or more details of the current situation. Then the writer wraps up with the effect, generally a look to the future or the impact of the event.

Look at this story:

IN ESPANOLA STUDENTS WILL RETURN TO FAIRVIEW ELEMENTARY SCHOOL TOMORROW AFTER ALMOST TWO WEEKS OF NO SCHOOL.

THE SCHOOL CLOSED MONDAY OF LAST WEEK AFTER A PLUMBER DOING ROUTINE MAINTENANCE WORK DIS- COVERED A GAS LEAK. THE SCHOOL WAS BUILT IN 1966, AND ADMINISTRATORS SAY EXTENSIVE REPAIRS WERE NEEDED.

SCHOOL OFFICIALS PRICED THE REPAIRS AT MORE THAN 20 THOUSAND DOLLARS. THEY SAY THE SYSTEM'S OTHER SCHOOLS WILL BE CHECKED FOR LEAKS, TOO.

The message clearly lets parents in the audience know that children will go back to school, and it gives other general-interest members an update on a story that has been in the news. The writer follows the lead with context by giving background on why the school was closed. The next sentence says why the school was closed for so long. Listeners then learn that the repairs were expensive. The effect or impact is an investigation of other schools' plumbing.

As for language, all words are simple. According to the readability for- mula discussed in Chapter 3, this story is easy for viewers to understand. The most complicated words are "maintenance" and "extensive."

Writing Guidelines

Basic writing principles apply for broadcast stories. Because timeliness is cru- cial to electronic media, writers should use the present tense if possible. Even if they have to shift to past tense later in the story, they find present tense preferable in the lead.

Avoid:

A convicted rapist was executed today after months of appeals failed.

Prefer:

A convicted rapist dies after months of appeals.

Avoid:

Sixteen winners were declared in the long-awaited state lottery.

Prefer:

Sixteen people are winners in the long-awaited state lottery.

Some other writing rules to follow:

- Avoid strange names or those of little-known people. Describe people in terms of employment or life's work, then name them in the second sentence. Use names only with prominent people.

A ROCKLAND SECOND-GRADE TEACHER IS THE NATION'S TEACHER OF THE YEAR.
RONNIE MILLER,...

Or

ROCKLAND MAYOR JOAN TILLIS IS IN GOOD CONDITION AFTER BACK SURGERY.

- Avoid tongue-twisters that can cause problems when reports are read on air. Always read copy aloud before it is aired or broadcast. "The clandestine clan committed continual crimes" or "the player's black plastic pants" may look clever on paper, but it may be difficult for an announcer to enunciate.

- Use action verbs. Remember that verbs can paint pictures, an especially important aspect of radio reports. "Race car driver Rusty Wallace roared to victory" has more life than "Race car driver Rusty Wallace won."

- Use quotations sparingly. Paraphrased statements are more easily understood. If a quote is particularly good, use it live from the source. Make sure that the writing does not imply the statement is from the reporter or newscaster. Direct quotes that use "I" or "we" can cause such confusion. Consider this quote: "Chamber of commerce president David Fall says, 'I have doubts about the town's development practices.'" Listeners who miss the attribution may infer the reporter is doubtful. Instead, write: "Chamber of Commerce President David Fall says he has doubts about the town's development practices."

- Put attribution at the beginning of a quotation: "Medical experts say the new treatment may cause cancer cells to die." If you must use a direct quote, try "Johnson said in his own words, 'The new treatment may cause cancer cells to die.'"...

- Avoid writing that uses a lot of punctuation. Punctuation—even a question mark—cannot be heard. Listeners may miss the inflection.

- Avoid long introductory clauses with participles, like this one: "While doing a routine maintenance check at the school, a plumber found…" The story example used earlier puts that information at the end of the sentence.

- Avoid separating subjects and verbs, particularly with phrases in apposition. "Marian Johnson, a director for the Rockland Little Theater, will leave her job in two weeks" becomes "Rockland's Little Theater director will leave her job within two weeks. Marian Johnson…" Don't leave verbs at the end of the sentence. Follow subject-verb-object order as much as possible.

- Break up lengthy series of modifiers and adjectives, "Police described the man as blond, long-haired, blue-eyed, and five-feet, six-inches tall." Rather, write: "Police say the suspect has long blond hair and blue eyes. They also say he is about five feet, six inches tall."

- Avoid negatives. A listener may miss the negative words "no" and "not" in a broadcast and thereby be misinformed. Use alternatives: "Police could find no motive for the shootings" can be translated "Police say the motive for the shootings is unknown."

- If your report runs long, say more than 30 seconds, look for ways to unify the story. Repetition of key words is one way to help listeners and viewers follow along.

Style in Copy

In Chapter 2, we looked at copyediting style for print. Electronic media have style rules for preparing copy.

- In the case of a word that might be mispronounced, spell it phonetically, just as you would with complicated names. For example, if you are reporting about lead content in paint, write it "led." Even though it is misspelled for the usage, you don't have to worry about an anchor reading "lead" as "leed" paint.

- If a name is difficult, spell out in parentheses following the name how to pronounce it. Anchors and reporters can stumble in stating people's names. Sound it out. For example, names with "ei" or "ie" can be confusing, such as Janice Weinberger. Write out "Wine Burger" so the announcer will use a long "i" pronunciation. For Iraqi leader Saddam Hussein, the pronunciation spelling is "Who Sayn."

- **Put titles before names and keep them short.** Use "Florida Governor Jeb Bush" rather than "Jeb Bush, the governor of Florida." A person who is a university vice chancellor for institutional research services becomes "a university administrator." You can use a descriptive title if audiences easily identify a person that way, such as, "evangelist Billy Graham" or "singer Sheryl Crow."

- **Use people's names the way they are commonly cited.** Former President Clinton is known as Bill Clinton, not William Clinton. Former vice president Dan Quayle was rarely called Daniel T. Quayle.

- **Write out most numbers between zero and 9.** Use numerals for 10 through 999. Above 999, you can combine numerals and words as long as they can be read clearly. For example, write "10 thousand two hundred" and "22 billion."

- **Round off numbers.** Say "more than 10 thousand" rather than "10 thousand two hundred and thirty-two subscribers."

- **Write out amounts for dollars and cents, percent, and fractions:**

    Gasoline prices are three to four cents a gallon higher.

    Three-fourths of town residents say they are pleased with the mayor's performance.

    About fifty-five percent of what you read, you remember.

- **Use numerals for phone numbers and years:** 919-555-1212, 1999, or 1865.

- **Keep statistics to a minimum.** Put them in a format people will understand. If a poll says 67 percent of the state's residents support NASA's plan for a lunar space station, report that "two out of three state residents say they favor NASA's plan for a lunar station."

- **Write out Roman numerals.** Write out "Harry Holland the third" rather than "Harry Holland III," or "Queen Elizabeth the second," not "Queen Elizabeth II."

- ~~Avoid acronyms~~. Use the full name, such as Department of Housing and Urban Development, not HUD, and Environmental Protection Agency, not EPA. Some acronyms can be used on second reference, such as FBI after Federal Bureau of Investigation has been the first reference. For local or state law enforcement, it is better just to say police or law officials on subsequent references.

Broadcast Formats

A major difference between print and electronic media is the format for the final message, as noted earlier. Broadcast media use a script format that indicates the text along with the sound bites or visuals. Time is critical in broadcast writing. Scripts indicate how long the total story runs plus the length of specific segments within the story. Radio reports are typed across the page, much like a print story, with audio cues. Following is an example of a radio news script:

7/30 MK Road Construction

SPEEDING ALONG HIGHWAY 86 IN NORTH CHAPEL HILL COULD COST YOU AS MUCH AS 165 DOLLARS. THAT'S THE WARNING FROM THE CHAPEL HILL POLICE TRAFFIC UNIT. OFFICER CHUCK QUINLAN SAYS A CONSTRUCTION WORK ZONE WILL STRETCH FROM ASHLEY FOREST TO INTERSTATE 40 FOR THE NEXT YEAR-AND-A HALF. QUINLAN SAYS THE WORK ZONE WILL HAVE A UNIFORM 35-MILE-PER-HOUR SPEED LIMIT WITHIN WEEKS. THAT MEANS DRIVERS NEED TO PAY ATTENTION.★

#145 QUINLAN:21 A:....ROAD, ETC.

QUINLAN SAYS HE AND HIS COLLEAGUES HAVE BEEN DEALING WITH REAR END COLLISIONS IN THE WORK AREA. AND HE SAYS THE SITUATION COULD GET WORSE, AS CREWS CONTINUE MOVING DIRT NEAR THE ROADWAY.★

In television reports, the cues on the left-hand side of the page give such information as the title or slug of the story, what newscast it will appear on,

---

★Reprinted with permission from Mitch Kokai, WCHL-AM radio, Chapel Hill, NC.

the tape number, the length of the story, the name of the anchor, and any graphics to be used. After the story text begins, cues will tell whether the story has a voice-over that is read by the anchor along with the visuals. Cues also indicate who is speaking—for example, a source who is interviewed for the story, the reporter, or the anchor. The following example shows cues:

Cues	*Explanation*
REALESTATE PG.8	Story slug and page of newscast script.
NEWSCAST=6PM	Tells computer in which newscast to find script.
TAPE#=95-1001	Edited stories are put on numbered tapes for the computer reference system.
ANCHOR=TERESA	Cue for the computer system to connect directly to the TelePrompTer when the anchor is speaking.
CK=TWO SHOT A7N 6	Tells the director and graphics operator what to put in the Chroma-key. TWO SHOT A7N 6 means the camera operators are to frame both anchors in the shot. The Chroma-key or label is to appear between them on the screen and read "Action 7 News Live at Six."
LIVE IN DROPKEY	A computer-generated box somewhat like the Chroma-key but in which a reporter appears as he or she waits to deliver a live report.
TAKE LIVE	Tells the director and technical director to put in the live shot.
ROLLCUE="TO THE OFFER"	Tells the director and the person rolling the tape when to start the videotape to play the story.
RUNS=1:30	Tells the computer how long the package is so it can take the introduction and the tag line and estimate the total run time of the piece.
OUTCUE	Cues the director to return to the anchor desk or to a live shot.

When the story text is typed, sometimes all capital letters are used. That helps clarify writing where a lowercase "l" might resemble a capital "I" and create problems for announcers. Capital letters are also easier to read from a distance. But some writers are moving to upper- and lower-case letters, as in print journalism.

When students study electronic journalism, they learn the codes and copy preparation style early on. The complete radio story may seem to be longer than a story typed for print because cues take up space on the left-hand side of the page. The goal is to make the copy legible for the anchor and the reporter who read from the copy.

Television News Script

DOTOFFICE PG.3
NEWSCAST=6PM
TAPE #=98–1056
ANCHOR=DAVE
CK=JOHNSON

<<(D) SOME CONSUMERS ARE CALLING FOR THE STATE TO ABOLISH THE STATE BOARD OF TRANSPORTATION. THE MOVE CAME IN THE WAKE OF A DEPARTMENT OF TRANSPORTATION HEARING TODAY. BUT AS MARGARET STEELE REPORTS, POLITICS MAY MAKE THAT DIFFICULT.

CVTR SOT FULL (✶✶✶✶✶✶PKG✶✶✶✶✶)

SUPER=14–Secretary's office/
Raleigh; at:03

SUPER=21–Norris Tolson
Transportation secretary; at :15

SUPER=@SSMR–Raleigh; at :46

RUNS=1:06
OUTCUE="…Action 3 News."

P-DOTOFFICE PG.3P   TWENTY-FOUR STATES DO
NOT HAVE TRANSPORTATION
BOARDS MADE UP OF POLITICAL
APPOINTEES. THOSE CALLING
FOR THE CHANGE WANT STATE
OFFICIALS TO INVESTIGATE
OTHER OPTIONS.

Online Writing

Since the early 1990s, more and more people, including writers, have become dependent on the Internet and Web sites to find information. Online sites supplement what readers and viewers find in newspapers and magazines and on television. Audiences have a wealth of news sources. They can access news.yahoo.com, which provides links to other news organizations' sites, or original-content news sites such as CNN.com and MSNBC.com. Newspapers of all sizes have Web sites, such as USAToday.com and NYTimes.com, as do television stations and other media.

The Value of Web Sites

Every day Web sites spring up to cater to specific audiences or to support a company's new venture. Sites are used to educate, to entertain, to sell products and services, and even to find a virtual date.

The value of Web sites became more focused during and after the terrorist attacks on the United States in 2001. Audiences looked to news Web sites for more information. Media organizations could update information on their Web sites faster than they could in print publications. Companies used Web sites to give employees and others information and to post their condolences to victims of the attacks. Many altered their sites to include links to data on anthrax and Islam. New sites were created to solicit donations, to track the events, and to serve as clearinghouses for information.

Several studies prior to the attack had documented an increase in Web site use people, particularly younger readers. It is expected that audiences' desires for online news will continue to grow. When news breaks, audiences will seek initial information from television then move to online news sites—as they did in September 2001. They will supplement their knowledge with newspapers and magazines—media that do not have the ability to get news out as fast as television and online reporters but that can provide in-depth information. Online sites, with their ability to link to other sites across the Internet, offer a breadth that print publications cannot match.

Most news Web sites, like other Web sites, face financial issues because they are not self-supporting through advertising revenue. In fact, most depend on their traditional media link, be it newspaper or television, for the revenue necessary to sustain them. As online media become more established, they face other challenges that are familiar issues for print and broadcast: ethics, conflicts of interest, credibility, and quality control. Traditional values of accuracy, clarity, fairness, and completeness will be paramount as online media take their place among electronic options for audiences.

Writing Is the Key

The advent of the Internet has captured the attention of journalists—particularly younger journalists—who are attracted by the appeal of a new medium. Internet site editors lament that some media Web sites don't have enough reporters and writers with experience to catch errors and to edit stories well. Their complaint reinforces the need for good writing on the Internet.

What makes for good writing on the Internet? The same tenets outlined in Chapter 3: short words, short paragraphs, lack of jargon, accuracy, completeness, conciseness, and fairness, to name a few. Anyone who creates a Web site may fancy himself or herself a writer. That's not true. The Internet has become a repository of too much bad writing.

As noted earlier in the text, headlines and stories on news Web sites are often pulled from stories in related media, such as the newspaper or television station. But online publications can't rely on using stories from other media. Writers may need stories that offer a new angle to readers or fit their particular Web site design. Stories may need to conform to the Web site's style rules. In other words, online writers must know how to develop a story from start to finish.

In addition to knowing guidelines for good writing, online writers must have a real understanding of the great potential of hypertext. *Hypertext* is the underlying code that can link an image or even a single word that is on the screen to other stories, to e-mail, and even to visuals and sound. Online writers must constantly think of ways that text can be enhanced by companion media that come along with hypertext. In online writing, formats call for text as only one component, and sometimes a small one at that. Much online news consists of briefs and headlines. Full texts sometimes are hard to find and are rare on Web site "fronts" or home pages.

Writers benefit from hypertext. They can describe new legislation or building plans, then link directly to original text documents that are online. Breaking stories can be updated moment by moment and supplemented with either live broadcasts or videotape as it becomes available. Events of September 11 unfolded on the World Wide Web. Stories linked to stunning live images, streaming video, recorded speeches, time lines, and even lists of names as the dead and missing were accounted for.

In a sense, good online writing highlights and exploits all the benefits of online communication: brighter pictures, links to original documents or sound, and the potential for instant feedback from an active audience. Readers expect to move quickly among media when they are online—from photos to text to sound to e-mail and back again, many times over in a single seating. Audiences appreciate the extras that come with online stories: more choices, more control, interaction, and variety. Writers must deliver these benefits and remember that one story on a given topic could end up being the only story that a reader may see. Writers must make each story self-sufficient and fully connected to related materials and sites.

When it comes to feeding content to any Web site, writers function as part of a team that includes artists, editors, photographers, videographers, and others. Even archivists and museum curators get involved when original documents become part of online news. The entire team is important because audiences gravitate toward sites that have strong design or that are easily navigated. Content is important, but so is the packaging.

Trends in Electronic Media

Television is a regulated and competitive medium that depends heavily on technology. And in the past decade, it has been on a roller coaster of change. Audiences use television primarily as an entertainment medium but also for news. Almost every household in the United States has a television set, and about three out of four homes have more than one.

In the last quarter of the twentieth century, the television industry went from a handful of networks, little cable or satellite service, and no Internet to almost a dozen major networks, cable and satellite distribution that increased channels to more than 200 and to Internet connections everywhere.

With so many choices for consumers—who also could turn to videocassette recorders and DVD players for entertainment—television has experienced declining audiences who have focused their attention elsewhere. Fewer viewers have meant less money to invest in programming that could bring audiences back. One option some stations are pursuing as a way to cut expenses and to have more money to put into programming is convergence.

Convergence

Convergence is one of the latest trends that is evolving particularly in the electronic media. It can take several forms, such as shared information or shared staffs. In *shared information,* a news reporter for a television station might give information about an event to a reporter from a sister newspaper with whom it has a sharing agreement. A television station might do a promotion for a story in a sister newspaper. With *shared staffs,* a television reporter may write a story and then rewrite it for the station's Web site. Or a newspaper reporter may write versions of a story for the newspaper and for the online site.

Convergence is evolving. Some see convergence as a permanent fixture in U.S. media; others see it as just an experiment. Some media observers say that online publications and sites represent convergence: the melding of print and electronic media. Convergence is getting support from publishers and media owners who see shared staffs as a way to reduce newsroom expenses. A plus for the business side is the ability to sell advertising packages that include ads for all media in a certain market: newspaper, radio, television, and online. Advertisers get a reduced rate to advertise in more than one medium. The package approach particularly helps online sites that haven't been able to support themselves financially. Supporters say that each medium—newspaper, radio, television, Internet—can maintain its values and basic structure but have the benefit of broader resources and expanded reach among audiences.

Executives considering convergence realize that logistics are just one piece of the puzzle. Combining newsrooms requires money and staff training on issues from responsibilities to technology. One of the biggest challenges may be the cultures of each medium and how to combine staffs of a certain mindset and institutional history. That conversion may take time, persistence, and progressive attitudes.

Tampa, Florida, and Phoenix, Arizona, were among the early ventures into convergence. Reid Ashe, former publisher of the *Tampa Tribune,* said that the benefits of convergence in its early stages have been to Internet operations first, then to television, and lastly to newspapers. In the *Tampa Tri-*

bune-WFLA-TV agreement, Ashe noted: "Each still had its traditional format but increased its resources. Advertising sales increased through multimedia packages. The partnership allowed the two to exploit the strengths of each medium. There was some institutional investment because we had to build trust among staff and an environment where people can experiment."

The *Arizona Republic* and Channel 12 news, owned by Gannett Inc., referred readers and viewers to coverage on the other medium. The *Republic* could provide the deep content while the television story had the visuals. In addition, newspaper and television stations could refer audiences to the online site, which in turn could link readers to additional information.

The trend toward convergence has prompted some schools of journalism and mass communication to teach students to write across platforms or different media styles. At the very least, those hiring students want them to know how writing styles differ and how to be comfortable with different media. Phil Currie, vice president of news for Gannett, commented at a journalism educators' meeting that he wants newspaper reporters to be comfortable being interviewed on television even if they were not trained specifically to write television copy.

Other Trends

The television industry is in the midst of a massive transition to a new technology: digital television (DTV). The Federal Communications Commission adopted in December 1996 yet another new standard for transmitting television signals, called DTV. Under that standard, television signals will be transmitted in digital rather than the existing analog format.

The highest form of DTV is called *high-definition television* or *HDTV.* It can transmit more than six times the information of the old analog system, which means higher-quality pictures and sound. HDTV screens are one-third wider than existing television screens; the picture is much crisper and more detailed, giving viewers the feeling of seeing images in a three-dimensional form. With HDTV, the television picture is studio quality, whether the viewer's television set is 6 miles or 60 miles from the broadcast station's antenna, points out John Greene, station manager for WRAL-TV in Raleigh, North Carolina. In 1997, WRAL established WRAL-DH, the first HDTV station in the country.

What do the changes mean for viewers? Eventually, new television sets, videocassette recorders, and camcorders. None will pick up the new digital signals, although HDTV sets will pick up older analog station signals. The first HDTV sets—as with any newly introduced technology—are expensive, averaging $3,500 to $7,000. But prices are expected to drop as manufacturers compete for customers. A set-top converter box will allow viewers to pick up digital stations on their analog TV sets, but pictures will be smaller and not as crisp as with HDTV equipment.

The FCC has set 2006 as the date finally to turn off all analog television sets, but some industry analysts expect Congress to extend that date until more people—at least 85 percent—have access to digital television signals.

What do the changes mean for professionals? Although writing styles will remain the same, pictures will change dramatically, Greene notes. Because the pictures will be wider and show detail greater, news videographers—those people who take the pictures—will have to adapt to the new wide-screen format and improved clarity.

Wrap-Up

Whatever field students choose and whatever jobs they ultimately hold in a converged newsroom or not, they must be good writers. The immediacy of broadcast will always attract audiences first—even before audiences check online sites. Radio and television can be accessed quickly, as was seen when people in the United States and abroad sought information about the terrorist attacks on September 11, 2001. People went to online sites and ultimately newspapers for additional links and information. But television continues to compete with other information-age technology, and writing must be compelling to keep audiences tuned in beyond the breaking news.

EXERCISES

1. Write a broadcast lead for each of the following stories:

> Sam Snyder, president of the Rockland Chamber of Commerce, has been elected to the board of directors of the National Chamber of Commerce.
>
> The Federal Reserve Board raised interest rates one-quarter percent, which means consumers will be paying

higher rates on their adjustable-rate home mortgages if they are seeking mortgages.

David Parkinson of Waverly County won first place at the county fair yesterday for the largest squash. It weighed 6 and ½ pounds. David is 6 years old.

Competition begins Thursday for the National Collegiate Athletic Association title. The tough competition has been dubbed March Madness.

2. Using the formula that a 60-space typed line equals 4 seconds of air time, write a 20-second radio script for the following information:

A masked man robbed the university dining hall of $3,000 and escaped after locking the dining hall manager in a closet.

Tony Jones, the manager, escaped unharmed. Police are looking for a heavy-set white man about 5-feet, 5 inches, and weighing about 175 pounds. He has a round face and broad shoulders. Jones could give no description of the man's facial features because he had a stocking pulled over his face.

Jones was preparing the payroll when he heard a noise in the kitchen. When he went to investigate, he said, the man came charging at him. The man ordered him to open the safe and put money in a blue sack. Jones complied, and the robber locked him in a closet before leaving.

3. Write a 20-second radio script for the following information and indicate an audio you could use to illustrate the spot:

The legal age for minors to buy cigarettes in most states is 18. Studies show that underage youth or

>minors still buy up to 500 million packs of cigarettes
>a year, despite the states' laws. About 25 states have
>agreed there should be stricter laws on tobacco
>products, and even tobacco industry officials claim
>their advertising is not geared to teenagers.

4. Write a 30-second television script for the following information. Type the copy in the right-hand column and indicate what visuals you would use.

>A coalition of child-care advocates marched on the
>state legislature today. They distributed flyers
>encouraging legislators to approve monies during the
>current session that would subsidize the cost of day
>care for families earning below $16,000 a year. They
>claim that day-care costs in the state have skyrocketed,
>and even working families are finding it hard to pay for
>quality day care out of their salaries. The coalition
>estimated 15 percent of the state's population fell
>below the federal poverty level guidelines last year.
>The coalition officials said that last year it had
>to turn away almost 400 families who needed financial
>assistance, because funds just were not available.

5. Watch the local evening news. Do a tally that covers the number of stories, story topics, whether they were local or based on a national event, the length of each, and numbers and types of sources used. Write several paragraphs on whether you felt adequately informed about news items from the television account.

6. Based on the information collected in Exercise 5, look at the local or regional newspaper the following day. See how many stories from your evening television newscast were covered in the newspaper. Look at the length of those stories and what new information you learned.

REFERENCES

Reid Ashe, keynote address, Association for Education in Journalism and Mass Communication, Washington, DC, August 5, 2001.

Felicity Barringer, "Growing Audience Is Turning to Established News Media Online," *The New York Times*, August 27, 2001.

Phil Currie, panel on convergence, Association for Education in Journalism and Mass Communication, Washington, DC, August 6, 2001.

Seth Finn, *Broadcast Writing as a Liberal Art*. Englewood Cliffs, NJ: Prentice-Hall, 1991.

Cecilia Friend, Don Challenger, and Katherine C. McAdams, *Contemporary Editing*. Chicago: NTC/Contemporary Publishing Group, 2000.

John Greene, Personal interview, written communication, Raleigh, NC, December 1997.

Radio-Television News Directors Association web site. Available at: http://www.rtnda.org.

Sabrina Smith, Personal interview, written communication, Raleigh, NC, January 1998.

Mitchell Stephens, *Broadcast News,* 2nd ed. New York: Holt, Rinehart and Winston, 1986.

C. A. Tuggle, Forrest Carr and Suzanne Hoffman, *Broadcast News Handbook*. New York: McGraw-Hill, 2001.

Leslie Walker, "Web-Page Collection Preserves the Online Response to Horror," *The Washington Post*, September 26, 2001.

11

Public Relations Writing

A student in an introductory writing course told her classmates that she wanted to pursue public relations (PR) as a career. Why? "Because I want to talk to people about the organization I work for," she said.

Her professor quipped, "You won't do much talking; you'll be much too busy writing."

Writing is the single-most important skill in public relations, all experts agree. Good writing is at the heart of every successful and effective public relations campaign and event, regardless of who does the talking.

Public relations practitioners must be able to communicate information about their organizations to targeted audiences. People will call an organization only when they know that it exists and what it does. The public relations practitioner must send the news release on company earnings before reporters will call. The mother must read the brochure on a community's child-care offerings before calling for more details. The college student must peruse the company's home page to learn about its internship program.

Being a successful public relations practitioner takes more than talking and a ready smile. Public relations practitioners must identify audiences to determine the best methods to communicate with audiences, conduct research, plan and carry out communication strategy, and evaluate plans. Writing is crucial at each stage, but particularly in communicating messages to important publics.

This chapter looks at the importance of

- Good public relations writing,
- Audiences that public relations professionals call *publics,*

- Communications tools used by public relations practitioners,
- The media as a major public, and
- Methods of reaching audiences.

What Is Public Relations?

Professor James Grunig at the University of Maryland defines *public relations* as the management of communication between an organization and its publics, or audiences: employees, clients, customers, investors, or alumni. Grunig emphasizes the importance of strategy and thinking in approaching those relationships.

Successful public relations builds and maintains good relationships between an organization and its publics through balanced, open communication. Public relations may be as simple as an announcement by the local literacy council about its success rate for the past year. Or it may be a complicated integrated marketing program that incorporates public relations with advertising, investor relations, and market research.

Diverse organizations use public relations: local, state, and national nonprofit organizations such as the American Heart Association; schools and universities; small companies; multinational corporations; and local, state, and federal government, including the president and the armed services. Public relations practitioners share information with the public to help the organization achieve its objectives. The objective of public relations efforts may be to announce new products or to show how a company works as a good corporate citizen or as a leader in its field. The objective may be public service, as in a broadcast message to reduce teenage pregnancy or to warn smokers about the risks of heart attacks.

Some people erroneously think of public relations as free publicity, believing that there is no cost. But real public relations—ongoing programs of communication with various publics—is expensive. Organizations must pay salaries and production costs, buy supplies and equipment, and cover additional overhead expenses, such as office space, computer support, and utilities. Most are hidden costs that the public does not see or consider.

Public Relations Tools

Public relations practitioners often use the term "public relations tools" or "communications tools" to describe the techniques or methods they use to reach audiences. All require solid writing skills. Among the more common communications tools are these:

- *News releases.* Articles that describe newsworthy events and are sent to media outlets. They are written in a style ready to be used.

- *Feature releases.* More in-depth, less timely articles about organization employees, projects, or services. These generally are targeted to a specific publication.

- *Media kits.* Folders that contain relevant information on the organization or company or a special event. Included are fact sheets, backgrounders, photographs, reprints, biographies, and other material.

- *Direct mail letters.* Letters written to targeted publics, generally to solicit support for a project or event.

- *Brochures.* Booklets or folders that include general information or targeted information about an organization or a special project. These are designed to be easily mailed or distributed at events or in racks.

- *Web sites.* Full-service Web sites that give information about an organization and invite the public to interact via e-mail and links to other sites.

- *Face-to-face contact.* Speeches or appearances at meetings, conventions, or other programs.

- *Audiovisual presentations.* Slide shows and multimedia shows that supplement information in speeches and visually depict an organization or its services.

- *Specialized publications.* Newsletters, annual reports, and magazines produced for internal audiences such as employees or for external audiences such as customers and the general public. In some corporate settings, annual reports are produced by the investor relations department; the public relations practitioner may help with some writing. Many specialized publications are online and linked to Web sites.

- *Video news releases.* Actual film footage with or without sound, especially voice-over, to give television stations ready-to-use material.

- *Public service announcements (PSAs).* Short announcements, generally sent ready-to-read to radio stations or posted on Web sites. These PSAs may be produced in video form.

- *Image advertising.* Attempts by an organization to improve an audience's perception of it. Such advertising is often done in conjunction with marketing departments.

Communications tools are incorporated into plans that serve as guides for public relations activities or campaigns. Corporate communications departments, for example, begin work in the fall on the next year's plan to support goals, specific actions, and target dates. Communications plans are discussed later in the chapter.

Of course, not all public relations is planned. A reporter may call the corporate communications department about a story idea, and the public relations practitioner will respond or arrange for a company executive to reply. The practitioner may send the reporter a media kit that contains a mix of communications tools, often called *collateral materials,* such as a news release, a fact sheet, and a brochure.

Public Relations Stages

In the late 1960s, Scott Cutlip and Allen Center identified four stages of a public relations campaign: research, planning, communication, and evaluation. Public relations practitioners still follow those stages today.

For example, a bank plans to change its checking service in three months. The public relations department is charged with informing the bank's publics of the change. Look at how the public relations practitioner would use each stage.

- *Research.* Research is essential to enable the bank to state public relations goals, identify relevant publics, describe the service, and identify its strengths and weaknesses. For example, the bank's reputation would be a strength; competition from other banks' services would be a weakness. Research could use focus groups to determine what the bank's customers would like in a checking account.

- *Planning.* In planning, the practitioner devises a communications plan or strategy. The practitioner determines what communications tools will be used during the next three months and sets deadlines for each one. For example, dates for news releases to trade publications differ from those for statewide media. Magazines usually need copy two months before publication dates; daily newspapers can print information within 24 hours of receiving it.

- *Communication.* In the communication stage, the practitioner carries out the plan. Information is written and distributed via the communications tools: news releases, brochures, fact sheets, annual reports and other publications, Web site, and speeches, just to name a few. Although writing is important in developing the plan, good skills are critical in the communication stage.

- *Evaluation.* In evaluation, the practitioner uses qualitative and quantitative ways to evaluate the success of the communications plan and strategy. For example, the bank can use focus groups of customers to determine how well they understood communication about the service. After the news release is distributed, the public relations staff can count the number of newspaper clippings to determine how many times the news release information appeared in newspapers. The Web site manager can count the number of hits or visits to the site.

The Role of Good Writing

Public relations practitioners must be good writers. They must be able to adopt different styles and tones when writing because they have many more audiences than the writer for a newspaper or specialized publication. In the morning they may write a general-interest news release and in the afternoon a speech in the language style of the company president. Or they may write an article for the employee newsletter and later consult with a production company on a video script for an upcoming stockholders meeting.

Much of public relations writing is grounded in journalistic writing. Many mass communications programs require public relations students to take media writing courses to learn the inverted pyramid and other formats. The courses also teach the fundamentals of grammar, punctuation, and style, and they stress the need for clear, concise, accurate writing that interests and attracts targeted audiences. Some public relations professionals are also trained in building and maintaining web sites for specific publics. A university, for example, will have sites for students, faculty members, donors, friends, alumni, and so on.

The need for accuracy in all aspects of public relations work is critical. Consider the public relations nightmare for CNN, the Atlanta-based cable news network, when it set up an 800 number so viewers could call in their questions and comments about programming. The number is 1-800-TALKCNN. But when CNN advertised the number, it mistakenly published it as 1-800-CNNTALK.

The latter number dialed into a sex service. Or the correction Warner Bros., the film giant, had to make in its promotion of *In the Garden of Good and Evil*. Publicity materials and even the film's final credits referred to author John Berendt's nonfiction work as a "novel." A novel is fiction. The misnomer required the film company to send out a correction that the movie was based on Berendt's book.

Informational versus Persuasive Writing

Public relations practitioners generally divide writing into two categories: informational and persuasive. The company's objective will determine the tone of the writing.

Informational writing is just what it says: It presents materials in a straightforward, factual manner—just as in journalistic writing. A brochure can be informational, simply listing an organization's history, services, address, and telephone number. A brochure may give specifics about an upcoming program.

A brochure can also be persuasive. *Persuasive writing* clearly pitches a particular point of view. Some public relations tools are deliberately persuasive. A direct mail letter to university alumni will try to persuade them to donate to endowed professorships. A public service announcement on radio will encourage listeners to donate canned goods to the local food bank.

Persuasive writing follows the tenets of good writing: accuracy, clarity, and conciseness. A brochure can be persuasive and still be informational, using facts and graphics to portray positively the company's position.

Most public relations writing adheres to journalism standards of fairness and impartiality. Experienced public relations practitioners know that arguments explained factually will have more impact than those that are biased and long-winded.

Considering Audiences, or Publics

Just as in any other mass communication field, public relations practitioners must consider their audiences, or what they call *publics*. The publics are the people who will be reading news releases or viewing video news releases. They may be employees, customers, other businesses, town residents, lawmakers, reporters, or officials in local, state, or federal government agencies. Public relations practitioners must identify and know which publics are important to their organization.

Imagine you are the public information director for a university system that is planning a capital campaign to raise funds for new buildings. The university administration has set a goal of $120 million. In planning a public relations campaign, you would have to consider the university's publics: alumni, faculty members, staff members, students, students' parents, potential students, donors, legislature (if the university is public or state supported), the general public, and the media. From that list, you might identify five key or important publics.

Practitioners use research such as informal surveys or focus groups to learn about their publics. Specifically, practitioners need to know how their publics get information. Then they can decide which media, or communications tools, are most effective in reaching them. And they can decide the tone and style of the message.

The Media as a Public

An important public for any public relations practitioner is the media. The media learn about an organization through standard communications tools found in media kits, such as news releases. But they also use annual reports, Web sites, investor publications, executive speeches, brochures, and other means to find out information about companies. In turn, practitioners must know the media. They must know the media's audiences, formats, and content. They must convince the media to use information. Media are essential audiences because through newspapers, magazines, radio and television, specialty publications, online sites, and others, the practitioner reaches many publics. Two primary tools for public relations practitioners are media lists and media kits.

The Role of Media Lists

Media lists are necessary equipment for public relations. Developing a media list can be time consuming, for it should include the name of the reporter, editor, or producer; title; address; telephone and FAX numbers; and other useful information, such as videotape requirements, kinds of stories considered, deadlines, and Web site and e-mail addresses. Information should be updated every three months.

Obviously, media lists provide the addresses for mailing, e-mailing, or fax-
ing news releases. But many practitioners use their media lists to keep track of
their media contacts. Reporters and editors are notorious for moving every
few years to different jobs in different locations. Practitioners can also note on
the media list when they have called to pitch a story idea or even personal tid-
bits, such as the names of reporters' children or favorite hobbies. Such knowledge serves as an icebreaker or a friendly way to wrap up a conversation.

Apart from media lists, most practitioners keep media logs. They note
when a reporter called, the media outlet represented, the story or summary
of questions, and who responded. The log can be a quantitative way to assess
public relations efforts.

The Contents of Media Kits

Many organizations, whether major companies or nonprofit groups, produce materials for media kits. Among the standard pieces are fact sheets,
backgrounders, news releases, and reprints of articles about the organization.
Each may be subdivided further. These pieces may also be available at the organization's Web site. Even if the content of the Web site and the media kit
are not identical, they need to be coordinated in appearance and tone. For
example, the company logo and any slogan would appear in both places. All
printed materials should show the address of the Web site; likewise, the Web
site should offer printed material.

Once the basic pieces are developed, a practitioner can build a media kit
depending on audience need. A reporter new to the financial services beat
would get a package with backgrounders, fact sheets, the most recent annual
report, the latest news release on company earnings, and any other information the public relations manager believes to be educational. When the bank
announces a new retail service, fact sheets on the other services would be included in media kits distributed at a news conference.

The pieces together are called *collateral pieces;* that is, they have a similar
look. The look or image of these pieces represents that of the company. The
American Heart Association uses its identifiable single heart logo on all
pieces. The slogan, "Fighting Heart Disease and Stroke," appears below the
organization's name. The collateral pieces have unity, visual harmony, and an
identifiable look.

With increased technology, organizations no longer rely solely on the U.S.
mail to deliver media kits or information included in media kits. Companies

use faxes or even post news on Web sites to reach the media. Some public and private companies, agencies, associations, municipalities, and other institutions hire companies to transmit news to the media.

For example, PR Newswire sends full-text news releases to newspapers, magazines, TV stations, and radio stations throughout the United States and to even more around the world. Medialink distributes printed press releases and kits by mail or broadcast fascimiles. But it also uses video, audio, and the Internet to make news for its clients available to television newsrooms and financial institutions. U.S. Newswire is an online news wire service for government, association, and public affairs news sources. It distributes news to print, broadcast, and online media around the world.

Communications Tools

As discussed earlier, public relations practitioners have many ways to reach their important audiences. Some are used more often than others. The more commonly used ones, and those that require skilled writers, are discussed here.

News Releases

News releases provide timely information to media. They may announce a promotion or staff change; a service or product; new information, such as the effects of legislation or the results of a survey; financial earnings; an upcoming event; or community service, such as a new scholarship program. Some news releases, especially those concerning events, are presented in the form of media advisories. Consider the following news release in Figure 11.1.

The release follows the business format but news media may be more interested in the news about Enterprise's donation rather than the company and its toll-free number. News releases must contain some of the news values discussed in Chapter 4: prominence, timeliness, proximity, impact, and magnitude. They may also include conflict, oddity, or emotional impact. The lead should summarize the relevant information. The rest of the release should be organized in the inverted pyramid style of writing discussed in Chapter 5 and follow Associated Press style, which most news outlets use.

The practitioner's goal in sending a news release is to get publicity. But the practitioner must remember that news releases are uncontrolled; the final

FIGURE 11.1   *Sample News Release: Enterprise Rent-A-Car*

Press Releases

For more information contact:
Christy Conrad
314-512-2706
cconrad@erac.com

ENTERPRISE RENT-A-CAR DONATES $1 MILLION
TO RELIEF EFFORTS IN NEW YORK AND WASHINGTON, D.C.

-Company extends waiver of one-way drop fee to further assist customers in need-

ST. LOUIS, (Sept. 17, 2001) – Enterprise Rent-A-Car announced today that on behalf of its 50,000 employees worldwide, the company will donate $1 million to the disaster relief efforts in New York and Washington, D.C.

The donation will be made by the company's charitable arm, the Enterprise Rent-A-Car Foundation. In keeping with the Foundation's tradition of giving to local organizations that Enterprise employees support, the company will work with Enterprise's managers in New York and Washington, D.C. to determine how the funds will be distributed to local charities.

In addition to the donation, the company is extending its no-drop-fee policy on one-way rentals through Friday, Sept. 21. This extension is in response to the many calls the company has received from customers who are still in need of one-way transportation. The amended policy applies to all customers with an open Enterprise rental contract from Sept. 11 through Sept. 21, 2001. Customers should contact one of the more than 4,300 U.S. Enterprise offices directly at 1-800-Rent-A-Car to see if a one-way rental can be arranged. In addition, any Enterprise customer who incurred a one-way drop fee on or after Sept. 11, 2001 will have the cost of the drop fee refunded over the next month. Customers who have questions about their refunds should contact Enterprise at 1-877-905-7283 or via e-mail at oneway@enterprise.com.

#

Reprinted by permission.

---

story is up to the reporter's and editor's discretion. Reporters may use the release as a basis for an expanded story, or they may use the news release as is and even give the writer a byline. Reporters, editors, and producers need news releases that are complete, accurate, newsworthy, and appropriate for their audiences. Few will reject news releases in a ready-to-use format.

News releases should contain the public relations contact name, organization, organization address, organization phone number, fax number, e-mail address, and PR contact's home phone number. The information goes in the upper left-hand corner. If the organization's address is readily visible on letterhead, it can be omitted. Under this information go the date and the headline, setting up the contents of the news release.

Often PR practitioners will include a contact name and telephone number within the text of the news release, usually at the end, to ensure that further information is available to interested publics if the news release is run verbatim. Online news releases, such as those posted on PR Newswire or other online news services, often contain a link so readers can give feedback on whether the information was useful and understandable.

Media Advisories

A media advisory follows the same format as a news release. It is just what it says it is: an advisory. Advisories announce an upcoming event that could warrant media attention. They are short—no more than a few paragraphs—and give media logistical information: who, what, when, where, how, and why, plus how to get to the event, where to park, opportunities for interviews, and so on. They usually contain some type of disclaimer that the advisory is not for publication; it is for information. An example of a media advisory is in Figure 11.2.

Fact Sheets

Fact sheets are generally one page long—or the front and back of one sheet—and are designed to be read quickly. Information about the organization, a service, a product, or a special activity is highlighted in short segments.

An easy way to develop a fact sheet is to follow the news elements discussed in Chapter 4: who, what, when, where, how, and why. A statewide children's forum is planning its annual fund-raiser. The fact sheet would be organized:

Who: The Children's Forum

What: Annual fund-raiser—a black-tie dinner and dance

When: June 14

Where: Downtowner Hotel

How: Ticket prices $75 per individual for the dance and $150 for dinner and dance through the institute offices at 444-1234

Why: To raise money for administrative and program costs

Fact sheets should also contain the contact name, organization, and phone numbers for reporters and others who want additional information. When fact

---

FIGURE 11.2   *Sample Media Advisory*

CAROLINA

NEWS SERVICES
210 Pittsboro Street, Campus Box 6210
Chapel Hill, NC 27599-6210
(919) 962-2091 FAX: (919) 962-2279
www.unc.edu/news/newsserv

ADVISORY

<u>Not for publication</u>   October 16, 2001

MEDIA ADVISORY

The University of North Carolina at Chapel Hill will hold a press briefing on Tuesday, October 16, to discuss details of the University's new contract with Nike.

The press briefing is scheduled to begin at 1:30 p.m. and will be held in the Chancellor's Ballroom West at the Carolina Inn. Media parking will be available in the Carolina Inn Lot. Please let the parking attendants know you will be attending the press briefing.

Chancellor James Moeser and Director of Athletics Dick Baddour will be on hand to talk about the contract and take questions from the media.

If you need further information, please contact Mike McFarland at UNC News Services (962-8593) or Steve Kirschner at Athletic Communications (962-7258).

Reprinted by permission.

---

sheets are produced or updated, put the date at the bottom of the fact sheet to indicate how current the information is.

Facts sheets are also uncontrolled. Media can use the information any way they wish. See the example in Figure 11.3.

Backgrounders

Backgrounders are not news releases and do not carry news that has immediacy. A backgrounder supplements a news release and gives additional information a reporter may need about a company or its services. Information in

FIGURE 11.3   *Sample Fact Sheet: Enterprise Rent-A-Car*

Fact Sheet

Established:	1957
World Headquarters:	St. Louis, Missouri
Executives:	Andrew C. Taylor, President and CEO Donald L. Ross, Senior Executive Vice President and COO Pam Nicholson, Senior Vice President of North American Operations Mike Robertson, Vice President of International Operations John O'Connell, Executive Vice President and CFO Sandy Rogers, Senior Vice President of Corporate Strategy
Background:	■ Largest rental car company in the U.S. ■ Rates up to 20 percent lower than most airport rental car companies. ■ Nearly 4,800 offices located conveniently where people live and work. ■ Outstanding service that includes picking up customers at no extra cost. ■ Offices within 15 miles of 90 percent of the U.S. population.
Primary Activities:	Specializes in renting vehicles to customers who: 1) need a car because of an accident, mechanical repair or theft; 2) want to take a short business or leisure trip, or have a different car for a special occasion.
Operations:	■ More than 4,300 offices in the United States ■ More than 400 offices in Canada, United Kingdom, Germany and Ireland ■ 50,000 employees worldwide
Fiscal 2001 Revenue:	$6.3 billion (worldwide)
Fiscal 2000 Revenue:	$5.6 billion (worldwide)
Fiscal 1999 Revenue:	$4.7 billion (worldwide)
Fiscal 1998 Revenue:	$4.2 billion (worldwide)
Fiscal 1997 Revenue:	$3.7 billion (worldwide)
Rental Car Vehicles In Service:	2001: 525,000 automobiles 2000: 493,000 automobiles 1999: 427,000 automobiles 1990: 89,000 automobiles 1980: 6,000 automobiles 1970: 500 automobiles 1963: Started rental operation with a fleet of 17 cars 1957: Leasing operation opened as Executive Leasing
2000 & 1999 Awards:	■ Named by *CIO Magazine* as one of "100 Companies Most Likely to Succeed in the next Millennium" ■ Named by *Fortune Magazine* as one of the "100 Best Companies to Work For" ■ Ranked highest in customer satisfaction by J.D. Power & Associates for rental car companies operating at or near the airport ■ Largest College Recruiter in the U.S. as reported by *Black Collegian* magazine

Reprinted by permission.

a backgrounder does not have to be attributed as it would in a news release. The source is considered to be the company. The information is organized by section, such as introduction, history, specific services, demographics, and other information. The sections note specific information quickly.

Like a news release, a backgrounder must be well written and organized clearly and logically. Information must be accurate and should be updated periodically. Like news releases and fact sheets, a backgrounder is uncontrolled. The practitioner knows that anything in the backgrounder could appear in print or be heard on the airwaves and thus assimilated by the organization's publics.

Brochures

In writing and designing brochures, public relations practitioners are limited only by their talent, creativity, and budget. With desktop publishing and multimedia technology, many more organizations can produce high-quality, good-looking brochures for little cost. They can also publish brochure content on the World Wide Web. The more work that is done in house, the more money saved.

Here are some questions to answer when writing a brochure:

• Is the brochure persuasive or informative? If the brochure's primary role is to persuade, it will be written with emotional language, comparisons, and familiar concepts. If informative, material will be to the point and language straightforward.

• Who is the audience? Whether the audience is specialized or general will determine the level of language used.

• Will the brochure be read and thrown away or saved? Deciding how it will be used will affect the cost and design.

• Will the brochure be a stand-alone piece, such as those in a display rack at a state's welcome station, or a collateral piece in a media kit or with a related Web site? A stand-alone brochure must be complete because it cannot rely on information in other pieces or online links.

• What is the appropriate format? If the brochure is a self-mailer, it will need to have an address space. Information has to be arranged logically, and decisions have to be made on artwork, such as photographs, and on graphic elements and white space, the size, the number of folds or pages, and how the brochure will open. How will the brochure copy be formatted for a Web site?

Brochure copy should be short. Publics are looking for a quick read. Each panel should stand alone, and copy shouldn't jump from one panel to the next.

Brochures, whether printed or online, are appealing to public relations practitioners because they are controlled messages. The practitioner has the final say on copy and design. No one can change the content or wording; the only uncontrolled aspect is placement—for example, whether brochures are left at a doctor's office to be displayed or are given to volunteers to distribute. The concerns are visibility of the brochure rack and whether all brochures are handed out.

Newsletters

Some public relations practitioners debate the effectiveness of newsletters. They contend that they can be time consuming and costly to produce and that few people read them. But newsletters are a primary method used by organizations to communicate with publics, particularly employees and donors.

Newsletters can also be produced efficiently and rather cheaply with desktop publishing systems. They can be quick-printed or even photocopied and folded in the office. Many are transmitted online via web sites or e-mail.

Information for newsletters comes from other newsletters, employees, managers, news events, industry happenings, or seasonal topics. People within the organization or company may be correspondents, submitting ideas or actual copy from their departments. The newsletter editor writes stories based on the ideas or edits the correspondents' stories. The style can be news or feature, and more stories can have a beginning, middle, and end—not just written in inverted pyramid format. And all copy is controlled: The public relations practitioner ultimately determines the content and tone.

Newsletter editors must guard to keep publications interesting and lively. Many newsletters are deadly dull, containing column after column of information. To attract readers, newsletters must be enlightening, informative, and entertaining. Good design and lively technologies can capture readers, but good writing will hold them.

Speeches

Many people dread the thought of getting up in front of a crowd and giving a speech. The public relations practitioner who has to write a speech may be relieved that he or she doesn't have to deliver it, but the task of writing a speech for someone else can be daunting. Speeches are controlled, because they are delivered, but speakers must remember that they may be easy marks afterward for people who may have unflattering questions.

Speeches are needed for a variety of reasons: to educate, to state a position or advocate a certain belief, to praise someone's achievement, to entertain, to highlight a special occasion, or to establish rapport. Each one requires a special format and writing style.

Writing a speech is like other mass communications writing. The writer must have a subject and a purpose or reason for giving the speech and must know the audience. Knowing what the audience already knows about the subject and whether it is likely to favor, oppose, or be undecided about the subject will determine the approach and how best to illustrate it.

A writer must create a speech that fits the speaker's way of talking and delivery. The style, however, must fit the audience's level of understanding and interest. The writer must use speech patterns that are suitable for the audience. For most audiences, the best bet is to use simple, precise language as discussed in Chapter 3. Simple language will also help the speaker.

After you have completed writing a speech, read it aloud. Make sure the writing flows, the structure is appropriate, and the audience is addressed. Determine whether visuals, such as video or power-point presentation, are needed. Visuals should supplement what the speaker is saying and not detract from it. The speaker should be comfortable using visuals and should talk to the audience, not the screen. If possible, someone other than the speaker should be responsible for operating the electronic equipment.

As a public relations practitioner, remember that the speech will come back to you for changes and rewriting, perhaps several times. That's okay. One public relations practitioner, recalling a speech written for the company president, said she agonized over style and finally submitted a draft. A few days later it came back, completely revised and retyped. "When I read through the 10 pages, I saw one complete sentence that was my own," she said. "But the note from the president said, 'Great work!'"

Chapter 9 discusses speech coverage from the reporter's perspective. Many of the points there can benefit the public relations professional.

Public Relations and Advertising

As the public relations director for your town's historical society, you want to let many publics know about plans for the society's annual Christmas tour of homes. To send a controlled message to many audiences, you decide to place an ad in the local newspaper. You would write the copy, and you might also solicit a local company to underwrite the cost and give it credit within the ad copy.

Advertising gives organizations the opportunity to produce a controlled message in both copy and placement. Once the message is determined, the ad is written. The organization buys space in a specific magazine or section of the newspaper or air time at a certain hour. The ad is printed or broadcast just as the organization produced it.

Many advertising and public relations professionals are joined in what the industry is calling *integrated marking communications.* That requires input and planning for all aspects of communication from advertising to direct marketing to news releases—whatever is necessary to get a client's message to the audience. Advertising is discussed separately in Chapter 12.

Communications Planning

To implement a public relations campaign, practitioners need a plan. Plans are written during the second public relations stage, as discussed earlier in the chapter. Plans are critical because they guide practitioners about their publics, communications tools, and timing. Once research is completed, practitioners can set out to match the types of communications tools with audiences.

Making the Match

In matching specific communications tools to publics, consider the example of the university capital campaign. As the public relations director, you would consider which media or tools would reach your targeted groups. You might decide to produce a general information brochure that would go to all publics or a web site. But for meeting the needs of individual publics, you might start a list like this:

- *Alumni.* Direct mail letters; news releases or news features to alumni publications; public service announcements (PSAs) to major radio and television stations in states where large numbers of alumni live; speeches and presentations to alumni club meetings; news releases and fact sheets to statewide media

• *Faculty members.* News releases, feature releases, e-mail, and fact sheets to campus publications; direct mail; speeches and audiovisual presentations

• *Students.* PSAs to popular radio stations; news releases, feature releases, and fact sheets to student publications; speeches and audiovisual presentations; advertisements in campus media

If you continued the list, you probably would find that some communications tools serve the same publics. Different publics read newspapers and direct mail letters, watch television, and attend civic meetings. Each public has its own interests and language. The focus of the public relations message will vary depending on the audience.

For example, the direct mail letters to faculty members and alumni would carry the same message of the need for donations and would make a pitch for a contribution. But the faculty letter would explain how new buildings would add classrooms, laboratories, and offices—all to the benefit of teaching. The alumni letter would discuss how new buildings would benefit the university's reputation and thereby maintain the strength of degrees.

Writing a Plan for a Specific Occasion

Writing a plan requires thinking and often experience. Practitioners usually begin by brainstorming or listing random ideas for communicating with publics. Then they start refining, based on time constraints, cost of producing materials, and company style. The final plan includes a statement of the issue or problem, campaign objectives, strategies for reaching objectives, and specific actions. Specific actions are assigned deadlines and an individual responsible for carrying out each action.

Think about a wireless telephone company that wants to attract more college students. Your role as the public relations person is to support the paid advertising done by the marketing department. Research says you need to target students who live on campus and off campus. You decide in the planning stage to develop an insert for the campus newspaper and a brochure that can be distributed to students. You also want to have information in an online brochure on the company's Web site and a news release on company services to distribute to area media.

Communications Plan for Wireless Service Geared to College Students

Issue: First Wireless Company will begin a marketing plan to secure more college-age customers. It will offer 1,000 free minutes on weekends if students sign up by Dec. 31. The offer will extend for six months after service is initiated.

Objective: To increase the customer base and to position the company as a reliable but affordable way to have wireless phone service.

Strategy: To use communication tools that will reach students whether they live on or off campus.

Actions:

Date	Action	Responsibility
Sept. 1	Develop outline and content for the brochure and insert	PR manager
Sept. 5	Hire a writer, designer, and Web master	PR manager
Sept. 23	First draft of brochure copy	Freelance writer
Sept. 24	Design for brochure and insert complete	Freelance designer
Sept. 28	Copy/design sent for approvals	PR manager
Oct. 5	Final brochure and insert complete	PR manager
Oct. 7	Brochure copy to printer and Web master	PR staff
Oct. 15	Secure students' names from campus directory; begin developing mail list	PR staff
Oct. 20	Consider focus of local/statewide news release; get brochure from printer	PR manager
Oct. 30	Complete draft of local/statewide news release; complete mail list	PR manager
Nov. 7	Approvals returned on local/statewide news release	PR manager
Nov. 10	Arrange for insert in next week's campus newspaper	PR staff
Nov. 14	Mail release to local and statewide media, publish copies of release on Web site	PR staff

Nov. 15	Complete addressing and stuffing envelopes with brochures and mail	PR staff
Nov. 17	Insert appears in campus newspaper	PR staff

Crisis Planning

No organization expects or wants a crisis, but plans must be made in the event a crisis occurs. The crisis could be as large as an oil spill or as small as an error in a newsletter. If any event negatively affects audiences, an organization has a crisis.

A crisis plan can help an organization make lemonade out of lemons, says Joyce Fitzpatrick, senior managing director in the Southeast for RF/Binder Partners, a major public relations firms in the United States. A crisis plan helps a company be prepared. Plans should be easily accessible and reviewed periodically.

Fitzpatrick notes when conducting crisis communication seminars that in a crisis plan, organizations should identify a specific representative to meet with the media. If possible, the person should be someone who has been in a crisis before—and that person may not be the chief executive officer. Organizations should also establish a sequence of who will be informed first. Affected employees should hear about the crisis before they read about it in the media.

When the crisis occurs, Fitzpatrick advises the companies to respond within the first 24 hours. If the crisis is long-running, companies should set up a specific site and time each day for news conferences. The representative should appear, even if there is no new development, and be ready to say when the company has new developments or information to share.

Wrap-Up

This chapter is an introduction to the public relations field, its role, practitioners' responsibilities, and some communications tools. Students majoring in public relations will take specific courses on theory, case studies, public relations campaigns, public relations writing, and possibly video production and Web design. In each course, they will learn more about the field and its opportunities. At the core of each course will be the ability to write.

Public relations practitioners must be able to communicate quickly, accurately, and completely to be effective. They also must know their audiences. Public relations practitioners who can combine those two talents will be successful.

EXERCISES

1. You are the public relations officer for the Campus Literacy Program. You want to recruit more volunteers to serve as readers to children in the community.
   a. Identify the audience(s) you are trying to reach as potential volunteers.
   b. Knowing your audience interests and media usage, identify three communications tools you would use to reach each audience.
   c. What information would your audience(s) need to make a decision whether to volunteer? Make a list.
   d. How could you evaluate the success of your communications effort?

2. You are the public relations director for Bicycle World Equipment Co. You are to write a news release for the local newspaper based on the following information:

   Bicycle World is planning to sponsor bicycle safety clinics in the public schools that are located in Wayne County, the company headquarters. The clinics will be on two consecutive Saturdays from 10 a.m. to noon. Each of the county's six elementary schools will have the clinics. People who want to attend must call 555-3456 to register. The clinic is open to children 6-12 years of age. Each child must have a helmet.

   Bicycle World staff members will check each child's bicycle for safe operation and indicate on a check-off list any equipment that needs repair. Children will be advised of good bicycle safety, such as wearing helmets, riding in bike lanes, and using proper hand signals. Then each will be allowed to enter an obstacle course, which will test their riding proficiency. For example, as they ride down a "road," a dog may run out from between two cars. Children's reactions and reaction times will be monitored. After the road test, they will be briefed on what they did well and what they need to improve. At the end of the course, they will receive a certificate of accomplishment.

"We believe bicycle safety is crucial for children," said company President Dennis Lester. "With just a little guidance, children can learn habits and rules that could save their lives. Those of us in the bicycle business want to ensure that children who use our products do so competently and safely. We want them to enjoy bicycling as a sport they can continue into adulthood."

The clinics are free.

Bicycle World is a three-year-old company that produces bike frames, components, bike helmets, clothing, and road guides to bicycle routes. Company President Dennis Lester is a master rider and formed the company to provide quality equipment to bicycle enthusiasts.

3. From the above information, write a one-page fact sheet based on the bicycle clinics sponsored by Bicycle World Equipment Co. You would be the contact, 555-2345. The company's address is 67 W. Lane Blvd., Your town, Your zip code.

4. Bicycle World President Dennis Lester has been asked to speak to the local Girl Scout council about bike safety. The audience is girls 10 to 12 years of age. Develop an introduction that would attract them to the speech. Then write an outline of the information you would include when the actual speech is written.

5. Choose a nonprofit organization in your community. Contact the director about preparing a media kit for the organization. The kit could provide information about the organization itself or a special event. The kit

would include a fact sheet; a backgrounder; a news release on a timely, relevant topic; and a news feature about the organization or one of its services. Use existing materials on the organization as part of your research plus interviews with the director, staff members, and any users of the organization's services.

REFERENCES

Thomas Bivins, *Handbook for Public Relations Writing,* 2nd ed. Chicago: NTC Business Books, 1993.

Scott M. Cutlip, Allen H. Center and Glen H. Broom, *Effective Public Relations,* 7th ed. Englewood Cliffs, NJ: Prentice-Hall, 1994.

"Death of a Princess, Birth of a Thousand Press Releases," *Wall Street Journal,* September 10, 1997.

J. E. Grunig and Todd Hunt, *Managing Public Relations.* Fort Worth, TX: Harcourt Brace Jovanovich College Publishers, 1984.

Medialink Web Site. Available at: http://www.medialink.com.

Doug Newsom and Bob Carrell, *Public Relations Writing: Form and Style,* 3rd ed. Belmont, CA: Wadsworth Publishing, 1991.

PR Newswire Web Site. Available at: http://www.prnewswire.com.

Public Relations Society of America Web Site. Available at: http://www.prsa.org.

"Warner Bros. Issues Correction," CNN Custom:News [Online], November 24, 1997. Available at: http://www.cnn.com.

Dennis L. Wilcox and Lawrence W. Nolte, *Public Relations Writing and Media Techniques,* 2nd ed. New York: HarperCollins College Publishers, 1995.

12

Advertising

Advertising is probably the first form of media writing that children notice. Kids respond to ads, often before they can talk. Toddlers excitedly point at Ronald McDonald and "read" the golden arches as a sign for food even before they know their ABCs. By combining color, sound, movement, symbols, and language, advertising creates some of the most powerful messages in our world today.

Like all media presentations, good advertising depends on good writing. "Good advertising writers are writers first. They are personal writers—people who bring their own feelings and reactions to the product," observes Professor John Sweeney, former creative director for a major U.S. advertising agency. "Good advertising slogans are some of the most effective communication available today. They have a concise, pithy, sensory quality that other writers would do well to study and adopt."

Clear, direct communication is and always has been required of ad writers, who are usually referred to as copywriters. Although many people think of ad writers as zany creative types—which they may be—copywriters primarily are just that: writers. Advertising copywriters learn to hook their audiences with the first sound or word of an ad. And, as Sweeney says, other writers can benefit from studying their techniques.

This chapter will explain

- Advertising goals in the information age,
- What is in an ad,
- Advertising strategies, including branding and product placement,
- The fate of Internet advertising, and
- Guidelines for effective ad writing.

By reaching these goals, the ad writer fulfills the client's goal, which is to sell the product or service.

Advertising in the Information Age

Volney Palmer is generally credited with being the first advertising "agent." In 1841, he began selling newspaper advertising space for a profit. Advertisers prepared their ads; Palmer and other agents placed the ads for them. Such advertising agents became concerned with copy and artwork for the ads several years later. In 1869, F. W. Ayer started N. W. Ayer & Son, an advertising agency that provided writing, art, and media placement to its clients.

Advertising agencies have changed throughout the years, but the seeds of the modern agency were planted with N. W. Ayer & Son and other early agencies that still exist today. Advertisers also have myriad ways to reach consumers, not just newspapers or billboards. One company may advertise in newspapers, on radio and television, and on the Internet. The overwhelming number of new media and the changing media habits of audiences allow advertisers to funnel product information directly to specific and special audiences.

The goals of ad writers, regardless of medium, have remained constant over the years:

- To communicate availability of products to audiences
- To communicate product benefits to audiences
- To provide accessible information about products
- To communicate main ideas about products in a few words

Other goals include image building, when a company wants consumers to view it as a good corporate citizen; response to a disaster, such as a utility company telling customers how soon power will be restored after massive hurricane damage; or public service messages, such as alerting audiences to the dangers of unprotected sex or the benefits of low-fat diets.

Like other media, advertising is a field that is changing daily. But almost all advertisements—whether print or online—are made by combining the same four elements:

1. A headline
2. An illustration, which may be graphic (pictures) or dramatic

3. Advertising text—from a few words to a few pages—describing the product
4. A signature or logo, usually at the close of the ad

But simply putting these elements together will not create an advertisement. Advertisements that work must carefully select and intertwine these four elements.

Is Advertising Propaganda?

Some people think of advertising as propaganda—as distorted information designed to lead, or mislead, its audience. Propaganda is manipulative, and so is advertising, some people say.

Unlike most other forms of published writing, advertising is one-sided by its very nature; no one wants to spend his or her advertising budget extolling the benefits of a competitor's product. But the absence of other products from ads does not have to mean that an ad is unfairly biased if the information presented is accurate in and of itself.

"An advertisement is a known one-sided form, like a résumé," explains Professor John Sweeney. "It is not a sinister hiding of information; rather, it is a presentation of your best information."

Advertising writing has work to do; it substitutes for personal, face-to-face contact in the sales process. Like professional salespeople, advertisers deal with factual information and must never forget that they have a public responsibility. Once an advertiser loses public confidence in the accuracy of its claims, that confidence may not be recovered.

Presenting your best to the public, Sweeney explains, is a core value of advertising culture. Advertising that is less than ethical is not advertising; it is propaganda or huckstering or manipulation. Professional advertising writing is an accepted form of argument—a fair argument—and it abides by an ethical code. A one-sided presentation need not be an unfair presentation, and understanding that aspect is part of being an effective professional, Sweeney says. He encourages advertisers to set ethical limits for themselves, adding, "We don't want billboards in the Grand Canyon."

Advertisers are subject to many government rules and regulations. The Capital Council of Better Business Bureaus advises that all advertisers stay abreast of regulations through subscription services, such as Do's and Don'ts in Advertising or the National Advertising Case Reports. Such subscription services are quite expensive and typically are used by large agencies or companies. The industry has self-regulators, such as the National Advertising Review Council (NARC). The Federal Trade Commission has information on how advertisers should behave, whether advertising in print or online. More information for advertisers—and consumers—can be found on the commission Web site at www.ftc.gov/bcp/conline/pubs/buspubs/ruleroad.

Advertising and Today's Audiences

The environment for advertising has changed tremendously in the past decade. New media and new products compete for audience attention, so that advertisers may no longer assume that mere publicity will lead to success or consumers using services and buying products. Today's advertisers must pay attention to audiences and audience's attitudes. Only through selecting likely audiences and streamlining ads for those groups can advertisers reach consumers of the information age.

Ad production is seldom the work of the writer. In most cases, the copywriter is part of a team. For an advertising agency, the team could include market researchers, who determine audience interest and product competition; an account executive, who oversees the account and serves as the liaison with the client; the copywriter, who takes the research and theme and creates text; the art director, who designs ads and other collateral pieces for the client; the creative director, who oversees the concept and production; and the media buyer, who places ads. All members of the team must know the others' roles. The copywriter often works mostly closely with the art designer on aspects such as typeface, length of copy, size of the ad, and graphic elements.

Newspapers still design ads for advertisers who do not have agencies or cannot afford to pay agencies to do the work. The newspaper staff would include an ad sales representative, art designer, and copywriter.

Advertising Strategy

Before a writer sits down to write an ad, an advertising strategy, which is part of and guided by an overall marketing strategy, is already in place. In short, the advertising strategy is made up of the media strategy (where the ads should be placed and when to place them) plus the creative strategy (what should be in the ads and how they should look). Generally, the ad strategy is a written document that also lists advertising goals, such as gaining more sales or improving corporate image; target audience; positioning, or how consumers perceive the service or product vis-à-vis competitors; benefits; creative approach, such as tone of the advertising message; and appropriate media to reach audiences.

The plan will enable the copywriter to know what structure will have the greatest appeal to the target audience. The creative approach is affected by the goal—selling a product, providing general information about a company, positioning a product as superior among its competitors, or boosting a corporate image. Target audiences will determine the tone of language and whether the ad must be serious or can have humor. Even corporate image will affect how a copywriter pitches an ad.

One of the copywriter's first responsibilities to support the advertising strategy will be to come up with a theme. Philip Ward Burton notes in *Advertising Copywriting* that the theme "is the central idea—the imaginative spark plug—that will give your advertisements continuity, recall value, and thus, extra selling power. Your theme is the lifeline of your campaign."

Targeting Audiences

The process of identifying and communicating with specific audiences is often called *targeting*. Clinique may target girls aged 13 to 15 as a likely audience for messages about a new tinted lip gloss. With the target group in mind, Clinique's ad writers design messages that will appeal to young teens and place these ads in publications and time slots of which teens are likely consumers. Clinique, for example, might place an ad for its new lip gloss in *Seventeen* magazine and between scenes on the show *Buffy: Vampire Slayer.*

Targeting is a necessity in an era of budget consciousness. Advertisers no longer can afford to waste funds by advertising to broad audiences that may contain only a few potential customers. To get maximum benefit from advertising dollars, advertisers select target audiences for specific products. Beer, tires, and trucks are advertised in sports sections and broadcasts; toys and sweet cereals are advertised with Saturday morning cartoons; and pain relievers, laxatives, and investments are sold with financial news.

Professional market research is used by major corporations to identify the best possible markets for particular ads. *Cluster marketing* attempts to impose some order on the new media-and-audience mix, dividing Americans into subgroups and predicting specific media behaviors, products, and services that each group is likely to use. Michael Weiss describes in his book, *The Clustering of America,* the nation's 40 neighborhood types. One cluster commonly used by advertisers is the "Blue Blood Estates" group. It reads the *New York Times* and watches David Letterman; smart advertisers will place ads for upscale products here. Educated viewers know that such products already are advertised in appropriate places; David Letterman's sponsors include many luxury cars, such as Infiniti and Lexus, whereas ads for furs and jewelry abound in the *Times.*

A common system is VALS, established in 1978 as one of the first major consumer segmentation systems based on lifestyle characteristics, according to its web site. Companies throughout the United States use VALS for assistance in audience targeting, product development, product positioning, advertising, promotion, focus groups, media planning, and corporate image. In targeting, for example, VALS helps identify what audiences to target, what the audience buys, why it does what it does, where concentrations of the targeted audience live, and the best methods of reaching the targeted audience. You can take the survey at www.future.sri.com/VALS/presurvey.shtml.

Tom Burrell, chairman of Burrell Advertising in Chicago, recognizes the need for all communicators to address specific audiences. He was one of the country's first advertising executives to focus his clients' advertisements on the needs, attitudes, interests, and even behaviors of a single ethnic group, African Americans.

"The future is destined to be more complex, more complicated, more diverse, and more segmented for media," Burrell predicts. He believes that the whole idea of mass marketing is dying and that agencies more and more will respond to the needs of specific consumer groups such as women, ethnic populations, seniors, urban dwellers, and rural residents.

Placement of Advertisements

Today's advertisers cannot afford to waste ad dollars on placing messages that will not reach their audiences; therefore Huggies, maker of disposable diapers and training pants, does not advertise in large newspapers or in general-interest magazines. Rather, the company advertises in magazines for parents; more specifically, it chooses magazines that appeal to consumers who value its product and can afford it. Huggies' ads for its Pull-Ups disposable training pants would appear in *Parents* magazine to reach conscientious parents of both genders working both in and outside the home.

For years, standard forms of advertising were limited to a few familiar media. Advertisers had access to audiences through television, radio, newspapers, magazines, billboards, and direct mail. Audiences for these forms were large and homogeneous: "middle America" for television, billboards, and general-circulation newspapers and magazines; "teen America" for radio and teen magazines; and "older Americans" for direct mail and specialty magazines.

Today, advertisers have more options as a result of audience fragmentation and new media development. They use faxes, voice mail, and online services in addition to the traditional mix. Each may indicate other ways to reach the company. For example, Princess Cruises and Princess Tours advertises its Alaska tour in *Travel and Leisure* magazine. The ad includes a toll-free number and a tear-out, postage-paid card that can be sent for a free Alaska planning kit. The Ritz-Carlton hotel gives a toll-free number and its web site address, www.ritz-carlton.com. Businesses are also flashing web addresses in television commercials, such as a cookie ad with www.chipsahoy.com as part of the visuals.

Product Placement

You are watching a movie, and the scene moves to the kitchen. On the counter are cereal boxes, diet soda, and cans of spaghetti. All the product names are clearly visible. Having real products seen in movies is called *product placement*. The benefits of product placement seem obvious: product reinforcement and possible recall when consumers shop.

Product placement has been around for years and is a fairly well accepted advertising tool. Popular television game shows, such as *The Price Is Right,* award specific products to participants. The product names and logos are repeated during each broadcast. Companies have sponsored events, such as bicycle races, and have their products and logos included with promotional materials. Some consumers associate brand names on athletes as product placement, but the advertising industry generally considers such label wearing as another aspect of marketing.

When product placement first came into vogue in movies, skeptical viewers wondered about the effects of certain products on younger viewers. For example, the war on tobacco and smoking among teens included criticism of tobacco product use in movies. The phenomenon of using specific products in movies and on television is becoming more prevalent. Viewers saw Target's red bulls-eye logo on boxes opened by *Survivor* team members. Mel Gibson tried numerous products, such as a WonderBra, in *What Women Want.*

In many cases, products that appear on the screen are not put there by the companies that make them. Filmmakers can select any brand of cereal and place it on the breakfast table—whether the manufacturer likes it or not. Executives who do want their products to be in the movies, however, can hire companies whose sole business is to place products on movie sets.

Whether product placement actually works is still debated. Research has shown that in some instances, cross-cultural differences prevent audiences from connecting with the products they see. As more and more products are included within television programming, some observers are concerned about consumers' reactions to their top picks becoming more commercial-laden. Most companies, however, like the idea of product placement as yet another way to create brand recognition. But researchers are still assessing whether product placement does increase brand recognition and sales. Seeing a product for a fleeting second on a movie screen or in the hands of a celebrity may not be enough to put it in a consumer's shopping cart.

Targeting and the Writer

When copywriters begin to write, they must consider the target audience and the medium or media that will be used. That information is in the strategy. As noted earlier, the audience's likes, dislikes, and even educational level will determine the approach and tone of the ad. Where it will be placed and that medium's style and approach must also be assessed. Royal Caribbean, which offers luxury cruises, targets its ads to different age groups. Scenes of activity appeal to younger vacationers, whereas serenity and sunsets attract older voyagers. The simple language is also directed to audience appeal. All ads end with the Royal Caribbean logo and the slogan "Like No Vacation on Earth."

Copywriters have great pressure to keep advertising lean, direct, and on target so that no advertising words and minutes are wasted on an unlikely customer. This pressure affects the advertising writer at every point. The ad message must be structured as carefully as the placement. If an ad is directed to a specific audience, it needs to appear in the correct medium and to convey concepts immediately that are meaningful to the target group.

Here is effective ad writing pitched to its specific audience:

"I never worried too much about nutrition.

"Then, my doctor told me I was HIV positive.

"Now, I do everything I can to maintain my energy, strength, and quality of life."

The advertisement pictures a handsome, athletic man. The product is Advera, a nutrition supplement. The three written lines from the ad demonstrate how specific today's advertisements can be. For the most part, ads today strive not for mass communication but for complete communication with a particular group. The copywriter and art director work as a team, combining language and graphics in a powerful way to produce effective advertisements.

Branding

Branding has become a primary factor for companies in their advertising strategies. Consumers are branded every day as they walk around with the Nike swoosh on T-shirts, Lexus logos on cars, Gap on baby overalls, Bruegger's on coffee cups, and Patagonia on backpacks. Branding can inspire depths of customer loyalty, and companies rely on such loyalty to maintain sales and marketshare.

When a product has a brand or identity, it is immediately recognizable to consumers. Part of the immediate recognition is an icon, a slogan, a jingle, and even colors that can trigger in consumers' minds the product—McDonald's golden arches, Volkswagen's "Drivers Wanted," the Army's "Be All That You Can Be," or Ben & Jerry's black and white cow colors. Once consumers recognize the product, then they ascribe certain feelings or values that create brand loyalty.

Companies have determined that brand loyalty is a combination of overall satisfaction and confidence or trust. Another component is emotional attachment. Think about brands that you use and why you use them. You may use a certain deodorant soap because that's the one you always found in the shower's soap dish at home. Whoever did the grocery shopping in your family had a loyalty to that particular brand. Perhaps you prefer a certain type of fast-food pizza because of the crust, the toppings, the service, or the group of friends you usually eat pizza with. People develop a familiarity with a product, and they may oppose any changes to it. Companies bank on consumers and their ties to certain products.

Companies use criteria that represent loyalty factors when assessing what makes consumers like you become attached to a product. Looking at the soap example above, you may have loyalty to Soap X because it brings back good feelings about home—the emotional attachment—plus you like the way it cleans your skin. In the quest for determining customer loyalty, researchers have gone so far as to develop indexes that rate customer satisfaction. Gallup, known for its polling, has developed a measure of what it calls *customer engagement.* A list of questions measures customer loyalty as well as emotional attachment.

More and more in the last decade, companies have considered branding as a key to retaining customers and profits. Research has shown that the cost of attracting new customers is five times the cost of keeping current ones. As a result, companies are investing more research dollars into what makes customers stick with certain products or brands. Businesses have adopted practices so that they can determine which products and services customers buy and why. They can even track individual customers to find out more about their habits and needs. Such information is invaluable in focusing advertising—and in developing other areas that provide customer service.

As an exercise to show CEOs the importance of branding, the American Advertising Federation (AAF) in 2001 launched a campaign called "Advertising. The way great brands get to be great brands." Four companies with outstanding brand recognition—Coca-Cola, Sunkist, Energizer, and Anheuser-Busch—agreed to have the names on their products replaced with the word "advertising." Ads with the modified logos were placed in key advertising locations in print and television. The point is to show CEOs who control advertising dollars that advertising built the brand recognition for these four products. Regardless of the lettering on each icon, any consumer can immediately name the product.

"While CEOs appreciated that advertising drove sales, they didn't have a complete and compelling understanding of its importance in building brands, market share and share value," said Wally Snyder, AAF president. "We felt we had an opportunity here to direct a campaign at CEOs to help explain [advertising's] value."

The AAF began the campaign to stress the importance of advertising, which is often cut when sales drop. AAF President and CEO Wally Snyder noted: "Advertising is the compass to consumers in a marketplace that's changing course. The need for the discipline has never been greater" (see AAF Web site).

Branding is important for anyone writing or designing ads. Armed with customer research, a copywriter can develop an ad that shows the product's character and appeal. Part of branding may be the slogan for the product, its name, or its logo that creates recognition and positive feelings. The brand elements add value and differentiate the product from similar products.

Another aspect may be choosing spokespeople to represent the brands. For example, Tina Wesson, the mother from Tennessee who won the second

Survivor show in Australia, suddenly was the top choice for several products, from milk to cars. Her success evokes qualities of determination, stamina, down-homeness, and just an average American who wins big.

Advertising on the Internet

The introduction of the Internet commercially and its subsequent growth spurred the hopes of entrepreneurs and even established media companies of an another source of advertising revenue—and profit. The Internet provides a threefold opportunity: a channel to market, a channel to sell or conduct business, and a channel for online-only companies to be born and prosper.

Established companies have found that they can expand their marketing efforts through the Internet. Web sites provide information about the company to potential investors and customers. Visitors can provide feedback on products and company behavior. For media companies, online sites provide more depth to broadcast news reports and another outlet of giving audiences information. Even some media companies, such as the *Wall Street Journal,* have found that their content is so valuable that audiences are willing to subscribe to the online site and pay for information.

As to selling, e-commerce has prospered fairly well, particularly with sales that are extensions of an existing brand. E-commerce sites work like a store, allowing people to shop online. Consumers see products, fill a shopping basket, and complete an order. The shipment arrives on their doorsteps in a few days without consumers ever leaving home. Convenience sells products, and the more customers have used credit cards securely to order online, the more willing they have been to spend via the Internet.

Where the Internet has not been as successful is in start-up companies that base their entire revenue model on the advertising—and subsequent sales—they can attract. These start-ups provided content and relied on making a profit from the ads around the content. Some had elements of advertising-based sites and e-commerce. In the late 1990s, thousands of companies formed and began marketing themselves and their products on the Internet. Most had short life spans and died, millions of dollars in debt. They weren't offering anything better or different than their competitors.

For example, etoys.com offered consumers online shopping for children's toys. The company failed in two ways: It had substantial competition from existing toy companies, such as Zany Brainy and Toys 'R Us, and toy manufacturers had more established companies with Web sites where they could advertise. The newcomer didn't make it because it couldn't offer its advertising as cost effective as its competitors.

Companies That Found Success

A few online companies have found the recipe for success on the Internet. They market a unique, cost-effective service, or they have a service that provides value and produces a profit. Among the basic components are a good business plan that focused on a niche and a company structure that they could afford. Successful companies range from the big to the small.

Among the big successful companies are yahoo.com and msnbc.com. Each has millions of viewers or visitors, a fact that attracts advertisers. A site such as Yahoo delivers a mass audience cheaply; for example, a company such as Procter & Gamble might expect an audience of 40 million or more. Another larger niche company is amazon.com, which serves as an online middleman for customers, retailers, and distributors. Also, ebay.com, an on-line auction site, has produced success through its initial venture as well as spin-off services. Ebay is one of the few—if not only—interactive, stand-alone businesses to survive in the new Internet e-commerce environment.

Smaller, more targeted companies such as dvdtalk.com or imdb.com (Internet Movie Data Base) have been successful because they can deliver specific audiences to advertisers. Dvdtalk.com started in a basement and hired only a handful of employees. Revenues of several hundred thousand dollars a year, although not in the league of a yahoo.com's income, made the company profitable. Another example is Cnet.com, a computer-oriented Web site where computer enthusiasts hang out. Such an audience appeals to companies that make computer products.

Internet Advertising Copy

Often when a visitor accesses a Web site, the first thing to come into view is a banner ad streamed across the top of the page. Then the rest of the page appears. For example, after clicking on msnbc.com, a Nieman-Marcus link might flash in the upper right-hand corner of the page. Another blinking headline might offer the latest Internet access from Nortel Networks. That type of advertising format has been the most prevalent and one of the longest-running ad types on Web sites.

But that has changed. Now icons link audiences to corporate sites. For example, on yahoo.com's home page—in addition to news, classifieds, and dozens of other services—a visitor could click on a company logo that powers the site and see products and services. A click on music, for example, will pull up an information site with Britney Spears's latest CD, price, songs, and options where to buy it.

Ads are squeezed onto Internet pages in the corners and between stories. Blinking lights or rolling screens are designed to catch a visitor's eye and tease him or her into clicking on the company's Web site for more information. Headlines have to be catchy, and writing has to be clear.

Some advertising professionals believe that Internet advertising has not been the success that some had hoped. They point out that so far, most businesses have used the Internet as another piece of their advertising plan and haven't abandoned more traditional forms, such as television, newspaper, and direct mail. Internet advertisers also must contend with software that can block ads. Others are optimistic that as research shows how audiences are using the Internet and as technology continues to evolve, the Internet can be a more profitable marketing tool.

Tips for Ad Copy That Sells

Advertising Professor Jim Plumb, who has 30 years of experience in all aspects of advertising, gives the following broad tips to copywriters:

1. *Touch on selling points.* Focus on concrete reasons for purchase. An abstract reason to buy a Subaru wagon is safety, but a concrete selling point is that buying a Subaru keeps the driver from shoveling snow or paying a tow truck.

2. *Sell the benefits.* Find and list the benefits of your product that are important to your audience. Build your ad writing around these benefits. List them in the ad if you can, but be sure to mention them in some way. Don't forget to look for intangible benefits. Sometimes the most powerful benefits are intangibles, such as the mood that a perfume creates or a feeling of belonging that comes from a health club. Again, the viewer or reader should experience the product.

3. *Identify the single greatest benefit of your product and feature it in the headline.* Research should identify the quality of your product that is most meaningful

to your intended audience. Then create a headline or slogan that will convey this benefit to your audience. With "Mmmmm, good!" Campbell's is selling the benefit of good taste. With "Just Do It," Nike sells discipline, an intangible benefit, as its star quality. A slogan in ads for the *Washington Post* reads, "If you don't get it, you don't get it." That is, if you don't take the *Post* regularly, you'll be left out socially. By communicating benefits in a few words, ad writing has the power to modify attitudes and behaviors. The same technique, among others used by copywriters, can work in all forms of writing.

Other experts in the field remind copywriters of more specifics. In their book, *The New How to Advertise,* advertising executives Kenneth Roman and Jane Maas list elements of good advertising strategy. They note that a good ad will show solutions to a problem; effective ads will aim for target audiences; and every good ad projects the tone, manner, and personality of the product. Other experts also recommend that ad copy note details; use well-chosen language; have strong, clear words; have one unifying idea or theme; Contain a beginning, a middle, and an end; and, for the most part, use correct grammar.

But some contend if such rules are followed, the result will be well-produced but boring ads. Other techniques are needed for fun or zany, truly creative advertisements. George Felton in his book, *Advertising Concepts,* discusses *reversal* as an approach to writing ads. He notes:

> *All great ads employ reversal: Something significant has been put in, left out, inverted, photographed oddly, colored wrong, talked about differently, or in some way had violence done to its ordinariness. Otherwise, if our preconceptions have been fulfilled instead of violated, we'll be looking at clichés.*

He gives as an example the classic Volkswagen ad that took the maxim "Think big" and reversed it to "Think small." The print advertisement used exceptional white space and put a small Volkswagen near the upper lefthand corner. "The ad reversed our expectations twice: once as user of clichés and once as viewers of ads," Felton notes.

If copywriters want to use reversal, among the questions they should ask are: Who doesn't use the product? Where don't you find it? When isn't it used? What's an unusual use for it? When is the one time it won't come in handy? The answers would be clues to an ad. Reversal would also allow a copywriter to capitalize on negatives or liabilities.

All Writers Can Learn from Advertising

Many advertising students argue that there is no connection between newswriting and advertising writing. Likewise, newswriting students argue that their work has nothing to do with advertising technique. But Associate Professor Katherine McAdams and Professor John Sweeney studied prize-winning ads and news stories and found that the two have much in common.

"Award-winning news competes for the reader's attention, as does ad copy; both kinds of writing require techniques that catch and reward readers with concise, informative, pleasurable reading," McAdams and Sweeney concluded. They list five factors that they found in both groups of award-winning writing:

1. *Audience.* Both newswriting and ad writing aim messages at specific audiences and demonstrate a clear knowledge of audience interests and concerns.

2. *Distillation.* News articles and advertisements both must distill large amounts of information into very limited space, resulting in careful, early placement of key information.

3. *Freshness.* Excellent news writing is involving and rewarding for the reader. The same is true of advertising. The means to success in both fields lies in presenting information with interest and liveliness.

4. *Substance.* Both kinds of writing depend on substantive writing that presents facts. Information—especially new or surprising information—is top priority in both advertising and news.

5. *Easy access.* Unless facts are presented with the reader's ease in mind, the information may not be read. That's why both newswriting and advertising writing emphasize short words, short paragraphs, and simple sentences. Both may have one-sentence paragraphs.

Advertising copy may have some quirky differences, however. Necessary transitions may require starting sentences with "because" or "which." Because rhythm is key, just as in newswriting, sentences will vary in length. Ad copy may contain more sentence fragments. A sentence in a news article might use semicolons between independent clauses when ad copy would use periods. Because of its persuasive nature, ad copy language can be bolder, more suggestive, even "cuter" than that found in a news article. And that aspect sells many students on striving to become copywriters—or to have some advertising job in the information age. In producing good writing for any medium, today's writers must be concerned with reaching audiences. Because of competition among products and brands, ad writers were first to identify and target audiences. Today, as all media become conscious of competition, we can learn from their techniques how to satisfy the public hunger for new and relevant information.

EXERCISES

1. Imagine that you have been asked to create an ad that describes the benefits of dining in your campus cafeteria. The ad will appear in your campus newspaper. The audience is undergraduate students.

    a. Begin by doing product research: Visit the cafeteria for a meal, and take note of important information and impressions. List the facts and impressions you gathered in your research visit. Be prepared to discuss the items on your list.

    b. Supplement your product research with audience research. List at least five questions about cafeteria dining that you could use in brief interviews with students. Discuss your questions with your professor and classmates, then use your best questions in interviews with six or more students.

    c. Consider what you learned from your efforts in product and audience research. Divide a blank sheet of paper in half. On one side, list the major benefits that you could write about for your advertising copy. On the other side, list prominent characteristics of your audience. Turn the page over and write at least three possible headlines for your ad. Each headline should feature at least one cafeteria benefit and appeal to at least one audience characteristic.

2. Invite an advertising professional from your campus or community to visit your class. Ask this person to talk briefly about advertising in today's competitive media environment. You may also want to ask your speaker to look over any headlines or advertising copy the class has written and to select some examples of good writing.

3. Imagine that you have been asked to write a headline and three paragraphs of advertising copy about the car that you drive most often. Your

audience is your fellow students; the ad will appear in a student publication. Begin by taking a research drive and listing the benefits of your automobile; then develop the copy.

4. Find a poorly written advertisement in a newspaper or magazine. Clip the ad, then get out a fresh piece of paper. Rewrite the ad, improving the writing and targeting. Do any research that is needed.

5. Find a copy of an advertisement that you think uses reversal to make its point. Explain how the ad deviates from what would be the expected presentation. Take a product you use regularly and come up with a creative approach that uses reversal.

6. Choose a company and visit its Web site. How much of the site is information and how much is advertising? Does the site allow browsers to order products? Compare the company's Web site with the site for a nonprofit organization such as Save the Children at www.savethechildren.org.

REFERENCES

American Advertising Federation Web Site, Available at: http://www.aaf.com.

Bruce Bendiger et al., *Advertising: The Business of Brands*. Chicago: The Copy Workshop, 1999.

Tom Burrell, Reed Sarratt Lecture, UNC-CH School of Journalism and Mass Communication, Fall 1992.

Philip Ward Burton, *Advertising Copywriting,* 6th ed. Lincolnwood, IL: NTC Business Books, 1990.

Federal Trade Commission Web Site, Available at: http://www.ftc.gov.

George Felton, *Advertising Concepts and Copy.* Englewood Cliffs, NJ: Prentice-Hall, 1994.

Stephen J. Gould, Pola B. Gupta, and Sonja Grabner-Krauter, "Product Placements in Movies: A Cross-Cultural Analysis of Austrian, French and American Consumers' Attitudes Toward This Emerging, International Promotional Medium." *The Journal of Advertising,* vol. 29, no. 4, Winter 2000.

Jason Kilar, Vice President—Books, Music, DVD and Video, Amazon.com, interview, Chapel Hill, NC, October 2001.

"The Loyal Customer: The Care and Feeding of Your Most Valuable Business Asset," *Gallup Management Journal,* Summer 2001 at www.gallupjournal.com.

Katherine McAdams and John Sweeney, "Copy Writing and Newswriting Need Similar Skills." *Journalism Educator,* Winter 1987.

David Ogilvy, *Ogilvy on Advertising.* New York: Crown Publishers, 1983.

Carol Pardun and Larry Lamb, "The Presence of the Corporate Web Site in Traditional Print Advertising." Paper presented to the International, Interdisciplinary

Research Conference of the Public Relations Society of America, Baltimore, MD, June 1998.

James Plumb, "Writing Advertising Copy." Lecture. College Park, MD, University of Maryland College of Journalism, 1990.

Kenneth Roman and Jane Maas, *The New How to Advertise.* New York: St. Martin's Press, 1992.

John Sweeney, "Principles of Advertising." Lecture series. Chapel Hill, NC, University of North Carolina at Chapel Hill, 1986.

John Sweeney, Personal interview. Chapel Hill, NC, University of North Carolina, 2001.

Michael J. Weiss, *The Clustering of America.* New York: Harper & Row, 1988.

APPENDIX A

The Abused Words List

Writers must pay attention to words that sound alike but are spelled differently and have different meanings. The words can be confusing and can be used incorrectly. When writers fail to select the correct word, often readers know it, and the writers' credibility suffers.

Professor Thom Lieb of Towson State University has developed what he calls "the abused words list." Writers need to review the list periodically to ensure they use words correctly. Here is Lieb's list, with a few modifications by from the authors:*

accept, except: Accept means receive; except means exclude.

adapt, adopt: Adapt means make fit or suitable by changing or adjusting; adopt means take up and use, vote to accept, select.

adopted, passed, enacted: Resolutions are adopted or approved; bills are passed; laws are enacted when they go into effect.

adverse, averse: Adverse is poor or bad; averse is opposed to.

advice, advise: Advice is an opinion given; advise means to give advice.

affect, effect: To affect is to have an effect on; effect is the noun. But effect as a verb means "bring about."

after, following: After means next in time; following means next in order.

aggravate, irritate: Aggravate means make worse; irritate means to incite or provoke.

agnostic, atheist: An agnostic believes it is impossible to know whether there is a God. Atheists believe there is no God.

---

*Adapted from Thomas Lieb, *Editing for Clear Communication* (Dubuque, IA: Times Mirror Higher Education Group, 1996). Reprinted by permission.

aid, aide: Aides (assistants) give aid (help) to their bosses. Aid can also be a verb, but aide can only be a noun.

all ready, already: All ready means prepared: "The team was all ready for the game." Already means beforehand: "The opponents were already there."

allusion, delusion, illusion: Allusion is a hint, an indirect reference: "He made an allusion to her vanity." Note that to allude to something is not to name the thing specifically. Delusion is a false belief, especially a psychotic one. Illusion is unreal perception, misconception, unreal image perception: "He had an illusion he could fly across the sea." And there is also, of course, elude, meaning avoid.

alot: It's a lot, and it's best saved for real estate stories.

alright: It's not; it's all right.

alternative, alternate: Alternative involves a choice; alternate, a verb or an adjective, means in turns.

alumna, alumni, alumnus: An alumnus can be of either sex, but is typically male. An alumna is female; plural is alumnae pronounced with a long e sound. Plural of both sexes or males is alumni.

amateur, novice: Amateur is a nonprofessional; novice is a beginner.

amount, number: Amount is the quantity of things: "The amount of testimony was small." Number refers to individual or separate units in a group: "The number of times she testified was too small to make a difference."

anxious, eager: You can only be anxious about something; you cannot be anxious to do that thing. Anxious implies fear and anxiety. If you are stimulated and excited at the prospect of doing something, then you are eager to do it.

assume, presume: Assume means take to be fact without a basis for belief; to presume is to regard as true because there is reason to do so and no contrary evidence. Presume also means take upon oneself without permission or authority.

bad, badly: Bad is an adjective, used when you want to describe the subject: "He felt bad about the report of campaign irregularities." Badly describes some quality of the verb rather than the subject: "She took her defeat badly."

bale, bail: A farmer's hay is baled; water is bailed out of a boat; a prisoner is released on bail. (Bond is cash or property given as a security for an appearance or performance.)

bi-, semi-: Bi means two; semi means half. Bimonthly means every two months; semimonthly means twice a month. However: Biannual means the same as semiannual—twice a year. Biennial means every two years.

capital, capitol: Capital means the city that is official seat of government; it also means wealth. Capitol with a capital "C" means the building in which Congress meets in Washington, DC; with a lowercase "c," it means the building in which a state legislature meets.

carat, caret, karat: Carat expresses the weight of precious stones; caret is a proofreader's mark; karat is the proportion of pure gold used in an alloy.

censor, censure: A censor is a person who can censor a publication, cutting out anything offensive, obscene, etc. To censure is to condemn as wrong or to strongly disapprove.

cite, site, sight: Cite means refer or quote; site is a location; sight is a view.

collision: Violent contact between moving bodies. A car cannot collide with a telephone pole or other unmoving object.

compared to, compared with: When you put one thing in the same class or category without examining it closely, use compared to: "The inflation rate can be compared to a hot-air balloon with an endless supply of fuel." When you put things side by side to examine similarities and differences, use compared with: "The inflation rate is 8 percent, compared with last year's figure of 10 percent."

compliment, complement: They both can be nouns or verbs. Compliment is praise; complement adds to something to make it complete.

compose, comprise: To compose is to make up; to comprise is to include. "Fifty states compose the United States." "The United States comprises 50 states."

confidant, confident: Confidant is a close, trusted friend in whom one can confide; confident is sure of oneself.

conscious, aware: We are conscious of what we feel and aware of what we know.

contact: As a verb, it means the physical touching of things: "His toe contacted the football."

continual, continuous: Continual means repeated or intermittent; continuous means unbroken.

council, counsel, consul: Council is an assembly, usually a legislative body; counsel is advice, a lawyer; consul is a person appointed by his or her government to serve his or her country's interests abroad.

couple of: Like "a pair," needs the "of." Never "a couple tomatoes."

data: Is plural, as are media, strata, phenomena, criteria, and alumni. When the group or quantity is regarded as a unit, it takes a singular verb: "The data is invalid." If the word refers to individual items, use plural verb: "The data were collected by a team of 20 scientists."

dilemma: An argument necessitating a choice between two equally unfavorable or disagreeable alternatives.

discreet, discrete: Discreet means prudent, circumspect; discrete is detached or separate.

disinterested, uninterested: Disinterested is impartial; uninterested means lack interest.

disorganize, unorganized: Disorganize is a verb, meaning disrupt the organization of; unorganized is an adjective, meaning lacking order, system, or unity.

due to: Not a synonym for "because of." It should modify a noun: "It was an omission due to oversight." BUT: "The name was omitted because of oversight."

egregious: (pronounced i gre jes): Outstanding for undesirable qualities; remarkably bad.

either: Not synonymous with both. Incorrect: "The teams lined up at either end of the field." Correct: "The teams lined up at both ends."

emigrate, immigrate: Emigrate means leave a country; immigrate means enter.

enrage, outrage: Enrage is a verb meaning put in a rage; outrage is a noun, meaning an act of extreme violence or viciousness.

ensure, insure: Ensure is guarantee: "A good writer takes every possible measure to ensure accuracy." Insure is used in references to insurance. And let us not forget assure, which means to make a person sure of something, or convince.

envelop, envelope: To envelop is to wrap up, obscure, hide. An envelope is the paper product that envelops your letters and bills.

epitaph, epithet: Epitaph is an inscription on a tombstone; epithet is a descriptive adjective applied to someone.

farther, further: Farther refers to physical distance; further refers to degree, time, or quantity.

faze, phase: Faze is embarrass or disturb; phase is an aspect or stage.

feel: Generally, best saved for touching and feeling things. Don't use as a synonym for thinking or believing. It is acceptable when you mean to be convinced emotionally rather than intellectually: "The parents of the kidnapped girl feel certain she is safe."

fewer, less: The general rule is that if you can't count it, use less: fewer students, but less interest.

flair, flare: Flair is a conspicuous talent; flare means blaze with sudden, bright light or to burst out in anger. Also a noun meaning flame.

flaunt, flout: To flaunt is to show off; to flout is to mock, scoff, or show disdain for.

flounder, founder: Horses flounder—struggle or thrash about—in the mud; ships founder or sink.

gantlet, gauntlet: A gantlet is a section of railroad tracks over a narrow passage where two lines of track overlap (two lines using only three rails). A gauntlet is a former military punishment in which an offender had to run between two rows of men with clubs. It is also a long glove.

get: Often used instead of a more precise verb. Get around—evade. Get behind—endorse. AND get does not substitute for become: "I become cold" rather than "I get cold."

gibe, jibe: Gibe is to jeer, taunt, or flout; jibe is to shift sails, alter a course, or be in harmony.

gorilla, guerrilla: Gorilla is an ape; guerrilla is a soldier or raider.

hanged, hung: Hang, hung, hung refers to objects; hanged refers to people.

hike: What a Boy Scout takes. Not synonymous for increase.

historic, historical: Historic means famous in history; historical pertains to history, such as historical sites and historical novels.

holdup, holed up: A person with a gun can commit a holdup by forcibly stopping another person and robbing him or her. If the robber hides out at the place of the holdup, he or she is holed up.

hopefully: Full of hope. "The hungry child sat hopefully on the steps of the candy shop."

imply, infer: The speaker implies; the listener infers.

in, into (also: on, onto): If you're in the lake and feel like jumping, you jump in the lake. If you're in a boat on the lake and you feel like jumping overboard, you jump into the lake.

ironically: The contrary of what is expressed—for example, calling a stupid plan clever. Irony is a form of sarcasm.

last, latest, past: Last few days, one's latest book, in the past.

launch: Send into space, not begin, as in "New Sewer System Launched."

liable: Not a good substitute for likely, unless the event designated is injurious or undesirable. "It is likely to be sunny and clear." "It is liable to rain."

lie, lay: To lie is to recline; to lay is to place. Confusion results mainly from past and past perfect tenses: lie, lay, lay (or lain); lay, laid, laid.

like, as: Like joins nouns and pronouns: "He blocks like a pro." Use as with verbs: "Winston tastes good as a cigarette should."

likewise: Avoid using as a transition. WRONG: "He went home. Likewise, his sister went." CORRECT: "He went home. So did his sister."

loath, loathe: Loath means unwilling; loathe means hate.

mad: Means insane, not angry.

masterly, masterful: Masterly means skillful; masterful means domineering.

mean, median, average, mode: Mean and average are generally interchangeable: the sum of the units divided by the number of units. Median is the number in the middle (such as the middle score or income); half lie above, half below. Mode is the most commonly occurring number.

moral, morale: Moral refers to ethics; morale to mood or spirits. "The moral life is the good life." "His morale was lifted by the phone call."

nauseated, nauseous: If you are nauseated, you feel or become sick. Something nauseous is sickening or disgusting.

negotiate: You negotiate a loan or treaty; you climb a hill.

noisy, noisome: Noisy is making or accompanied by noise; noisome is injurious to health, noxious, harmful, or foul smelling.

off of: Off suffices: "Get off my back."

only: Almost invariably misplaced, altering the meaning of the sentence. Try it in front of each word in this sentence to see how it alters meaning: "I hit him in the eye yesterday."

oral, verbal: The use of the mouth is essential to oral communications; verbal means simply "using words."

penultimate: The next to the last: "The penultimate month of the year is November."

persuade, convince: Persuade means induce someone to believe or do something, plead with, or urge. Convince means bring someone to belief or conviction beyond doubt, satisfy by proof. "Grace has tried to persuade her to change her story. Finally, she was convinced that Grace was right."

podium, lectern: Podium is a footstool or platform; lectern is what speakers thump.

populous, populated, populace: Populous means crowded or thickly populated; populated means inhabited; populace means common people of a community.

portentous: Ominous, portending evil.

precipitate, precipitous: Precipitate means cause to happen before anticipated; precipitous is steep like a precipice.

presently: Means soon, not now. Not synonymous with currently.

pretense, pretext: Pretense is a false show, a more overt act used to conceal personal feelings: "Her compliments were all pretense." Pretext is something put forward to conceal a truth: "They said he was dismissed for tardiness, but that was just a pretext for incompetence."

prior to, in advance of: Use "before" instead.

prone: If a man is lying prone on the beach, no one can step on his stomach. Prone means lying face down. Supine means lying face up.

prostate, prostrate: Prostate is of or relating to the male body; prostrate is lying with the face downward in a show of great humility or abject submission.

quell, quench: Uprisings, disorders, riots, and the like are quelled; a fire is quenched.

quintessential: Quintessence is the pure, concentrated essence of anything.

rack, wrack: To rack is to trouble, torment or afflict, or to oppress by unfair demands. Also, you rack your brains, and something exasperating is nerve-racking. Wrack is properly used as a noun meaning ruin or destruction.

raise, rear, raze: Raise animals, rear children. To raze is to destroy.

ravage, ravish: To ravage is to destroy or ruin: "The tornadoes ravaged the town." To ravish is to fill with joy, carry away forcibly, or rape: "The army ravished the Trojan women."

record: You do not set a new record or an all-time record; neither is it a record first. It is simply a record.

refute: Means disprove—almost always implies editorial. Generally, rebut or dispute is better.

regime, regimen, regiment: A regime is a political ruling system; a regimen is a system of diet, etc., for improving health; a regiment is a military unit consisting of two or more battalions.

reign, rein: Reign is royal power, authority, or rule; rein is a strap of leather used to control a horse.

reluctant, reticent: Reluctant is unwilling to act; reticent is to speak.

role, roll: Role is a part assumed by an actor or a function assumed by someone; roll is a noun and verb meaning more than a dozen different things—but not what role does.

sensual, sensuous: Sensual refers to the gratification of the grosser bodily senses of appetite (sex, food); sensuous suggests a strong appeal of that which is pleasing to the senses. A sensuous person is susceptible to the pleasures of sensation: "She was given to sensual excesses." "The music playing was sensuous."

set, sit: To set is to place: "Set the book here." Sit is what you do when you take a seat: "Please sit down for the performance."

sewage, sewerage: Sewage is human waste, sometimes called sanitary waste; sewerage is the system to carry away sewage.

since, because: Since is best used when it denotes a period of time, either continuous or broken. Because gives a reason or cause.

tall, high: A building, tree, or man is tall; a plane, bird, or cloud is high.

temperature, weather: The temperature can move higher or lower, but only the weather can become warmer or cooler.

than, then: Than is a conjunction of comparison. Then is an adverb denoting time.

their, there, they're: Their is the possessive form of the pronoun "they." There is an adverb denoting place or, when used to begin a sentence, it is called an expletive or a false subject: "There are only 20 shopping days left until Christmas." They're is the contraction of they and are.

til, till: Use until.

try and: The correct usage is "try to."

wasted words: These words add nothing: kind of, little, pretty, rather, really, some, sort of. The most wasted: VERY.

would, could, should: Saying a child *could* remain in an institution until age 18 is different from saying he *would* remain there—or *should*. Be careful with these.

APPENDIX B

Keys to Grammar and Style Quizzes

After years of working with these exercises, we recognize that no single answer exists for any exercise item. Each answer we provide is what we consider to be the *best* or *preferred* answer, rather than the *only* answer.

Grammar Diagnostic Quiz (pages 27–29)

1. Puctuation error. A comma replaces the semicolon because clauses on either side of a semicolon must be independent.
2. Subject–verb agreement error. The subject of the sentence is list, so the verb must agree. It is the LIST that HAS BEEN TRIMMED.
3. Punctuation error. A period or semicolon replaces the comma because commas may not separate independent clauses. Some would label this a comma splice; others, a run-on sentence.
4. Punctuation error. Comma needed after OCTOBER 25 because commas follow all elements in a complete date.
5. Sentence structure error. The modifying phrase, TRADITIONALLY EXPECTED TO BE IN CONTROL OF THEIR SURROUNDINGS is misplaced and needs to follow the word STUDENTS. In its present position, the phrase modifies THE INSECURITY.
6. Word use error. LIE instead of LAY when no action is taken.
7. Word use error. Modifying the word COUNCIL with the word HOPEFULLY leaves the council filled with hope. It is preferable to say, "We hope the council...."
8. Punctuation error. Semicolons are used to separate punctuated items in a list.

9. Word use error. Use neither and nor as a matched pair. The same goes for either and or.
10. Pronoun error. Use the pronoun IT to agree with the noun COMPANY, a singular thing.
11. Punctuation error. Phrases that rename subjects (appositives) are nonessential and therefore set off by commas. Place a comma after COMMITTEE.
12. Subject–verb agreement error. LIVES is the verb that agrees with the true subject of the sentence, which is ONE.
13. Punctuation error. Commas follow both elements of a city and state combination that occurs in midsentence, even if the state abbreviation ends in a period.
14. Word use error. The past tense, USED, is correct usage in this idiom.
15. Sentence structure error. Including WILL PLAY in this list of parade items makes for faulty parallelism. Delete WILL PLAY.
16. Sentence structure error. This sentence is incomplete. It is a sentence fragment. Even though it is lengthy, it has no verb.
17. Comma error. Semicolon or period needed.
18. The coordinate conjunction AND is used where a subordinate conjunction, such as BECAUSE or THAT, is needed.
19. Modifier problem. His muscles are not being a weight lifter.
20. Agreement: ITS SKIN.

1. Correct. Your princiPAL is your PAL. PrincipLES are LESSONS.
2. Correct. A waiver is a document of permission; a waver is a person who waves.
3. Incorrect. A bore is a dull person or event. A boar is a wild pig.
4. Incorrect. A navel is a belly button. Naval means pertaining to the Navy.
5. Correct. StationERy is sold by stationERs.
6. Incorrect. A role is a part in a play. A roll is something rolled up, even a class list.
7. Correct. Note also bookkeeper and withholding.
8. Incorrect. Canvas is cloth. To canvaSS is to cover thoroughly, as in a canvass of the neighborhood.
9. Incorrect. Complement is a verb that means to complete. A compliment is a flattering statement.
10. Correct. Cite is correct in this case.

Slammer for Commas, Semicolons, and Colons (pages 33–34)

1. 4. Comma after Bowl.
2. 2. Commas after Blimpo and man.
3. 9 and 10. Semicolon after strings; comma after basses.
4. 2. Comma after fall, after dark, after reading, and after fishing.
5. 2, 5, and 6. Colon after concern; comma after 2 and 4; comma after 1991 and yours.
6. 8. Comma after Dad.
7. 4 and 10. Semicolon after halftime; comma after however.
8. 1. Comma after bill.
9. 7. Comma after well.
10. 10. Semicolon after disappointment.
11. 6 and 7. Comma after 3 and 1972; comma after Baltimore and Md.; comma after birth.
12. 2 and 12. Colon after semester; comma after journalism, after English, and after political science.

Slammer for Subject–Verb Agreement (pages 37–38)

1. includes
2. appear
3. gives
4. results
5. have
6. do
7. is
8. are
9. exhibits
10. are
11. constitute
12. was
13. believes
14. is
15. decides
16. typifies
17. are
18. are
19. is
20. is
21. teach
22. is
23. consider
24. disagree

Slammer for Pronouns (pages 39–40)

1. his or her
2. its
3. himself
4. its
5. its
6. is
7. was
8. was
9. their
10. is
11. its
12. it
13. are
14. himself or herself
15. his or her

Slammer for Who/Whom and That/Which (page 42)

1. whom
2. who

3. whom
4. who

5. whose

1. gun, which sale,
2. that
3. car, which plates,

4. Texans, who drawl,
5. gun, which com-
   partment,

6. who
7. gun, which
8. that

Slammer for Modifiers (pages 43–44)

1. The waiter served ice cream, which started melting immediately, in glass bowls.
2. Correct.
3. On the way to our hotel, we saw a herd of sheep.
4. Correct.
5. The house where Mrs. Rooks taught ballet is one of the oldest in Rockville.
6. Correct.
7. Without yelling, I could not convince the child to stop running into the street.
8. The critic said that after the first act of the play, Brooke's performance improves.
9. While we were watching the ball game, Sue's horse ran away.
10. Correct.
11. The bank approves loans of any size to reliable individuals.
12. After I was wheeled into the operating room, the nurse placed a mask over my face.
13. Correct.
14. Aunt Helen asked us to call on her before we left.

Slammer for Style (pages 50–51)

1. Lt. Gov. Stanley Greene was stripped of his powers by the N.C. Senate.
2. William Williams, dean of the Graduate School of Journalism, will speak to students about graduation requirements on Wednesday afternoon.
3. The students are expected to begin the test at 9 a.m. Tuesday.

4. The president lives at 1600 Pennsylvania Ave., but his mail is delivered to the U.S. post office on 22nd Street.
5. The state Senate is expected to pass a bill to require polio vaccinations for children under the age of 2.
6. The airport in Medford, Ore., was closed yesterday after an Alaskan airlines jet made an emergency landing on the runway.
7. The attorney general has a bachelor of arts in history from American University.
8. The then-Soviet bloc countries sponsored the Friendship Games rather than attend the 1984 Olympics in Los Angeles.
9. The city and county used 13 buses to transport the children to the July Fourth picnic.
10. Water freezes at zero degrees Celsius.
11. Three houses on Sims Street were destroyed by the fire, which began at 112 Sims St.
12. Following the Federal Reserve action, three banks announced a 1 percent increase in the prime rate, putting it at 6 percent.
13. Longtime Sen. Jesse A. Helms, R-N.C., used to be city editor of the *Raleigh Times.*
14. John L. Harris, 48, of 1632 Winding Way Road was charged Tuesday with cocaine possession.
15. The champion wrestler measured 6 feet 6 inches tall and won four-fifths of his fights.
16. Army Sgt. Willie York was charged with misappropriating $1 million in construction equipment.
17. Hurrican Diana, blowing from the east, caused millions of dollars in damage to the East Coast of the United States.
18. Col. Max Shaw, who has served as a national guardsman for more than 20 years, is Ed's commanding officer.
19. Ability with a Frisbee is not a valid measure of IQ.
20. We heard the kickoff announced over the radio at the Laudromat.
21. The stockings were hanged by the chimney with care, in hopes that Kriss Kringle soon would be there.
22. Travelling the 30 miles, or 48 kilometers, to Kansas City, we got 32 miles per gallon in our new minivan.
23. The 5-year-old boy got on the wrong bus and was missing for two hours.
24. Sarah sold 202 boxes of Girl Scout cookies to her neighbors on Sweetbriar Parkway and Pantego Avenue.

APPENDIX C

Key to Math Test

1. a. The ratio of men to women is 9:4. Subtract the number of women from the total to get the number of men.
   b. To get percentage, divide the difference by the base. In this case, 4 (the number of women) is divided by 13 for a percentage of 30.8 percent (the actual number is .30769 but is to be rounded to the nearest tenth for 30.8).
   c. The same process is used to figure the percentage of Hispanic men on the jury: Divide 1 by 13 for an answer of 7.7 percent.
   d. Again, divide the number of African American men (1) by the base of 13 and you get the same answer as 1c: 7.7 percent.

2. a. To get the cost for the center alone, multiply the number of square feet by the cost per square foot, or 15,000 by $85 for a cost of $1,275,000.
   b. The cost follows the same formula: Multiply 15,000 square feet by $25 for a cost of $375,000.
   c. To get the total cost, add the cost of the building to the cost of the furnishings for a total $1,650,000.
   d. To round off, remember that you round up after 5, 50, 500, 5,000, etc. So rounded to the nearest 100,000 would be $1.7 million.

3. a. To get the size, multiply 12 by 8 to get the size of one booth (96 square feet) then double it because each booth is two parking spaces. The answer is 192 square feet. *Note:* You can't double both measurements then multiply because the booth will grow only in width, not in depth. So the booth actually measures 16 by 12, which is 192 square feet.
   b. The company can rent 120 booths. Divide the number of spaces in the parking lot by 2 because each booth is two spaces.

    c. Multiply the number of booths (120) by $30 to get $3,600.

    d. Go back to 3a. One booth is 192 square feet. If you get two booths, you get 384 square feet.

4. a. First you have to calculate how many units per $100. So divide the house value of $175,000 by 100 and you get $1,750. Then multiply by the tax rate of 85 cents (.85) to get a tax bill of $1,487.50.

    b. Under the new tax rate of 88 cents, Sarah will pay 1,750 times .88 or $1,540.

    c. To calculate the increase in her tax bill, you need the difference between the old bill and the new bill. So subtract $1,487.50 from $1,540 to get $52.50. To find the percentage increase, remember difference divided by base or $52.50 divided by $1,487.50, or a 3.5 percent increase in value.

    d. To find out how much her property would increase, multiply $175,000 by 5 percent (0.05) to get $8,750. Add that amount to $175,000 to get the new value of $183,500. To find the tax bill, follow the steps in 4a. Remember to use the new tax rate of 88 cents per $100 to get the answer: $1,617.

5. a. The total female respondents were 275. Add the female counts of 107, 137, and 31.

    b. Total respondents are 627. (Add all the individual counts for male and female.) Divide the total number of women respondents, 275, by 627 and the percentage is 44.

    c. You cannot add rows of percentages to get this answer. You have to go back to your counts. Fifty-four respondents (male and female) supported Tucker. Divide by total 627 and the percentage is 8.6.

    d. The same rule for 5c applies here. A total of 274 supported Small, divided by the total respondents of 627, and you get 43.7 percent.

6. The key here is that if she has a 75 percent chance of band practice, she has only a 25 percent chance of going to the fair. Multiply the two probabilities, 50 percent (.5) and 25 percent (.25). The likelihood she will get to the fair is 12.5 percent.

7. The answer is C; $270. If he earns $6.50 an hour, 25 cents more means $6.75 an hour. Multiply by the number of hours, 40.

8. The answer is 61.29. You multiply the number of pounds by 0.454 to get the number of kilograms.

INDEX